HELLS ANGELS AT WAR

YVES LAVIGNE

HELLS ANGELS AT WAR

HarperCollins*Publishers*Ltd

HELLS ANGELS AT WAR
Copyright © 1999 by Yves Lavigne.
All rights reserved. No part of this book may be used or reproduced
in any manner whatsoever without prior written permission
except in the case of brief quotations embodied in reviews.
For information address HarperCollins Publishers Ltd,
55 Avenue Road, Suite 2900, Toronto, Ontario,
Canada M5R 3L2.

http://www.harpercanada.com

HarperCollins books may be purchased for educational, business,
or sales promotional use. For information please write:
Special Markets Department, HarperCollins Canada,
55 Avenue Road, Suite 2900, Toronto, Ontario,
Canada M5R 3L2.

First HarperCollins hardcover ed. ISBN 0-00-200024-5

Canadian Cataloguing in Publication Data

Lavigne, Yves, 1953–
Hells Angels at war

ISBN 0-00-200024-5

1. Hell's Angels. 2. Motorcycle gangs – North America.
3. Organized crime – North America.
I. Title.

HV6453.N73H44 1999   364.1'06'07   C99-931144-1

99 00 01 02 03 04 HC 6 5 4 3 2 1

Printed and bound in the United States

To the passage of time, which allows for reflection, grants perspective, and enables understanding. Truth has no better ally.

"To give light to them that sit in darkness and *in* the shadow of death."
Luke (King James Version), Chapter 1; Verse 79

"There are a thousand hacking at the branches of evil to one who is striking at the root."
Henry David Thoreau

"The only thing necessary for the triumph of evil is for good men to do nothing."
Paraphrase of lengthy Edmund Burke passage
by an anonymous writer

"The blood-dimmed tide is loosed, ... and everywhere ...
The best lack all conviction, while the worst are full of passionate intensity."
William Butler Yeats, "The Second Coming"

"The greatest single enemy is the misuse of information, the perversion of truth in the hands of terribly skillful people. The manufacture and distribution of the sophisticated lie must be one of the worst legacies of the Cold War." [It is unfortunate that we are often ruled by mental tyranny] "where there is only one respectable opinion about anything. If you don't have it, you are on the wrong side of the fence."
John le Carré, April 1999

ACKNOWLEDGMENTS

After more than two decades of investigating outlaw motorcycle gangs and other forms of organized crime, I have developed a network of contacts that both law enforcement agents and criminals have sought to identify. The contents of this book, particularly internal police and Hells Angels documents, will prove so controversial that in the interest of protecting the lives and careers of my sources, I decided it would be unwise to list any of them. There is no point giving prying eyes even a shred of information to fuel their investigations and witch hunts.

Thank you to all who helped in support of the cause. Although your professionalism dictates anonymity, I am gratefully indebted to you for sharing my belief and conviction that the Hells Angels are a threat not only to our way of life, but to national security as they amass wealth and power to rival that wielded by politicians and captains of industry.

I am also grateful for the adversity I faced throughout my journey. The challenge shook me out of my torpor, kept me alert, and motivated me to plumb the depths of my resourcefulness. Life within the smallest seed, even when covered with a heavy rock, will seek and attain the light.

AUTHOR'S NOTE

My lifelong goal has been to write literature. As a one-year-old, I scratched stories in the frost that caked the windows of my home. The scratches were indecipherable, but the intent was clear.

As I grew older, I could not separate my heart and soul from the pains and needs of the world around me. Today, I morally cannot allow myself the luxury and indulgence of writing literature while the varied societies that make up our world succumb to an ever-increasing array of man-made ills. The greatest difficulty I faced as I wrote this book was to witness daily on television the horrors of Kosovo. Evil has so many faces. As one is exposed, another continues its vile work.

At century's end, I hope for peace in my time in the hearts of all so that for a brief moment I may allow my soul to express itself through writing and leave behind a testament of joy to temper my chronicles of despair.

CONTENTS

INTRODUCTION

Good and evil will always war. Neither side can be eradicated, as the existence of each is defined by the presence of the other. But in the ebb and flow of battle one force can dominate, even conquer—not forever, but long enough to ensure the liberation of peace or the enslavement of tyranny. This never-ending struggle scars every era. Evil knows no limit in deed. Good is boundless in sacrifice.

War is art. It must be fought with intelligence, insight, and passion. It tries, tests, and tempers the soul. Each side is constrained only by the desire and determination of its warriors. Those who fight purely will prevail. The weak, who succumb to the frailties of heart, ego, or character, expose to the enemy their soft underbelly and betray the cause. The evil succumb to their personal demons before they seek war. The good can succumb to their demons while at war.

This, my third book about the Hells Angels, is an exploration of man at war.

It is a dirty war, where everyone gets hurt. Gangs fight each other for territory. Cops fight gangs. Gangs fight cops. Cops fight cops. And both sides wage a war of words against the truth, to woo society and maintain their comfortable status. The line is fine between bikers and cops, and it doesn't get any thinner than in the heat of war, where truth is the first casualty. Both sides distort and suppress facts to deceive the public and themselves.

Hells Angels: Taking Care of Business (1987) dealt with the evolution of the Hells Angels and the evil they embody.

Hells Angels: Into the Abyss (1996) revealed in minute detail how biker evil functions from day to day.

1

Hells Angels at War is a journey into the public world of violence and the secret realm of deception. It documents wars waged around the world by the Hells Angels during the past six years. The Hells Angels warred with the Rock Machine in Quebec, against the Bandidos in Scandinavia, and with the Outlaws in Illinois and Indiana. These clashes produced blood and brotherhood, and a horrible menace that will haunt society for decades to come.

The four books I have published in the past twelve years are my attempt to create a substantive, thoughtful public literature on organized crime to combat ignorance and self-serving myth, and to undo the Hells Angels' public relations efforts, which garner so much support and launder their filthy image. I want to place in the public eye books that make it difficult, if not impossible, for the Hells Angels to continue to lie. I hope to demystify gangs in the eyes of the gullible, shock awake the somnolent, and expose those who would surrender us to evil as befits their selfish needs. My books strive to bring order to chaos, and reason to the unfathomable, by putting into perspective the apparently random bursts of violence from the biker underworld that momentarily startle and blind rather than enlighten. My writings are also an attempt to save society from itself: from the ravages of greed, sloth, and complacency.

I strive to shed on evil the desiccating light of truth. Without truth, there is nothing, just a fictitious world of posers and fake characters who continually re-invent themselves to suit their needs and times. Descartes was so right, yet so superficially misunderstood when he stated: I think, therefore I am. We can think honestly or dishonestly. Self-delusion alters one's perception of reality, but does nothing to affect reality. Truth is consistent and grounding. It forces us to look inward and outward realistically. It teaches us that evil is an energy that can be turned against itself.

Our parents fought the enemy without to secure the world for us. We must fight the enemy within.

The Hells Angels are a global menace to all races and cultures. The gang's seventeen hundred members in 137 chapters in twenty-one countries on five continents run a criminal empire so wealthy and powerful they laughingly fend off attempts by law enforcement agents and the courts to curb its growth. The Hells Angels have branded their trademarked symbol of fear into the public consciousness for more than half a century through explosions of violence strategically tempered with acts of staged kindness calculated to defuse anger and confuse opinion.

It is not enough to chronicle the Hells Angels' deeds. The public needs to know why the gang has doubled in size since publication of my first book. Law enforcement has failed to curb their expansion. In fact, inaction by authorities has allowed the Hells Angels to flourish.

A small number of cops with personal agendas have criticized me during the past four years for revealing and speaking out against questionable police tactics and abysmal failures in the war against outlaw bikers. It is both my right and duty as a journalist and a citizen to scrutinize those we pay to protect us. Too many good cops fight the Hells Angels on the front lines to let the dishonorable deeds of some police and politicians go unnoticed.

As the Hells Angels strive to complete their takeover of Canada, a task begun on December 5, 1977, rival biker gangs have done more than police to keep the Hells Angels out of Ontario. The police, contrary to the public image they present, have capitulated to the Big Red Machine. They prance ahead of the pack and shrilly announce their impending arrival, instead of creating a climate inhospitable to the bikers' survival. These exercises are crafted to scare citizens and manipulate politicians into opening public coffers.

The Canadian public has been deceived into thinking that police want to end the biker problem. In reality, police want to manage the biker issue and build bureaucracies and careers on the public fear the police themselves fuel.

Administrations, bureaucracies, and the public have short memories. They continually need to be re-educated, not only over their individual lifetimes, but from one generation to the next. Like individuals, systems must forever strive to overcome the numbing inertia of complacency.

The public allows itself to be deceived and has not been very helpful in the fight against the Hells Angels. Few people have the courage to look evil in the eye and acknowledge the danger it poses to them. Recognition of a threat requires action, and that entails consequences. Few follow this course because it requires a trait that has become foreign in our world: accountability. It is much easier for most people to turn a blind eye to reality, however horrible it may be.

I have been told I'm not a team player. Well, I don't belong to any team, but I'm on a side: the right side. People who hide on teams are as weak and gutless as those who live in gangs. They need to be accepted by the team. They give in to group-think, suppress criticism, censor themselves, succumb to style, and forsake substance.

Intimidation works only if you allow yourself to be intimidated. I have no need or desire to be accepted by my peers or anyone else. I need only to seek and expose the truth. I trust my instincts and my reward comes from within.

We live in a world that fears individuality, a wannabe culture that accepts and bows to the will of peer groups and gangs. Most people see themselves through the eyes of others. They fear being alone, not only with their thoughts, but with themselves. They foster and engender the leveling effect of group-think and the snotty, disrespectful gang mentality that breathes an arrogant sense of entitlement.

Style once set the individual apart. Today, style is what the majority wears, does, or says. People no longer discuss ideas or share thoughts; they spout labels and slogans. Words are meant to convey ideas and be forgotten once the idea is grasped. In a world without ideas, the medium has become the message. And the message rings hollow.

In a world bereft of belief, conviction, and direction, the victor in war doesn't win; the loser capitulates.

PART I:
HELLS ANGELS AT WAR

Chapter 1: Quebec
Red, White, and Bloody

Hells Angels vs. the Rock Machine

1980s and Early '90s

The history of biker violence in Quebec is long and tortured, and bathed in more blood than flowed on the Plains of Abraham when Wolfe sneaked in the back door and took Quebec City. Like the tension between French and English, the feuding of biker gangs seems interminable. Although the Hells Angels and Rock Machine have dominated the headlines since 1994, every decade has been branded by bloody biker wars. Because of their guerrilla nature and the public's short memory, the body count does not take a political toll. Quebec police have conveniently sanitized such deaths over the last forty years with the phrase: "*C'était un règlement de compte.*" The belief that a settling of accounts in the underworld affects only criminals takes the onus off police to solve crimes, and creates no political pressure from the public to safeguard the streets. Except for one brief moment in 1995, when shrapnel from a Hells Angels bomb ripped the life from an innocent boy, Quebeckers have become inured to biker violence.

The events that led to that short-lived flash of consciousness, and the events since, are not only a study in the profit-driven politics of the criminal underworld, but a mirror that reflects a self-serving, short-sighted society.

In *Hells Angels: Taking Care of Business*, I documented the rise of the Hells Angels—known as the "Red and White" in the underworld—in Quebec and the sadistic history of the gangs across the province that they gradually took into their fold. The Hells Angels who terrorize Quebec are not outsiders, but punks who cut their teeth in the fast-talking, double-dealing criminal underworld that operates in large cities and rural communities. My first book ended two years after the March

7

24, 1985, slaughter of the Hells Angels' drug-addled and violent North chapter of Laval. Six of the chapter's members were shot in the head, wrapped in sleeping bags, weighed down with concrete blocks and weightlifting plates, and dumped in the St. Lawrence Seaway where they rotted for sixty-nine days before police found them. The sensational inquests and trials in the following years, bolstered by the testimony of three Hells Angels who informed on the gang in the face of death, brought unwanted attention to the bikers and should have branded them forever as undesirables.

But the Hells Angels are driven. The trials and imprisonment of their members after the North chapter slaughter did not slow them down, although their high public profile prevented them from opening a new chapter in Laval to replace the one they had liquidated. They resorted to the time-honored tactic of installing a puppet gang in that part of Quebec to do their dirty work and sell their drugs, then torched the old Laval North chapter clubhouse on November 29, 1988. The Death Riders, formed in the early 1980s, succumbed to the Hells Angels' advances. They would not be hounded as much by the police, and could establish and maintain drug and prostitution networks in the area. They were forced out of Laval by police in 1987 and built a fortified bunker in nearby Sainte-Thérèse where the police force is smaller and less well funded.

Police also targeted the Missiles in Jonquière in 1988. After a series of busts, they moved to Chicoutimi and changed their name to Satan's Guards, a Hells Angels puppet gang. Later they were moved to Trois-Rivières to take over the area's drug networks. They became an official Hells Angels chapter on June 14, 1991.

The Vikings gave up their colors and became a new Hells Angels chapter in Saint-Nicolas, outside the provincial capital of Quebec City, on May 26, 1988, to take over the area's drug trade. In dozens of radio interviews in 1987 and 1988 I predicted that recalcitrant dealers and bar owners who refused to deal with the Hells Angels would be dealt with harshly. I told listeners that the area death toll would increase considerably as the Hells Angels killed where intimidation failed to gain cooperation. Police did not stand idly by. They raided the Saint-Nicolas clubhouse on October 17, 1989, smashing two outside walls, inside walls, and a ceiling with a backhoe. They wanted to get in quickly before any drugs were flushed down the toilet. They found little and the Hells Angels, predictably, sued under sections 8 and 24 of the Charter of Rights and Freedoms which protect against unreasonable searches and seizures. The court ruled in favor of the police.

The negative public image garnered by the liquidation of the North chapter did not curb the traditional Hells Angels' practice of drowning members deemed no longer profitable to the organization. Hells Angels disappeared one by one in the late 1980s and 1990s. The bikers never complained that one of their brothers went missing. Some bodies were inadvertently found. Others are still wrapped in sleeping bags on the bottom of the St. Lawrence Seaway. Two members of the Sorel-based Montreal chapter disappeared on September 10, 1989. On the last day of March 1990, fishermen found the body of Jocelyn (Le Prof) Girard, 34, near Louiseville in a canal that links the seaway to Lac Saint-Pierre. Seventy-two hours later, police divers found the body of Marcel (Polpon) Blackburn, 38, floating nearby. Both men were bound and tied inside sleeping bags.

The Hells Angels also waged their ongoing low-profile guerrilla war with their arch enemies the Outlaws in the 1980s. The Outlaws' fortified bunker in Danville, near Asbestos, was torched in 1989. That chapter's former president, Darquis Leblanc, quit and defected to the Hells Angels. Though he would never be allowed to wear Hells Angels' colors, he did their dirty work. Leblanc, six-foot-two and tough, started his life as a hood on a ten-speed bicycle with a gang called the Marauders. When they were old enough to ride motorcycles, they called themselves the Quidams. The Outlaws told them to join their gang or dump the Harleys. They built the bullet-proof Danville bunker in 1985, at the height of their power and war with the Hells Angels. Leblanc sold the bunker to 2549–4444 Quebec Inc. for $1 in 1988. His $150,000 home was torched in April 1989. The bunker was bombed on September 15 of that year. The city bought the building for $21,900 in April 1990 and tore it down.

The Hells Angels tackled the Outlaws in their Joliette stronghold and whittled the chapter down one biker at a time. A confident and cocky contingent of fifty Hells Angels and supporters toured Joliette bars on August 2, 1990, in a show of force and defiance they knew the Outlaws could not match. They would not rest until all Outlaws were dead.

Outlaws leader Claude Meunier, 39, parked his bike outside a motorcycle repair shop in Montreal's Côte-Saint-Paul one day during the first week of September 1990. He was riddled with bullets fired from a passing car before he could get off. Police found a semi-automatic pistol in a storm drain a few blocks away—the trademark disposal of a professional hit. Darquis Leblanc showed up at his funeral in Joliette despite the presence of a hundred Outlaws, but beat a hasty retreat when they spotted him and gave chase. Police stopped a van nearby and arrested two Evil Ones—a Hells Angels puppet gang—and one Hells Angels' associate who were carrying a machine gun and two .44-Magnum revolvers. The Hells Angels moved more of their associates into the Joliette area as they killed off members of that city's Outlaws chapter. Meunier's friend, Tony Mentore, who lived near the Outlaws' Montreal clubhouse on Cazelais Street, was shot to death the following month as he sat in a van outside his family's restaurant supply business in Park Extension.

By the end of 1990, there were only ten Outlaws in Quebec, and they kept to themselves in south-west Montreal, in Valleyfield, and in Châteauguay. Quebec Outlaws president Johnny (Sonny) Lacombe, 46, would not leave his Chateauguay house without bodyguards. The Hells Angels had blown up his mother's car in early November in an attempt to kill his brother, Bertrand.

Darquis Leblanc, as a show of devotion to the Hells Angels, tried to lure me into an ambush and kill me in 1990. He wrote me under pretext of being a reformed biker who had quit the Outlaws and wished to write a book about his exploits to discourage wayward youth from following his path. He assumed I was unaware he had become a Hells Angels associate. In a show of good faith he gave me his home telephone number and asked to meet. Right.

Darquis Leblanc died a turncoat's death at 1:25 p.m. on February 20, 1991, in an alley near a Harley-Davidson dealership and three buildings from the Hells Angels' clubhouse on Boulevard Taschereau in Longueuil on Montreal's South Shore. Leblanc, 34, and his right-hand man and brother-in-law, Yvan Martel, 36, were gunned down and left a trail of blood as they crawled in the snow. Their vehicles were in the Hells Angels' parking lot. The Hells Angels denied through a lawyer that Leblanc belonged to their organization. They did not lie. He was an associate, not a member.

*   *   *

A guard at Montreal's Archambault federal prison conducted a routine search of a prisoners' refrigerator on May 16, 1992, and found a piece of paper that sent shudders through the corrections establishment: a list of 260 prison employees' names, their job positions, social insurance numbers, and home addresses. Nearly sixty of them were underlined or marked with an asterisk. Prison officials and the union played down the incident. The source of the information and the existence of duplicate lists were never confirmed.

The Hells Angels forged strong ties with Montreal's Italian mobsters in the early 1990s. They used their main puppet gang—the Rockers—to participate in drug deals with the Montreal mafia, thereby insulating themselves from prosecution. But when a scheme was devised to import five thousand kilos of cocaine into Canada, the Hells Angels' heavy hitters came out of the shadows to oversee the operation.

The first part of the plan involved smuggling ten sealed drain pipes that contained 740 kilos of cocaine worth $750 million into Canada through Halifax. That deal went sour on August 25, 1993, when the RCMP wrapped up an undercover operation that had begun in May and arrested nineteen people for importing the cocaine into Nova Scotia. Among those arrested were Reynald Desjardins, 43, right-hand man to Vito Rizzuto, boss of Montreal's Sicilian clan; eight Hells Angels and associates, including Saint-Nicolas chapter leaders Richard Hudon and André Imbeault; and Rocker Luc (Bordel) Bordeleau, 32, confidant of Hells Angel Maurice (Mom) Boucher, godfather to the puppet gang and responsible for Hells Angels' activities in the Montreal area. Police seized a Venezuelan freighter, two trawlers, a boat, and $500,000 in cash. It took months for a navy submarine to locate and raise the drain pipes that the smugglers had accidentally dumped in deep water off Halifax when the ship's electrical system malfunctioned. Police had infiltrated the gang with an Acadian fisherman they had trained to con the smugglers into believing he could help them.

Police spent years trying to shut down the successful hashish- and cocaine-smuggling operations of the Montreal mafia and the Hells Angels. They had intercepted trucks full of hash, but failed to arrest the major players. After years of frustration, they finally had a big haul.

The bikers and mafia weren't the only bad guys the Mounties had trouble catching. A series of aborted investigations in Quebec in 1991 convinced them they had a mole. Someone was tipping off major drug smugglers before they were arrested. Pointing a finger at their own is not something cops do lightly. The brotherhood precludes such accusations. Familiarity also makes it difficult to suspect a partner, especially among people who trust each other with their lives. But by 1991, the RCMP conceded internally that they had a rat.

Like most momentous events, the RCMP's corruption problem had innocuous origins. Policy dictated to make the Mounties more inclusive and more reflective of society meant they were hiring a higher percentage of people from visible minorities in the 1980s. There was already dissent in the ranks because it seemed that only bilingual officers got top jobs, and only French-Canadian Mounties were fluently bilingual. But, except for the clipped mustaches, they didn't look any different from English-speaking Mounties. The new hiring policy changed that, and Mounties now came in all shapes, sizes, and colors.

Jorge Leite was five-foot-four and 37 years old when he applied to join the RCMP in 1987. He had dual Portuguese-Canadian citizenship, spoke French, English, Spanish, and Portuguese, had served five years with the Portuguese army in Angola and Mozambique, and had worked on North Sea oil rigs. He made $60,000 as a millwright in Cambridge, Ontario, before he decided to take a $25,000 pay cut and join the force.

Upon graduation from the RCMP academy in Regina, Leite was posted to Spain to work on an international drug investigation. He eventually ended up on the cocaine squad in Montreal, where he earned a reputation as a gung-ho cop on busts. But he also dreamed of financial success, and often complained about not having enough money. He started a limousine service that failed. He talked about opening up a restaurant and bar in Portugal. It was a curious attitude for a new man on a job that doesn't pay that kind of money. Leite's behavior should have raised eyebrows, but it didn't. Police nowdays spend much time complaining about money and sharing their investment schemes and dreams with co-workers.

Early in 1991, Leite's best friend, Luis Lopes, asked him for confidential police information on a drug dealer. It didn't bother Leite that Lopes was a convicted cocaine dealer. Leite asked him for an introduction to Inés Barbosa, described by police as the Cali drug cartel's boss in Montreal. From March to May, Leite sold Barbosa confidential police information forty-nine times. He received $500,000 in cash, vehicles, and a condo in Portugal. Leite opened a U.S.-dollar checking account at a CIBC branch in La Salle, Quebec, for Barbosa on which she wrote $880,000 (U.S.) in checks that bounced. He also returned her passport, which police had seized pending her trial on drug charges. Barbosa, also known as The Godmother, smuggled cocaine inside bowling balls. She and eight employees were arrested in 1990 with $75 million in cocaine.

But the RCMP had trouble nailing the players in bigger busts. They seized 545 kilos of cocaine worth $410 million in a shipment of hammocks from Colombia in April 1991. They seized five hundred kilos of cocaine worth $340 million in a shipment of aluminum silicate powder in May. In both cases, they watched the drugs for days before they realized they had been burned and no one would show up to pick up the cargo.

Leite called the office on May 12 and said he wouldn't be in because of marital problems. He secretly flew to Cartagena, Colombia, where he helped smugglers plan routes into Canada. He suggested Labrador. Leite had met smugglers in Venezuela on an earlier trip.

On May 13 Barbosa's lawyer, Sidney Leithman, was assassinated in downtown Montreal. Montreal's highest profile criminal lawyer—he defended underworld crime boss Frank Cotroni and a Hells Angel at a murder trial—he'd spent two years defending Colombian smugglers, with little success. That doesn't cut it with Colombians. They want guarantees. They want a lawyer who can buy judges, juries, and witnesses. In a trial of three people charged with importing five hundred kilos of cocaine into Canada, two men he defended got twenty-three- and twenty-five-year sentences. The female client he promised to get acquitted got eighteen years in jail. The hit man approached Leithman's black Saab at a red light and shot the 53-year-old lawyer in the head and heart. He left a plastic bag of raw meat inside the car, probably to symbolize a pound of flesh.

The RCMP had suspected for months it had a mole. During raids they found confidential information from their offices. Some information was transmitted on a police fax machine equipped with a scrambler. They fed false information to different officers in the hope of finding out who leaked it. Attention eventually focused on Leite, and he was put under surveillance.

At the time, Leite was a bodyguard for the RCMP's main witness against members of the Medellin cartel caught smuggling cocaine into Canada. A Colombian hit team sent to Canada to kill the informant had already been caught in Nova Scotia after their skin color and light clothing made them stand out from local residents. The witness, Doug Jaworski, had supplied planes for the cartel in the late 1980s and knew their operations. On the police risk scale of one to seven, he rated 6.5.

Leite spotted surveillance on his friend Lopes, and realized he had been targeted as the Mountie mole. He faxed his resignation on May 22, and said he hoped his quick departure would not affect his pension. He shipped several vehicles to Portugal. His wife, who stayed behind to tie up loose ends, had earlier in the year carried $100,000 to the country in a briefcase. Leite would elude the RCMP and justice for years.

The man who ordered Leite put under surveillance was Inspector Claude Savoie, head of the RCMP's Montreal drug squad from 1989 to 1991. He targeted Leite when informed there was a mole in the force. Leite's flight from Canada confirmed the RCMP's worst suspicions and explained the unacceptable failure rate of high-level drug investigations.

A more comprehensive explanation—albeit one that opened a whole new range of possible problems—was offered on December 28, 1992. Inspector Savoie, by then assistant director of the RCMP's intelligence service—one of the most sensitive police posts in Canada—killed himself with a shotgun in his Ottawa headquarters minutes before he was to meet internal affairs investigators who had suspected for the past year that he had links with criminals.

Inspector Savoie, 49, was a twenty-seven-year veteran of the RCMP's Criminal Intelligence Service. He had accepted $200,000 from Montreal crime boss Allan (The Weasel) Ross, head of the West End Gang, for confidential police information. Inspector Savoie, without alerting his superiors, had met with Ross and his lawyer in 1990. He first tried to explain his actions by saying he'd hoped to persuade Ross to become an informant. There are specific policies for such approaches and Inspector Savoie adhered to none of them.

The U.S. Drug Enforcement Administration caught Ross as he tried to import and traffic ten thousand kilograms of cocaine and three hundred tons of marijuana in Florida. He was fined $10 million and sentenced to three life terms in May 1992. RCMP in Burnaby, British Columbia, arrested Hells Angel Jacques (Jack) Émond on September 4, 1993. The 37-year-old biker was wanted by the U.S. Drug Enforcement Administration in Florida for alleged participation in a smuggling scheme.

Three separate investigations were conducted into the Savoie affair. The RCMP looked into Savoie's links with Ross, and also examined the overall operations of its Montreal drug squad. The Ottawa police conducted a separate investigation of Savoie's suicide.

No one knows how many police officers in all levels of law enforcement were recruited by Inspector Savoie to provide information to drug smugglers and sabotage investigations, or whether these moles are still in place. No one knows how many cases or informants have been compromised. Inspector Savoie had unlimited access to files and the heads of the world's criminal intelligence services. He kept more secrets in death than he did in life, and his legacy may still haunt the RCMP today, as his hand-picked moles gnaw away at its effectiveness in the war against drug-rich criminals.

Leite evaded RCMP investigators until 1998, when he gave them a signed confession of his treachery. He was arrested in Portugal, which does not extradite its citizens. However, he was tried there on Canadian charges of breach of trust, corruption, and fraud. Then Leite recanted his confession and concocted a tale which had him working as an honest cop for Inspector Savoie in an attempt to infiltrate the Cali cartel. He said he turned over to Inspector Savoie all payments received for leaked information. His bank accounts and assets told another story, but Inspector Savoie was in no condition to testify. Leite was found guilty of corruption on January 19, 1999, and sentenced to four years in jail. The sympathetic judge suspended the sentence because the crimes had been committed long ago and far away by a man who was nearing 50. Leite is free to spend the proceeds of treason as he wishes.

Origins of the Rock Machine

The Hells Angels was not the only motorcycle gang to expand and consolidate its criminal empire in the 1980s and early 1990s. Bikers from half a dozen gangs that dissolved or were absorbed during the Hells Angels' expansion drive in the 1980s plied their drug trade anonymously, but successfully, in Quebec City and Montreal. Despite their financial gains, they longed for the recognition and respect accorded to outlaw bikers in the underworld. They missed the ability to intimidate. Once a biker, always a biker. A punk can't be a punk without a gang.

Salvatore Cazzetta was 30 when his SS biker gang dissolved in 1984 and its members got sucked into the monolithic Hells Angels empire. Cazzetta was a charismatic leader and couldn't see himself in an organization where the gang came ahead of the individuals. He convinced his 27-year-old brother Giovanni to quit the Outlaws and help him form a new biker gang, one with all the trappings—tattoos, clubhouse, symbols—but without the pitfall of colors which identify them to the public and police. The Cazzettas were born to crime. It was a business to them, and they discriminated against no one. In their short lifetime, the trilingual (Italian, French, and English) brothers cultivated powerful contacts in Montreal's Italian mafia, among the French-Canadian mob of the Dubois brothers, and with the predominantly Irish West End Gang.

The Cazzettas built their networks assiduously and by 1990 called their low-profile biker gang the Rock Machine. That name and their crest—a black, stylized eagle's head—appeared on all gang members' businesses and on a gold ring members used instead of colors to identify themselves. Prospective members wore the same ring, without the gang's name engraved on it. The Rock Machine did not have weekly meetings like the Hells Angels and did not keep membership lists with addresses and phone numbers, lists which identified Hells Angels to police. Because they did not show up at biker functions and did not live the traditional biker lifestyle, the Hells Angels had only a vague idea who some of the Rock Machine members were. Police did not consider them a motorcycle gang and would not for a decade. They called them the Cazzetta clan. It was to become a sore point that haunted some gang members in need of notoriety.

The branch of the Rock Machine that operated in Quebec City was made up of former members of the Pacific Rebels, a group dissolved by gang warfare in the late 1970s. The Montreal branch numbered about ten former SS, Merciless Riders, and Exécuteurs members. The Rock Machine had a network of more than a hundred associates that smuggled and distributed drugs in both cities.

Although the Italian Mafia and the Hells Angels controlled drug trafficking in Quebec, both groups had a good working relationship with the Cazzettas. This was unusual for the Hells Angels. They were monopolistic and shared territory with no one. But the Cazzettas were well connected—they had grown up in the tough streets of Saint-Henri—and had a large army of supporters to draw on. The Hells Angels didn't dare start a war that would cost them more than a victory would give them. Intimidation, which worked so well against most criminals, was useless against Salvatore Cazzetta. He was a cold-blooded, violent man driven to success. He provided leadership that inspired loyalty, and to attack such a man was foolish, even for the Hells Angels. So they bided their time and waited for the Rock Machine to show weakness.

The Rock Machine fortified a $1.3-million clubhouse at 2025 rue Hudon in south-west Montreal. Salvatore Cazzetta's house in L'Épiphanie was worth more than $2 million. Gang members had access to lawyers, accountants, and financial advisors. These were not a bunch of punks who decided to become criminals. They were established criminals who added the punk cachet to their resumes.

Nine years of success brought no public notoriety, but did attract police attention. Giovanni Cazzetta was charged with possession of three kilos of cocaine worth $2.25 million in April 1992, and pleaded guilty in the face of overwhelming evidence in the spring of 1993. With one brother down, the RCMP and the U.S. Drug Enforcement Administration issued an extradition warrant for Salvatore Cazzetta in late March 1993, on charges he had imported eleven tons of cocaine. Cazzetta, associate Nelson Fernandes, 28, and another man had allegedly paid a double agent $600,000 for cocaine in Florida. Three members of the West End Gang were also arrested in the deal. Salvatore Cazzetta eluded police until May 8, 1994, when he was arrested in Fort Erie, Ontario.

The Hells Angels smelled blood. Maurice (Mom) Boucher ran Montreal for the Hells Angels, which he joined on May 1, 1987, three years after the SS gang he belonged to with Salvatore Cazzetta had folded. Boucher and his right-hand man Normand (Biff) Hamel got their Hells Angels' colors several days after Death Riders president Martin Huneault was killed, which allowed the Hells Angels to take over the gang and expand their drug territory into Laval and the lower Laurentians.

Boucher decided the Rock Machine was an easy target with its two leaders in jail. Boucher, though violent, was not given to impulsive actions. He had long watched the Rock Machine make money in downtown Montreal, and figured he was due a cut of the action. He enlisted a handful of members to help him plan the takeover. The dirty work was relegated to puppet gangs, the Montreal Rockers and the Evil Ones from the South Shore. Both gangs already had drug networks in central Montreal that overlapped with those of the Rock Machine. The Hells Angels and Rock Machine's favorite bars were kitty corner from each other at a downtown intersection.

Biker strongmen wasted no time trying to wrest control of drug distribution in bars from the Rock Machine in central Montreal, along the boulevard Saint-Laurent, rue Sainte-Catherine, and rue Saint-Denis. Some readers might recognize these streets from some of Canada's finest literature. For the rest of the world, these streets are home to Montreal's criminal underworld. The Rock Machine sold an estimated $5 million in cocaine alone in this area. That does not include hash, marijuana, PCP, and LSD.

The Hells Angels greatly outnumbered the Rock Machine on the eve of a war that could have been averted if the Angels had not been so greedy. But the Hells Angels are monopolistic. They refuse to share. They looked at the gangs they had assimilated over the years and figured the Rock Machine would be just another trophy. Of the 315 outlaw bikers in Quebec—the numbers varied throughout the war as some were killed, others jailed, and new members were recruited—264 were linked to the Hells Angels (72 were full-fledged members) and 51 were Rock Machine. The Hells Angels were outnumbered only in Quebec City, where their Saint-Nicolas chapter had 14 members and 1 prospect. The Rock Machine had 19 members.

Hells Angels:
- Montreal chapter in Sorel: 19 members, 1 prospect. Puppet gangs under their control: Rockers: 17 members, 9 prospects; Evil Ones in Drummondville: 9 members, 2 prospects; Evil Ones in Rive-Sud: 18 members, 1 prospect; Death Riders in Laval: 11 members, 15 prospects.
- Nomads chapter: 9 members (formed during the war's first year).
- Saint-Nicolas chapter: 14 members, 1 prospect.
- Lennoxville chapter in Sherbrooke: 22 members, 2 prospects. Puppet gangs under their control: La Meute in Abitibi: 4 members; Bucks in Malartic: 8 members; Pow Wow in Val-d'Or: 11 members; Pacifiques in Evain: 12 members.
- Trois-Rivières chapter: 8 members, four prospects. Puppet gangs under their control: Satan's Guards in Saguenay: 11 members, 2 prospects; H.D. Riders in Sept-Îles: 10 members; Rowdy Crew in Lanaudière: 9 members; Rowdy Crew in east Montreal: 8 members; Jokers in Saint-Jean: 8 members, 2 prospects; Blatnois in Mauricie: 14 members, 3 prospects.

Rock Machine:
- Montreal: 25 members.
- Quebec: 19 members.
- Rimouski: 7 members.

Puppet gangs do the dirty work for the Hells Angels. They kill, bomb, burn, intimidate, extort, all at the behest of their Hells Angels godfather. They not only provide the gang with a pool of prospects, but with a layer of insulation from prosecution. When a puppet-gang member gets caught, he takes the rap. If he rats, he gets killed. The more people criminally active Hells Angels have working for them, the richer and more powerful they become.

The most successful Hells Angels never get their hands dirty. They just plot and give orders. Each one is a godfather to a criminal empire within the gang's larger international network. None enter the Hells

Angels without a godfather—someone to teach them the ropes and guide their progress. Seasoned members only accept prospects who will help them achieve their goals. Though a prospect must obey all full-fledged members, he controls anyone below him on the hierarchy, be they hangarounds or sympathizers.

The more ambitious Hells Angels set up puppet gangs, usually by taking over an existing gang, peacefully or violently. The Hells Angels godfather teaches his underlings the gang rules and how to do business the Hells Angels way. Contrary to the beliefs of proponents of an anti-gang law, no one inside the Hells Angels organization gives orders to commit crimes. The gang itself does not commit crimes. Those members who are criminals operate in isolated cells and have no contact with other members, unless they cooperate on specific ventures. However, the gang's international networks and its power and ability to intimidate allow each cell to be successful. That is why membership in the Hells Angels is so important. Few organizations inspire fear and trepidation as do the Hells Angels.

The Rock Machine laughed at Hells Angels' attempts to verbally intimidate them. They showed the Angels on July 13, 1994, that they would stand their ground. Two hit men walked into a Harley-Davidson motorcycle repair shop in Rivière-des-Prairies owned by 34-year-old Hells Angels sympathizer Pierre Daoust and shot him dead. The next day, July 14, five Rock Machine members planned to blow up and shoot members of the Evil Ones in Saint-Basile-le-Grand. Police arrested them at their hotels with three radio-detonated bombs, twelve pounds of dynamite, and two pistols. Among those arrested were Frédéric Faucher and Martin Blouin from Quebec City.

Rock Machine sympathizer Michel Boyer, son of Bernard (Big Ben) Provençal, one of Quebec's most notorious informants, was arrested in east Montreal on July 17, as he and an accomplice prepared to assassi-nate Montreal Hells Angels president Maurice (Mom) Boucher. The men were armed, wore body armor, and had balaclavas. They also had dynamite, detonators, and a remote control device able to trigger three separate bombs. Big Ben Provençal ratted on dozens of underworld figures in the 1980s, including his brother Roger.

Police prevented another bloodbath when they arrested three armed Rockers wearing bullet-proof vests in central Montreal on July 27 as they planned to attack the Rock Machine.

Quebec Hells Angels decided in August 1994 to order the Rock Machine to stop calling themselves a motorcycle gang. The Hells Angels had, through decades of violence, appointed themselves the makers and enforcers of rules for outlaws. Newly elected national president Robert (Tiny) Richard personally delivered the edict to the Rock Machine clubhouse. The Hells Angels have had the arrogance and audacity since the 1960s in California to determine who could be a biker gang and who couldn't. The Rock Machine, who were more businessmen than bikers, laughed at this tight-assed side of the Hells Angels. Rather than be intimidated, they picked up the pace of battle.

Hells Angels associate Maurice Lavoie, a former dealer for the Pelletier brothers' gang, was gunned down with a 9-mm pistol on October 19 as he arrived home in Repentigny.

The following week, Rock Machine sympathizer Sylvain Pelletier, 32, a major drug trafficker in the Hochelaga-Maisonneuve quarter of Montreal who operated a successful drug network with his two brothers, was shredded when a bomb exploded inside his Jeep Cherokee on rue Notre-Dame in Repentigny. He was a good friend of the man charged in Lavoie's death.

On November 4, Rock Machine associate Daniel Bertrand, 29, was machine-gunned in the Sainte-4 bar on rue Sainte-Catherine.

On December 5, Rockers prospect Bruno Bandiera, 28, died when his stolen Plymouth Voyageur van exploded half a kilometer from the Hells Angels clubhouse in Longueuil.

On December 16, someone parked a bomb-laden truck in front of a restaurant frequented by Hells Angel Maurice (Mom) Boucher. The truck was towed before Boucher arrived. The Hells Angel was wary. He wore body armor and installed bullet-proof glass in his house.

1995

Six Hells Angels from the Trois-Rivières chapter and two prospects flew to Acapulco, Mexico, on Friday, December 23, with an entourage of fourteen people. Normand Baker, 34, one of five Rock Machine members stopped in July with bombs and guns, was also in Acapulco with his girlfriend. On January 4, 1995, they had lunch with another couple at the Hard Rock Café. A man who had followed Baker around Acapulco all morning on a motorcycle allegedly walked up to their table, wearing a bathing suit, and shot him in the head. The man jumped through a plate-glass window and scampered down the street, only to be tackled by waiters who gave chase. He was taken to the police station across the street from the restaurant. Hells Angels prospect François Hinse, 30, was charged with the shooting.

The Quebec Hells Angels and their puppet gangs

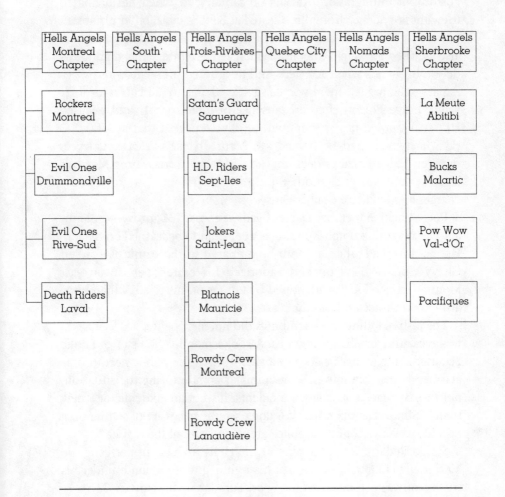

Hells Angels Montreal Chapter	Hells Angels South Chapter	Hells Angels Trois-Rivières Chapter	Hells Angels Quebec City Chapter	Hells Angels Nomads Chapter	Hells Angels Sherbrooke Chapter
Rockers Montreal		Satan's Guard Saguenay			La Meute Abitibi
Evil Ones Drummondville		H.D. Riders Sept-Iles			Bucks Malartic
Evil Ones Rive-Sud		Jokers Saint-Jean			Pow Wow Val-d'Or
Death Riders Laval		Blatnois Mauricie			Pacifiques
		Rowdy Crew Montreal			
		Rowdy Crew Lanaudière			

vs.

The Alliance

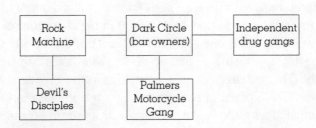

Rock Machine	Dark Circle (bar owners)	Independent drug gangs
Devil's Disciples	Palmers Motorcycle Gang	

Mexican judge Edmundo Román Pinzón released Hinse into the custody of immigration officials on January 14 when he dismissed eyewitness evidence from those seated at Baker's table, other restaurant patrons, and a waiter as insufficient to charge Hinse in the killing. He also ascribed no weight to police evidence that Hinse had had gunpowder on his hands when arrested. And he ignored prosecutor José Vélez Zapata, who argued there was enough evidence to jail Hinse for forty years. Judge Pinzón cited an "absence of direct proof" and released Hinse. Acapulco newspapers within days reported that a $700,000 (U.S.) payment had been made to secure Hinse's release. Lawyers branded Judge Pinzon's decision "absurd." The stories stung Mexico's legal authorities, and another judge was appointed to review the charges and evidence against Hinse.

Rock Machine member Daniel (Dada) Senesac, 31, proved on January 15, 1995, that bomb-building is not a craft to be learned on the job. He lost his head when a bomb he prepared in the trunk of a stolen Chevy Corsica blew up and vaporized his extremities on an east Montreal street. He was identified by tattoos on his torso, which body armor had protected from the blast.

The rash of killings and bombings did not alert politicians that a war was escalating on their doorsteps. A spokesman for Minister of Public Security Serge Ménard said on January 19 that the public need not be alarmed by the bombings. "The minister is monitoring the situation, but they appear to be isolated incidents. It's not an epidemic or a new trend," Simon Lacroix said. "We don't see the necessity of setting up a task force. We're confident police are taking care of the matter."

Simon Bédard, 26, a member of the Hells Angels puppet gang the Mercenaires in Quebec City, lost his right leg when a bomb under his truck seat was detonated remotely on Tuesday night, January 31.

Earlier in the day, the Montreal Urban Community police anti-gang squad found two hundred sticks of dynamite when they stopped a car and fifty detonators during a raid on a house.

Later that day, Claude (Le Pic) Rivard, 38, a member of the Pelletier gang that did business with the Rock Machine, walked out of his house and got into his white Suzuki 4×4 at 3:30 in the afternoon on Friday, February 3. Two men, one of them a member of the Rowdy Crew, a Hells Angels puppet gang, pulled up next to him in a pick-up truck at a red light. The passenger, Serge Quesnel, shot Rivard with a revolver. The Rowdy Crew, based in Lanaudière, have a clubhouse in Lavaltrie. They competed with the Pelletier gang for drug turf in Montreal's east end and became more aggressive with the death of Sylvain Pelletier, their leader. His brothers operated more discreetly after his Jeep Cherokee was bombed.

*   *   *

The Hells Angels committed a tactical error when they asked their puppet gangs to target independent networks like the Pelletier gang. The Angels got greedy, and in the heat of war decided to go after the entire drug market in Montreal instead of the portion controlled by the Rock Machine. As the Hells Angels threatened bar owners and killed gang members through their associates, they created more anger than fear in the underworld.

Montreal gangs have traditionally shared the lucrative drug market. Since their arrival in Quebec in 1977, the Hells Angels had taken over eighty percent of a drug market worth hundreds of millions a year. Other gangs watched their revenues decrease, but were powerless to take on the Hells Angels. These different gangs realized in early 1995 that they had a common enemy and the battle for drug turf turned into a fight for survival. The Rock Machine, independent drug gangs, and a group of bar owners called the Dark Circle, who allowed the sale of narcotics in their establishments, banded together to create the Alliance to fight off the Hells Angels and even take back from the biker gang drug territory they felt was theirs.

The Dark Circle became the hit squad for the Alliance. During the course of the war they created their own biker gang—the Palmers—to fight the Hells Angels puppet gang, the Rockers. Palmers were sponsored, meaning controlled, by two members of the Dark Circle and were identified by a pendant worn around their necks that showed a palm tree and an island. White members had white palm trees, black members had black palms. Members of the Dark Circle wore rings with an engraved claw. All members of the Alliance were allowed to wear a ring engraved with an acronym of the Alliance motto: ALVALM—À la vie, à la mort. For life, until death. As the war progressed, the easiest way to spot a gangster was to look at his hands.

The Hells Angels had bitten off more than they could chew. They arrogantly believed when they started the war that the Rock Machine would cave in to intimidation. When that failed, they expected them to fearfully beg for mercy after a few assassinations. The Hells Angels were caught off guard when the Rock Machine and associates fought back. The Hells Angels had become so complacent they neglected the first duty of any ruling power: they failed to gather intelligence on potential enemies in case they ever needed it. As the war escalated, the Hells Angels found they had few targets, while the Rock Machine and Dark Circle knew who the Hells Angels, plus their associates and sympathizers, were, and where to find them. The balance of power favored the Alliance, and the Hells Angels ran scared in 1995.

*   *   *

The Rock Machine stockpiled an arsenal of weapons and explosives to tackle the Hells Angels. Thieves stole nearly 2,500 kilos of dynamite in broad daylight from a Joliette construction site on Sunday, February 12.

By mid-February 1995, enough Hells Angels and Rock Machine sympathizers had been arrested that the war for the streets of Montreal carried over into prisons. Each side tried to force inmates into its camp in a battle to control drug trafficking behind bars. It is a sad testimony and an indictment of the prison system that it is easier to buy drugs while incarcerated anywhere in the world than it is on the streets. Prison officials often look the other way as inmates bide their time smuggling and selling drugs. Busy minds and busy bodies don't start trouble for guards and administrators. The drug business inside Bordeaux prison north of Montreal was worth $7 million a year. Some dealers had their associates lob drug-filled tennis balls into the prison yard.

About twenty prisoners in Bordeaux who refused to support either warring gang were severely beaten during the first two months of the year. The four Hells Angels associates and four Rock Machine associates behind bars recruited fifty sympathizers and wannabes among the inmate population to fight their war. Sympathizers on the outside committed petty crimes to be sent to jail to bolster the forces. Prison officials finally segregated gang sympathizers in separate wings.

Montreal police found two powerful bombs in a van in a South Shore garage used by the Hells Angels on Monday, February 20. One of the devices was a shrapnel bomb, made with three four-pound sticks of dynamite, thousands of three-inch nails, detonators, and batteries. A twelve-pound dynamite bomb without a detonator sat next to it. A remote control box to trigger the bombs was found in the van. Another stolen van in the garage yielded two four-pound sticks and twenty-eight quarter-pound sticks of dynamite. "Many people could have been killed or maimed if the bomb had exploded on a public street or open area," said Det.-Lt. Michel Gagné of the anti-gang squad, which had five investigators and a fifteen-man task force working to stop the war. "It's no longer just a war between gangs. All bombs are dangerous, but the danger to citizens increases when you start messing around with powerful nail bombs."

Later in the day, the anti-gang unit found a Hells Angels' arsenal and seized thirty-three kilos of marijuana, four machine guns, and four bullet-proof vests.

The next day, Tuesday, February 21, the Montreal Urban Community police added a second fifteen-man task force to its arsenal. That night, a bomb damaged an empty dance club—l'Énergie—in east Montreal. The bar was a hangout for Hells Angels' associates and sympathizers. The five-kilogram dynamite bomb mixed with 9-mm bullets was detonated at the building's front door. The bar had been bombed two years earlier, in April 1993.

On Monday, February 27, Claude Cossette, a 50-year-old east Montreal gang leader, rolled down the window of his van outside his house to talk to a man who approached him. The man pumped three bullets into his head. Cossette was part of the Rock Machine alliance against the Hells Angels. He had contacts in the Dubois gang in Saint-Henri and the Provençal gang in the east end. Cossette's leg had been broken on August 4, 1994, when his car exploded as he turned on the ignition.

Between March 9 and 12, someone stole 571 of 70,000 detonators stored in a sand pit in Charlesbourg, near Quebec City. On Friday, March 10, two Rockers opened their rue Guilford clubhouse door in Montreal and found a bomb on the steps. The remote-controlled bomb contained twenty pounds of explosives. They carried it across the street to prevent damage to their clubhouse. Rocker André (Toots or Peanuts) Tousignant, Maurice (Mom) Boucher's chauffeur, pulled the detonator out of the bomb and tossed it down the street, where it exploded. That night, police disarmed a parcel bomb left in a Val-Belair bar.

The Rockers' clubhouse had been financed with a $105,000 loan from the Federal Business Development Bank when they took over the mortgage on the building after the original holders moved out. The mortgage applicant was Guy Lepage, a former Montreal policeman who became a bar owner, then a biker. Lepage applied for money to buy a warehouse to repair and distribute vending machines. His references and credit rating checked out and the bank transferred the mortgage to his name. At the time, Lepage was serving a two-year prison term for laundering drug money. The bank called back the loan in August 1994 when Lepage was deemed in default of the conditions of the loan for not using the building for the purposes stated on his application. He was released in 1995 and shortly afterwards the bank found out the building was the Rocker clubhouse to which two bombs had recently been delivered.

The federal bank was not the only financial institution to fund a biker clubhouse. The Caisse populaire Sherbrooke-Est had contracted six mortgages totaling $353,500 since 1988 on the Hells Angels' clubhouse in Lennoxville and two houses owned by Hells Angel Claude (Burger)

Berger. The North chapter had been slaughtered at the clubhouse in 1985, but the killing was still in the news because of ongoing trials. A $60,000 mortgage was taken out on the clubhouse in March 1990 and a $50,000 mortgage in June 1992. Claude (Burger) Berger and 2314-3639 Quebec Inc., which promotes motorcycle shows and real estate, contracted the mortgages. Hells Angels Charles Filteau and Guy Auclair are the company's secretary-treasurer and vice-president.

Hells Angel Maurice (Mom) Boucher returned to Montreal on Monday morning, March 13, after a two-week holiday in Ixtapa, Mexico, with Patrick Lock, son of the Rockers president. The previous fall, someone had parked a truck loaded with dynamite in front of his house. The RCMP seized an arsenal at his girlfriend's house. That Monday night, a Rock Machine member in Quebec City found a bomb in his parked car.

Tuesday night, March 14, Rock Machine associate Denis Marcoux, 39, nearly lost a chunk of his left leg in Quebec City when his Chevy S-10 truck blew up as he drove to work at a bar he managed. The bombers placed the bomb on the driver's side of the truck rather than in the center, and the remotely detonated explosion dissipated when the door popped open. The truck's running board was flung through an apartment window across the street and landed next to a sleeping 18-month-old baby's crib, which was filled with glass. The baby, who wasn't hurt, wouldn't stop crying. His 10-year-old brother stood in the middle of his bed surrounded by broken glass. All the building's windows were blown out.

The next day, Wednesday, March 15, public security minister Serge Ménard assured fellow cabinet ministers that police were doing all they could to curb the biker war. "We're taking special measures," Ménard said. "All the latest incidents are being scrupulously analyzed. We're trying to determine which gangs are involved in these attempts. This is one of our priorities and I'm certain that the Sûreté du Québec, as we speak, is doing everything that is humanly possible to do in a democratic society to fight these gangs." Pressed, Ménard admitted: "It's a war between the Hells Angels and the Rock Machine for control of drugs."

*   *   *

While a handful of Montreal Hells Angels orchestrated the war with the Rock Machine, others pursued the gang's long-term plan to control drug trafficking across Canada. Mindful of the police ability to raid clubhouses and easily follow members who meet regularly, nine hand-picked Hells Angels who had proven their worth over the years formed a rootless Nomads chapter that wasn't bound to a clubhouse or territory. Lack of a clubhouse also gave enemies little chance to find them. Their aim was to conquer Ontario, which was controlled by six established biker gangs and six lesser gangs that did their bidding. Police labeled the Nomads chapter the Hells Angels' "dream team" or "SWAT team." It is a weakness all police exhibit. It is easier for them to deal with labels.

The Nomads chapter was formed on June 24, 1995, of tough businessmen who were all leaders in their own right. It was Quebec's fifth chapter after Montreal, Sherbrooke, Saint-Nicolas, and Trois Rivières. The Nomads used the Trois-Rivierès mailing address. Its members were Wolodumir (Walter, Nurget) Stadnick, former national president and graduate of the Wild Ones from Hamilton, Ontario; his best friend Donald (Pup) Stockford, also a Hamilton boy and the only Quebec Hells Angel without a criminal record; Maurice (Mom) Boucher, Montreal chapter president and sponsor of the Rockers puppet gang. He was also Nomads president; Louis (Mélou) Roy, Trois-Rivières ex-president; his right-hand man, Richard (Rick) Vallée; Denis (Pas Fiable) Houle; Gilles (Trooper) Mathieu; David (Wolf) Carrol, formerly of the Halifax chapter and interested in the northern Ontario drug network; and Normand (Biff) Hamel, who controlled the Death Riders and drug networks in Laval and the lower Laurentians.

Quebec now had five Hells Angels chapters with seventy-five members.

*   *   *

The Quebec public finally woke up to the seriousness of the biker war on March 17, when a bomb damaged the Rockers' clubhouse in Montreal and shattered windows as well as the peace of mind neighbors had lulled themselves into. People who live near biker clubhouses always describe the bikers as quiet men who treat them well. That's because bikers want neighbors on their side. They don't want complaints to the police and they want the eyes on the street to work for them. The bombing of the Rockers' clubhouse prompted a public outcry against bikers never before seen in Quebec.

Police followed Hells Angel Maurice (Mom) Boucher Friday night, March 24, because they suspected he was about to make a drug deal. If they had not known him, they would have guessed the short-haired, polite man was a businessman out on the town. They stopped Boucher's car and found a loaded, unregistered 9-mm pistol with the serial number filed off tucked in his belt. He was on his way to a Hells

Angels' motorcycle show in Sherbrooke with his right-hand man, Rocker André Tousignant. Boucher was already at odds with many Hells Angels for the negative publicity his war with the Rock Machine brought the gang. To avoid giving the press more fodder, he pleaded guilty Saturday morning to two of the three charges he faced: carrying a concealed firearm and being inside a vehicle containing a restricted firearm. He was sentenced to six months in Bordeaux jail. He would be out in two months if he behaved. He was also put on probation for three years and prohibited from owning a weapon for ten years. (Boucher, 42, was released in late July.)

Around this time, the Hells Angels began to plot a publicity campaign used by the gang elsewhere in the world during times of conflict. They anonymously circulated tracts that accused police of starting the war. One of these tracts read: "For several months, through its numerous mouthpieces and certain court reporters . . . the Sûreté du Québec, to achieve its ends, has flooded the biker milieu with falsehoods, leading them to believe, among other things, that their lives were threatened by other gangs, thus provoking the current bloody war. Furthermore, just as the conflict is about to be resolved, the SQ does not hesitate to stoke the flames by planting incendiary articles, even going as far as exploding a bomb (Bar L'Énergie), as the RCMP used to do during the FLQ period."

I have witnessed similar allegations made by Hells Angels in Scandinavia, the United States, and other parts of the country. They seem to share the same public relations firm.

As part of their campaign to discredit press reports of the biker war, the Hells Angels complained to the Quebec Press Council in late March about a January article in the *Journal de Montréal* which published a group photograph of the Hells Angels to illustrate a year-end wrap-up. It seemed the Hells Angels were concerned about their enemies being able to identify them. Their lawyer asked the council: "Will we see the publication of personal addresses or a list of schools attended by the children of Hells Angels Inc.?" The lawyer complained that readers could conclude that all persons in the photograph were active Hells Angels and drug traffickers. He said five men in the photographs had quit and "reoriented" their lives and that the article harmed them. Curiously, none of these former members complained. He concluded that all persons, including the Hells Angels, have a "right to have their private life, their honor, and their dignity respected." It's amazing what some people say for money.

Public reaction to the bombing of the Rockers' clubhouse led to my participation in a live television program on Friday, March 31, in Montreal. Guests included frightened neighbors, several levels of law enforcement, and public security minister Serge Ménard. The politician said police had the war under control. I called his bluff: "I challenge you, Mr. Minister, to make the streets of Quebec safe for its citizens or quit your portfolio and give the job to someone who can do it."

Quebec police announced in April that they had convinced the Hells Angels and Rock Machine to agree to a truce.

*   *   *

Montreal police arrested six Rock Machine sympathizers in a hotel room on Wednesday, May 3, as they plotted to kill two Hells Angels. Michel Bertrand, 30, head of the Bertrand gang, whose twin brother Daniel had been shot dead in a bar the previous November, was the group's leader. Four of the six men were hit men, members of a Haitian street gang that dealt drugs in Bertrand territory. They had divided themselves into three groups to carry out the killings. The first group planned the hit; the second had to find the victims; the third was to carry out the assassination. Police seized two Cobray machine guns, a twelve-gauge shotgun, a Luger pistol, a .357-Magnum revolver, four 9-mm semi-automatic pistols—all loaded, and a tool box full of ammunition.

Police found a Hells Angels' stash of 103 sticks of dynamite on Tuesday, May 9, in Larouche in the Saguenay region of northern Quebec. The dynamite had been stolen from a construction site near Chapais the previous summer. The dynamite had been wrapped in plastic and buried under moss by members of the Satan's Guards, a Hells Angels puppet gang.

Despite the killings and bombings, the Hells Angels pursued their public relations efforts and lawyer Gilles Daudelin seized on every opportunity to deflect attention away from his clients. He denied the existence of a turf war. "It's all a set-up by the police so that they can get more public money and increase their power," he said.

Further proof of a Hells Angels public relations campaign was caught on a wiretap of Maurice (Mom) Boucher's phone. Boucher discussed details of a private conversation public security minister Serge Ménard had had four days earlier with former Sûreté du Québec corporal Gaétan Rivest, who criticized police tactics in handling the biker war and recommended a public inquiry to expose objectionable police behavior toward bikers. Boucher said over the phone that the gang must enlist the aid of communications specialists so the operation to sway the minister is carried out without a hitch.

*   *   *

Police acted on a tip and found a van in Lachine on Monday night, July 3, that had been stolen from the McGill University campus in January and converted into a war wagon. It contained a seven-pound fragmentation bomb, 122 sticks of dynamite, fifty detonators, two sawed-off twelve-gauge shotguns, a semi-automatic .30-caliber M-1 rifle, four 9-mm Cobray machine pistols—three equipped to handle silencers—and a Belgian 1.762-caliber anti-tank, anti-aircraft machine gun loaded with a six-foot-long ammo belt and bolted to a metal table fastened to the van's interior with chains. More frightening, the truck contained Sûreté du Québec decals—stolen during a 1993 burglary of a Saint-Laurent supplier—which would have made the van look like a police vehicle. Bikers hide their guns when police approach a clubhouse, and would have been taken off-guard by the war wagon. Police would have been blamed for the shooting. The guns were shipped to the Hells Angels from Mohawk Warriors on the Kahnawake Reserve.

Police used their remote-controlled $65,000 robot to remove the bomb from the van and spray it with a jet of water, which normally defuses explosives. The bomb exploded, vaporized the robot, and sent debris crashing through houses half a mile away, narrowly missing two chlorine reservoirs at a nearby water-treatment plant. The area had not been cordoned off or evacuated. Neighbors woke up as pieces of metal the size of footballs tore through bedrooms. Only the robot was hurt.

Montreal Hells Angel Michael (L'Animal) Lajoie-Smith was godfather to the Death Riders who had replaced the slaughtered North chapter in Laval, then moved to Sainte-Thérèse because of police pressure. He ran a network of thugs who intimidated bar owners into letting Hells Angels' dealers sell drugs in their establishments. Those who weren't intimidated verbally were beaten, shot, or bombed. The owner of the disco-bar Le Pot didn't cave in to intimidation, and Lajoie-Smith got violent. During a fight on July 22, he beat innocent bystander Alain Cadieux, 32, so badly the man must spend the rest of his life in an institution.

*   *   *

Hells Angels' attempts to discredit police and gain public support continued on Sunday, July 30, when gang lawyer Martin Tremblay released to a newspaper photographs of informant Serge Quesnel and his girlfriend taken in police headquarters. Tremblay had had the photographs since May, but chose to release them one week before

Quesnel was to testify against members of the gang. Quesnel, a Hells Angels' contract hit man, was the triggerman who killed Claude (Le Pic) Rivard on February 3. He was charged for this and numerous other crimes on April 3 and struck a deal to testify against the Hells Angels in exchange for $390,000 over fifteen years and a new identity. He confessed to five murders and thirteen murder conspiracies.

"I saw that they had me," he said after he was caught with $10,000 in jewelry and shown evidence that linked him to dozens of crimes. Fifteen years is better than life, so he ratted out. He invested the money and estimated he would leave jail with nearly $1 million. The government also allowed him to keep the jewelry, and agreed to pay for his change of identity and the removal of his tattoos. Besides regular biker tattoos on his body, Quesnel had tear tattoos under his eyes.

Quesnel was to testify on August 7 against Rowdy Crew member Mario Lussier, 32, who had been the wheelman in the Rivard hit. Tremblay gave a newspaper a photograph of Quesnel, 25, with his girlfriend, 21-year-old exotic dancer Sandra Beaulieu, sitting on his lap, as well as photos of the suggestively clothed woman posing for the camera. He also handed over an affidavit signed by Beaulieu in which she claimed to have had sex, PCP, and alcohol with Quesnel in an office at police headquarters. Quesnel was such a valuable informant police dared not entrust him into the prison system. Quesnel was such a valuable informant police dared not entrust him to the prison system. They kept him in cells at headquarters. Tremblay also gave the newspaper a copy of Quesnel's informant contract with the Quebec government which fixed his salary at $500 a week for fifteen years.

Quesnel told police that Tremblay had plotted to have former client Roger Aubin killed. Aubin blamed his lawyer for making a bad deal with the prosecutor when jailed for murder in 1990. Tremblay denied Quesnel's allegation and accused police of trying to sully his reputation. "They don't want to see me in this case against those fingered by Quesnel. Quesnel is their only witness and the defense knows well that I'm in a position to ruin his credibility. They're trying to get me off this case. They asked me by phone. They asked me by letter. I've always refused. Now we're bringing out the heavy artillery."

Police interviewed Aubin in prison after Quesnel revealed that Tremblay had plotted with him to kill Aubin. Police told Aubin that the Hells Angels had taken a contract on his life, but did not reveal Tremblay's name. Tremblay took offense and wrote public security minister Serge Ménard on May 2.

I can understand that the police might not like me. But to visit Donnacona [prison where Aubin is held] on "false information" from informant
Serge Quesnel, to meet a prisoner, mention that I had placed a contract
on him, just makes it so that he could, when freed, in these circumstances kill me or members of my family, nearly all at the request of the
Sûreté du Québec.

That's why, Mr. Minister of Public Security, I formally notify you to
insure my full and complete protection following the situation created
by your subordinates. Should something happen to me during the next
few years because of actions taken by your subordinates, you can rest
assured my heirs will take legal action for damages, with interest.

. . . if you support your police and believe Mr. Quesnel's lies about me,
it might be better to charge me so that the matter be made public so I
can answer the charges rather than let the Sûreté du Québec secretly
provoke my assassination.

A response from the minister's assistant said: "Your allegations . . .
require reasonable verification time. . . . Rest assured you will be
informed as quickly as possible of the results of this undertaking."

Two police officers who had taken the suggestive photographs of
Beaulieu were reprimanded for allowing Quesnel to have sex in the
office, although conjugal visits are allowed in prisons. They were not
found liable for the drugs used by Quesnel because they had no authority to body search the informant's girlfriend when she visited him
during debriefings at police headquarters. Beaulieu said she smuggled
the drugs inside her vagina when she visited Quesnel from April 11 to
May 22. Quesnel was charged on July 19 with conspiracy to traffic
drugs because of the incident. Quesnel pleaded guilty the next day,
violating his government contract, which enjoined him not to commit
criminal acts while a paid informant.

The judge at Lussier's preliminary hearing made a ruling on August
8 that Tremblay must have expected. She deemed Tremblay inca-
pable—due to conflict of interest—of defending Lussier against Quesnel's testimony in the murder case because Tremblay was at one time
Quesnel's lawyer. Tremblay did not argue.

Nearly two hundred inmates in Montreal's Bordeaux prison were
confined to their cells for three days in early August because of
increased tension between Rock Machine and Hells Angels supporters.
So much for the truce in the gang war police announced in April after
the arrest of 13 Hells Angels and associates for 12 unsolved murders.

*   *   *

While their lawyers fought in court, the Hells Angels fought in the streets. Six men, including a Hells Angel from the Montreal chapter who planned the operation, decided to kill a drug dealer in the Pelletier gang. One man made the bomb, two others planted it, another kept watch. On August 9, they planted a remote detonation bomb under the driver's seat of a Jeep parked on an east Montreal street. The men with the detonator parked no more than three hundred yards away, so they could trigger the device. They could see 11-year-old Daniel Desrochers and his 10-year-old friend Yan Villeneuve playing in front of the school across the street from the Jeep. Driver Marc Dubé, 26, jumped into the vehicle while his friend Jean Côté, 22, returned to the apartment to retrieve something he had forgotten.

The blast blew both of Dube's legs off and killed him instantly. Glass shattered in apartments and cars along the street. Debris whistled through the air fifty yards away. Daniel Desrochers lay on the ground, clinically dead: a piece of metal had pierced his skull and sliced his brain. He underwent a four-hour operation to stem a brain hemorrhage and was put on life support. Yan Villeneuve was treated for minor injuries, as was Côté.

The fourth casualty in this incident after the man, the boy, and public security, was the truth. Police initially said that Dubé and Côté were not known to them, meaning they were not criminals. But the media were so hungry to link the bombing to the biker war that subsequent stories labeled the dead man as a drug trafficker. The truth is, the poor man two weeks earlier bought a black Jeep similar to that of an Alliance member—Normand (Bouboule) Tremblay, an associate of the Pelletier gang—the man targeted by the Hells Angels. They placed the bomb in the wrong vehicle and killed the wrong man.

Police warned the biker gangs on Thursday, August 10, to fight without bombs that endanger innocent bystanders. Inspector Pierre Sangollo, assistant director of investigations for Montreal police, told a press conference police can't end the war and that the public should expect more bombings as long as the drug market exists. He said police warned the bikers months ago about using explosives. "I cannot order them to use something other than explosives. But I wish they would listen. You can take care of someone without having bystanders killed."

To cover up their mistake and avoid a public relations fiasco, the Hells Angels hired a black hit man—assuming the police and public would never suspect a white supremacist gang like theirs of dealing with blacks—and had him walk into the Rock Machine motorcycle shop, a gun in each hand, and shoot two bikers. Rock Machine Luc Deshais, 44, died. The Angels hoped the incident would be interpreted as the Rock Machine killing the two idiots who bombed Hells Angels sympathizers and injured a boy in the process.

Some police adopted this theory. Others put their own incorrect spin on the shooting. They said the shooting was to avenge the murder of Dubé, "a suspected drug dealer with links to the Hells Angels. . . . Another man in the blast is also suspected of being involved in the drug trade." This was a lie. By creating fiction to fit their theories, police locked their brains into a rut and failed to consider other possible scenarios. Bad detective work let the Hells Angels off a hook that could have pierced deep into the gang's heart, had the public known the truth at a time when emotions ran strong against the bikers. Police often attempt to manipulate the media. This tack not only reflects the moral make-up of the deceivers, but their sense of impotence.

The public was now frightened and angry. An innocent boy lay in critical condition in a hospital bed while bikers controlled the streets. Police administrators and unions fought each other in the newspapers in a power struggle. Lawyers and former cops alleged abuses of power by the police. It seemed Montreal was on the verge of anarchy.

"They're killing children in the streets of Montreal," said former provincial cabinet minister and now talk-show host Jean Cournoyer. "A society that tolerates that is a society that doesn't deserve to exist." Cournoyer used his platform to criticize police unions for fighting the public, politicians, and their bosses rather than catching criminals. Police politics would follow the same path in Toronto three years later.

Inspector Jean Ostiguy, head of the Montreal police major crime unit, made the first public request on Friday, August 11, for a draconian anti-gang law that would allow police to stop and arrest anyone belonging to a gang. He misinterpreted to reporters that the United States Racketeer-Influenced and Corrupt Organizations (RICO) statute gave that power to police. It was the first attempt by police to invoke laws that arbitrarily stripped away the rights guaranteed in the Charter of Rights and Freedoms. During the coming months, Quebec police would lobby for the power to arrest anyone without proof, and lock them up. They did not understand that an anti-gang law does not make it easier to arrest and convict criminals. It makes it more difficult. Not only do police have to gather evidence against an individual and prove his criminality in court, they must prove that the organization planned and participated in the crime. That's a lot of leg work. But Quebec police hoped for a law that would allow them to arrest and convict people without proof they had committed a crime, just for belonging to a gang. Only in Quebec.

Sunday, August 13, proved to be a turning point in Quebec's biker war. Daniel Desrochers died in hospital without regaining consciousness. Police labeled the boy the first innocent victim of the Hells Angels/Rock Machine war. Daniel Desrochers was the first child killed, but Marc Dubé had been the first innocent victim. The public reacted with outrage never before seen in Quebec. If only they had known the Hells Angels killed the boy. They would have burned down their clubhouses. The public turned on the police, who had until then publicly stated they didn't mind that bikers and criminals killed each other. The public demanded that police serve and protect, and stop the war before more innocent casualties were tallied.

Federal justice minister Allan Rock had reservations about an anti-gang law as requested by Quebec police and politicians. The day after Daniel Desrochers's death, Montreal mayor Pierre Bourque asked Ottawa for such a law to end the biker war. Police said they lacked the tools to stop the fighting. Rock answered that a draconian law would violate civil liberties and interfere with the rights of bikers and anyone else to gather freely. He feared the law would be used against any group the police targeted. Quebec public security minister Serge Ménard said current laws were adequate to deal with the problem.

When Daniel Desrochers died, the hospital issued a brief statement. "The family wishes to live through this event as privately as possible." Josée-Anne Desrochers, in the years to come, would be anything but a private person. At his stepson's funeral, Desrochers's husband said he wanted Ottawa to adopt an anti-gang law that would allow police to charge motorcycle gang leaders even if underlings commit the crimes. Family friends circulated a petition calling for the law.

*   *   *

A powerful bomb severely damaged the heavily fortified bungalow the Hells Angels puppet gang the Rowdy Crew used as a clubhouse in Le Gardeur on Tuesday, August 22. The gang dog died.

A five-kilogram bomb blew the back wall off the Hells Angels' best known motorcycle shop, Bob Chopper in Longeuil, at 2 a.m. Saturday, August 26. A faulty grenade had only cracked the front window the previous week. The Hells Angels in the clubhouse next door quickly called their lawyer to the site to prevent police from entering the bombed building. Police had to get two search warrants before they could pursue their investigation. The Hells Angels refused to cooperate. Half an hour before the explosion, the police bomb squad had been tipped off that a car some distance from Bob Chopper was rigged to blow up. Police found a wire running from the motor into the gas tank. By the time they figured it was a diversion, the motorcycle shop blew up.

The following night, Sunday, August 27, the front wall of a north Montreal tattoo parlor linked to the Rock Machine was blown out by gasoline bombs placed next to the front window. This type of warfare was unusual for biker gangs, who usually shot or blew up people, not property. A bombed building attracts attention; a dead body sends a message. But earlier messages had not been heeded, and the bikers seemed content to keep the other side on edge and whittle away at each other's assets.

*   *   *

A damning report of an inquiry ordered by Corrections Canada concluded on Wednesday, September 6, that organized crime bosses ran Quebec's Leclerc medium-security penitentiary in Laval and were treated like royalty by prison officials. Investigators said that Montreal and New York mafiosi, Hells Angels and affiliated gang members, as well as members of the prisoners' committee lived well above prison standards. These gangsters rarely or never ate institutional food, but were catered to by chefs. Their cells were filled with furniture to be used only by prison employees, and they had clothing and goods well beyond the set prison limit. Hells Angels and their associates were housed together. They controlled telephone use in their wing and forbade other prisoners from using the telephones. The gangsters decided who got which cells and who got transferred into or out of any area.

Although prisoners were restricted by policy to seven visits a month, some gangsters were allowed twenty visits a month. Conjugal visits, which allowed several days of privacy for couples or families, were also hogged by the hoods, who booked forty-three percent of these visits, though they made up eighteen percent of the prison population.

Crime bosses got the choice paid jobs in the gym, recreation department, canteen, and radio room.

Raynald Desjardins, right-hand man to Vito Rizzuto, the Sicilian mafia boss in Canada, was sentenced to fifteen years in Leclerc along with several Hells Angels convicted of smuggling 740 kilos of cocaine into Canada. His cell contained a hand-crafted bookcase lit with a lamp "borrowed" from the prison gym and installed by an electrician. A computer sat on his desk. In the summer of 1995, he paid a contractor to restore the prison's run-down jogging track.

Desjardins and his Hells Angels friends sat in the contractor's truck and shot the breeze while workers toiled on the track. On another occasion he ordered a truckful of seafood for a party. Police called prison officials and politely suggested they turn it away.

Montreal mafiosi Frank Cotroni's violent driver, Raymond Fernandez, beat and stabbed a 17-year-old stripper to death when he was 21. After a few years in jail, he took up with Vito Rizzuto. He was sent to jail again in 1991 for trafficking cocaine. When he married behind bars, Raynald Desjardins, who was then a free man, attended. Fernandez was allowed to visit his mother on special passes. He never saw her, but hung out with his underworld buddies.

Frank Cotroni was sent to prison for eight years in 1987 for a murder committed by one of his underlings. In 1991 he was sentenced to six years for heroin trafficking. He became chairman of the Leclerc prison recreation committee. During the summer, when he was supposed to be cleaning river shorelines on work duty, he walked the streets of Laval, hung out with businessmen, bought popsicles for kids, and treated fellow prisoners to meals.

Rockers president Guy Lepage, a Hells Angels associate, pleaded guilty to laundering cocaine money in British Columbia. He was sentenced to two years in jail and fined $200,000. He missed Quebec, so he paid $5,700 for a one-way plane ticket for himself and two two-way tickets for prison guards to escort him to Bordeaux prison. Fifteen days later he asked for and was granted a transfer to the nicer Waterloo prison. If only all bureaucracies were so accommodating.

Not to be outdone by the inquiry's investigators, the vice-president of the Canadian Public Service Alliance, speaking on behalf of the prison guards' union, revealed that mafia and Hells Angels had sex with a different woman every week.

One festive group of criminals ordered $3,000 worth of lobster on April 28.

A Corrections Canada spokesman said the privileges "developed over time. These prisoners are influential in society and in the penitentiary system. We accorded them privileges to keep the peace in the building. They are able to start riots or, conversely, have a positive influence on the other prisoners."

Prison officials said the privileges were revoked after the inquiry findings were made public. Mafiosi and Hells Angels threatened prison officials. They threatened to poison employee food, which they prepared. Employees stopped eating in the cafeteria. Riots were a constant threat. Fights and drug use increased. The Hells Angels informed officials that without their help, order could not be maintained. They demanded their privileges back.

*   *   *

While bikers partied carefree behind bars, those in public bars chugged at their own risk. Members of the Dark Circle, the group of bar owners who joined the Alliance of drug dealers to support the Rock Machine battle the Hells Angels, bombed a bar frequented by associates of the Death Riders at 10:15 p.m. on September 11. The bomb, placed near an outdoor patio table, was remotely detonated when the waitress walked back into the building. Among the nine persons injured in the blast at Le Harley in Boisbriand, twenty miles north of Montreal, was Mario Lepore, former manager of the Caisse populaire de Saint-Placide, convicted on April 29, 1994, in a $1-million fraud. The 42-year-old accountant was given forty-eight months to pay a $25,000 fine and was put on two years' probation. His Harley-Davidson motorcycle, parked outside the bar, sported three decals that read: "Support local Hells," for the Montreal, Trois-Rivières, and Nomad chapters. Lepore, a friend of Maurice (Mom) Boucher, lost part of a leg in the blast. An off-duty policeman who helped the injured found another bomb made of ten sticks of dynamite in a kettle placed near the bar wall.

During the first fourteen months of war, both sides shot and bombed associates, sympathizers, and street-level drug dealers to spread fear through the gangs. Before long, every criminal in Quebec checked under his car and looked over his shoulder. Targets were picked for convenience, and anyone could be next. It was a war of nerves unlike that fought by any biker gangs before. The top-ranked bikers in both gangs did not get involved in the dirty work, which they farmed out to associates who also bore the brunt of the damage. The strategists tried to deplete their enemy's income and confidence, hoping they would capitulate.

The Hells Angels underestimated the support the Rock Machine would gain in the underworld. The Hells Angels, who equated fear with respect, had no idea how much they were hated. Their primary weapon—intimidation—was nullified by their enemies' anger and need for vengeance. The Hells Angels never cared that they had stripped many dealers of their fortunes when they took over Quebec's drug market. Montreal's $5-million cocaine market was all these dealers had left. They would defend it to the death.

*   *   *

On September 15, the Alliance served notice on the Hells Angels that the war was no longer for the drug market, but for survival—only one gang would be left on the battlefield. An Alliance hit man assassinated

Hells Angel Richard (Crow) Émond, the second most powerful Angel in the Trois-Rivières chapter, as he got into his car at a shopping mall in north-east Montreal at 3:15 in the afternoon. The killer fired six shots. Three hit Émond, 39, in the chest and he fell in the parking lot next to his Pontiac Bonneville as his girlfriend looked on. His revolver was under the driver's seat. Émond, a former Missile, was a founding member of the Trois-Rivières chapter on June 14, 1991, and sported the Filthy Few patch on his colors which meant he had killed for the Hells Angels.

Only killers can wear the black-and-white Filthy Few patch or the black-and-white SS lightning bolts. These symbols can also be found on rings and motorcycles. Because police now recognize the significance of the patch, some Hells Angels have replaced it with the numerals 666— the number of the Beast—which represents the sixth letter of the alphabet: FFF—Filthy Few Forever. Only the most daring Hells Angels wear the patch today. Nine members of the Hells Angels' Sherbrooke chapter sign their Christmas cards as Filthy Few.

Émond controlled the Jokers puppet gang in St. Jean. He was the war's twenty-second victim, but the first Hells Angel to die. The effect was instantaneous. Police and politicians knew that the Hells Angels had to slaughter mercilessly to save face. For the first time in the war, the Canadian flag and the Hells Angels' flag flew at half-mast over Hells Angels' clubhouses. Both flags, ironically, are red and white. The Hells Angels had known the war would come to them eventually. Two weeks earlier, they had stacked sandbags along the clubhouse's inside walls to shield against bullets and bombs.

Hells Angels lawyer Gilles Daudelin took advantage of the heavy media presence at Émond's funeral on Wednesday, September 21, to lambaste the police for checking bikers at roadblocks during the days leading up to the funeral. "There are provisions in the Charter of Rights and liberties that protect against abusive searches. We're going to start by filing a complaint with the police commission." Police seized a 9-mm semi-automatic pistol in the car of two Undertakers bikers from Nova Scotia.

The Alliance blew up another bar hours before Émond's funeral and the Hells Angels tossed a Molotov cocktail into a clothing store owned by a Rock Machine sympathizer, causing $160,000 in damage.

Later that night, at 2 a.m., three Rock Machine bikers blew themselves up as they tried to bomb the Jokers' clubhouse in Saint-Luc. Four would-be bombers approached the clubhouse in a van with the lights turned off. Two Jokers watched them on their intricate video security system. One man got out and sneaked up to the clubhouse. Two others unloaded the bomb, while the fourth sat in the truck with the detonator. One of the Joker security guards ran out with a sub-machine gun and startled the bombers. Either a bullet detonated the explosive, or the man in the van panicked and pressed the detonator button. No one will ever know what happened. The two men holding the bomb were vaporized. Flesh and blood sprayed over a hundred-yard radius, the biggest piece no larger than a fist. The man in the van was blown into the woods. The scout was seriously injured. The two Jokers stashed the guns and waited for police. It took three weeks to gather all the body parts to bury Benoît Grignon, 28, Daniel Paul, 26, and Pierre Patry, 27.

The death toll reached twenty-five, and politicians knew it was a matter of time before another innocent victim would rouse the public against them. The public pressure created by Daniel Desrochers's death forced policians into action. Public security minister Serge Ménard knew he must give up his portfolio. Montreal police had fought valiantly to stem the war, with fifty cops on three anti-biker squads, but they needed more manpower. A joint-forces squad was created on Sunday, September 24, to go toe-to-toe with the warring bikers. It was made up of RCMP, Sûreté du Québec, and Montreal cops. They called themselves Carcajou, French for wolverine, a creature legendary Quebec folk singer Félix Leclerc once described as "devil of our forests." The first Carcajou squad had thirty provincial cops and thirty Montreal cops. The RCMP would soon join the squad, and total manpower would eventually be boosted to one hundred.

The squad raided an illegal after-hours club in downtown Montreal in the early hours of September 29. An anonymous caller had sent police there on August 27 with a false bomb scare; they returned to see if it still operated, and discovered that the owners were Hells Angels: Gilles (Le Vieux) Dumas and Claude (Burger) Berger, 46, of the Sherbrooke chapter. Berger, who had no criminal record and played third trumpet in the Quebec symphony, is one of the gang's major public relations spokesmen. He told reporters at a motorcycle show he promoted in 1990 that "the Hells Angels, like the Knights of Columbus and even the clergy, have had to collectively suffer for acts committed by certain elements of the club. It happens in all organizations. We can't avoid that." When the orchestra downsized because of budget restraints, some members feared reprisals if they fired Berger, so they offered him a part-time contract.

*   *   *

A Rock Machine associate survived two bullets, one to the head, outside a downtown Montreal bar on September 31. The next night, Sunday, October 1, the Rock Machine's main clubhouse on rue Huron near the Jacques-Cartier bridge was bombed at 10:30. A ten-kilogram bomb placed next to the building's front window blew out windows and the aluminum roof. It was the war's twenty-first explosion. A bold thief stole out of the gathered crowd and drove off in an unattended police cruiser, number 33-27, and spent the night taunting police over the car's radio.

Another Hells Angels' drug dealer was shot to death on Tuesday, October 3.

On Wednesday, police found a booby-trapped minivan parked at a suburban shopping mall in Montreal. It took police twelve hours to defuse six gas cans packed with dynamite. The bomb's detonator was rigged to explode when the van's doors opened.

The home of the deputy warden of the Sorel prison was torched on Thursday, October 5. The previous June, the warden's house in Saint-Lambert had burned down while Hells Angel Maurice (Mom) Boucher was incarcerated in the prison on a weapons conviction. Boucher complained frequently about the institution's food, especially the shepherd's pie. He was transferred to Cowansville penitentiary after the first fire. Prison officials were growing increasingly fearful of repeated threats made against them by Hells Angels and their associates.

Two Rock Machine snipers set up 350 feet from the barbed wire fence at Leclerc medium-security penitentiary in Laval on Monday night, October 9, and fired eleven shots from a semi-automatic rifle at Hells Angels leaders Richard (Bob) Hudon, 34, and Denis (Pas fiable) Houle, 32, as they walked in the prison yard with sixty other prisoners. The second sniper didn't fire, but kept watch over the first. Both men fled in a car stolen the previous day. A police dog found a pair of gloves, two rifles, and the stolen car nearby where the shooters changed vehicles. Hudon, of the Hells Angels' Saint-Nicolas chapter, had been jailed for thirteen years for importing (with the Montreal mafia) 740 kilos of cocaine into Nova Scotia in August 1993.

The Carcajou squad arrested six Rockers and seized fifty detonators, a machine gun, shotguns, and drugs in raids on the gang's clubhouse and an apartment in Lachine on Thursday, October 12.

The following week, on Wednesday, October 18, four people were injured when a bomb found attached to the wheel of their van in Terrebonne blew up as a man picked it up and tossed it away.

Rock Machine sympathizer Michel Boyer, arrested on July 17, 1994, in an attempted assassination of Hells Angel Maurice (Mom) Boucher, kept plotting the man's death for eighteen months. He arrived home in Lanoraie Tuesday night, October 17, with his wife and four-month-old baby when two men hidden in the hedges behind the house opened fire and killed him.

While police waged war against Montreal's warring bikers, the Hells Angels and Rock Machine solidified their hold on bars in the Quebec City area. More than forty bars allowed drug dealers from one or the other gang to sell on their premises in return for a cut of the action. Hells Angels' bars were easy to spot, as the color-wearing bikers did not try to hide the fact that this was their territory. Their high profile also allowed them to intimidate. Of the seventy-three Hells Angels in the province (those behind bars are not counted), thirty-five sported the Filthy Few patch over their breast pocket.

*   *   *

There are nearly twenty biker clubhouses in Quebec, all of them fortified, with bullet-proof glass, steel plates in the walls, and surveillance equipment ranging from video monitors to infra-red motion sensors and vibration sensors placed in the ground. Clubhouses have at least one guard twenty-four hours a day. Hells Angels' clubhouses in Lennoxville, Trois-Rivières, Sorel and Saint-Nicolas are strategically placed. So are those of the Rockers and Rock Machine, both close to the Jacques-Cartier bridge. The Sherbrooke chapter's clubhouse in Lennoxville is on twelve acres and worth about $1 million. It is protected on two sides by a river and a train track. Guards and dogs patrol the grounds. The Montreal chapter's clubhouse in Sorel is in a renovated furniture factory; chapter members, as is the tradition world-wide, have bought dozens of neighboring houses and buildings. The Saint-Nicolas clubhouse is fort-like, with a parapet on the roof. Hells Angels puppet-gang clubhouses are no less fortified. The Jokers are in Saint-Luc, the Rowdy Crew are in Le Gardeur and also have an impressive fortress in Saint-Antoine-de-Lavaltrie, the Death Riders are in Sainte-Thérèse, and the Rockers are in Rosemont.

The Hells Angels raised eyebrows in Quebec on October 20 when they chose to support the "No" vote in the Quebec referendum to separate from Canada, and posted signs indicating their choice in front of the Trois-Rivières clubhouse. Theirs were the few that weren't vandalized by separatists. At the clubhouse, a friend of the gang's explained the Hells Angels' rationale, which could as easily have been applied to their business practice of assimilating competing gangs. Guy, 31, said:

We're proud Canadians. Everybody is voting "No". Strength is in numbers, in unity. This whole separation business, I don't get it. I don't understand why anyone would want it. It's more a question of the laws and our rights. We want to keep the same rights. If Quebec was to take control, they'd scrap all the Canadian laws. Premier Jacques Parizeau would just spit on us. He'd use the opportunity to crack down and justify all sorts of repression, anti-gang laws and stuff, to throw us in jail. We don't want to end up with borders between Quebec and Ontario. We don't want to end up with more borders everywhere.

Some Montreal residents were more stressed than others by the biker war. The third attempt to bomb Bob Chopper next to the Hells Angels' clubhouse in Longueuil on Wednesday, October 18, pushed Marcel Blondeau over the edge. The poor man lived next door to the buildings and was desperate to get his family out of the neighborhood. He tried to sell his house, but no one would buy. Mayor Claude Gladu, in an unprecedented humanitarian display, offered to temporarily house the Blondeau family until they could sell their house. The generosity was probably prompted by lawyers, after the chief of police said police couldn't do any more to protect the neighborhood.

*   *   *

Police were convinced that continued pressure on the Hells Angels, the Rock Machine, and their associates would curb the violence. They were right, although history has shown that once they succeed and the threat of violence has passed, public fear eases and politicians become complacent. Budgets get cut and police are assigned to other tasks. Then the war resumes. This scenario was predictable from the start, as I had witnessed it before, but the players were in motion and the game had to be played.

Police decided that Maurice (Mom) Boucher was the Hells Angels warlord and that putting him behind bars could slow the war. They jumped on every opportunity to take him to court. Under normal circumstances, some people might argue that police were splitting hairs. But he was now president of the new Hells Angels' Nomads chapter and responsible for taking over drug trafficking in Montreal. If they didn't attack him, who could they tackle?

Snivelling Hells Angels sympathizer and drug dealer Steven Bertrand, 27, complained to Boucher on a wiretapped phone on September 25 that a man he'd picked a bar fight with on September 23 had severely beaten him and had to be pulled off at gunpoint by another associate. The man had flirted with Bertrand's girlfriend. Boucher advised him to get a baseball bat and take care of business.

Police issued an arrest warrant for Boucher for breaching his probation by counseling violence. Boucher was on probation for a weapons offense. When he failed to surrender, police visited clubhouses and homes in search of the Hells Angel. This rattled the gang. Police raided the club-houses of the Jokers, the Evil Ones, and the Death Riders on Tuesday, October 24. Boucher surrendered to police on Wednesday, October 25, with longtime Hells Angels lawyer Léo-René Maranda.

Crown attorney René Domingue argued against bail for Boucher, call-ing him a killer with enormous power and influence in the criminal underworld. Defense lawyer Maranda rebutted that "it's not illegal to be a Hells Angel." The lawyers had confronted each other during the trials of the Hells Angels charged with the 1985 slaughter of the North chap-ter. Both knew the Hells Angels well.

Domingue told the court that Boucher counseled a violent act and that his criminal record warranted he not be granted bail. Boucher had been convicted fourteen times since 1973 for theft, fraud, and posses-sion of a firearm. He was sentenced to twenty-three months in jail in 1984 for armed sexual aggression. He also failed twice to show up for court proceedings. When he surrendered Wednesday, Boucher was under two probation orders. One was to expire on November 3, the other on March 25, 1998.

The judge ruled on Friday, October 27, that the Crown had not proven Boucher was a threat to society; he was released on condition he stay away from bars, biker clubhouses, and people with criminal records. He could not communicate, directly or indirectly, with seven-teen persons on a police "black list," he had to report to police head-quarters every Monday and Friday, he had to be home by eleven o'clock every night, he surrendered his passport, and he couldn't own a cell phone or a pager.

*   *   *

Police did not rest on their laurels. They continued their investigations and on Wednesday, November 9, charged twenty-two Rock Machine members, associates, and sympathizers arrested in twenty-five raids with crimes that ranged from murder to drug possession.

Patrick Dupuis, 27, an associate of the Hells Angels puppet gang the Evil Ones on Montreal's south shore, was arrested while delivering four sticks of dynamite on Sunday, October 22.

Police raided eight clubhouses and homes of Hells Angels associates on Thursday, October 26, and arrested two Death Riders and thirteen Hells Angels sympathizers on weapons and drug charges. They found eleven guns (two of them assault rifles fitted with bayonets), one grenade, three remote-control detonators, three kilos of marijuana, and three ounces of cocaine.

As the war progressed, the Hells Angels realized they couldn't afford to lose members to the judicial system. Several gang leaders were jailed pending trial on drug and murder charges. The most potent weapon against them was former Hells Angels' associate-turned-informant, Serge Quesnel.

They needed to discredit Quesnel to neutralize his testimony against gang members. Hells Angels lawyer Martin Tremblay had already given a newspaper compromising photos of Quesnel, as well as documents showing his informant's salary. Tremblay hired private investigator Jules Livernois during the summer of 1995 to dig up more dirt on Quesnel. Livernois, 51, was well known in Quebec for uncovering scandals inside the Sûreté du Québec. As the scheduled 1996 murder trial of three Hells Angels loomed, the gang hoped Livernois could get more information on Quesnel. Hells Angels lawyer Gilles Daudelin approached the investigator. "My clients wanted me to sign a ten-week investigation contract with him," Daudelin said. "We were to pay him, but I didn't want to personally get involved in the financial negotiations. I told Robert Savard [a friend of Maurice (Mom) Boucher] to arrange that, and that I would prepare the contract." Savard and Livernois met on Saturday, November 17. Livernois said he had a lead that could discredit Quesnel, and they agreed on a fee. "Savard called me at 10:15 and told me the deal was done," Daudelin said. The three men planned to meet at 2 p.m. in Laval to sign the contract. Livernois drove away in his red Thunderbird and stopped at a phone booth in Saint-Léonard to call Gaétan Rivest, the former Sûreté du Québec corporal who spent his days denouncing the police on behalf of the Hells Angels. He spoke a few words to Rivest's wife. As she handed the phone to her husband, a hit man put four bullets in Livernois's back. He survived.

* * *

Police arrested Gilles Frenette, 47, leader of a new chapter of the Devil's Disciples biker gang on Thursday, November 23, in connection with the bombing of a Montreal bar on May 23. The Disciples are enemies of the Hells Angels and fought a vicious, bloody war with the Popeyes in the 1970s before they became Angels.

Although car bombings were a regular occurrence that caused an increase in the sale of small mirrors that bikers used to check the undersides of their vehicles, some criminals were more cautious than others. Hells Angels associate Giuseppe Ierfino, 30, didn't check his Suzuki Sidekick, left unattended in a parking lot, before he drove home at 3:30 a.m., Friday, November 24. An Alliance member had fastened a bomb to the electrician's vehicle and followed it to a highway intersection in Laval before he detonated his handiwork. Ierfino was blown out of the vehicle and died instantly.

Police used information provided by a second informant who, like Quesnel, had defected from the Hells Angels camp, to take more bikers off the streets. Martin (Satan) Lacroix, right-hand man to Hells Angel Michael (l'Animal) Lajoie-Smith, became an informant after his arrest on October 26. He gave police the names of Lajoie-Smith's network of thugs and drug dealers who intimidated bar owners into letting gang dealers sell drugs in their establishments. Police arrested ten members of the network on Wednesday, November 30, in Cartierville, Montreal, and Sainte-Thérèse. Lajoie-Smith was charged behind bars, where he was serving time on a weapons charge. He asked to be jailed in Saint-Jérôme because the Rock Machine had taken control of the Bordeaux prison. He also awaited trial on a charge of paying $400 to Lacroix to plant a bomb in the Le Gascon bar. The bomb had failed to explode.

Police who raided the Jokers' clubhouse in Saint-Luc on November 30 found human body parts preserved in a jar of formaldehyde, and also in the freezer. They belonged to three Rock Machine members who had blown themselves up in September in a botched attack on the clubhouse. The Jokers kept a thirty-centimeter section of a human spine in a jar on a shelf.

* * *

Several persons who schemed to sanitize the Hells Angels' image and discredit informants against the gang were arrested on Monday, December 18, on charges that ranged from extortion to murder. They included Hells Angels' lawyer Gilles Daudelin, 45, former Sûreté du Québec corporal Gaétan Rivest, Robert (Bob) Savard, 44, and Gilles Giguère, 45, the latter two business associates of Hells Angel Maurice (Mom) Boucher.

Daudelin was charged with plotting with Savard and Giguère the death of a 50-year-old woman whose business they had tried to extort unsuccessfully over several months. Daudelin was also charged with counseling a witness to lie in Giguère's upcoming trial for possession of four machine guns and fifty pounds of marijuana. (The charges were dropped on February 26, 1996, after the Crown revealed police hinged their case on the testimony of a compulsive liar.) Daudelin was convicted in 1991 of drug possession and received an absolute discharge after he paid $500 to a charity.

Rivest, who had worked in the Sûreté du Québec's crime-against-persons section, awaited trial on a December 1994 charge of threatening.

He once admitted in court he was a big-time cigarette smuggler. He was charged with Savard and Giguère for threatening a former business partner, Gerry Etchevery, who owned an east Montreal restaurant. Etchevery, 51, was part of a fraud investigation that saw the former provincial politician for Laval-des-Rapides, Guy Bélanger, charged in September. Several months prior, Bélanger had arranged for Rivest to meet public security minister Serge Ménard to voice his complaints about the way police treated the Hells Angels. Ménard accused both men of being on the Hells Angels' payroll.

Savard and Giguère were also charged with extortion in a case brought by a west Montreal restaurant owner.

The bikers continued to deliver exploding packages as Christmas approached. Car dealer Ronald Snyder, 46, was nearly cut in half when a remote-detonated bomb blew his Jeep Cherokee apart as he drove out of his Beaconsfield driveway on Thursday, December 22.

1996

The year 1996 began much as did 1995, with Hells Angels prospect François Hinse in Mexico awaiting trial for the killing of Rock Machine Normand Baker. Hells Angels lawyer Roger Bellemare complained on Friday, January 6, that Canadian officials were pressuring the Mexican justice system to convict Hinse. "I've been holding back for a long time, but now I'll tell you. There's a lot of pressure by the RCMP and the Canadian embassy against Hinse, which is kind of crazy. An embassy should be there to ensure a Canadian citizen's rights are respected. The RCMP is pressuring Mexican authorities to convict him." Asked how he knew this to be true, he replied: "I can't tell you." The RCMP had asked the Mexicans why Hinse had been released in January 1995. He was subsequently arrested and committed for trial after allegations were made that someone received $700,000 U.S. before the judge, Edmundo Román Pinzón, let him go.

Montreal courts were so busy in 1996 processing bikers busted by Carcajou that Hells Angels and Alliance members often crossed paths and police had to prevent fights.

Obesity killed the first Hells Angel in 1996. National president Robert (Tiny) Richard, 46, felt queasy at the clubhouse on Friday, February 23, and was taken to hospital where he died of a heart attack. Richard, the former owner of Bob Chopper next to the clubhouse, was the only Hells Angel acquitted in the 1985 slaughter of the Hells Angels' North chapter. He succeeded Walter Stadnick as national president in

August 1994. Tiny was not: he was six feet tall and at one time weighed three hundred pounds. He died at 230.

Shortly after Tiny Richard bought the farm, two Hells Angels sympathizers wounded in the September bombing of a Boisbriand bar bought the most celebrated and notorious property in Quebec: the Lavigueur mansion in Laval. The house was a tabloid favorite after the Lavigueur family paid $850,000 for it in August 1986 from proceeds from the $7.6-million 6/49 lottery jackpot they had won. All of Quebec followed the family's foibles as they drank and squandered their money in a squalid lifestyle right out of *God's Little Acre*. On March 3, the house was up for sale. Richard Turcot and Michel Gagné applied for renovation permits for work that included a steel door, after they paid $400,000 for the chateau, $200,000 for a nearby house, and $15,000 and $5,000 for adjacent properties. Turcot had denied on Tuesday, February 28, that he was a Hells Angels sympathizer.

The first indication of police infighting was sparked by Tiny Richard's funeral. The leader of the provincial police union, Luc Savard, complained on Thursday, February 29, that twenty local police forces had illegally sent reinforcements to Sorel during the funeral. He said the Sorel police department of twenty-nine men, supplemented by the Sûreté du Québec, could provide security for the event that attracted thousands of onlookers despite the possibility of an attack by the Rock Machine on the 150 Hells Angels and associates in attendance. The union official said these police officers had no jurisdiction in Sorel and communications would have broken down during an emergency. "Officers of the SQ were able to do all the work without the help of municipal forces," Luc Savard said. His attack seemed out of place and self-defeating to anyone unaware of the tensions that boiled below the public veneer of cooperation between the municipal, provincial, and federal forces that made up Carcajou. Police are known to back-stab each other, but not in public. His complaint was moot. The Hells Angels literally controlled Sorel during the funeral, and police could do nothing about it. People were embarrassed to see police stand by as the Hells Angels patrolled and closed off streets.

While police bickered over who can best cover a funeral, François Hinse was acquitted in Mexico because of insufficient proof that he had killed Normand Baker. He immediately boarded a plane to Montreal, having spent thirteen months in a Mexican jail.

*　　*　　*

Carcajou was so successful in Montreal that police expanded its anti-biker operations to Quebec City on February 6, to put pressure on the Hells Angels and Rock Machine there. On Thursday, March 14, they arrested Hells Angels sympathizer (Clément Allard, 57), with $20 million in counterfeit $20 bills that he produced on a stolen $57,000 laser photocopier. In six weeks, police conducted 24 raids, arrested 35 persons, laid 78 charges, seized 2 handguns, 22 rifles, a machine gun and ammunition, 170 grams of cocaine, 154 grams of liquid hash, 31 grams of marijuana and 440 plants.

Fighting started on Friday, April 26, in Quebec City, when a man walked into a pool hall linked to the Rock Machine at 9:10 p.m. and fired a handgun. A panicked employee jumped through the plate-glass window to escape. Eight minutes later ten masked men burst into the L'Entrée bar, also linked to the Rock Machine, and destroyed the interior with baseball bats. The Hells Angels' baseball team had just made its presence known.

The following week, on Wednesday, May 1, police found twenty sticks of dynamite in a leather bag on the steps of a house trailer. Hours later, at 3:51 p.m., someone tossed a Molotov cocktail at the back wall of a bar owned by a biker linked to the Hells Angels, causing minor damage. Minutes later, another bar owned by the same biker was severely damaged by another Molotov cocktail.

Police arrested eight members of a drug network run in Baie-Comeau by the Saint-Nicolas Hells Angels chapter on Thursday, June 20.

Eight months after the assassination of Giuseppe (Joe) Ierfino by the Rock Machine, his drug trafficking and money laundering partner, Guiseppe Ruffolo, was shot ten times in the head and torso by two hit men who waited outside his house in Saint-Léonard with machine guns at 9:45 a.m. on Tuesday, July 30. One killer stepped out of a 4×4 and grabbed Ruffolo out of his car, pulling him toward the 4×4. They gunned him down as he tried to escape. Ruffolo, 30, owned a driver training school. Both men were influential members of Montreal's mafia and were close to the Hells Angels. Their money runner, Giuseppe (Joe) Tanaglia, was a frequent visitor to a currency exchange business set up by the RCMP to infiltrate the money laundering underworld.

*   *   *

A relative peace in Montreal did not go unnoticed by municipal politicians who, like all politicians, are not concerned with problems unless they upset the electorate. Sucking at the public tit seems to desiccate souls and hearts. City politicians told police privately in the spring of 1996 they would cut their share of subsidies to Carcajou in September. I revealed this during a radio interview and explained the folly. Fighting bikers is like bailing water out of a leaky boat. The water never stops seeping in. If you stop bailing, you drown. Society isn't perfect. Bikers

exist because a drug market buys their drugs. Men pay for their prostitutes. As long as humans are humans, someone will capitalize on their
faults. Constant vigilance is the only way to survive. The war against
bikers is not a war that will be won once and for all. Organized crime
has existed for thousands of years. Bikers are just a North American
expression of gangsterism.

Montreal politicians were ready to reduce subsidies until a massive
Hells Angels' bomb was found in Verdun on Friday, August 23, after a
botched attempt by the Angels to bomb the new Rock Machine clubhouse in that city. Pedestrians watched a stolen van disguised as a
Hydro Quebec vehicle veer out of control and hit a telephone pole after
its driver steered it toward the Rock Machine clubhouse and bailed out
in the middle of an intersection a block away. He hopped into another
waiting van and escaped. Police found ninety kilograms of dynamite
attached to detonators inside camping coolers in the van.

Politicians quietly shelved their plans to cut subsidies in September
because media attention focused the public's attention on the war. Officials waited for a lull in the biker war to cut the funds so they could
spend the money elsewhere. By the end of August, 36 people had been
killed in the two-year-old war, fifty-five attempts had been made to kill,
and there had been forty bombings and acts of arson.

*   *   *

The Rock Machine had so many members in prison they tried to break
a member out of Donnacona on Sunday, August 25. Police were tipped
off on Friday that four Rock Machine would try to free Roger Hardy, a
breakout expert. They found Hardy in a plastic recycling bin in the
prison yard shortly after midnight. He had used the prison workshop
to make spikes to climb a post, a three-pronged grapple, and most
impressively, had woven sewing thread into a seventy-foot-long rope.
Hardy fashioned a dummy which he stuffed into his bed and his cell-
mate pulled a cord to make him move when guards looked in. Four
Rock Machine members in two vehicles were caught cruising nearby
roads, waiting to pick up Hardy.

*   *   *

The federal government announced on Tuesday, August 27, that it was
considering new laws to help police combat organized crime. "The
fight against organized crime is a priority for the government," Solicitor General Herb Gray said. The stance was made to appease police
officials who indicated that organized crime had become a threat to
national security.

"The day it becomes a national threat is when it's all over the country ... That's what's happening right now with outlaw motorcycle gangs, who are the most, I would say, visible organized crime syndicates," said Captain Richard Philippe, assistant director of the Criminal Intelligence Service of Canada. The agency's 1996 report predicted that the Hells Angels/Rock Machine turf war in Quebec would spill over into Ontario. "Police expect increased violence in Ontario in the forthcoming months."

*   *   *

Hells Angel Michael (L'Animal) Lajoie-Smith pleaded guilty on Friday, August 30, to plotting to bomb the Le Gascon discotheque in Lachenaie in September 1995. Testimony from his right-hand man (turned informant), Martin (Satan) Lacroix, was too overwhelming. Lacroix had helped plant the bomb, which did not explode.

Lajoie-Smith made a surprise court appearance on Wednesday, September 18, to be informed he was charged with possession of goods obtained from the proceeds of crime. The Hells Angel couldn't suppress his anger as the Crown announced that a Quebec court had ordered his assets frozen. Police seized his two houses, jewelry, one Cadillac, and two Harley-Davidson motorcycles—one valued at $70,000 which sported the Hells Angels' death head—all worth half a million dollars. His bank accounts, with $35,800, were also frozen.

Another Hells Angel was iced a few weeks later, but in different circumstances. Sylvain Vachon became a member of the Hells Angels' Sherbrooke chapter in 1995. "It's like a big family. And you have to be honest. They're all honest guys," he said. Vachon worked as a structural technician in his father's factory and raced a Harley-Davidson drag bike. Norman Lapointe, president of the Windsor Papetiers of the new Quebec Semi-Professional Hockey League, watched the 30-year-old Vachon play pick-up hockey and liked what he saw: six-foot-one, 235 hard pounds. "He was tough, a good fighter, but he had hockey skills, too. We thought Sylvain would get us some respect." He signed Vachon to a contract and the Hells Angel played his first game on October 5. His fellow Hells Angels did not wear their colors to the game for fear of focusing attention on their friend.

There was no second game for the Hells Angel. The Louisville Jets refused to play against a member of a criminal gang. The twelve other teams announced they would not play Windsor as long as a Hells Angel was on the team. The RCMP ordered Windsor general manager Sylvain Parent to quit the team. It did not look good to have a Mountie and a biker on the same team.

One man didn't let money get in the way of logic. League vice-president Claude Lavoie explained why Vachon had to go. "This was a matter of security, not just for the players, but for the spectators. The teams had told us they were afraid of what would happen to their players if they got into a fight with Vachon. And what if there were other Hells Angels in the stands? Would they start fights, too? Let's be honest. The Hells Angels are a criminal organization. They've got a war going on in Montreal and in Quebec City. We have teams that play around those cities. What if they started throwing bombs at the games?"

Vachon's Hells Angel colors were seized twice in six months by the Sudbury police when the gang rode through town. His second set had a cheap, plated death's head rather than the solid-gold version of his original colors. He also had a Filthy Few patch and the SS metal bars.

*   *   *

A murder on Friday, October 18, raised serious questions in my mind about the police in Quebec—questions I didn't find answers to for several months, but which proved crucial in understanding how politics got mixed up with law enforcement in the Quebec war on bikers, and seriously jeopardized public safety.

Renaud Jomphe, 37, was the second-in-command of the Rock Machine and head of its Quebec City operations. He was effectively the gang's leader after Salvatore Cazzetta was jailed. Carcajou officers had been tailing all major players in the war since the anti-gang task force had been formed 14 months earlier. Jomphe dined at the Kim Hoa Restaurant in Verdun at 7:30 that Friday night with Rock Machine Christian Deschesnes, 38, and associate Raymond Laureau, 49. They sat in an enclosed booth at the back of the restaurant. A man walked up to the table, shot all three men, and ran out the back door. Jomphe and Deschesnes died. Laureau was hit in the shoulder.

What struck me about the killing was that police were not watching Jomphe that night. He should have been under surveillance. Why wasn't he? Although several avenues remained to be explored, I discovered that the politicians had effectively pulled the plug on Carcajou a few weeks earlier and drastically reduced its funding. The squad's manpower had been reduced from a hundred to about twenty-five. Most of them were in Quebec City. I revealed this on television in Montreal the following March, although not before a terrified Quebec public had been manipulated by political machinations. But everything in its time.

It was revealed in the Quebec National Assembly on Wednesday,

October 24, that Quebec's associate deputy justice minister, Mario Bilodeau, had been a Hells Angels lawyer before the Parti Québécois appointed him to the job. Bilodeau was responsible for criminal and penal matters. Liberal justice critic Thomas Mulcair demanded Bilodeau be removed from cases involving the Hells Angels. "I don't say that a lawyer doesn't have the right to defend the client they want," Mulcair said. "I am a lawyer, too, and I defend clients. But I would never put myself in a position to take an administrative or legal decision concerning one of my ex-clients."

Mulcair accused Bilodeau in question period of halting the Crown's prosecution of officers of the Caisse populaire Sherbrooke-Est, "despite overwhelming proof that an agent of the Sherbrooke-Est caisse populaire had prepared false declarations" that ruined businessman Robert Proteau. "We underline also that, curiously, the caisse populaire had financed the construction of the Hells Angels' hideout in Lennoxville and that one of the lawyers who defended the Sherbrooke-Est caisse populaire, Conrad Chapdelaine, in addition to being a former lawyer for the Hells Angels, was the defeated candidate for the PQ nomination in Sherbrooke. Faced with such troubling facts, ... does the justice minister still believe that he did well to name, among the 17,000 lawyers in Quebec, Mario Bilodeau, former lawyer for the Hells Angels, when it appears clear that this was not liable to favor the protection of the population?" Premier Lucien Bouchard praised Bilodeau's "integrity and competence."

Mulcair pursued Bilodeau's alleged conflict of interest again in the National Assembly in early December. "He defended the Hells Angels and he decides whether or not charges will be laid against them. As we speak, his office is blocking a pile of Carcajou cases this high. There's the problem of public perception. People say it doesn't make sense for a former Hells Angels lawyer to be the Crown prosecutor's boss and the one to decide if court actions are stopped. We're not saying he doesn't have a right to earn a living, but he doesn't have a right to that job. It's no good for the public image of the administration of justice, or for the public confidence in our institutions."

*   *   *

The biggest bomb in the biker war failed to go off outside the Saint-Nicolas Hells Angels' clubhouse on Friday, November 8. Fifty pounds of dynamite and five gas cans were hidden inside a stolen Jeep YJ parked against the fence next to the clubhouse. The remote-control detonator was left on the right front seat. The Hells Angels were angry that someone would park so close to their fence, and pushed the vehicle into the street. Then they looked inside and saw the bomb. They called police, who said the bomb would have destroyed the building.

Hells Angels associate Dany (L'Animal) Lizotte pleaded guilty on Tuesday, November 12, to killing and burying Gilles Fournier, a Rock Machine sympathizer, the previous summer. He agreed to testify against the Hells Angels and was sentenced to thirteen years in jail.

Tension between the Hells Angels and the Rock Machine in Quebec City was so all-consuming that even a trip to the corner store to buy cigarettes was a risky venture. A masked hit man shot at Rock Machine leader Marcel Demers five times and hit him on the back and arm on Thursday, November 14, as a payback for the attempted bombing of the Hells Angels' clubhouse. The 39-year-old biker tried to drive away, but swerved into a ditch.

*　　*　　*

Informant Serge Quesnel provided an inside look at the killing operations of the Hells Angels as he testified against two of them on Tuesday, December 3. (Both men, Louis [Mélou] Roy and Sylvain [Baptiste] Thiffault, were later acquitted.) Quesnel became a career criminal at age 15. He worked legitimately for two weeks as a cook when he was 18. One day in 1993 he was bored, so he stabbed a garage-owner in the back. It was his first murder. His second victim was biker Martin Naud, who talked about Quesnel's first killing. Eric Fournier ripped a shoelace from Naud's boot and strangled him with it while Quesnel rammed scissors into his eye and slit the artery in his neck. Quesnel poured alcohol on the body and torched it.

While imprisoned in Donnacona on other charges, Quesnel was asked in 1994 to join the Pelletier brothers' east Montreal gang as a hit man. In addition to the two murders under his belt, he had stabbed and beaten numerous prisoners with a steel bar. He dropped a gram of PCP into one prisoner's coffee before midnight mass at Christmas and tried to crush another's neck with a weightlifting bar. He offered one inmate a massage and plunged a homemade pick into his back.

The east Montreal gang leader offered Quesnel $500 a week and $10,000 to $20,000 a hit. Quesnel discussed the offer with his lawyer, Martin Tremblay, who discouraged him and suggested he could find him other work upon release. (Tremblay had become Quesnel's lawyer in 1993 at the request of Michel Guérin, a childhood friend of the hit man.) Tremblay arranged an interview for Quesnel with Hells Angel Louis (Mélou) Roy at the Trois-Rivières chapter clubhouse. Roy hired Quesnel as a hit man and paid him a $500-a-week retainer. Quesnel testified that Roy told him, "There's a lot of work."

The Hells Angels took him into town to buy new clothes and get a haircut so he wouldn't stand out. They gave him a room at the clubhouse next to the watch room where members and prospects took turns monitoring cameras. The watch schedule and photographs of "targets" were posted on a bulletin board. Quesnel was to be paid $10,000 to $25,000 for every murder he committed. The Hells Angels gave Quesnel $2,000 and a 9-mm semi-automatic handgun with two magazines that day.

Quesnel described Roy as his boss. "He told me not to do anything without talking to him and to never do anything for the Hells in Quebec (City)."

Roy asked Quesnel to meet with Hells Angel Sylvain (Baptiste) Thiffault, who gave him a security file in December 1994 with information on where to find and kill his first victim, Jacques Ferland. He wasn't told why the man had to die, and he didn't ask. Quesnel was to be paid $10,000 for the hit, ten percent of that to be deducted for the operations fund of the Hells Angels' Trois-Rivières chapter. He was given a down payment of $2,000.

Quesnel used ten rented, borrowed, or stolen vehicles in January 1995, as he scouted out the Grondines area west of Quebec City where Ferland lived. On one outing he dinged another car and paid the driver $20. He hired a getaway driver for $1,500, but he later backed out. Then he offered Michel Caron, a former member of the Mercenaires biker gang, $4,500 to drive him. Caron convinced Quesnel that the best way to avoid capture was to drive to Ferland's house and return to Quebec City by snowmobile after the hit.

As he approached the house Quesnel met André Bédard, who went into the house to advise Ferland he had a visitor. Bédard walked out, Quesnel slipped in and shot Ferland as he was walking downstairs. Quesnel had been ordered by Roy not to kill Ferland's wife. She was about to come downstairs behind her husband when the shots rang out and she hid.

In March, Thiffault contracted Quesnel to kill Richard (Chico) Delcourt for $10,000. Quesnel was given a .357-Magnum revolver and a vehicle rented by the Blatnois biker gang in Grand-Mère. Quesnel scouted Delcourt's home in Sainte-Thérèse several times before he settled on a way to kill him. Caron agreed to drive the car again, but failed to show up, probably because he thought Quesnel was going to kill him for having witnessed the Ferland killing. A second driver also backed out. Quesnel finally called Delcourt late at night and told him

someone in Quebec City wanted to talk to him. Delcourt hesitated. "If
we wanted to kill you, we would have done so long ago," Quesnel reas-
sured him. Delcourt agreed to accompany Quesnel, even though it was
obvious he wore a long-haired wig, a toque, glasses without lenses, and
slippers.

On the way to Quebec, Delcourt explained that he imported drugs
on a small scale by paying travel fare for couples. Quesnel was at wit's
end. He'd planned to kill Delcourt in his house. "I tried to figure out
what to do with him. I didn't want to go all the way to Quebec." Quesnel drove slower and slower, and told Delcourt he didn't have a driver's
license. Delcourt offered to drive. As they got out of the car to exchange
seats, Quesnel said "Good night," and shot him three times.

*   *   *

Rock Machine sympathizers were so numerous in Montreal's Bordeaux
jail that they controlled the institution—from drug sales to politics.
Hells Angels supporters had to be isolated in a separate prison wing for
their own protection in the second week of December. They seemed
more concerned about being unable to get their daily fix of drugs in
their new cell block and complained about the loss of privileges, to
which prison authorities conveniently turn a blind eye. "All the other
prisoners can consume while we, because of our affiliations with the
Hells Angels, are being punished, supposedly to protect us," one Hells
Angels sympathizer said.

Prison officials, like the public at large, believed that the drug problem behind bars did not affect them. As far as they were concerned,
inmates who dealt and used drugs were so busy they couldn't cause
trouble for guards and administrators. While this was one short-term
effect of turning a blind eye to drugs, this policy also allowed inmates
to create a power base in prison and wield power over the institution:
dealers controlled the users, and could order them to riot or make life
miserable for authorities. Prison officials had, over the years, turned
over the institutional reins to inmates who no longer feared or
respected their jailers. Power was voluntarily abdicated, not won by the
prisoners.

A sad testimony to this topsy-turvy state of affairs was the federal
government's acceptance of a proposal by Corrections Canada to
supply inmates with syringes to reduce the number of AIDS cases
behind bars. Prison guards were afraid of catching the disease during
bloody fights with prisoners. The only way to rectify the situation is to
stem the drug flow into prisons, fire all officials who tolerate and

encourage drug use behind bars, and let the inmates withdraw cold turkey. Prisons no longer protect society or rehabilitate criminals. Prisons create and nourish addicts who are released into society to commit more crimes to fund their habit. Prisons create their own business. In the process, they create thousands of victims.

* * *

Hells Angel Michael (L'Animal) Lajoie-Smith, 34, pleaded guilty on Thursday, December 5—the Hells Angels' nineteenth anniversary in Quebec and Canada—to severely, and arbitrarily, beating Alain Cadieux, 35, in Le Marsolais bar in Cartierville on July 22, 1995, condemning the man to a life in an institution and a wheelchair. Lajoie-Smith was sentenced to six years in jail, his third prison sentence in one year.

Molotov cocktails were thrown at the Hells Angels-linked Lady Mary-Ann strip bar at 4:30 a.m. on Friday, December 13. At 2 p.m., two masked gunmen walked into the Rock Machine-linked Bagdad Café, trashed several times already by thugs with baseball bats, and ordered the waitress and three clients out before they tossed three Molotov cocktails against the walls.

Hells Angel Scott Steinert, 24, moved into the Lavigueur mansion on Île-Jesus in December and immediately surrounded the property with an eight-foot-high fence. He also strategically placed huge concrete blocks at the main entrance and installed security video cameras near the steel doors. Richard Turcot, who denied being a Hells Angels sympathizer when he bought the building, applied and received from city officials a building permit to erect three or four single-family houses worth $250,000 each on the property. One of Steinert's business ventures was the Sensation stripper agency in Montreal. Steinert, a native of Wisconsin, had moved to Quebec with his family at age 8; currently he was appealing a deportation order on the humanitarian ground that he had a young child.

One of Steinert's first visitors was Hells Angel Normand (Dog) Labelle, who was one of fifteen bikers to buy the gang's first Canadian clubhouse in 1977. He had been a business associate in Laval of Hells Angel Michael (L'Animal) Lajoie-Smith before his incarceration.

Hells Angel Richard (Rick) Vallée, of the Nomads chapter, had a good-news/bad-news day on Tuesday, December 17. First he was acquitted of conspiracy to murder an associate of the Jokers, a Hells Angels puppet gang; the victim had been targeted for his lack of loyalty to the Jokers. The Jokers in the audience applauded in support. Then Vallée was taken to another courtroom when the smile was wiped off his face by an extradition request from U.S. authorities to face charges in the July 28, 1993, murder in Champlain, New York, of a man who had been scheduled to testify against the Hells

Angels. Vallee, 39, was accused of planting the car bomb that killed Lee Carter, an informant for the U.S. Drug Enforcement Administration.

The Rock Machine retaliated for the shooting of a sympathizer on Monday, December 16, by gunning down 42-year-old Hells Angel Bruno Van Lerberghe as he ate in a Vanier bar the next afternoon. The hit man dropped his gun in the lobby of the Rest-O-Broue II bar and fled. Professional killers leave their guns at the scene, to ensure they are not caught with them and to prevent their use in other crimes which could then be linked by police. The gunplay marked an escalation of the biker war in the Quebec City area, which so far had been fought with bats and bombs. Van Lerberghe was the second Hells Angel killed in the biker war.

Four days later, on December 20, a hooded gunman shot Pierre Beauchamp, 46, in his car at a downtown Quebec City intersection. The year's violence in the Quebec City area ended with the curbside shooting of two Rock Machine sympathizers early Monday morning, December 30.

*   *   *

The biker war heated up in the Quebec City area as the weather chilled. Another bar had been torched with a Molotov cocktail on Tuesday, December 19, and normally festive residents began to pressure police to release a list of bars frequented, controlled, or owned by the Hells Angels and the Rock Machine. Police were stuck in a bind. Most of the bars' owners had no criminal records, so publishing a list could give rise to lawsuits. Other bar owners were victims of extortion, and anyone who complained to police would be killed by the bikers. Residents began to feel like hostages in their own homes. Until the spate of bombings, the Quebec public accepted underworld deaths as a fact of life. They didn't care about the biker war as long as the violence didn't affect them. People don't realize that turning a blind eye to crime only allows it to flourish and eventually affect everyone's lives.

Quebec City mayor Jean-Paul L'Allier pleaded with the province's public security minister for the second time in six months on Wednesday, December 18, for help in protecting his city's residents from warring bikers. He asked for an anti-gang law like the U.S. RICO statute, which he mistakenly believed made it illegal to belong to a criminal gang. Behind the mayor's seemingly altruistic gesture was a more practical goal. Because the bikers fought for control of drug turf, he deemed the war a provincial and federal responsibility and believed his taxpayers shouldn't have to pay the bill by having their cops take part in the battle. The mayor didn't understand that special squads like Carcajou are successful only with the help of local police, who know the criminals on their turf and who will continue to fight them after the squads move on. L'Allier repeated a refrain chanted by many head-in-the-sand politicians and demanded a public inquiry to expose the dirty doings of bikers.

I became an active participant in the public debate on how to curb biker warfare when the media came to me for an unbiased view on the issue. "Back-to-basics arduous detective work over the long term is the only way to hurt the gangs," I told *Le Soleil* in Quebec. "The war moved from Montreal to Quebec City when Carcajou turned the heat up on the bikers." As for Mayor L'Allier's request for a public inquiry, I said, "The situation is too critical to waste time with an inquiry. A public inquiry helps define a problem. The problem of gangs warring over drug turf is very clear."

Federal justice minister Allan Rock also broached the subject of Quebec's biker war on Wednesday, December 18. Rock had been pressured by the separatist Bloc Québécois to introduce an anti-gang law to stop the war. Rock said he sympathized with the frightened public, but did not believe an anti-gang law would solve the problem, especially the draconian law requested by police and politicians. Rock suggested that better cooperation between different levels of law enforcement would be more productive. "An anti-gang law is not one of our options," Rock said, "because the real problem consists of gathering proof against gang members. The solution, as I see it, is for police agencies to work together more effectively."

1997

The new year in the Quebec City area nearly began with a bang, but police were able to disarm a twenty-pound bomb left in a garbage bag at the front door of a Lac-Saint-Charles strip club linked to the Hells Angels on Wednesday, January 1. The manager opened the garbage bag to find nine plastic cylinders full of explosives wired to an alarm clock.

Saint-Nicolas mayor Richard Blondin took a more proactive tack in his city's fight against bikers. City councilors drafted a by-law that banned the construction of fortified buildings such as clubhouses, and made bullet-proof windows and shutters illegal. The by-law could not be used against existing buildings, but would prevent new clubhouses from being built and would require purchasers of existing clubhouses to renovate the buildings to current specifications. "This is a preventative measure," Blondin said. "It's clearly dissuasive in nature. We'd like to shed the reputation of housing the Hells Angels. We already have their first clubhouse. We're not going to make it easier for them to buy a new property."

The by-law was prompted by news that the real estate agent for a huge property adjacent to the city put money ahead of civic responsibility and contacted the Hells Angels to ask if they would like to buy the land because it would be "a nice location" for bikers. Business owners are the last to complain about bikers, because they profit from the money they spend in their towns. Many owners like bikers because they pay cash. The property covered 3.5 million square feet and boasted a 5,844-square-foot house with fifteen rooms, seven bathrooms, five garages, a guest house, and a stable—all valued at $700,000 by the city and offered for sale at $950,000.

The Quebec government succumbed to pressure in mid-January 1997 and agreed to fund municipal police efforts to keep track of bars owned, controlled, or used by the Hells Angels and Rock Machine. The cost of the task was pegged at $1.2 million, with $800,000 paid by the cities and $400,000 paid by the Ministry of Public Security—half to municipal forces, half to the Sûreté du Québec. It was the first time the provincial government had given money to municipal police.

The deal was struck after twelve police chiefs wrote public security minister Robert Perreault, who replaced Serge Ménard after the death of Daniel Desrochers. I had challenged Ménard in March 1995 to make the streets of Quebec safe or resign and give the job to someone who could do so. He assured me and the public that the biker war was under control. The chiefs asked Perreault to pay the salaries of the police officers they contributed to the bar identification operation. The provincial government also authorized municipal police to enforce liquor laws as a way of shutting down bars. Provincial liquor inspectors were not up to the task.

Citizens of Quebec City feared at the end of January that the Hells Angels were renovating the rock pub Le Repaire—damaged by a four-pound dynamite bomb on July 22, 1996, a blast that vaporized the Quebec police bomb-disposal robot—into a new clubhouse. On January 25, 1997, someone parked a truck stuffed with 75 pounds of dynamite outside Le Repaire. Coincidentally, *repaire* means clubhouse. The new building sported surveillance cameras and steel doors, but then, most of the bars in the area had installed surveillance equipment to watch for people leaving bombs at their front doors.

*   *   *

The biker war returned to Montreal early Friday morning, January 17, when the Hells Angels detonated a ten-pound bomb at the front door of the Champlain bar, frequented by the Rock Machine, and blew out its front wall. A Molotov cocktail had been thrown against the bar in November as a warning.

The following week (Friday, January 24), Rock Machine drug dealer Marc Belhumeur was assassinated at mid-day on his twenty-fifth birthday in an east Montreal pub frequented by the gang and the Pelletier brothers. Belhumeur ran a drug network in northeast Montreal and was a suspect in two biker war murders. The masked killer tried to shoot Belhumeur outside, but he crashed through the door and ran to a pay phone at the back of the pub. He was shot before he could dial the number.

*   *   *

Back in Quebec City, Mayor Jean-Paul L'Allier kept trying to reassure the public that the war would soon be under control. Unbeknownst to the public, the Sûreté du Québec had turned against public security minister Robert Perreault after he ordered the first-ever public inquiry of the provincial police force in the wake of allegations of systemic corruption and incompetence.

Mayor L'Allier and Minister Perreault also incurred police wrath when they refused to pressure Ottawa to pass an anti-gang law (as demanded by Quebec police) because it would certainly be appealed and defeated in court in a challenge under the Charter of Rights and Freedoms. Police wanted gang membership to be made illegal so they could arrest without proof of criminal activity anyone they suspected of belonging to a gang. So much for the freedom of association and the presumption of innocence. Perhaps politicians should be reminded of the phrase uttered by the Athenian historian Thucydides: "A man will go to the limit of his power."

To set the record straight on the U.S. Racketeer Influence and Corrupt Organizations statute, it does not criminalize membership in an organization. The act requires police and prosecutors to demonstrate a "pattern of racketeering activity." The prosecution is more difficult, as is the detective work, but the increased penalties ensure the criminal is locked up for a long time.

The Hells Angels were charged and tried under the RICO statute in 1979 and 1981 in California. The prosecution was not properly prepared and the police failed to conduct investigations to corroborate the testimony of paid informants. Both cases failed miserably. (I detailed them in *Hells Angels: Taking Care of Business*). The Hells Angels have learned through experience and, with the help of lawyers, have structured themselves to be impervious to anti-gang laws. I have preached this for many years, to no avail. The Hells Angels are structured hierarchically for the club part of their interests. But their criminal operations are compartmentalized into isolated cells, much like terrorist groups and spy agencies. The organization does not give orders to Hells Angels to commit crimes. The organization does not want to know what individuals do. Most Hells Angels operate on their own with associates. If they are caught, their activities cannot be traced back to the Hells Angels. The individual takes the rap. And because people mind their own business, even if a Hells Angel wanted to rat, he knows little about other members' activities. So it was frustrating to watch politicians and police in Quebec plead for an anti-gang law. They had little knowledge or sense of history, and fought in a vacuum.

*   *   *

Carcajou scored a major victory in Montreal on Wednesday, January 29, when three members of the Alliance who had become police informants earlier in the year gave them information that allowed the arrest of five persons involved in the attempted killing of Hells Angel Maurice (Mom) Boucher on November 24, 1994. A stolen truck full of explosives parked near the Cri-Cri restaurant was to be detonated as Boucher walked by. Rock Machine associates hid nearby, detonator in hand, and watched for Boucher. A busy-body called police to tow the illegally parked truck, which was taken to a compound where the trigger men detonated the bomb a few hours later to prevent the death of innocent bystanders. Boucher never knew there had been an attempt on his life. He led a charmed life. Police foiled several attempts to kill him as he pursued his expansionist policy.

The Alliance members who became informants were highly placed: Harold Pelletier, a hit man whose brother Sylvain had been blown up in his vehicle in Repentigny; Denis Bouthillette, tasked with protecting the Alliance explosive stashes; and Normand (Bouboule) Tremblay, whom the Hells Angels had been trying to kill when they blew up the wrong Jeep and killed Marc Dubé and Daniel Desrochers. Tremblay was part of the team that had tried to kill Boucher with the truck bomb.

By January 30, police in Quebec City had temporarily closed (for reasons of public security) Le Repaire and La Causerie, two bars frequented by Hells Angels. The new police bar squad—le Groupe régional d'intervention sur le crime organisé (GRICO); or, in English, the Regional Organized Crime Intervention Group—convinced the

Liquor Control Board to order the bars closed until owners could prove at a hearing that they should be allowed to operate. A two-pound bomb blew out La Causerie's front window on Tuesday, January 14. Police were granted the power to seize the bars' liquor licenses and to confiscate their stock.

Hells Angels lawyer Roger Bellemare successfully argued to have La Causerie re-opened on Tuesday, February 4, and threatened to sue the Liquor Board for damages caused by the January 29 closure and loss of clientele scared by the publicity. Bellemare told reporters outside the hearing it was a coincidence that a Hells Angels lawyer was arguing the bar's case. Several lawyers representing half a dozen bars closed by police in the previous week argued—and the commission agreed by reinstating licenses—that the Liquor Board had acted precipitously and failed to query bar owners before suspending their licenses.

One of the Dark Circle's major strategists, sought by Carcajou for a year, was arrested off the coast of Ireland in mid-February by the military coast guard who answered a distress call from a thirty-five-foot boat being tossed around in a violent storm. His false passport prompted authorities to check Interpol for an arrest warrant, and they found that Carol Daigle, 48, a former Devil's Disciple in the 1970s, was wanted for ordering the killing of Hells Angel Normand (Biff) Hamel in October 1995. He was the last member of the Dark Circle sought by police and was connected to the Italian mob, the Dubois brothers, and the West End Gang. The Dark Circle plotted the elimination of the Hells Angels' Nomads chapter whose president, Maurice (Mom) Boucher, had instigated the war they were forced to fight. Hamel, Boucher's right-hand man, was targeted for a hit in the Galeries d'Anjou shopping center, but Carcajou foiled the operation. Dark Circle member Louis-Jacques Deschênes, 55, was sentenced to seven years in jail in January 1996 for his part in the plot.

Montreal police quietly withdrew from Carcajou in February and pulled their thirty-nine detectives from the joint-forces operation, leaving the Sûreté du Québec and RCMP to carry on. Montreal police officials said they thought Carcajou had accomplished its main goals—goals that were never publicly stated, but which included stopping the biker war—and wanted to use the police investigators elsewhere. The Montreal police still had its own anti-biker squad. It was a curious gesture for a police force whose city was in the throes of the world's largest and bloodiest biker war.

*   *   *

American authorities began to wonder in 1997 why it was so difficult to get Hells Angel Jacques (Jack) Émond, 41, extradited to Florida to face charges of conspiracy and trafficking of large quantities of hash and cocaine. Émond also faced charges of belonging to a continuing criminal enterprise from January 1976 to February 14, 1990. The law was used to sentence West End Gang leader Allan (The Weasel) Ross, to life in prison on the same charges Émond faced.

Those charges were laid after the 1987 arrest of four of Émond's alleged accomplices, one of them being Robert Leclerc, his main drug supplier in the United States. Leclerc, who owned a Miami diving shop, testified he was introduced to Émond in 1979 by Georges (Bo Boy) Beaulieu, then president of the Gitans in Sherbrooke, which became a Hells Angels chapter in 1984. (Beaulieu was convicted in the 1985 slaughter of the North chapter after living the life of a fugitive.) Leclerc said Émond and other bikers wanted cocaine to party in 1979 and he gave them four ounces. The following week, Émond and Beaulieu paid Leclerc $18,000 (U.S.) for eight more ounces of cocaine. Until his arrest in 1987, Leclerc provided Émond once a month with cocaine destined for Canada. The largest amount he sold him was 135 kilos, and after 1984 Émond always bought hundred-kilo lots. Emond was convicted of drug trafficking in Quebec in 1987 and sentenced to nine years in jail. He was released in December 1991.

The U.S. government sought his arrest in 1993. He was released on $150,000 bail by a Vancouver Immigration tribunal. Émond had moved to British Columbia after his release from prison in 1991 and transferred to the Hells Angels' East End chapter. He bought a $350,000 house in North Burnaby, studied business administration, and worked at a motorcycle shop owned by Hells Angel John Bryce of the same chapter. Émond needed a steady job to meet parole requirements.

Émond's extradition hearing was postponed eight times by the federal crown prosecutor, who is entrusted to act on behalf of the U.S. attorney general.

Another Hells Angel facing an unwanted trip to the United States had his hearing postponed for the second time in three weeks on Monday, March 3, when his lawyer failed to show up. Scott Steinert, 34, a Wisconsin-born member of the Montreal chapter, had been ordered deported on November 14, 1996, by the immigration minister.

Several Montreal chapter Hells Angels consulted gang lawyers and read the fine print in Bill C-95. They decided it was better to anticipate police use of the law against the gang, and they took preventive measures to foil cops and courts. Eight Hells Angels who had no criminal convictions within the past five years—an inportant point in the proposed law—broke away from the Montreal chapter and formed, along with two prospects, the "South" chapter on March 1. Unlike other Hells Angels' clubhouses around the world, their building was not painted red and white but black and white. They ordered new patches from Vorarlberg, Austria, where all Hells' Angels patches are made, and had them shipped UPS after paying directly into the Hells Angels' Swiss bank account.

*   *   *

Carcajou investigators worked hard to find the thirty cases of dynamite stolen by the Rock Machine from the Dyno Nobel company in Rimouski in November 1996. Five of the cases were accounted for by March: some of them had been used in bombs, others were found by police. The remaining 1,200 pounds of dynamite could fill seventeen vans. Compared to the Rock Machine, the Hells Angels had detonated only a handful of bombs, notably the October 1995 blast of a 25-pound bomb that gutted the Rock Machine clubhouse in Montreal.

The Hells Angels feared another innocent victim, and when the war moved to Quebec City, they used tactics less likely to inflame the public: Molotov cocktails, false bomb scares, shootings, and their pick-up baseball team. Nevertheless, the Hells Angels nearly killed another innocent bystander in early March when they pumped ten bullets into Rock Machine sympathizer Alain Proulx at the Chez Yollande café in Quebec City. Marcel Lagrange, who nursed a coffee at a nearby table, was seriously wounded by a stray bullet.

By March 1997, the war in Quebec City was being waged by about two hundred Hells Angels and Rock Machine, including their associates and sympathizers. Some of these people could be found by using only a telephone book. The Hells Angels have always been crazy about numbers. The number eighty-one means Hells Angels—H is the eighth letter of the alphabet and A is the first. Many Hells Angels and associates tried to get telephone numbers ending in 4355: HELL. A Montreal Rock Machine had the cellular phone number 862-ROCK.

The driver of a Jeep Cherokee aimed his vehicle at the Hells Angels' clubhouse in Saint-Nicolas and jumped out, pressing the remote-control detonator that triggered a twenty-five-pound bomb on the back seat. The blast not only damaged the clubhouse but blew doors and windows out of dozens of houses. Flying glass pelted a one-month-old girl in her crib. She wasn't even scratched. Hard-packed snow banks absorbed much of the blast.

The Bloc Québécois tried to embarrass federal justice minister Allan Rock on Tuesday, March 11, by asking in the House of Commons why the extradition hearing of Hells Angel Jacques Émond had been put off eight times by a Crown prosecutor. Rock said he was unfamiliar with the case, but would look into it.

The Rock Machine retaliated on Friday, March 14, for the January bombing of the Champlain bar in Montreal by bombing the Monte Carlo bar frequented by the Rockers with a ten-pound bomb that not only destroyed the building but damaged twenty-two neighboring businesses. The Rock Machine had thrown a Molotov cocktail against this bar on November 20, 1996, as a warning. It was the sixty-sixth bombing or attempted bombing in the biker war.

Public fear over the bombings erupted on Sunday, March 16, when six hundred residents of Saint-Nicolas marched around the Hells Angels' clubhouse and chanted for the gang to leave town. Masked Hells Angels stood on the building's parapet and videotaped the crowd. "Does it take children blown to bits in the streets for people to show solidarity?" asked organizer Michel Arnautovitch. Saint-Nicolas mayor Richard Blondin gave a short speech: "Go away." Quebec City mayor Jean-Paul L'Allier, who complained that the government was not doing enough to stop the war, said he would not attend the protest—an unusual decision for a politician who claimed that a public inquiry was needed to educate the public. The bar La Décroche in his city, frequented by the Hells Angels, was burned to the ground the previous Friday.

The Rock Machine in Montreal seemed to know the Hells Angels celebrated their forty-ninth anniversary on Monday, March 17, and they threw some fireworks into their celebrations. They planted a bomb wired to two twenty-liter gas cans outside l'Énergie, a bar frequented by the Hells Angels. Ninety minutes later, a Pontiac Eagle blew up in front of Custom Cycle. The building's former owner, Pierre Daoust, 34, had been linked to the Hells Angels puppet gang the Death Riders. Hit men with shotguns made him one of the biker war's first victims in July 1994.

*   *   *

The momentum for an anti-gang law accelerated in mid-March after four attempted bombings in Montreal in ten days. Montreal deputy police chief Pierre Sangollo re-ignited his three-year campaign for the law. Police had wanted this kind of legislation long before the biker war. Bikers are just one type of criminal gang. Canada is host to a multitude of organized criminals including Vietnamese street gangs, Chinese triads, the different Italian mafias, aboriginal gangs such as the Mohawk Warriors, street gangs like Winnipeg's Warriors, the Russian mafia, Jamaican posses, Colombian cartel cells, countless ethnic terrorist groups that raise funds through crime to subsidize wars in their homelands, and more. "We can get along day to day," deputy chief Sangollo said on Tuesday, March 18, "but we'll never be able to dismantle these gangs with existing legislation. The drug business is at stake here. It's a multi-million-dollar market. They won't stop because public opinion is against them."

Police worries were compounded by the impending release from jail of eight members of the Dark Circle, the Rock Machine's muscle. The men had been sentenced to thirty months in jail in January 1996.

A small-time Quebec hood didn't think twice when he killed a Rockers associate on February 11 because he felt the man—an expert tow-truck thief—didn't give him his fair share of the proceeds. The criminal and his friends threatened Marc-André Trépanier, a drug-dealing Rockers associate. Trépanier, a friend of Hells Angel Maurice (Mom) Boucher, asked the Nomads chapter president for help on February 7. Boucher told him his fears were groundless, but offered protection for several thousand dollars. Before he could pay, Trépanier, 36, was beaten and burned and wrapped in plastic, then dumped on a country road on February 11. The killers, having vented their anger, realized their error and ran scared that they had angered Boucher. They drove to Ottawa to steal a truck with Ontario plates and continued their trip to the west coast. On Tuesday, March 18, Winnipeg police arrested and charged five people armed with a bomb and a .25-caliber pistol, in connection with the murder.

Allan Rock promised in a letter to a Bloc Québécois politician on Tuesday, March 18, to make a decision on the extradition of Hells Angel Jacques Émond. Rock admitted he became aware of the Émond case in 1994, when Émond's Toronto lawyer, Clayton Ruby, asked Rock to dismiss the extradition request before it was heard by a tribunal. Rock ordered officials to get more details from American prosecutors "in light of allegations made by Émond's lawyers." The federal government decided in 1999 not to extradite Émond to the United States to face drug smuggling charges.

The Rock Machine killed two innocent bystanders with a car bomb behind the Valleyfield bar, Place à Moustache, the night of March 18. The bar owner and an employee tried to move the bomb before it exploded outside the Hells Angels' hangout. They became the biker war's thirty-first and thirty-second victims.

*   *   *

I appeared on sixteen different CBC radio and television shows on Tuesday, March 4, including the *National News* and the *National Magazine*. A CBC reporter in Vancouver who resurrected a months-old story in the print media about the large number of Hells Angels and their associates employed at the Vancouver port had his apartment broken into and found his stereo receiver wrapped in a plastic bag and left in a bathtub full of water. The reporter and police called this an act of intimidation by the Hells Angels, and the reporter went into hiding. The story immediately took on a high profile, as did the reporter's week-long series of reports on the gang, and I was called upon to comment on the gang and put its operations in perspective for CBC listeners in different parts of the country.

I took advantage of the situation to point out that the police had failed to put the damper on the Hells Angels when they had the opportunity, mainly because police administrators never took the biker problem seriously. Some highly placed police officers had also been bought by the Hells Angels, I warned.

*   *   *

The Hells Angels put their Saint-Nicolas clubhouse on the market for $350,000 on Monday, March 24.

Attempts to shut down biker clubhouses across Quebec with municipal by-laws were temporarily successful, but the resourceful bikers found ways to keep their fortresses. The City of Montreal invoked fire regulations to close the Rockers and Rock Machine clubhouses, both bomb targets. Fire officials said steel doors and bullet-proof glass would foil attempts to break into the building to douse flames or save lives. The bikers made modifications to conform to the fire code and re-opened the clubhouses two days later.

Chicoutimi city officials had passed an anti-noise by-law four years earlier to tackle the Hells Angels puppet gang the Satan's Guard, whose clubhouse was built between two farms. The city banned loud motorcycles—bikers pierce the muffler or strip the baffles inside the pipe. "This law does not target only the Hells," said a local policeman. "It targets all those who like to shatter the air. When a motorcycle doesn't conform, we seize it and the owner has to get a proper muffler installed at his expense." The Hells Angels, who like to have their own way, fought the by-law in court for four years with the help of legitimate motorcycle clubs. The gang boycotted Chicoutimi, moving its annual party and spending its money in Jonquière instead. Citizens of Chicoutimi did not miss their dirty money.

The trick to devising laws to tame bikers is to ensure the laws are not aimed at bikers alone, as the courts strike down such laws for being discriminatory. The court struck down a 1937 by-law, for example, that forced citizens of Saint-Hugues to muzzle all dogs that weighed more than fifty pounds. There was only one such dog in the village.

Quebec's public security minister deemed the thirty-two-month-old biker war a crisis on Wednesday, March 19, and asked Ottawa to help the province end the slaughter. Politicians from all levels were slated to meet the next day to find ways to ensure public safety and ease the fear which panicked Quebec residents.

Allan Rock rejected the request by eighteen Quebec mayors, provincial public security minister Robert Perreault, and Quebec justice minister Paul Bégin at their Thursday, March 20, meeting, for a law that would have made it illegal to belong to an outlaw motorcycle gang. Such a law would never survive a challenge under the 1982 Charter of Rights and Freedoms. "I share the objective," Rock said. "We all want to find measures that are both effective and valid. There's no sense proposing a law which in a month or in six months might be struck down by a court as invalid. That would be a cruel hoax for the families and for the citizens who are looking to us for hope and to restore tranquillity." Rock promised to toughen up the Criminal Code.

Politicians and police from Quebec City and Montreal created a task force on Friday, March 28, to examine ways to end the biker war. Montreal police chief Jacques Duchesneau attacked Allan Rock for not passing an anti-gang law. Officials targeted Rock because the federal government was due to call a spring election, and the last thing Rock wanted was a yoke to drag along the campaign trail. Quebec officials knew this and took advantage of the weakness in Rock's armor to get their way. There's no better time to pressure a politician and put him on the hot seat than just before he faces the public for re-election. The task force examined by-laws and zoning laws they could use against the bikers.

I appeared again on the Montreal television show *Droit de Parole* on Friday, March 21, 1997: two years less ten days since my 1995 appearance on the show when I had challenged public security minister Serge Menard to make the streets of Quebec safe or quit his job. He was transferred to another portfolio after Daniel Desrochers's death.

The citizens of Montreal were on the verge of hysteria now that the biker war and its bombings had resumed in the city after a hiatus of nearly a year. The politicians and police who were guests on the program argued in favor of an anti-gang law. I explained that such a law would be futile, as the Hells Angels were structured to be impervious to anti-gang laws and the RICO statute had failed against them twice in the United States. But the politicians, police, and Josée-Anne Desrochers refused to listen.

I referred to the previous day's press conference, when politicians of all stripes stood together on a stage and told the media they were in agreement that such a law was needed. "It's always a danger sign when politicians from all parties agree on something," I warned. "It means they're screwing the public for their own benefit." The politicians in the audience cringed. Justice minister Allan Rock's parliamentary secretary, who joined the program via satellite, waited for the bombshell he knew I was about to deliver.

I pointed out that politicians did not mind making political hay out of the public fear generated by the biker war. Then I revealed that the politicians had failed to inform the public that the war had resumed in Quebec City in October 1996 and moved to Montreal in early 1997 because the politicians who pretended to tackle the problem had agreed to secretly cut Carcajou funding in October. The bikers resumed the war in Quebec City when they realized they were no longer under intense surveillance. They returned to Montreal when it was obvious Carcajou had less manpower. In fact, I revealed, Carcajou staff had been reduced to twenty-five from a hundred.

The two innocent men who died in the Valleyfield bomb blast would be alive if the war had not returned to Montreal, I said. Then I accused the police, who always complain when budgets are cut, of remaining silent when Carcajou was eviscerated because they had been promised an anti-gang law by politicians. Allan Rock began to consider the law because he wanted to pacify voters and bolster his party's standing in Quebec for the election, which was to be called days after the law was passed.

Josée-Anne Desrochers was so traumatized by her son's death that, rather than grieve his loss, she succumbed to police pressure to lobby politicians and garner public support for an anti-gang law. The woman had lived through hell since her son's death and it was unconscionable of the police to pin their public relations efforts for new tools on the sleeve of a grieving mother. When I talked to her that night, nearly two years after her son's death, the woman's soul was dessicated by the relentless battle she waged. She had not yet dealt with Daniel's death. She needed time alone, and wouldn't allow herself to heal. She is a good woman with a good heart, but the battle she waged would have been more fruitful if it had been fought with reason rather than through the uncauterized wounds of a broken heart. I grieved for her and told her she owed it to herself to take that long journey inward and set a new path for the future. She sat with the police and politicians during the program and argued passionately for an anti-gang law as they looked on, pleased to have a spokesperson who could tug at the public's heart-strings.

That night also marked the last time I saw my friend, Sorel police chief Brian Lannigan. As always, he quietly melted out of the darkness on a Montreal street mottled with moving shadows and greeted me with a smile. We spent hours at Ben's eating smoked meat sandwiches and talking anything but business. He was a good man and a great cop and died much too young.

*   *   *

The trial of Hells Angels Louis (Mélou) Roy and Sylvain (Baptiste) Thif-fault ended with the final summation of their lawyer on Thursday, March 27. The two had been fingered by two informants—Serge Ques-nel and Michel Caron—who pleaded guilty to numerous crimes, including contract murders, then agreed to go on the government payroll and testify against their former employers. The final argument by Hells Angels lawyer Jacques Larochelle illustrates the pitfalls of using criminals to testify against criminals, especially if a case is not bolstered with more substantive evidence gathered by detectives. Juries are not sympathetic to criminals. The men on trial are assumed innocent until proven guilty. The people who testify against them have their entire criminal past described in great detail in court. Juries don't sympathize with such witnesses. When it's one man's word against another, they can't be expected to convict on a killer's say.

"People don't tell the truth just because the government pays them," Larochelle said. "If they only said they killed two people, they would serve at least twenty-five years, wouldn't get a penny, and would be mistreated. But if they drag down someone the police want, the picture changes: they become heroes, informants. They are acquitted when they plead guilty. . . . .It's tempting to give a version that gets us out of prison and gives us money. . . . .What a crafty ruse. He's bought himself a quiet little life. His victims don't receive money. The noble state, to the contrary, even pays the informant's lawyer to defend him against lawsuits by the victims."

Another Hells Angels lawyer, Pierre Poupart, continued the attack on the validity of informant testimony. "The state pays the criminal's expenses," he said. "Quesnel will walk out of prison at 37 a millionaire, or nearly, after pleading guilty to five murders. That's extraordinary. He's assured himself a public salary until his last breath if he isn't freed. So he's willing to say anything to get his way."

The use of informants is a necessary evil. Police can't infiltrate gangs, because they should never be allowed to commit crimes to gain credibility in the criminal underworld. So informants become their eyes and ears. The drawback to using informants is their credibility. The justice system loses legitimacy when it pays society's most depraved criminals to help achieve justice. And police who rely too much on informants get lazy, stop seeking the truth, and forgo other measures that would solve the crime.

*   *   *

Eight Hells Angels associates crushed the skull of 19-year-old Sylvain Brazeau, a Rock Machine sympathizer, with baseball bats on Easter Sunday, March 30, then carried him to his apartment and left him in a pool of blood. The comatose man was hospitalized.

Police charged Hells Angel Louis (Mélou) Roy of the Nomads chapter on Wednesday, April 2, with ordering the February 1995 murder of Claude (Le Pic) Rivard, whom Serge Quesnel admitted killing.

Police found a van with a ninety-kilogram bomb outside the Rock Machine's new clubhouse in Verdun on Sunday, April 6.

Rock Machine bomb and escape expert Roger Hardy failed to show up in court on Monday, April 7, after prison guards at Donnacona put him in a paddy wagon with Hells Angels Louis (Mélou) Roy and Sylvain (Baptiste) Thiffault who were on their way to court to await the verdict of their murder trial. A bleeding Hardy was taken out of the vehicle on a stretcher. Hardy escaped from Donnacona in 1980 and 1982. He failed in a 1992 attempt to flee through the sewer system.

The owner of the Donnacona Hotel, Denis Lavallée, was shot to death in his third-floor office on Tuesday, April 8. Although the hotel was a Hells Angels' hangout, it appeared an Angel hit man killed the 31-year-old man then dropped his gun at the scene.

Louis (Mélou) Roy and Sylvain (Baptiste) Thiffault were acquitted in the murder of two drug dealers on Wednesday, April 9. The jury didn't consider Serge Quesnel to be a credible witness, especially without corroborating evidence. Criminology professor Jean-Paul Brodeur, who teaches at the Université de Montréal, said the case shows the need for strict informant guidelines. "The police forces have been shown to lack basic policing skills and . . . they are resorting to gimmicks like [informants] to get a quick and cheap victory."

The Rock Machine were also in court, but this time they were the complainants. The numbered company 2857-6684 Quebec Inc., which operated under the name Les Investissements Rock Machine Enr., sued police for $28,291 for damages caused by a raid on the Rock Machine clubhouse on

March 9, 1994. Police found no drugs or guns and laid no charges. They tricked the Rock Machine by arriving in a fire truck. The numbered company lists its officers as Giovanni Cazzetta, imprisoned Rock Machine leader, Gilles Lambert, his right-hand man, and Renaud Jomphe, murdered in a Verdun restaurant in October 1996.

Carcajou officers caught two Rock Machine sympathizers in mid-April who admitted they burned and bombed bars for the gang and stole numerous vehicles, mostly Jeep Cherokees, to be used in the attacks on Hells Angels' clubhouses and hangouts. Patrick Villeneuve, 22, and Alain Pilote were sentenced to jail terms.

Hours after his arrest on a gun charge early Tuesday morning, April 22, Sherbrooke Hells Angel Claude (Burger) Berger lost his ten-year position as third trumpet with the Quebec Symphony Orchestra when the band abolished the position. Berger was arrested after police saw a man flee a bar and try to hide a gun during a raid.

*   *   *

Quebec politicians increased the pressure on Allan Rock on Tuesday, April 1, weeks before Ottawa's Liberal government was expected to call a federal election. Bloc Québécois leader Gilles Duceppe and Quebec justice minister Paul Bégin blamed Rock for the continuing biker war. Typical politicians: pass the hat, pass the buck. "I am worried because I don't feel he has the will to lead the attack," Bégin told a news conference. The politicians repeated their demand that Ottawa pass a law that would allow police to immediately arrest all bikers. "Now is the time to pressure the federal government," Duceppe said, admitting they were using the biker war as a political issue. Bégin failed to mention that he had recently cut $140 million from Quebec's public security budget.

The anti-gang law as desired by Quebec politicians and police curiously resembles a 1936 French law "Relative to Private Militias and Combat Groups," drafted to empower the government to attack and disband right-wing gangs modeled on Fascist groups fighting wars in countries such as Spain. The law still exists. It was rewritten in 1992 to read much like the law Bégin and Duceppe wanted in Quebec: to outlaw "any group of persons holding or with access to arms, structured in a hierarchical manner and likely to disturb public order." In an ironic twist, the separatist Quebec politicians must have shuddered if they read the original law, which outlawed separatist groups "whose goal is to harm the integrity of the national territory."

While Quebec police waited for a new anti-gang law, some officers undermined existing laws by breaking them. The already soiled reputation of the provincial police took a beating at the freshly minted inquiry into the Sûreté du Québec, which probed, for the first time in fifty years, allegations of corruption and wrongdoing in a force perceived by the public and media as operating above the law.

Serge Barbeau stepped down as Sûreté chief for the duration of the inquiry. He testified that his senior officers kept him in the dark about charges that police planted evidence in the bust of twenty-six tons of hashish in the Port of Montreal, which prompted the court to set free some of Montreal's most notorious drug importers. Barbeau learned from a newspaper article on April 7, 1995, that four of his officers had planted incriminating evidence during the bust. A Quebec Superior Court judge threw out drug smuggling charges against Gerald and Richard Matticks and five others in June 1995. Barbeau ordered an internal investigation into the scandal in July, but senior officers and the police union stonewalled the hand-picked, senior investigators. "I was told there was a directive from the union to avoid giving information to the investigators," Barbeau said.

A Sûreté report showed that on August 26, 1996, two high-ranking officers tried to intimidate an internal affairs investigator into backing off. André Dupré, the Sûreté's second-in-command, and Michel Arcand, head of criminal investigations, took the investigator to task. "You're a two-faced bum," Arcand yelled at the investigator. "You're going to find it tough to investigate police officers. I'm going to fight to the end." Dupré appointed Arcand head of the anti-biker unit, but both men were later demoted.

Federal justice minister Allan Rock traveled to Quebec City to introduce his new anti-gang law—Bill C-95—on Thursday, April 17. True to his word, he did not outlaw gang membership, but he did make it illegal to "participate in a criminal organization." The law could be applied where a person knew that one or all members of the organization had committed crimes in the previous five years for the benefit of, at the direction of, or in association with the criminal organization. "People can be penalized for what they do and not for what they are," Rock said. "This will help police put out of business those whose business is organized crime." The bill defined criminal organization as any group that has as "one of its primary activities" the commission of a series of offenses punishable by five or more years in jail. The RCMP, as was revealed in the 1980s, once had as one of its primary activities the illegal opening of private mail.

Unfortunately, as I mentioned earlier, the Hells Angels are structured to be impervious to such laws. The organization does not participate in its members' crimes. The Hells Angels Motorcycle Club is not a criminal organization, but rather an organization of criminals. The Hells Angels will beat this law in court.

Rock believed the law would weaken gangs by locking up their leaders. This may work with some street gangs and other forms of organized crime, but each Hells Angel who participates in criminal activities runs his own empire; he is his own boss. The associates commit the crimes for the boss, even when the boss is behind bars. The police and politicians were looking for a magic pill, a quick and easy solution to a problem they had let fester for decades. While they looked the other way, the Hells Angels and other biker gangs evolved and set up near-impregnable empires. They would have been easier to fight twenty years ago. They can still be fought, but only the most dedicated investigators would be up to the task. Most police officers are not suited to such a long-term battle.

As a concession to Quebec, Rock increased the penalty for possession or use of explosives to a maximum fourteen years in jail. Accused gangsters would also be jailed pending trial unless they could prove they are not a menace to society. Previously, the Crown had to prove the accused was a threat. The bill made it easier for police to obtain income tax information on gangsters, obtain search warrants, and tap telephones. It also enhanced the powers of police to seize proceeds of crime from gangs.

Rock moved quickly to introduce the legislation to avoid accusations in the upcoming federal election that he had dragged his feet on the issue of public security in Quebec. Members of all parties, in a rare show of unanimity, passed the bill on Monday, April 21, to avoid being tagged with an unwanted election issue.

The Senate, encouraged by the government, passed the bill on Thursday, April 24. If the bill had not been passed before the election, it could not be reintroduced until the fall sitting of the House of Commons. The election was called a week later.

Hells Angel Maurice (Mom) Boucher reacted quickly to the passage of Bill C-95. He allowed Hells Angels to ride Japanese motorcycles, contrary to the gang's by-laws, and wear full-face helmets in an attempt to soften the gang image. By July, the Harleys were back on the road, although Quebec Hells Angels were seen at the Laconia, New Hampshire, motorcycle rally riding Japanese bikes while wearing shorts and running shoes.

*   *   *

The Hells Angels are always cleaning house, getting rid of unwanted riff-raff, potential snitches, gofers, hit men, and associates who know too much. The biker war gave them ample opportunity to dump their human dust-bunnies. The trial and acquittal of Trois-Rivières Hells Angels Louis (Mélou) Roy and Sylvain (Baptiste) Thiffault, who were arrested on the word of informants, sensitized the Hells Angels to threats from within. Six members of Hells Angels' Trois-Rivières puppet gangs disappeared in the spring of 1997. The missing: Ormand (Ti-Mine) Dorant, 38, a Joker from Saint-Jean; Guy (Ti-Cul) Mageau, 36, a Rowdy Crew from Lanaudière; Benoît (Ben) Lachance, 25, a Rowdy Crew from east Montreal; Clermont (Ti-Narf) Carrier, 35, and Edward (Cap) Villiers, 36, a Blatnois from Mauricie; and Sylvain Bernard, a Rowdy Crew associate in east Montreal.

All six men had been arrested by police many times during the previous two years for their complicity in the biker war. Although no explanation was ever given for their disappearance, bikers from their respective gangs visited the men's wives and girlfriends to retrieve all gang paraphernalia.

The Hells Angels' Nomads chapter moved their headquarters from the Trois-Rivières clubhouse to the Montreal Rockers' clubhouse to be closer to the battlefield. The Nomads did away with the traditional red-and-white paint scheme and re-painted the building with their chapter colors, black and white. They flew the Hells Angels' and Nomads' flags on the roof.

The Montreal chapter, based in Sorel, sold the Bob Chopper motorcycle shop in Longueuil, to distance themselves from the war. The shop, bombed in 1995, had been their meeting place in Montreal. By the end of April, the Hells Angels membership increased to the magic number eighty-one.

*   *   *

The arrest of six PCP traffickers in Quebec City on Thursday, May 1, showed police that while the Hells Angels and Rock Machine warred over drug turf, street-level dealers for both gangs worked together selling drugs. Money comes before loyalty in the underworld.

Hells Angel Scott Steinert's extradition hearing was put over once more on Thursday, May 8, when his lawyer sent a doctor's note that said he needed to take a two-week break from work. Steinert's second lawyer, Pierre Pannacio, photographed everyone in the hearing room with a disposable camera, but objected when a Swedish journalist tried to photograph the Hells Angel. "You don't have the right," Pannacio said. "It's forbidden. Return to your seat." He mocked a police officer who sarcastically commented on his ability to change the rules to suit his purpose and left the room chanting "Qué será, será."

The Quebec government passed a provincial law in early May that allowed municipalities to enforce a ban on bullet-proof windows, steel doors, and video security cameras in biker clubhouses. However, the less fortified buildings could still be used as clubhouses. Although some might argue that such a law does not hurt bikers, it shows them who's boss. It gives municipalities some control over the clubhouses which are a slap in the face to all citizens as they are known to house criminals. Law-abiding clubs don't need to hide behind steel walls and sandbags. There is no shortage of roads in Quebec that could justify killing competing bikers. Stripping clubhouses of their fortifications also exposed the entire gang to its enemies when gathered for meetings. It also made police raids easier.

A member of the Hells Angels puppet gang the Death Riders in Sainte-Thérèse illustrated with his suicide on Thursday, May 8, how much gang membership means to some bikers. Mario (Marteau) Martin, 32, had been a Death Rider since the mid-1980s. He was stripped of his colors and reduced in status to a prospective member in early May because of his consuming addiction to cocaine. Unable to live with the disgrace, he shot himself in the head after pumping several shots into the walls. Martin owned a motorcycle paint shop with another Death Rider and a former police officer.

Carcajou officers arrested several major Alliance bosses on Tuesday, May 20. Giovanni Cazzetta was charged with West End Gang member Richard Matticks, 63, with drug offenses. Matticks and his brother Gerald had charges of importing twenty-six tons of hashish into Canada dropped in 1995 after it was shown police planted false evidence in their attempt to convict them. Police also charged Rock Machine Serge (Merlin) Cyr, 39, with attempting to kill Hells Angel Maurice (Mom) Boucher.

The next morning, Wednesday, May 21, 562 police officers raided Rock Machine homes and clubhouses in twenty-four Quebec municipalities, arrested twenty-three people, and seized $4 million in assets. The largest police operation in Quebec history targeted the Rock Machine because they had a large stash of dynamite. Police found 772 pounds of explosives stolen from the Dyno Nobel company in Rimouski, 350 pounds of it in a cottage bomb factory near Sainte-Brigitte-de-Laval. They also evicted the Rock Machine from their two clubhouses, in Montreal and Beauport, near Quebec City.

Two Rock Machine members who slipped through the dragnet were arrested in Tilbury, in south-west Ontario, on Friday, May 23, with a kilo of cocaine, handguns, and body armor. An RCMP officer stretched the limits of credulity and said that pressure by Carcajou could force the Hells Angels and Rock Machine to set up outside Quebec.

The next day, the Saint-Nicolas Hells Angels emptied their clubhouse of all documents and potentially incriminating materials. Four Hells Angels went to a nearby bank and emptied four safety-deposit boxes. They also reduced the asking price for their clubhouse to $225,000.

Rock Machine associate Michel Patry was freed from prison in September 1996 after serving time for the June 11, 1990, murder of Hells Angels sympathizer Stephane Roy. Hells Angels carried the coffin at the funeral. Roy had had a part-time job cutting grass in cemeteries. Someone had wounded him with a rifle shot in the Sainte-Foy Jewish cemetery on Friday, May 23.

The Saint-Nicolas Hells Angels chapter celebrated its ninth anniversary on May 26 by granting prospect Jonathan (Grand Jos) Robert, 26, his colors as a full-fledged member. They also elevated two hangarounds to the status of prospect. Robert, a former Mercenaire, replaced Bruno Van Lerberghe, who had been shot to death on December 17, 1996. Robert was sentenced to three years in jail on April 15, 1993, for drug trafficking and possession of a dangerous weapon. He was fined $1,000 on January 29, 1997, for possession of a firearm while prohibited by court order, $800 for modifying its serial number, and $700 for possession of a restricted weapon. The Hells Angels were too wary to have their party at the clubhouse, so they used the Mercenaires' former clubhouse that night.

The Rock Machine set up a new clubhouse in Stoneham in June to replace the one seized by police in Sainte-Brigitte-de-Laval.

Hells Angel Richard (Rick) Vallée, 39, a member of the Nomads, was facing extradition to the United States on charges he murdered DEA informant Robert Lee, made a Hollywood-style escape from a Montreal hospital on Thursday, June 5. Vallée, who had undergone jaw surgery, told the two unarmed jail guards shortly before 8 p.m. that he wanted to take a shower. One guard stood at the door while the other followed Vallee into the shower room. An armed accomplice hiding in the shower put a gun to the guard's face while Vallée gagged and cuffed him with his own handcuffs. They left through another door and fled on motorcycles driven by two other men.

*   *   *

When Salvatore Cazzetta founded the Rock Machine, he envisioned a different kind of biker, one who had evolved beyond the ego-driven throwbacks who wore colors to advertise their toughness to the world. Outlaw bikers are the only form of organized crime to wear a sign that tells the world who they are. This leads to a frightening observation: if they are so visible, why haven't police been able to shut them down?

After all, they don't have to guess who the players are, as they must do with other criminals. The simple answer is that police really haven't considered outlaw bikers a threat until recently. The delay allowed the gangs to build crime pyramids where the underlings do the dirty work and the bosses at the top reap the benefits. Underlings often get caught, but even the most cooperative often can't see beyond one or two levels in a multi-level organization.

Cazzetta understood the importance of the structure that had been refined by the Hells Angels since their formation on March 17, 1948. The organization was nearly impregnable. Certainly, hundreds of Hells Angels have been jailed over the years, but the gang always comes out of prosecutions smarter and stronger. Cazzetta also knew that allegiance to a common cause (other than the money) was a powerful adhesive. But he thought wearing colors was just too obvious. So he took the best of the Hells Angels and tweaked it into his own vision of an organized crime gang.

Not all Rock Machine members thought this way, mostly because they didn't think much at all. Some younger members didn't understand biker history and had no long-term vision. They were impatient, and wanted to be granted immediate respect. In the biker underworld, that means people are deathly afraid of you.

Frédéric (Fred) Faucher, 27, was a full-fledged Rock Machine who was really a biker wannabe. Faucher didn't share Cazzetta's vision. He thought the Hells Angels were the big league. He couldn't join them, because they were the enemy. So he wanted to become a member of another big-league biker gang. The big five are the Hells Angels, the Outlaws, the Bandidos, the Pagans, and the Sons of Silence. Of these, the Outlaws have been the Hells Angels' mortal enemies since 1974. There were all but wiped out in Quebec.

Faucher was impressed by media reports of a war between the Hells Angels and the Bandidos in Scandinavia. I will examine the war in a later chapter, but suffice it to say that Faucher identified with the Bandidos and their fight against the Big Red Machine. Instead of buckling down and fighting his own battle in Quebec, Faucher dreamed of becoming a Bandido. The dream quickly evolved. The Rock Machine would become Bandidos and Fred Faucher would be their first Quebec president. From the first time Faucher voiced his dream publicly I challenged him to discuss it with me on radio, and he has never taken me up on it. I have told Faucher through the intermediary of radio that his goal of beating the Hells Angels as a Bandido is a pipe dream. He had no idea of the politics involved and was blinded to the pitfalls of his pursuit.

Faucher and several Rock Machine visited the Bandidos headquarters in Houston, Texas, and asked to be taken into their organization. He was told to go piss up a rope. The Bandidos, contrary to what police and media say every day in Quebec, are not the mortal enemies of the Hells Angels. The two gangs in the United States don't like each other, but they have never gone to war. Their territories don't overlap and each gang has a high-ranked member who keeps in touch with the other to prevent misunderstandings. Hells Angels' Ventura chapter president George (Gus) Christie, who will lead the gang when Ralph (Sonny) Barger dies, has talked regularly to the Bandidos president over the past decade. The war in Scandinavia was a European affair out of the hands of the Texas Bandidos, who provided no support for their Nordic brothers. In fact, the Hells Angels have targeted the Bandidos for takeover and have made political overtures to assimilate them which I will document and discuss later.

Faucher was not subtle or patient. He wrote to the Bandidos in Sweden and explained that his gang was at war with the Hells Angels in Quebec and that the Rock Machine wanted to become Bandidos. He was so overjoyed by the positive reply he received that he never doubted the Bandidos motives for embracing him so quickly.

Realistically, the European Bandidos were in no position to help the Rock Machine in Quebec. They couldn't provide manpower, because immigration laws kept them out of Canada. And they were so wrapped up in their own war that they couldn't spare manpower or money. The Rock Machine didn't need men or money. They had more than enough, plus a will to win. It seems Fred Faucher lost his focus and got caught up in his dream of being the leader of a new gang. He seemed to think that changing the Rock Machine name to Bandidos meant instant cachet, power, and respect. In reality, it would trigger a war in the United States between the Hells Angels and the Bandidos, something neither gang wanted.

Quebec Bandidos would never be able to attend runs in the United States because the great number of Hells Angels there would slaughter them. They also couldn't travel across Canada, because the Hells Angels control all provinces except Ontario. Even the American Bandidos would not accept Quebec Bandidos if it meant a needless war with the Hells Angels. More likely than not, they would lure the Quebec Bandidos to a function and then kill them, to maintain the fruitful peace south of the border.

Fred Faucher was out of his league and about to be used by a group of power-hungry rebellious Bandidos who sensed easy prey. Faucher never clued in that the Bandidos and Hells Angels in Scandinavia were on the verge of a truce in the summer of 1997 as the Danish government prepared to amend its constitution to ban outlaw motorcycle gangs. The three other Nordic countries considered taking the same route if the war continued. But Denmark was hardest hit by the warfare, and drastic measures were called for.

I speak with experience because I was part of talks and planning sessions in 1996 and 1997 aimed at ending the biker problem in Scandinavia. The Bandidos would not support a war between the Rock Machine and Hells Angels in Quebec if it jeopardized their agreement in Scandinavia, where they worked out a deal to share drug territory without fighting. But they could pretend to support the Rock Machine, who seemed too stupid to understand the changed political climate in Europe, take the gang over, then strike a deal with the Hells Angels and dissolve it after killing off dreamers like Fred Faucher. Or more bluntly, they could lead the Rock Machine into a Hells Angels' trap and wipe them out.

It seems unlikely that the Rock Machine, if they become Bandidos, would then join in being assimilated into Hells Angels, if that's what happens to the Bandidos world-wide. The Rock Machine, along with the Dark Circle and other Alliance members such as the east-Montreal Pelletier gang, went to war with the Hells Angels to protect and take back drug territory from them. All these gangs were tired of losing ground and money to the Hells Angels. Few of these guys are real bikers and they would never be accepted into the Hells Angels. To take this route, the Rock Machine would have to betray their Alliance friends. But, that's what being a Hells Angel is all about: you betray your friends for money.

Fred Faucher should have been aware of these scenarios when he traveled to Helsingborg, Sweden, on Wednesday, June 18, in hope of attending a Bandidos' memorial service for five members killed since 1994 in the war with the Hells Angels. Faucher traveled with Montreal members Johnny Plescio, 32, and Robert (Toutou) Léger, 39. The Bandidos' Memory Run attracted 150 Bandidos from across Europe. Swedish police stopped the Rock Machine members at Göteborg-Landvetter airport, detained them for 24 hours, and put them on a plane back to Canada because of their criminal records. From that day on, Quebec police and the RCMP put out the most interesting stories, interpretations and supposed analyses every time Fred Faucher or a Bandido farted.

*   *   *

The mystery of how jailed Rock Machine members obtained vast quantities of steroids and Valium to supply their network of buyers in Donnacona maximum-security penitentiary unraveled in June when investigators found that a former policeman and a homosexual priest had smuggled the drugs into the institution. The 46-year-old priest with a penchant for rough sex spent fifteen hours a week in the prison ministering to the needs of the needy. Prisoners who found him doing unpriestly things blackmailed him into smuggling the drugs in return for their silence. The pills were supplied by the former policeman, stepfather to an inmate.

Having struck a blow against the Rock Machine with a raid on the scale of a small war, police turned their attention to the Hells Angels and dismantled the drug network operated by Saint-Nicolas chapter president Marc (Tom) Pelletier on Wednesday, July 2, and Thursday, July 3. All levels of law enforcement were represented among the 270 police officers who conducted fifty-seven raids in thirty-two municipalities. They arrested the Hells Angels' leader and fifty associates and sympathizers who dealt drugs. Police issued a warrant for the arrest of the Quebec City Hells Angels' second-in-command, René (Will) Pearson, who avoided capture. Pearson, 44, surrendered on Monday, July 14. The one-year investigation saw an undercover operative spend $60,000 on sixteen purchases of cocaine, PCP, and ecstasy, with a resale value of $450,000. Police also arrested Pelletier's right-hand man, Jean René Poirier, on drug charges. He was the suspected leader of the Hells Angels' "Pitbull crew" that used baseball bats to ransack bars linked to the Rock Machine.

Prison guard Diane Lavigne climbed into her van at Rivière-des-Prairies penitentiary on Tuesday, July 1, drove briefly along the street that leads from the prison, and took the on-ramp to the Laurentian Autoroute, mindless of the motorcycle with two men that followed her. The motorcycle, a Japanese model no self-respecting outlaw biker would ever ride, pulled up beside her. The passenger raised his arm and fired at the woman until the motorcycle acclerated hard past the target. Lavigne died in her van.

*   *   *

The RCMP's top criminal investigator for Quebec said on June 18 that the Sûreté du Québec relied too much on rats and informants and failed to conduct proper investigations. Inspector Rowland Sugrue said Quebec police focused too much on the short term by racking up arrests and seizures with the use of informants. He said the RCMP preferred "to build solid proof to increase chances of securing a conviction in court. . . . We prefer to do less, but well."

Hells Angels' contract killer Aimé Simard followed a path well used by many hit men and became a police informant on June 12, 1997. He helped police round up alleged Hells Angels killers, mostly associates of the Rockers puppet gang in Montreal. By Tuesday, July 15, police had arrested Gregory (Picasso) Wooley, Pierre Provencher, Steven Falls, and Patrick Ménard-Pascone.

Simard, a short, stocky homosexual, explained in court how he'd ratted out drug dealers in Quebec City before he moved to Montreal and fell in love with the man who brought him into the biker underworld. The man was an associate of the Hells Angels puppet gang the Rockers. The Hells Angels told the Rockers in February 1997 to kill a Halifax drug dealer they no longer trusted. A Hells Angel will kill on mere suspicion anyone who might jeopardize his status, even his best friend. The lovers were sent to do the job. "I put one or two bullets in his head to finish the job," Simard said.

The Rockers gave Simard a list of five people to kill. The Hells Angels wanted to eliminate Jean-Marc Caissy, who undercut their prices in Montreal. The Rockers explained to Simard that the purpose of the hit was not only to eliminate Caissy, but to send a message to all other drug dealers that they shouldn't mess with the Hells Angels. "Killing them isn't everything," Simard said. "It has to be sickening, disgusting. You have to cut up their faces." He tracked Caissy and decided to kill him at the gym where he regularly played ball hockey. Simard held the door open as the drug dealer walked out. "Hey, Caissy," Simard said to get his victim to turn around. "I fired several shots at close range. I fired in his face. I think I fired five shots." One bullet and five empty casings were left in the barrel. Caissy paged the Rocker who had contracted his services and left a series of fives indicating he'd killed his target.

Simard kept his gun in the locker of a private gym. As a thief, he should have known that such gyms install video cameras because of the high rate of theft. He pulled the gun from his coat and put it into the locker as the caretaker watched. The caretaker called in police and gave them the videotape as evidence. They cut the lock off the locker and took the gun to test it for fingerprints and ballistics. Simard decided to inform on his employers rather than face a lengthy jail term. He would collect $400 a week for a total of $36,400 for his services.

*   *   *

Fred Faucher pursued his dream and traveled to Luxembourg with fellow Rock Machine members Paul (Sasquaatch) Porter and Johnny Plescio on July 17 to meet with the Bandidos international president from Texas, the European president, and chapter presidents from Australia and France during the Bandidos' Euro Run.

The dirty little murder of a Rock Machine associate in July showed the kind of scum that inhabits the underworld. Luc Laine, a sympathizer affiliated with the Hells Angels' Trois-Rivières chapter, contracted Dany (L'Animal) Lizotte and Stéphane (Le Roux) Alain to kill Gilles Fournier. They abducted him near the Quebec City bar Le Charest and took him to rural Frampton to bury him alive. The killers realized they had no shovels, so they drove to the home of a friend, André (Tonton) Vigneault, to borrow some. Vigneault tried to talk them out of killing the man, but ended up lending them two shovels, a pick, and a blanket, then telling them of a good place to bury the man. "All I wanted was for them to go." The killers returned to use his shower. He gave them clean clothes. The next day, Vigneault's roommate, Roger Gendron, burned the killers' clothing.

By August, police had jailed twenty-two of the Hells Angels' eighty-six members and prospects in Quebec. By contrast, of sixty-nine Hells Angels and seven prospects in five British Columbia chapters, only one had a criminal record: David James (Nick) Olinyk of the White Rock chapter. It was a sad reflection on the ability and dedication of police in that province.

Josée-Anne Desrochers continued to be a tireless crusader for an anti-gang law. She was a convincing, sympathetic speaker whose passion easily swayed listeners. The publicity-conscious Hells Angels offered her thousands of dollars to buy her silence. They even offered, before her son's funeral, sixteen motorcycles with riders to accompany the funeral procession. And they offered to pay for the funeral. This is a fact police did not pick up on, as it would have destroyed their theory that the Rock Machine had killed a Hells Angels' drug dealer. The Hells Angels wrote her and asked that she meet with their president. "They wanted to give me an exorbitant amount of money. I won't say how much, but I refused. I told them they could never buy my silence or compensate me for the sadness." The Rock Machine also tried to buy off Mrs. Desrochers. In all, both gangs made five offers in writing and over the telephone. "A life has no price," she said. "No one can buy Daniel from me."

*   *   *

Bombs and Molotov cocktails returned to Montreal and Quebec City during the third week of August. A homemade bomb was thrown into an empty variety store used as a drug den in the provincial capital. Two Montreal bars and Hells Angel Scott Steinert's escort-and-dancer service were torched with Molotov cocktails.

Hells Angel Louis (Mélou) Roy was shot four times with a revolver in the back and leg as he got out of his black Mercedes at his father's motel in Jonquière Saturday, August 23. Roy was on bail awaiting trial on charges of killing Rock Machine associate Claude (Le Pic) Rivard and had an 11 p.m. curfew. Court granted bail because Roy had been acquitted in April of the murder of two drug dealers. The 38-year-old Hells Angels leader refused to cooperate with investigators, calling them pigs. His lawyer, Martin Tremblay, said his client would not complain to police about the shooting. Police speculated that the Hells Angels may have tried to kill Roy for problems he caused the gang by hiring hit man Serge Quesnel, who became a police informant and fingered the organization's killers and drug dealers.

Police guarded the Saint-Luc hospital where Roy underwent a second abdominal operation on Monday, August 25. Police once again asked him about the shooting and he refused to talk or file a complaint, so they canceled their surveillance of the hospital.

Hells Angels hangaround Stéphane (Monroe) Carrier, 29, was severely cut on the face and neck with a broken bottle in the bar Chez Duff in Valleyfield on Sunday, August 24. The former member of the defunct Pirates biker gang refused to talk to police.

*   *   *

Police did their best to incite public fear over the Rock Machine dalliance with the Bandidos, often succumbing to wishful thinking, resorting to disinformation, or maybe they just didn't know any better. A Rock Machine was arrested on Wednesday, August 27, wearing a T-shirt that read "Support your local Bandidos." Here is a translated excerpt from the *Journal de Québec* that shows the inaccurate information fed to the media by police and my attempts, however abbreviated in this case, to counter it.

A member of the Rock Machine in Quebec, Martin Clavel, demonstrated yesterday that the links between this gang of bikers and the dangerous Bandidos have narrowed, when he was arrested in his Sainte-Foy apartment wearing a sweater of the Hells Angels' worst enemies.

Following the example of the California organization which allows only its members and close associates to wear a sweater "Support your local 666," a sign of their alliance with the Hells Angels, the other biker gang had T-shirts printed with a similar inscription "Support your local Bandidos," a product reserved, once again, for the initiated.

"It shows the Bandidos are closer to Quebec than certain persons believe," offered Richard Gagné, spokesman for the Sûreté du Québec.

According to information published in *Le Soleil*, Frédéric "Fred" Faucher, another Rock Machine member, wants to become the first Bandidos' president in Quebec. He succeeded in meeting Scandinavian Bandidos in July, along with two Montreal Rock Machine members, to establish links. Some observers of the biker underworld, like Yves Lavigne, openly cast doubt on the accuracy of these reportings.

The reporter, a favorite media mouthpiece of Sûreté du Québec biker investigator Sergeant Guy Ouellette, took umbrage to comments I made on a Quebec City radio show suggesting reporters dig up the truth instead of relaying slanted information from the police or bikers. Take the reporter's four paragraphs I just quoted, for example: the Bandidos are not the Hells Angels' worst enemies, the Outlaws are. The only clothing restricted to Hells Angels is that which reads "Hells Angels." The gang sells T-shirts to the public with a number of inscriptions, including "Support the Big Red Machine," "Free Sonny Barger," "Free the Hells Angels East Coast," *ad nauseam*. The "Support Your Local Bandidos" T-shirts are not reserved for "the initiated." They can be bought by anyone at dozens of biker events across the world. I saw them for sale in Sturgis, South Dakota, and in Stockholm, Sweden.

Police started scaring people in 1997 by predicting the imminent arrival of the Bandidos. I stood my ground and accused them of improper analysis and wishful thinking. By 1999, the Bandidos had not arrived, but Sgt. Ouellette continued to predict the event would happen soon. At the annual conference of the Criminal Intelligence Service of Ontario in September 1998, he predicted Bandidos' colors would fly in Quebec by year's end. It was curious to watch a man with access to so much information come to such conclusions. The answer to his behavior would come to me before long.

Montreal police introduced their new bomb disposal robot to the public on Monday, September 1. A biker bomb had disintegrated the first one in 1995. Inflation hiked the cost of the new gizmo to $150,000 from $65,000. The six-wheeled robot neutralizes bombs with a water cannon that shoots a stream of water so powerful it can dismember people.

Talks were afoot among biker gangs to cement alliances in case more

Hells Angels joined the war against the Rock Machine and to deter them from attacking other gangs. Fifteen Rock Machine members drove to Ottawa in two vans on Friday, August 29, for a weekend meeting with Outlaws leaders from Quebec and Ontario at their clubhouse on rue Lacouceur. Some European and American Bandidos accompanied them.

Sergeant Ouellette told his favorite Quebec City media mouthpiece he found it surprising that both gangs would flaunt their relationship so publicly, given they were involved in a war with the Hells Angels. Not if they wanted to give the Hells Angels something to think about.

Inspector Joe Dorricott of the Ontario Provincial Police predicted on Tuesday, September 2, that any biker war in Ontario would erupt in Ottawa. The RCMP's Criminal Intelligence Service of Canada followed suit on Wednesday, September 3, with a claim that it was "possible" for the Hells Angels and Rock Machine war to break out in the Ottawa-Hull area in the near future. The RCMP based the assertion on the previous day's arrest of eight area drug dealers affiliated with the Hells Angels. The RCMP deemed the area drug market "open" to many organizations that would try to take it over. Ottawa city police estimated the Hells Angels already controlled sixty percent of the area drug market through associates, and their biker expert saw no need for the Angels to move into the area, as they already got what they wanted from it. Sergeant Ouellette made a similar comment in July: "They don't need to come to Ottawa. They control it already."

The police and media speculated in the summer and fall of 1997 about the Rock Machine becoming Bandidos. They tacked onto their guesses dire warnings about a violent reaction by the Hells Angels. But there was no confirmation of what the gangs talked about. I wanted the Rock Machine and Bandidos themselves to state what they were up to. I taunted and baited Fred Faucher on several radio talk shows at the end of August, accusing him of being an ass-kissing wannabe that the Bandidos would use and chew up. I called him a typical no-life, low-life bootlicker of anyone or anything American.

Faucher contacted an accommodating reporter at the *Journal de Québec* and asked him to publish a photograph of Australian Bandido Mike Kay standing next to a Rock Machine with the Château Frontenac in the background. Kay was Michael Kulakowski, president of the Bandidos' Nomads chapter. (Like the Hells Angels, the Bandidos had an elite enclave named the Nomads.) In the photograph the men had their backs to the camera. Kay wore Bandidos colors. The Rock Machine had a windbreaker with the gang crest and name on it. (The photograph was taken

August 27. The bikers later had dinner at L'Astral restaurant at the hotel
Loews Le Concorde.) Faucher also told the reporter the Rock Machine
wanted a story published to show me that they indeed were friends with
the Bandidos. The story appeared on Wednesday, September 3.

At least four Bandidos leaders, two Americans and one Australian, Mike
Kay, spent four days in Quebec City last week. They weren't being tourists.

The Hells Angels' enemies were able to leisurely fraternize and
discuss with Rock Machine members from Quebec and Montreal the
creation of two new Bandidos chapters in these cities in the midst of a
war between these two biker gangs that has killed 50 people since the
summer of 1994.

These meetings were "very positive," two Rock Machine members
reported during an interview in the *Journal de Québec* offices. Our two
informants, who asked to remain anonymous, emphasized that the
meetings had not yet permitted the Rock Machine to receive Bandidos
colors. But "next time will be good," one of them assured us while giving
us a photograph taken last Wednesday when 40 Rock Machine, including members, sympathizers and hangarounds, took advantage of the
nice weather and took a cruise on the *Louis-Jolliet* with their illustrious
guests. In the photo are the backs of Mike Kay, an Australian Bandido,
and a Rock Machine who didn't want his identity revealed.

The Sûreté du Québec would not confirm this information. However,
officer Richard Gagné indicated that Carcajou investigators were
conducting many investigations into allegations of a possible presence in
Quebec of outlaw bikers from outside the country.

Notably, police are checking information indicating that two bikers on
motorcycles bearing Texas plates, [Texas is the Bandidos headquarters],
met, on Wednesday in an Old Quebec bar, an individual believed to be
a Rock Machine member and who wore the notorious black sweater with
the inscription "Support Your Local Bandidos," and that only certain
initiates are allowed to wear it. Last week, two Rock Machine members
wearing this sweater were arrested in Sainte-Foy and in Saint-Nicolas.

Our two informants, who voluntarily avoided all questions about their
war with the Hells Angels, also wanted to respond to journalist Yves
Lavigne, outlaw motorcycle gang specialist, who declared, lately, on a
local radio station, that the Bandidos would never affiliate themselves
with a gang as small as the Rock Machine. "They're the ones who invited
us," one of them said, referring to the July 20 get-together in Luxembourg, which included leaders of the Scandinavian Bandidos and three

Rock Machine members from Quebec and Montreal. To prove it, our informant showed us a letter clearly identified as being from the Bandidos in Helsingborg, Sweden, addressed in the spring to the Rock Machine at their Beauport clubhouse. The letter read: "It is with great interest that we have read about the situation in Quebec. It's much the same conditions here in Scandinavia. We would like to hear more."

The anonymous Fred Faucher failed to mention that the Bandidos' letter was a response to his initial letter introducing himself and the Rock Machine.

*　　*　　*

Prison guards Pierre Rondeau and Robert Corriveau drove the empty prisoners' bus to the local Tim Hortons at 6:30 a.m. on Monday, September 8, to pick up their first coffee of the day. Two Hells Angels' hit men ran out from a bus shelter toward them. Paul (Fon Fon) Fontaine stood in front of the bus, pointed his .357-Magnum revolver, then jumped onto its hood and shot driver Rondeau several times, once in the chest. Stéphane Gagné stood at the passenger door and pulled the trigger of his 9-mm semi-automatic pistol. It wouldn't fire. Corriveau shrunk down into his seat to make himself a smaller target. Gagné fiddled with the gun. It fired several times into Corriveau, who survived. The men jumped into a van and raced away.

Quebec prison guards lived in terror after the second murder of a guard in two months. They believed bikers killed Rondeau and also Diane Lavigne on July 1. More than two thousand guards walked off the job for twenty-four hours on Tuesday, September 9, to protest Rondeau's slaying. Public security minister Pierre Bélanger, the third man to hold the job in two years, announced on Wednesday, September 10, that guards would be allowed to wear bullet-proof vests and carry guns when they transported prisoners, to deter attacks and make them feel more secure.

Prison officials from across Quebec discussed segregating Hells Angels and Rock Machine members in different prisons to reduce tensions behind bars. The Centre de détention de Québec held more than a hundred Hells Angels associates and sympathizers and only fifteen Rock Machine sympathizers. The Rock Machine outnumbered the Hells Angels in other prisons. In Orsainville, the gangs were housed in separate wings.

Quebec City Rock Machine leader Claude (Ti-Loup) Vézina, 41, was sentenced to seven years in jail on Thursday, September 11, for drug trafficking. The gang's second-in-command, Dany Légaré, was sentenced to five-and-a-half years for possession of explosives found during the massive police raid in May.

Rock Machine Richard Parent, a drug dealer whose ambition was to take over an area of Quebec City controlled by the Hells Angels, was caught on camera telling Giovanni Cazzetta he wanted to treat himself to a Hells Angel and had plans to blow up the Lavigueur estate where gang members lived. Parent, 34, said he wanted to approach the island by boat and plant enough explosives to blow the whole place up. Hells Angel Scott Steinert lived there with his bodyguard Donald Magnusen. Steinert filmed several porno movies on the property, including one called *Babe's Angel* in which he starred with nine women.

In an attempt to take heat off the gang, the Rock Machine handed over to police in mid-September the last of the dynamite stolen in Rimouski. The news bolstered the Hells Angels' confidence and they dared hold a full-scale party at the Saint-Nicolas clubhouse on Saturday, September 13, for all Quebec members. The party ostensibly celebrated the one-year membership anniversary of Claude Morin, whose growing influence in the organization belied his recent arrival. Morin introduced indoor baseball to Quebec City bars and sported a large Filthy Few ring on his hand.

Hells Angels prospect Emery (Pit) Martin of the Saint-Nicolas chapter pleaded guilty on Monday, September 22, to charges of conspiracy and possession of twenty-seven tons of hashish.

The RCMP raided the Kahnawake Mohawk reserve on Tuesday, September 23, to arrest gun runners who armed both the Hells Angels and the Rock Machine. The raid was conducted without alerting Montreal police or the native Peacekeepers whom they feared would tip off the smugglers. The RCMP learned through double agents who bought guns and from wiretaps that the natives had sold seventy-five guns—from pistols to machine guns—to both gangs over four months.

The seized Rock Machine clubhouses in Montreal and Beauport were torched on Wednesday, October 1, and Thursday, October 2. By the end of October, the Montreal clubhouse would be set on fire three times. A surprise raid on the suburban homes of three associates of Hells Angel Maurice (Mom) Boucher netted police a small arsenal, drugs, equipment for methamphetamine and cocaine laboratories, and a bomb. They seized a silencer-equipped Uzi sub-machine gun, a semi-automatic rifle, a .223-caliber Mini-14; a 10-mm pistol, and a .357-Magnum revolver. The fragmentation dynamite bomb was laced with thousands of nails.

Three shootings in one week in Montreal after a relatively quiet month were part business, part war. The Hells Angels killed Serge Tailly, 54, on Friday, October 3, for resisting their attempts to take over his bar. They shot and wounded Rock Machine Guy Langlois on Monday, October 6. A 21-year-old man was shot by a passenger in another car as he drove through Saint-Henri on Friday, October 10.

An immigration board deported Danish Bandido Claus Hansen, 33, on Wednesday, October 15, because of his criminal record. Sergeant Guy Ouellette of the Sûreté du Québec testified at the hearing that Hansen and Swedish Bandido Jan (Clark) Jensen arrived in Quebec on Saturday, October 4, to finalize plans with the Rock Machine to create two Bandidos chapters in Quebec. Sergeant Ouellette testified that Bandidos chapters in Montreal and Quebec City would be established by the end of 1997 and that this would exacerbate Quebec's biker war. "By becoming Bandidos, the Rock Machine gain an international status that elevates them to the same level as the Hells Angels," Sergeant Ouellette testified. The Bandidos had 550 members in fifty-three chapters in the U.S., Europe, and Australia. Sergeant Ouellette told the tribunal that the two Bandidos and several Rock Machine members visited bars in Old Quebec City, one of them a Hells Angels' hangout, which he said signified an imminent deal between the two partying gangs. Hansen denied the existence of a deal to join both gangs. Jensen, who sports an "Aryan Pride" tattoo on his stomach, couldn't be deported because of his dual Canadian/Danish citizenship.

A hysterical story prompted by the immigration hearing and interviews with a police officer with the Criminal Intelligence Service of Canada appeared in the *Globe and Mail* on Saturday, October 18, under the headline, "New biker war on horizon, Canadian police fear": "A bloody biker war that has left a trail of bodies across Scandinavia may be about to explode into Canada, police say." The war in Quebec was deadlier, bloodier, and had more victims than the Scandinavian skirmish. A little knowledge and some thought can go a long way.

Prison guards were near panic in mid-October, when ten of them noticed their homes had been photographed by suspicious people. Thieves broke into a guard's home in Saint-Hubert on Tuesday, October 14, and stole his uniforms—four shirts and two pairs of pants—and his handcuffs. Some guards recalled that prisoners were found to have lists of their home addresses several years earlier. And the drivers of trucks that carried prisoners to and from prison noticed they were often followed.

Four Trois-Rivières chapter Hells Angels and a member of the Blatnois puppet gang represented by Hells Angels lawyer Jacques Larochelle pleaded guilty to murder conspiracy charges on Friday, October 17, on condition the Crown withdraw murder charges against Louis (Mélou) Roy, Quebec's second most powerful Hells Angel, who had allegedly ordered the killing of Rock Machine drug dealer Claude (Le Pic) Rivard in February 1995. Serge Quesnel, the Hells Angels' contract-killer-turned-informant, testified that he participated in the crimes for which the five bikers were convicted and that Roy ordered them. Hells Angels Mario Brouillette, 25, François Hinse, 33, Sylvain (Batiste) Thiffault, 40, and Claude (Macho) Giguère, 36, were sentenced to prison terms, as was Blatnois Clermont Carrier, 35. No sooner was Roy freed than Revenue Canada served him notice of claim for $189,000 in unpaid taxes for 1991, 1992, and 1993.

A judge presiding over the preliminary hearing on drug charges of Hells Angel Marc (Tom) Pelletier, president of the Saint-Nicolas chapter, had a pretty good idea that the police fed the media information that suited both their purposes. "The courts must not be manipulated by the media which try to pressure them," Judge Narcisse Proulx said. "We all know that the biker war sells well. The accused must not become victims of the court system because the public demands heavy sentences even before they are convicted."

Two Montreal bars linked to the Rock Machine were hit with Molotov cocktails on Thursday, October 23.

Quebec police and the RCMP's Criminal Intelligence Service of Canada showed once again on Thursday, October 23, that they did not have their finger on the pulse of the biker gangs. The television program *Quatre Saison*, quoting police, announced that thirty Rock Machine members in Montreal and Quebec would become Bandidos within weeks, and police believed this would lead to a bloody war. The CISC said that Fred Faucher, who conducted negotiations with the Bandidos, could become the leader of that gang in Quebec. It also said twenty Rock Machine members were ready to follow him. The program reported that the Rock Machine had already started flying Bandidos' colors in Quebec. Police predicted they would get their "vests" probably just before December 5, the Hells Angels' twentieth anniversary in Canada.

That television report is a perfect, albeit sad, example of media manipulation by police. The media itself must be blamed for not demanding proof. Although I will discuss in later chapters this disgusting police habit of needlessly inflicting fear on an unsuspecting public, the people who propagated the Bandido theories in Quebec are the same who predicted bloodshed in other Canadian provinces in a sordid attempt to boost their careers and their budgets.

The Hells Angels and Bandidos declared a truce on national television in Denmark on September 25 to halt a government move to ban outlaw motorcycle gangs in that country. The two gangs stopped fighting in all Scandinavian countries. I will describe these negotiations at length in the following chapter on the Nordic war, but mention the fact now because the truce was not secret, yet police and Rock Machine members failed to factor it into their plans and analyses. The police kept forecasting a bloody war when the Rock Machine became Bandidos—and they kept predicting this war until publication of this book. If the Bandidos were to grant charter rights to the Rock Machine, they would do so on the grounds the Rock Machine stop the war with the Hells Angels. The Rock Machine couldn't do that unless the Hells Angels stopped competing for drug territory. It's not in the Hells Angels' nature to share, but they might.

The Rock Machine should have thought long and hard about the Denmark truce. The Bandidos were now friends with the Hells Angels. Why would they want to align themselves with a gang at war with the Hells Angels? Bandidos trips to Quebec were most likely intelligence-gathering missions. Information is power. And the Bandidos probably traded what they learned from the Rock Machine with the Hells Angels in Scandinavia. The Rock Machine's secrets would then have been given to Quebec Hells Angels so they could better plot their war.

But Fred Faucher's foolish followers, who succumbed to his will only because the true Rock Machine leaders were in jail, tempted fate and fêted the Bandidos on their second trip to Quebec on Tuesday, October 28. A party of twenty-five bikers booked a large table at the l'Astral restaurant in the hotel Loews Le Concorde in Quebec City. The guests of honor were George Wegers, national vice-president of the Bandidos in the United States, and Bandido Jan (Clark) Jensen of the Swedish Nomads chapter. Wegers participated in the discussions with the Hells Angels that led to September's Danish truce. Whatever his stated purpose in Quebec, it had nothing to do with his ultimate goal. And only Wegers knew that.

Police intelligence had no clue the meeting had been scheduled, and failed to notice Weger's entry into Canada. Jensen had been in the country since early October and was slated to return home on November 18. A uniformed officer who watched a discussion between the drivers of two vehicles that slightly brushed each other outside the hotel recognized two Rock Machine associates. He then noticed a line of Harley-Davidson motorcycles outside the hotel. He called for backup. Police disrupted the dinner and arrested six bikers on weapons charges. Police interpreted the dinner as proof the Rock Machine were in the final phase of becoming Bandidos.

Immigration officials held Wegers on charges that he entered Canada illegally by failing to declare his criminal record. He was deported to Bellingham, Washington, on Friday, October 31.

The Rock Machine traveled to Ottawa for the second time in three months on Saturday, November 1, to meet with the Outlaws. Fred Faucher led the delegation. Faucher became Rock Machine leader after the jailing of Claude (Ti-Loup) Vézina on September 11.

* * *

Two secretaries of Rock Machine lawyer Gilles Thériault found a remote-detonated fragmentation bomb made with nuts, bolts, and 130 sticks of dynamite in his second-story office on Thursday, October 30. The bomb was in a box that previously held files and had recently been delivered to his office with other boxes. "If it's a warning, I'm saying right now I have no intention of giving in to anybody," Thériault said. "I'm not scared. Once again this morning, I was in court for one of their cases. I don't know who did it. A lot of people could have it in for me: the Ministry of Revenue, my two ex-wives, others. Who knows. For the moment, I'm not linking it to the Rock Machine." Disgruntled gangsters in Quebec have a history of killing their lawyers. The previous evening, Thériault held a press conference to announce that he had filed a claim with the government for repairs the Rock Machine had to make to their Quebec City and Montreal clubhouses after police seized them.

An immigration hearing in Montreal on Thursday, October 30, heard that a Haitian fighting deportation was a hit man for the Hells Angels puppet gang, the Rockers. Patrick Pinder, 27, was a crack dealer, pimp and suspected member of the Master B, Family, and CDP street gangs. He was sentenced to sixteen months in jail in December 1996 for trafficking crack. Pinder told the hearing he was approached by Rockers in 1994 who asked him to carry out two contract killings to repay a debt he owed the gang. Pinder said he was ordered to kill Rock Machine associate Luc Deshais, who was shot in a motorcycle shop on August 10, 1995, the day after Daniel Desrochers was injured by a bomb. He told police his friend Gregory (Picasso) Wooley carried out the hit. Wooley was charged and acquitted in the killing.

Hells Angel Scott Steinert phoned his bodyguard Donald Magnusen on the evening of Tuesday, November 4, and arranged a meeting. Magnusen cried as he left his apartment and said goodbye to his girlfriend. The Hells Angels beat both men to death that night with hammers, wrapped their bodies in plastic and duct tape and dumped them into the St. Lawrence Seaway at Beaufort near Quebec City. (Magnusen's body floated to the surface on May 23, 1998. Steinert's body was found on April 15, 1999.)

The Sûreté du Québec continued its search for the elusive Hells Angel Scott Steinert and on Wednesday, November 5, seized two houses near Sorel and a garage in the Laurentians that belonged to the biker. Seventy police officers conducted fifteen raids across Quebec in search of documents to prove that Steinert's assets had been acquired with the proceeds of crime. Police raided Steinert's stripper agencies and escort service: l'agence Artistique, l'agence Sensation, Sensation deux, and the .08 escort service. They also raided the home of porn producer Stéphane Chouinard.

One of the more curious sideshows of the biker war was the defense by Rock Machine lawyer Gilles Thibault of the rights of the English lesbo-porno-punk band Rockbitch to perform in Montreal after Montreal police asked immigration officials to deny them entry to Canada. Police also convinced the liquor board to prohibit the bar that booked the band from allowing their shows on November 8, 9, and 10. Rockbitch members describe themselves as liberated lesbians, former prostitutes, and strippers. They perform topless (courts have ruled that breasts are not sexual objects in Ontario), urinate on stage, whip each other, and throw a golden condom into the audience. The person who catches it climbs on stage and has sex with the Rockbitch of his or her choice.

Three Bandidos were assassinated in an Australian bar on Sunday, November 9: Michael Alexander Kulakowski (Mike Kay), 41, national vice-president and Nomads chapter president; Sancha Milenkovic, Inner City chapter president; and Sydney chapter member Rick Raymond. Kulakowski, who died on Monday, November 10, was Mike Kay, the Bandido who met with the Rock Machine in Quebec City on August 27 and whose photograph appeared with a story printed to prove the gangs were friends.

Hells Angels associate Alain (Lulu) Leclerc, 28, a man deemed violent even by biker standards, was shot three times in the head at the Ashton restaurant in Charlesbourg, near Quebec City, on Monday night, November 17, as he ate dinner with his girlfriend. Leclerc had contracted his friend, Michel Caron (both were members of the Mercenaires biker gang), to kill Serge Quesnel, contract hit man for the Trois-Rivières chapter, because Quesnel had killed Leclerc's other friend, Martin Naud. Quesnel became a police informant the day after Caron accepted the contract to kill him. Caron decided to become an informant also, because the pay was good.

Caron told the court about a rape Leclerc had committed. It illustrates the biker attitude toward women. Both men were at the L'Entre Nous bar when the owner, a woman, gave them the address of "two girls who want to get fucked." The men found "a 40-year-old girl, a big one, and all crooked," Caron said. She wanted sex, but Leclerc got weird. He was angry there was only one woman. He put his gun on the table and yelled at the woman, "We didn't come here for nothing. You're the one we're going to fuck, you big *crisse de lesbienne*." The woman took her clothes off, and didn't object. As she cried, Leclerc screwed her and encouraged Caron to get a blow job at the same time. Caron was never charged, and claimed he never touched the woman. "Anyways, she was real ugly."

Quebec City police tried to pull over a red Camaro for a routine traffic check at 10 p.m. Wednesday, November 19. The driver pulled a U-turn, crossed a median, and sped down a side street where he abandoned the car. Police found Hells Angels associate Dominique Gordon walking nearby. They took him back to his car and saw, through the tinted glass of the rear hatch, the corpse of 21-year-old Hells Angels associate Daniel Belanger in the trunk. Gordon, 20, said his friend accidentally shot himself in the head with a .357-Magnum revolver as he was playing Russian roulette and he was *en route* to hospital when police stopped him. More likely, police believed he planned to dump the corpse near a Rock Machine hangout to place the blame on them. Police raided a nearby Hells Angels' drug den where the shooting had taken place.

Customs officials at Vancouver International Airport seized an Australian shipment of 1,500 to 2,000 Bandidos' defense fund T-shirts and jogging pants shipped to the Rock Machine in Quebec in early November. The clothing sported the Bandidos' mascot, the Fat Mexican who brandished a machete and pistol, with the letters SYLB: "Support Your Local Bandidos." Once again, here was proof to debunk the conspiracy-theorist claims that the clothing was worn only by gang initiates. The shirts were destined to be sold to the general public to raise money. All motorcycle gangs do this. At the time the shipment was seized, the Hells Angels puppet gang, the Regulators in Burnaby, British Columbia, sold T-shirts to high school students that read "Support Your Big Red Machine." Students could do this by buying their drugs from Hells Angels' dealers.

Police used the new federal anti-gang law to seize the Hells Angels' Saint-Nicolas clubhouse on Saturday, November 21, and evicted members until courts could decide whether it was bought with the proceeds of crime. Three weeks earlier, the city granted the Hells Angels a building permit for renovations valued at $50,000 – $75,000 to a $239,000 building. Because the law had yet to be tested, investigators and prosecutors assembled a 200-page brief to support their request for a warrant to seize the clubhouse. They even had deputy justice minister Mario Bilodeau review their case before they presented it to a judge. To keep the clubhouse, police and prosecutors must prove that it was built or modified to facilitate the commission of a crime, that it is used by a group of at least five criminals, and that a criminal act had been committed since the law was enacted on May 5. The seizure was pegged to the arrest of chapter vice-president René (Will) Pearson, who needed to be found guilty for the Hells Angels to lose their clubhouse.

Quebec premier Lucien Bouchard's office was revealed on Sunday, November 23, to have channeled confidential tax information on federal Bloc Québécois MPs to the party's chief of staff in Ottawa. A member of the premier's staff told the separatist party's officers that MP and lawyer Ghislain Lebel, who defended Hells Angels, was involved in litigation with the Quebec revenue department.

Friday, December 5, was the twentieth anniversary of the Hells Angels in Canada. A dinner party for two hundred was planned for Saturday night at the Montreal chapter clubhouse in Sorel. Two Rockers ran into three Rock Machines in the hallway of a Montreal courthouse earlier in the day and exchanged knuckle prints.

Marc (Tom) Pelletier, 44, president of the Hells Angels' Saint-Nicolas chapter, pleaded guilty with his right-hand man Jean-René Poirier on Friday, December 19, to trafficking cocaine. They were arrested on July 3 after police mole Sylvain Duperron spent several months establishing himself as a drug dealer in Old Quebec City and made increasingly bigger drug purchases. After he gained Poirier's confidence, he bought five kilos of cocaine from him and Pelletier for $110,000 on June 25. Duperron wore a body transmitter as the three men negotiated the deal inside a car wash in Saint-Étienne.

* * *

Montreal police investigating street-level drug dealers arrested 32-year-old Steve Boies Thursday night, December 4, and were taken aback when he began to spill his guts. Boies was a suspect in several crimes, including the attempted bombing of the former Rock Machine clubhouse in Verdun on August 23—his pager was found in a truck full of explosives parked in front of the building. Boies told police he knew the killers of Steve Arsenault, 19, a country boy new to the city who was beaten to death on August 10 for ripping off a drug dealer. Then he said that his friend Stéphane (Godasse) Gagné, 28, had killed prison guards Diane Lavigne and Pierre Rondeau on June 26 and September 8.

Carcajou officers tracked Gagné to Berthierville where they arrested him on Saturday, December 6. Gagné realized that Boies had opened his big mouth and he told police the names of two men who had participated in the killings with him. As payment for the hits, Gagné had been given status as a Rockers prospect. The gang was godfathered in the Hells Angels organization by Nomads chapter president Maurice (Mom) Boucher. The two informants were put under heavy security while police investigated their allegations. Even the plainclothes officers who accompanied them to court for arraignment carried sub-machine guns.

Boucher shut down the Nomads' Montreal clubhouse on Tuesday, December 16. He feared police would search it using information provided by Gagné. Police arrested Boucher on Thursday, December 18, and charged him in his jail cell on Friday with two counts of first-degree murder. Boucher, who sometimes used the names Gérald Larose and Ghyslain Dufour, was to have been arraigned in court, at 2:30 p.m., but an irate janitor drove his dark-blue Firebird Trans-Am through the courthouse's plate-glass doors at 9 a.m., triggering police fears the vehicle carried a bomb.

Police also issued arrest warrants for Nomads prospect André (Toots) Tousignant, 33, and Rockers member Paul (Fon-Fon) Fontaine. Police had said for months they suspected bikers in the guards' killings. Forty investigators worked on the case. Sergeant Jean-Pierre Lévesque, biker expert for the Criminal Intelligence Service of Canada, said on Monday, December 22, that the killing of prison guards marked an escalation of the biker war. "Once you're at the level where you attack people who are supposed to protect society, I think you're at the point of no return."

Boucher's arrest stunned both the underworld and public, as he was seen to be untouchable. Several attempts by the Rock Machine to kill him were foiled by police. He led a charmed life in the middle of the bloodiest biker war the world has ever seen. Boucher, who turned 44 on June 21, was first arrested at 19 in 1973 for stealing $200. He was convicted thirteen times for thefts, break-ins, and possessing a weapon. His severest sentences were relatively light. He was sentenced to forty months in 1976 for armed robbery. He was sentenced to twenty-three months for armed sexual assault in 1984. Even in the midst of the biker war, he got six months in jail when caught with a handgun in 1995. In 1990 the same crime cost him $1,000. Police investigations showed he was so powerful in the Quebec underworld that he got $500 for every kilo of cocaine sold in Montreal. He was often seen in the company of mafia chieftain Vito Rizzuto.

Boucher had three children from two marriages. His oldest son, Francis, was president of the neo-Nazi White Power Canada group in Sorel and a member of the Quebec Ku Klux Klan youth wing. Francis Boucher, at age 17, organized Quebec's first neo-Nazi festival on July 31, 1992. Boucher the father was so embarrassed by the publicity the Hells Angels got from his son's activities that the gang wrote to the Anti-Fascist League in May 1992 to dissociate itself from the younger Boucher's racist activism: "The Hells Angels club is apolitical and is no way interested in the Aryan Festival '92. We are aware that all societies under Nazi or fascist domination are totalitarian and do not tolerate special-interest groups or non-conformist minorities. History has shown us this. We certainly wouldn't want to raise our children under such a regime."

Quebec public security minister Claude Ryan said police would not stop the festival, which was patterned after the 1990 neo-Nazi rally in Metcalf, Ontario. At that rally, 225 neo-Nazis from across North America spent three days listening to racist music and speeches by Ku Klux Klan leaders, and burning crosses. Today, Francis Boucher has followed in his father's footsteps and is a soldier in the Rockers biker gang.

1998

An arrest warrant for fugitive Hells Angel Scott Steinert was issued on Thursday, January 22, 1998, after he was charged with possession of goods obtained with the proceeds of crime. These were seized from the Lavigueur estate in October when the property was sealed off and video cameras were installed so Laval police could monitor the building and grounds from headquarters. Police feared the bikers might burn the building rather than let it fall into government hands. Steinert, for whom immigration officials had also issued an arrest warrant because he missed his deportation hearing on November 24, disappeared after his wedding in the fall of 1997. His wife returned to live with her parents.

The charred, fingerless body of Rocker Andrée (Toots) Tousignant, wanted in the murder of two prison guards, was found near Bromont, northeast of Montreal, on Friday, February 27. He wasn't identified until Wednesday, March 18, on the eve of Hells Angels Maurice (Mom) Boucher's preliminary hearing. Tousignant had been shot several times before being set on fire.

Courthouse security for Boucher's preliminary hearing on Thursday, March 19, was so stringent that every person who entered was video-taped and searched. Benches along thirty feet of corridor were removed so bombers had no hiding places for packages. More dynamite had been stolen from a Rimouski warehouse the previous week.

Earlier in the day, police informant Stéphane Gagné pleaded guilty to the first-degree murder of prison guard Diane Lavigne, 42, on June 26, and the attempted murder of guard Robert Corriveau, who was wounded when guard Pierre Rondeau was killed on September 8. The Crown dropped a second murder charge for Rondeau's death in return for Gagné's testimony against Boucher. The automatic penalty for first-degree murder is life in prison with no chance of release for twenty-five years. He also received a ten-year concurrent sentence for the shooting of Corriveau. Because the second murder charge was dropped, Gagné could ask a jury to grant him a conditional release after fifteen years. Gagné told the court the victims were randomly chosen, and didn't deserve to die because they were just doing their job. Gagné said he carried out the killings to get promoted within the Hells Angels organization. He was to have been made a full-fledged Rocker prospect on the Hells Angels twentieth anniversary, December 5, an honor that was to be bestowed at the gang's party on Saturday, December 6, the day Gagné was arrested.

Boucher was not brought to court because prison guards, who don't believe in the presumption of innocence until proven guilty, and who didn't behave professionally, refused to transport him. "It's like you're a father and someone has raped your daughter and then you're being asked to drive him to court," said Réjean Leguard, president of the provincial jail guard's union. "We have a problem with anyone who participates in the murder of a peace officer." Well, buddy, most people have a problem with killers, regardless of who they kill. The prison guards' behavior demonstrated the brotherhood among peace officers, who generally regard with contempt the citizens who pay them to serve and protect.

Boucher was kept in the new and empty Tanguay prison for women, where he was the only prisoner. Prison officials wanted to keep him away from other prisoners. "We don't want two hundred guys standing up and applauding when he shows up, like he's some kind of hero," Leguard said.

Maurice (Mom) Boucher, still waiting for his preliminary hearing to begin, asked through his lawyer on Wednesday, April 29, to be transferred to a regular jail filled with people because he was tired of being cooped up in the newly built high-security wing of the Tanguay women's prison in north Montreal. More than $1 million was spent to renovate the wing to hold prisoners such as Boucher, who were considered "very dangerous" by the ministry of public security. Boucher was kept alone in his cell twenty-three hours a day. Even when he was let out for one hour, he had no one to talk to.

*   *   *

In Ottawa, the Supreme Court of Canada refused to hear Rock Machine leader Salvatore Cazzetta's appeal of an extradition order sending him to the United States to face drug trafficking charges. Cazzetta pleaded guilty in the United States and was to be sentenced in late June 1999.

Quebec City restaurants proved to be favorite killing spots for hit men. Hells Angels associate Alain Bouchard was shot to death over dinner on February 10.

One of the Rock Machine founders, Denis Belleau, was shot on February 20. And Hells Angels associate Roland Ruel, 47, was shot four times in the head by a gunman who dropped his gun outside the Lotus Select Restaurant on Thursday, April 2.

*   *   *

Federal Solicitor General Andy Scott called a meeting of police, prosecutors, and justice officials on Thursday, April 23, to find ways to attack organized crime, especially outlaw bikers. "We certainly want to bring them to their knees. I think Canadians expect nothing less. Organized crime is a serious problem in Canada. We're going to put the strategy together to clear up this problem once and for all," Scott naively said, forgetting that organized crime gangs like the mafia have been around for hundreds of years, and the Chinese triads for thousands.

This was a surprising move by a government that knew nothing about organized crime, let alone cared for the damage it caused to Canadian society. The Liberal government had just disbanded the ports police, leaving both coasts open to smugglers who shipped drugs in cargo containers.

The outcome of Andy Scott's meeting was predictable. The cops, as they always do, asked for more money and better technology. Scott said the money wasn't available. When will these people realize that better cops are needed? The bikers have evolved to the point where they can outsmart and out-think the cops. You can't expect a radar trap expert to nab the head of an organized crime syndicate. Police recruitment and training are so far out of sync with the times that the handful of really good investigators on any force feel like they've walked into a Keystone Kops movie.

London police chief Julian Fantino (now chief in York Region, north of Toronto) is the main crusader for more money to fight outlaw motorcycle gangs. "We cannot be held accountable for public safety if . . . the political folk are not going to dedicate the resources that are necessary," he said after the meeting with Scott.

Bill C-68

One highly touted, high-profile law supposedly designed to take guns out of criminal hands was never mentioned by police or politicians during talks about the biker war. Bill C-68, the federal government's anti-gun law (implemented in October 1998 after years of controversial debate) which police supported, forced farmers to take their shotguns out of the hen house but did nothing to disarm criminals, who do not register their illegal guns.

Police and politicians knew Bill C-68 was just a ploy to strip guns from law-abiding citizens with a grossly overbudgeted financial sink-hole of a bureaucracy and would never prevent criminals from harming themselves. This is why the law was never mentioned during talks about a biker war that saw heavy public use of guns and explosives. To do so would be to invite scrutiny of the law and its ineffectiveness against armed criminals.

Bill C-68 was drafted by bureaucrats who had no idea what they were doing. Although they consulted both gun owners and anti-gun groups, they accepted at face value the rhetoric of the anti-gun movement and ignored the rational arguments of gun owners. The bureaucrats never let facts get in the way of a contrived, deceptive law. When RCMP figures failed to support their thesis, they fudged the figures to sway the Canadian public. Then they conducted polls and said their law was desired by the majority of Canadians. One of the few statements uttered by a Conservative politician that I agreed with was made by former prime minister John Diefenbaker, who said that polls were for dogs.

The RCMP took umbrage to the misuse of its statistics, and Commissioner J.P.R. Murray wrote a four-page letter to George Thomson, deputy minister for justice and deputy attorney general of Canada, on July 21, 1997, to outline his concerns. Note that the bureaucrats who drafted Bill C-68 and the information to support it were by definition anti-gun from the start: the Firearms Control Task Group. They just sought information to support a position already taken by government.

I am writing to request that the Department of Justice correct its representation of the 1993 Royal Canadian Mounted Police (RCMP) statistics on firearms involved in crime.

Around June 1994, the Firearms Control Task Group requested information on all files investigated by the RCMP during 1993 where there was a firearm associated with it. Since the RCMP does not collect statistics on firearms in this format, a special software application was written to extract the data for the Department of Justice. The data was provided in electronic format with the coding information necessary to interpret the data. The Firearms Control Task Group tabulated the data and produced reports without consulting the RCMP staff on the accuracy of their interpretation of our data.

The RCMP became aware that there was a problem with the representation of the 1993 RCMP statistics on firearms involved in crimes in February 1997, as a result of correspondence from Ms. Wendy Cukier of the Coalition for Gun Control, in which she requested an affidavit as to the accuracy of the data in Appendix "A," titled "RCMP (PIRS) Table 2. Firearms Involved in Crime: Type of Firearm Recovered According to Offense." Ms. Cukier required the affidavit for use in the province of Alberta's constitutional challenge respecting the Firearms Act. The Firearms Control Task Group created Appendix "A" from the statistics obtained from the RCMP in 1994.

Since the RCMP had not created Appendix "A," we extracted the 1993 data again and tabulated the number of firearms involved in a crime under the category of violent offenses. We believe that most people would interpret the Appendix "A" caption: "Firearms Involved in Crime: Type of Firearm Recovered According to Offense" to mean a firearm used in the commission of an offense. In some cases, without completing a more detailed review of the file, it was impossible to make a definite determination; therefore, we resolved some of the questionable decisions in favor of the Department of Justice findings. We determined that our statistics showed that there were 73 firearms involved in a violent crime compared to the Department of Justice findings of 623 firearms involved in a violent crime. A further analysis of the Department of Justice statistics has not been done due to the volume of work involved. However, a cursory review of the remaining 909 firearms cases revealed that only a very small percentage of these would meet the definition of a firearm involved in a crime.

In order to mitigate damages, the Firearms Research Unit, the Department of Justice, and Ms. Cukier were notified that the RCMP could not provided an affidavit on the accuracy of the 1993 firearms statistics presented by the Department of Justice.

At a subsequent meeting with the Firearms Research Unit staff to discuss the release of similar 1995 RCMP statistics, they presented a report entitled, "The Illegal Movement of Firearms in Canada." This report contains the same statistics as those in Appendix "A," however, the RCMP statistics are combined with those of other major Canadian police forces. The Firearms Research Unit representatives believed that the firearms identified in Appendix "A" had actually been used in committing a crime.

It is of particular concern that the Minister of Justice and the Canadian Association of Chiefs of Police relied on these statistics while Bill C-68 was being processed in Parliament as evidenced by statements in the report, "Illegal Firearms Use in Canada."

A quotation from page 2 of the report states that: "It can also be seen that rifles and shotguns were involved in 51% of violent firearms crimes, airguns were involved in 19%, and handguns were involved in 17% of violent crimes. The Firearms Smuggling Working Group was concerned with the significant number of long guns involved in crime." This statement is not significant when we consider that in 1993, the RCMP investigated 333 actual homicide offenses, including attempts, but only 6 of these offenses involved the use of firearms according to the statistics provided to the Firearms Control Task Group. Furthermore, the RCMP investigated 88,162 actual violent crimes during 1993, where only 73 of these offences, or 0.08%, involved the use of firearms. If we display the RCMP 73 offences in the same manner as the Firearms Control Task Group, we would say that rifles and shotguns were involved in 79.5% of violent firearm crimes investigated by the RCMP. This is not surprising when we recognize that rifles and shotguns represent 84.4% of all firearms in Canada. The difference between 623 violent firearm crimes credited to the RCMP compared to the actual number of 73 is significant.

The Canadian Firearms Center (CFC) staff were unwilling to meet to confirm where the problem occurred with the interpretation of the 1993 RCMP data. Their efforts were focused on producing a report on the 1995 firearms data. The CFC offered to make comparisons between the results of their current research project and other similar research conducted in the past. This proposal was not acceptable since there was no means to validate the 1993 data, only a possibility of some comments on differences between the findings of the two years. This would leave the 1993 data in circulation. The incorrect reporting of the RCMP 1993 statistics could cause the wrong public policy or laws to be developed and cause researchers to draw erroneous conclusions. Considering that the data is clearly marked as belonging to the RCMP, we must accept ownership and responsibility for the harm the data may cause. For these reasons, something must be done to correct the data or remove it from circulation.

Since the data in our Police Information Retrieval System (PIRS) and Operational Statistics Reporting (OSR) special reports is open to interpretation, it was necessary to suspend further release of firearms data pending an agreement on regulating this problem.

I am, therefore, requesting your assistance to resolve this issue. In addition, you may wish to inform the Minister of Justice about this issue to ensure that she does not refer to the RCMP statistics quoted in the Department of Justice report. [End letter]

In April 1999, it was estimated it would take the National Firearms Centre 233 years to register all the rifles and shotguns in Canada. Bill C-68 requires that these guns be registered by January 1, 2003. Staff at the center registered an average of 360 guns a day since December 1, their first day of work. To achieve the law's registration goal deadline, they need to register 7,300 to 22,000 guns a day, depending on the true number of long guns in the country. The federal government, which at one point in the debate over the bill promised its implementation would cost less than $50 million, admitted in December 1998 that $200 million had already been spent. Critics estimated it will cost $1 billion to register guns in the hands of law-abiding Canadians, money that could be better spent fighting crime.

*   *   *

Alleged hit man Gregory (Picasso) Wooley, 26, was acquitted on July 18 for the 1995 murder of a Rock Machine member. A Haitian, on July 24, he became the first black member of the Rockers bike gang. Members of the Hells Angels' Nomads paraded Wooley through their favorite haunts to show him off. Wooley will never become a Hells Angel, as both national and international rules prohibit "niggers" in the organization. He will remain a Rocker until he dies.

Rock Machine leader Richard (Bam-Bam) Lagacé, 32, was shot to death as he walked out of a northeast Montreal health club on Thursday, July 31. Alliance member Yvon Roy, 57, was shot forty-five minutes later outside his house. Rock Machine leader Johnny Plescio, 34, known for his strong-arm tactics and desire to become a Bandido with Fred Faucher, was machine-gunned in his Montreal home on Tuesday, September 8. A burned-out car with two machine guns in the back seat was found in the neighborhood. By mid-September, four years and two months after the war started, there were 89 murders, 89 attempted murders, 129 arsons, and 82 bombs that exploded or were defused.

Some bozo Montreal landscape-and-snow-removal company capitalized on the fear engendered by the Hells Angels in early September and sent bogus threats on Hells Angels' letterhead to 150 West Island residents who used a competitor's services. The letter-writer got the addresses of Bo Pelouse clients by driving around Dorval to look for the company's signs in people's drive-ways. The letter, under the logo "Hell's Angels—World, Ontario," read, "You have been observed as using the services of Bo Pelouse for either snow removal or lawn care. This company has done one of our members' mothers a disservice by not issuing proper refunds for unsatisfactory work. This eventually leads to medical problems. We are very angry. It is suggested not to employ their fucking services again. Consider yourself warned."

Even the Montreal Alouettes football team feared bikers. Three players got into a fight with Rockers outside the Kokino bar early in the morning of Tuesday, September 15. Linebacker Stefen Reid was whacked on the back of the head, in the neck and on the elbows with a pipe. Backup quarterback Anthony Calvillo and linebacker Brian Clark also got roughed up. Neither the players nor the team pressed charges.

Hells Angel René (Will) Pearson, administrator and vice-president of the Saint-Nicolas chapter, was sentenced to seven years and seven months in jail on drug charges on Wednesday, September 30.

Montreal lawyer Carole Lepire, 33, was charged on October 1 with selling $32,000 of drugs to Richard Cardin in the Hells Angels' cell block of Donnacona maximum-security penitentiary in early October. Guards found 221 grams of hash, 20 grams of heroin and 15 grams of an unknown substance on the prisoner after the visit. Montreal police also charged her with fifteen drug-related offences. She quit the Quebec bar on April 14, 1999, and was slated for trial that summer.

Hells Angel Michel (Sky) Langlois, 52, one of the founding members of the Hells Angels in Canada and a former fugitive who surrendered after two years on the run in Morocco to serve time for the killing of North chapter members in 1985, was charged on Tuesday, October 13, with importing and conspiring to import 178 kilos of cocaine worth $71 million. Langlois allegedly bankrolled fifteen percent of the operation which saw Richard Savard, 44, smuggle the cocaine from Mexico to Quebec in the walls of a house trailer he pulled behind his van. A man called "Le Grand manitou" by Langlois supplied the rest of the money to buy the drugs. Savard, arrested on January 18, pleaded guilty to smuggling charges and was sentenced to seven-and-a-half years in jail. One of his eight accomplices, Raymond Demers, 29, also pleaded guilty and was sentenced to nine years.

Police evidence from a double agent inside the organization included videotaped meetings. Police said Langlois was extremely cautious when he discussed business and always used code words and hand signs. He often wrote words on paper, which he immediately destroyed. Langlois and the mole often used mechanical terms when they spoke about drugs. Langlois's girlfriend, Micheline Blanchard, 42, described him at a bail hearing as a good father and a man of his word. Blanchard had been the girlfriend of Hells Angels president Yves Buteau when he was assassinated in Sorel in 1983. The self-described housewife offered to put up the $186,000 family home as bail surety.

Sergeant Guy Ouellette of the Sûreté du Québec got way ahead of the facts in an interpretation he gave to media on November 3, of talks between the Hells

Angels and the Bandidos in the United States. Ouellette said the September 1997 truce in Scandinavia was partly responsible for U.S. talks between the gangs, who realized that peace was better for business. "If talks between these two gangs go further ahead, we may have the first Bandidos chapter in Canada," Ouellette said. "After one or two chapters in Quebec, the next step will be to open a chapter in Kingston, Ontario." Ouellette, who failed to grasp the international perspective of the Hells Angels, didn't realize that the Hells Angels wanted to assimilate the Bandidos, not allow them to expand.

Police charged twenty-two Hells Angels and associates with offenses ranging from drug trafficking to attempted murder on Thursday, November 5. They seized $3 million in drugs and $45 million in counterfeit U.S. money. Hells Angels Claude (Burger) Berger, 49, Marc Bordage, 35, and Gilles (Le Vieux) Dumas, 47, secretary of the Quebec City chapter in Saint-Nicolas, were charged with drug offenses. Dumas, Sylvain Gagnon, 38, and Jean-Pierre Ross, 24, were charged with the attempted murder of Rock Machine Francis Gagnon, shot on a Quebec City highway in December 1996. A weapons charge laid against Berger in 1997 was dismissed in October when a judge ruled his arrest had been unconstitutional.

The Quebec Treasury Board announced on Monday, November 9, that the seized house of Hells Angel Michael (L'Animal) Lajoie-Smith in the Laval suburb of Fabreville would be auctioned in December, with bids starting at $72,000. The house, valued at $220,000, had suffered $100,000 in damages caused by arson on October 14. The thirteen-room, two-story house had a two-car garage and an in-ground pool. Sale of the house by its owner was blocked in 1996 under the proceeds of crime legislation, which police used to seize the house on the grounds that it had been bought with drug money. Quebec legally confiscated the building in June.

Rock Machine members Stephane Morgan and Daniel Boulet, both 30, were shot to death in a car in Montreal on Tuesday, November 10. Several blocks away, the killers set fire to the van they had used.

* * *

Hells Angel Maurice (Mom) Boucher's trial began in earnest on Tuesday, November 17, after two weeks of legal arguments and a surprisingly quick one-and-a-half days of jury selection. Police told media that Boucher was their biggest catch in ten years, and his conviction would severely damage the Hells Angels. Boucher's defense team was led by Quebec City lawyer Jacques Larochelle, a man of few but correct and precise words, who had represented Canadian Armed Forces soldier Denis Lortie, the man whose shooting spree in the province's National Assembly in May 1984 had been recorded by the room's television cameras. Larochelle was also defending Theoneste Bagosora, alleged architect of the 1994 genocide in Rwanda.

Crown prosecutor Jacques Dagenais, just as meticulous, precise, and well prepared as his opponent, brought thirty years of experience, including an inquiry into organized crime, to the courtroom. The trial was heard by legendary Superior Court judge Jean-Guy Boilard, no stranger to the Hells Angels, as they had bought one of his jurors in the 1986 trial of four Hells Angels charged with the murder of the Laval North chapter. Boilard did not suffer fools, be they lawyers, police, or witnesses during his twenty-one years on the bench. He was quick to deflate blowhard lawyers and his grasp of the law kept him one step ahead of the lawyers who argued before him, so much so that his rulings were immediate and to the point.

Dagenais explained in his opening statement that he hoped to prove, mostly through the testimony of informant Stéphane (Godasse) Gagné, that Boucher ordered the assassinations of two prison guards, picked at random, to stem the wave of informants produced by the biker war. "By making his soldiers kill prison guards, the accused believed he guaranteed their silence," Dagenais said. "He was certain that the minister of public security would never, in such cases, negotiate away first-degree murder charges."

Gagné, 28, testified that he first met Boucher at the beginning of the biker war in July 1994, when he asked the Hells Angels leader to get the Rockers off his back. This Hells Angels puppet gang wanted Gagné, who sold drugs in the Hochelaga-Maisonneuve area, to buy his drugs from them. Gagné aligned himself with the Hells Angels. "I'm not stupid. I knew that the Hells would win the war. They're richer, better organized, and certainly more disciplined."

Gagné was arrested for selling a kilo of cocaine to a police informant, sent to Bordeaux prison for two years (less a day), and placed in C Wing with the Rock Machine. They asked him to stomp on a photograph of Boucher; Gagné refused, and was severely beaten. He later pounded one of his assailants into a coma with a steel pipe. "In this environment, there's only one rule: win." He fought often with prisoners and guards, who refused to transfer him out of Rock Machine territory because he wasn't on Carcajou's list of Hells Angels sympathizers.

Gagné said he next met Boucher early in 1995 when he was finally transferred out of Bordeaux after guards realized he would continue beating Rock Machine sympathizers. In Sorel penitentiary, Boucher greeted Gagné with respect for having shown support for the Hells

Angels in Bordeaux. They spoke during prison Alcoholics Anonymous meetings.

The men next met early in 1996 when both were out of prison. Gagné said Boucher gave him $1,000 in a restaurant to "stay accessible, because he had a job to be done." Gagné had just gained hangaround status with the gang—the first step in a series of promotions that leads to full membership. If he proved his mettle, he would then be made a prospect. Gagné said he planned to blow up the Rock Machine clubhouse in Verdun with a stolen van full of dynamite, but the scheme failed on its third attempt. Gagné was convicted for the theft of the van and sentenced on October 4, 1996, to six months in jail. He would be out in the spring of 1997. Boucher advised him to join the Rockers' "football team," tasked to take control of Montreal's drug trade. "Our orders were to kill the Rock Machines and scatter others with violence," Gagné testified. The Hells Angels' "football teams" killed and bombed. The "baseball teams" used baseball bats and violence to intimidate.

Two weeks later, Boucher assigned Gagné to the Rockers team of André (Toots) Tousignant and Paul (Fon Fon) Fontaine, which controlled drug trafficking in Montreal's gay quarter. Tousignant informed him that their main mission was to kill prison guards, saying, "We have screws to do in Bordeaux."

The Rocker kept watch on Bordeaux, north-west of Montreal, while Gagné photographed and noted guards' schedules at the Rivière-des-Prairies jail. Their first attempt to kill a guard was aborted because the motorcycle they picked (from a garage full of stolen bikes destined to be used in hits) malfunctioned. The Hells Angels rented garages in Plateau Mont-Royal and Saint-Hubert full of stolen vehicles, disguises, and guns to be used in the biker war and to commit crimes.

For their second attempt, on June 26, 1997, Gagné and Tousignant dressed in black polyester jogging suits and donned gloves inside their green Ford Escort getaway vehicle, which also contained two guns. Gagné, who had purchased $3,000 of motorcycle helmets from different dealers during the previous weeks, wore a nylon stocking over his head to prevent leaving hair inside the helmet that could give police DNA evidence. The killers boarded a Japanese motorcycle and followed four guards in a car, but the vehicle turned down a side street rather than embark on the Laurentian Autoroute, where they planned to rake it with gunfire.

The next van to come out of the prison took the expressway on-ramp and the bikers followed prison guard Diane Lavigne, 42, a mother who was on her way home. As the motorcycle pulled up beside the driver's door, Gagné extended his arm and shot the woman. "I stopped shooting when the motorcycle accelerated."

The killers abandoned the motorcycle in a shopping mall parking lot and fled in a getaway car. Gagné burned his clothing. Gagné said he visited Boucher at his office with three Rockers the next day. Gagné told Fontaine about the hit—"Me and Toots, it's done." Fontaine relayed the information to Boucher, who turned to Gagné and said, "That's good, Godasse. It's not serious even if she did have tits. You can't talk about this with anyone. Killing a prison guard, that's twenty-five years. If we had the death penalty, you'd get hanged."

Gagné explained to the court that anyone who aspired to become a Hells Angel had to be cautious, disciplined, and respect gang hierarchy. The first rule was to never talk business on the phone or in a car, a house, or a clubhouse. Even at home, Gagné used a blackboard to converse with biker friends and his wife. The safest way to talk to someone was during strategic walks in laneways or remote areas. And even then, everything was done in codes and hand signs in case police had parabolic microphones set up in parked vans or rented apartments. Nicknames, rather than proper names, were always used.

Gagné testified that Fontaine became his partner for the second hit on September 8 because he wanted a "uniform" to his credit, to earn prospect status with the Hells Angels' Nomads chapter. Fontaine was jealous that Tousignant chose a mere Rockers hangaround for the first hit. Despite his envy, Fontaine chose Gagné for the second hit and they started in late June to plan the murder of a guard from Rivière-des-Prairies prison. Their plan was delayed two months when Gagné was seriously injured by a Rock Machine who rammed his motorcycle with a car. Gagné became a Rockers prospect on August 21.

The killers scouted the area and aborted three attempts to kill guards because the route they took leaving the prison didn't give the bikers enough time to get to the getaway car. "To do twenty-five years for a Rock Machine, that's okay," Fontaine explained to Gagné. "But for a guard who hasn't done anything to us, that bothers me." They modified their plan and chose to carry out the hit at an intersection used every day by guards who drove the prison bus on their way to Tim Hortons.

Gagné and Fontaine, dressed in their black jogging suits, waited inside a bus shelter at 6:30 a.m. "We didn't know who we were shooting, just that they were wearing the blue uniform of prison guards."

Fontaine walked out in front of the prison bus, took a three-point stance with his .357-Magnum revolver aimed at the driver, then jumped up on the hood and shot driver Pierre Rondeau three times. Gagné ran up to the passenger door and pulled the trigger on his semi-automatic pistol. It jammed. (More likely, he forget to disengage the safety.) He fiddled with the gun until it fired several rounds into Robert Corriveau, who scrunched up in his seat to present as small a target as possible. They fled in a green van, which they torched—Gagné burned his face when he set fire to the van. Then they drove away in a gold Mazda 323 provided by Boucher and supplied by a South Shore garage. Gagné had put his prison-taught skills to good use and made a fake license plate. The getaway car was chopped in a garage recommended by Tousignant. Fontaine and Gagné then drove to Saint-Luc hospital for their shift as bodyguards for Hells Angel Louis (Mélou) Roy.

A Hells Angel from the Nomads chapter gave Gagné $5,000 to take his wife and son, Harley-David, to the Dominican Republic. In the following months, Fontaine became a Nomads prospect, and then he and Gagné flew to Boucher's home in separate helicopters for a meeting. Boucher wanted to kill more prison guards, as well as Crown prosecutors and judges. "You know we did that so that people around us don't become informants," Boucher told Gagné. Gagné testified the Nomads president also wanted to kill the parents and loved ones of gang members he suspected could become informants. He asked Gagné to compile a security file on all members, associates, prospects, hangarounds, and sympathizers—the hierarchy in the biker underworld—that included the names and addresses of everyone in their families, as well as their home and business addresses, phone numbers, and social insurance numbers.

Defense lawyer Jacques Larochelle tried to undermine Gagné's credibility. His questions focused on Gagné's violent streak, his drug dealing, and his propensity for theft. Gagné dealt and sold drugs in grade school at age 13. He broke into countless homes and businesses to fund his use of cocaine and PCP. He was jailed eleven times from 1990 to 1997. Prison reports showed that Gagné lied repeatedly to gain early release. "All criminals are bluffers," Gagné said in his defense. "If we don't bluff, we're dead."

Larochelle accused Gagné of inventing a tale that would allow him to strike a deal he knew police wanted. "Boucher is a cunning man, intelligent and competent," Larochelle said. "You'd have us believe he confided in you about killing prison guards. That's impossible."

"Sometimes," Gagné replied, "even if we're bikers, we are human, not fish, not robots. Sometimes we talk, we err."

"You're taught not to talk, to be circumspect in case police are eaves-dropping, and you're saying that Boucher told you this about killing prison guards. That's not true," Larochelle countered.

"Ask him," Gagné replied. "He's there," he said, pointing to Boucher.

Gagné explained why he became a police informant: "I understood that if I went to prison, I was a dead man. They would have been afraid that I'd talk. Look at what happened to Toots and Paul. It wasn't easy. In a few seconds I had to confide to the police and the system I have hated since I was 15 years old."

Larochelle asked why he waited to tell police about Boucher.

"I kept Mom for later. I didn't want my family killed before I signed the informant contract."

Larochelle turned to the jury and told them that Gagné would receive $140 a month during his stay in prison and the Crown promised not to oppose his parole after fifteen years. His wife also continued to illegally collect welfare payments of $1,298 a month.

Judge Boilard told the Crown (in the absence of the jury) that it needed to corroborate several key points made by Gagné. He asked lawyers for both sides to immediately research case law on corroboration. Larochelle stood and announced he was prepared to admit into evidence without question all statements from the remainder of the Crown's witnesses. "We've already done it for forty witnesses, we can do it for the rest." Larochelle was a canny operator. Dagenais was caught off guard, and said he would consider the offer. He had no choice. The decision to object was the defense lawyer's prerogative.

The Crown was in a bind. It had no direct proof that Boucher had ordered the murder of the prison guards. The two men who had accompanied hit man and witness Stéphane (Godasse) Gagné, Tousig-nant and Fontaine, were Boucher's associates and Gagné told police they claimed Boucher gave them the orders. But there was no way to confirm this. Tousignant was dead, and Fontaine was missing. Since Gagné had much to gain by pinning the blame on someone else, his testimony was useless without corroboration. The case boiled down to his word against Boucher's, and the Hells Angels didn't even need to testify. I explained this on Radio-Canada television's national news in Quebec on Wednesday, November 25, and predicted that Boucher would be acquitted and would celebrate Friday night at the Molson Center where Stéphane Ouellette, the Hells Angels' favorite fighter, was to defend his Canadian middleweight title against perennial favorite Dave Hilton, Jr.

The Crown's case now rested on thirteen wiretaps of Boucher's cellular telephone. During conversations with Tousignant and Fontaine, he alluded to the prison guards. Conversations between these two men and Gagné were also recorded. The Crown's case also hinged on the jury's acceptance that the strict hierarchy within the Hells Angels would preclude any murders by associates, prospects, sympathizers, or puppet gangs unless ordered by a Hells Angel.

Judge Boilard poured cold water on the Crown's case when he ruled that five of the conversations could not be entered into evidence because police had obtained their warrant to tap Boucher's cellular phone under false pretenses. Police illegally lied (information is sworn to be true when applying for warrants) when they told a judge they were seeking information on a fire at the home of Nicole Quesnel, wife of police informant Serge Quesnel. Judge Boilard declared such subterfuge unacceptable, and not only excluded calls made by Boucher on his cellular phone, but also calls made to Gagné by Tousignant when he borrowed the phone. The judge stated that Boucher had a reasonable expectation of privacy under the Charter of Rights and Freedoms. It was the first ruling in Canada on an illegal wiretap warrant that took into account not only the person designated on the warrant, but also other users of the telephone.

Larochelle surprised the court by announcing he would call no witnesses, implying the Crown had not proven its case.

The Crown used the eight remaining conversations as best he could. Boucher told Gagné on Friday, December 5, the day before his arrest, that he wanted him and Tousignant to come to Sorel for a meeting. Boucher told Gagné to send someone else to the airport in his place to pick up guests for the Hells Angels anniversary banquet on Saturday, December 6. On Saturday, the day Gagné was arrested, Boucher asked an unidentified man about the charges against Gagné. He asked the man to dig up information and to bring him the day's newspapers. Later in the day, Boucher called associate Normand Robitaille several times. They agreed during one conversation that "Godasse" was not a "rat." Robitaille informed Boucher in another conversation that the gang's lawyers could not reach Gagné because he had rolled over.

"Why was Mr. Boucher interested in the fate of Stéphane Gagné?" Dagenais asked the jury. "Why was he so worried?"

Dagenais plied the jury with irrelevant information on the Hells Angels structure and hierarchy and ballistics evidence that the guards had been shot the way Gagné said they were. But he was short on evidence that Boucher ordered the hits. He stretched credulity when he reminded the jury that the Nomads chapter (of which Boucher is president) is incorporated as H.A.N. Quebec Inc. He even entered the gang's rules into evidence.

Judge Boilard instructed the jury that neither the Hells Angels nor Boucher's membership in the gang were on trial. He told the jury they must convict Boucher on all three charges he faced—two first-degree murder charges and a charge of attempted murder—or acquit him. Judge Boilard directed the jury to determine whether they could believe a career criminal, who dreamed of wealth and power, beyond a reasonable doubt.

Boucher was acquitted on Friday, November 27, and rushed out of the courthouse to the cheers of Hells Angels and their supporters. He sat ringside at the Molson Center that night to watch Stéphane Ouellette lose to Dave Hilton with eighteen seconds left on the clock in a hard-fought, but honest fight. If only the police had been so honest in their investigation. They just had to tell the judge the truth: they were investigating a murder. The lie was so blatant, it appears someone wanted to sabotage the case.

André Vincent, the chief crown prosecutor for Montreal who signed Boucher's arrest warrant, had expected to win. "We're shaken by the verdict, because we were convinced we had enough proof," he said as Boucher walked out of the courtroom. "Our proof wasn't that bad since it took jurors two days to decide. Boucher benefitted from reasonable doubt. It wasn't an easy trial. A lot was at stake. The element of fear was always there."

Vincent defended the use of informants, stating that Gagné was questioned by a team of lawyers and passed lie-detector tests. "Each case is unique. The Crown prosecutor's job is not to win at all costs, but to evaluate the proof and present it to the court. Failing to do this would be a betrayal of public trust. Informants are the only way to penetrate the secrets of large criminal organizations. All the world's democracies use informants. They're a necessary evil. We lost Boucher, it's true. However, we solved the murder of two prison guards by arresting Stephane Gagné."

The Sûreté du Québec's Sergeant Guy Ouellette couldn't let go of his pet Bandidos theory, and linked it to Boucher's acquittal. "If Boucher, instead of being acquitted, had copped twenty-five years in penitentiary, maybe the Bandidos would have been inclined to more quickly finalize their deal with the Rock Machine and the war would have ended in Quebec."

*   *   *

Earlier in the day, the house seized from Hells Angel Michael (L'Animal) Lajoie-Smith in the Fabreville district of Laval was destroyed by fire. Police stepped up security on the Lavigueur estate seized from Hells Angel Scott Steinert, and the government put it up for sale on Friday, December 4, with an opening bid of $450,000. To keep nosy people away, prospective buyers had to pay $20 to view the property.

Hells Angels associate Lawrence-Louis Bellas, 38, was shot to death by a masked killer in an east Montreal restaurant on Monday, December 21. Stray bullets wounded two bystanders. Bellas was charged with Maurice (Mom) Boucher and Hells Angels associate Steven Bertrand in 1995 with conspiracy to commit assault. Bellas and Bertrand pleaded guilty to the charge. The restaurant where Bellas died was destroyed by fire after a Molotov cocktail was thrown through a window on Tuesday, December 29.

By the end of 1998, there had been 103 murders in the 4-year-old biker war, 124 attempted murders, 85 bombings, and 130 attempted arsons. Nine bikers were missing and presumed dead.

Paybacks are a way of life in Quebec. After all, the provincial motto, stamped on all vehicle license plates, is: "Je me souviens."—"I remember."

1999

Prosecutors and police who had pressed the federal government for an anti-gang law for years finally decided on Monday, January 25, 1999, to test the law enacted on May 2, 1998. Quebec City prosecutors decided to charged six Rock Machine members with "associating, under the direction of, or profiting from a gang."

The first trial in Canada for gangsters charged under the new anti-gang law was scheduled for Winnipeg, Manitoba, where forty members of the Warriors street gang were charged in 1998. By February 18, 1999, taxpayers' costs for the trial had skyrocketed to an astounding $8 million in legal aid funds for thirty-five lawyers to represent the defendants and $6 million to build a high-security courthouse for the proceedings. And this is before a single argument was heard. It seems the bureaucrats who drafted the law failed to consider its financial implications. The high-security courthouse was a needless knee-jerk reaction. Gangsters have been tried for decades without attacks on courthouses. All that was needed in Winnipeg was a secure way of getting the accused to and from court, and a special team to secure the building.

*   *   *

The Poitras Commission, created in 1997 to scrutinize the questionable investigative practices of the Sûreté du Québec's 4,100 members, recommended on January 28, 1999, that control of the police force be given to civilian authority. The commission concluded in its 1,700-page report that the Sûreté du Québec routinely broke the law during criminal investigations, lacked professionalism, and was locked in destructive turf wars with local and federal police agencies. "A crisis of values has shaken the Sûreté du Québec from the beginning of this decade," the report noted. "The concepts of loyalty, integrity, and equality are poorly understood. Any criticism of the organization or its practices made by a member seems suspect." The commission, headed by Lawrence Poitras, former chief justice of Quebec Superior Court, made 175 recommendations.

About the seizure of 26.5 tonnes of hashish for which the Matticks brothers faced smuggling charges (that were thrown out of court because police planted false evidence), the report said: "In the eyes of many, with the Matticks Affair, the Sûreté du Québec had set an unenviable record among police forces that had become infamous through scandals or corruption and abuse."

The Poitras Commission heard evidence of police wrondoing during the investigation of the biker war. Although the commission's voluminous report details mind-boggling corruption, ineptness, and unprofessionalism in the Sûreté du Québec, I will refer only to a few examples that touch directly on Carcajou, as they give a look behind the scenes of an operation that was presented to the public as a major inter-agency success. The commission concluded otherwise.

Under the heading, "The use of media as an offensive weapon," the commission quoted testimony by Inspector Rowland Sugrue of the RCMP as he commented on the use of Quebec media by the RCMP, the Sûreté du Québec, and Montreal police to boost the profiles of their police forces:

> The main problem is that everyone wants to give their own police organization higher visibility in biker-related operations. The provincial task-force strategy is often by-passed. For example: Carcajou, through the media, wants to reassure the public. Others, through their comments, want to upset the public. Everyone knows that Quebec is where the action is and everyone wants a piece of it, whether for personal or professional profit.

There was so much back-stabbing within Carcajou, the commision found, that the three major police agencies never formed a cohesive, effective team to combat the biker war.

True partnerships can't be based on connivance or condescension. In this sense, the recent past and the future of Carcajou are not reassuring. On this issue, the Commission doesn't share the enthusiasm expressed by the Sûreté du Québec in its October 13, 1998 memorandum that states that "Carcajou, despite certain irritants, has been, according to all, a success." To quote but only one example of the real or potential frictions between the Sûreté du Québec, the Montreal police, and the RCMP: while the Sûreté du Québec forwarded to the Minister of Public Security a report containing allegations about the quality of RCMP and Montreal police investigators attached to the squad, the head of the Sûreté du Québec admitted to the squad's steering committee that, in such a focused project, "the caliber of the investigators leaves much to be desired. The SQ investigators, with the exception of perhaps one investigator, don't have the necessary expertise to work lengthy cases." Furthermore, in additional comments aimed at correcting the wrong impression created about the RCMP and Montreal police in his December report, the author explained in these terms the differing objectives of the Montreal police and the Sûreté du Québec: the first "wants to profit from this joint project by showing its worth outside the island of Montreal in order to extend its territory" while the second "wants to assume the leadership that comes with the role of being a provincial police force." With such partners, who needs enemies?

The report pursues the topic under the heading "Deviance: derogatory and incompetent practices."

We asked ourselves about the ability of a police force to produce propaganda in response to public queries of its actions. . . . The consequences of operations to manipulate information destined for the minister or the Ministry of Public Security are without doubt. They can poison already tenuous relations between partners who see themselves more as rivals. They can even corrupt the spirit of ministerial responsibility.

In January 1998, the Sûreté du Québec forwarded to the Ministry of Public Security a document entitled "Status report on outlaw motorcycle gangs, Carcajou." Now, it seems that this document reprints, without quoting, portions of a September 1997 report by the Montreal police destined for city politicians. This qualifies, in some circumstances, as plagiarism, at least partially. But it could be a relatively minor act of plagiarism if credit had been given to the Carcajou squad. However, what really sours this attempt at information manipulation is the difference between the original report and the second. Essentially the second report adds derogatory comments about the other police agencies involved in Carcajou in an attempt to magnify the Sûreté du Québec's contribution to the squad.

Evidence gathered by the Commission shows that the Ministry of Public Security received only that version of the report sent by the Sûreté du Québec, without the input forwarded to the Sûreté du Québec by the Montreal police and the RCMP. We know that the Montreal police withdrew from the Carcajou operation in 1998 saying that the biker war "had ended, public peace has returned." It is impossible to imagine that this report did not directly contribute to the Montreal police withdrawal from Carcajou, if it was not in fact the only reason.

The commission questioned the Sûreté du Québec management's ability to foresee problems the force would need to tackle to enable them to plan and budget properly. "The kind of strategic management and planning practiced by the Sûreté du Québec is illustrated by the events involved in the creation of Carcajou. . . . The public was worried, the media demanded action and police forces were in the hot seat: was anyone going to be able to bring these criminals under control?" The mood of crisis forced the Sûreté to respond. "Political authorities at the highest levels intervened and asked the director of the Sûreté du Québec for a plan of action."

Sûreté director Serge Barbeau, in testimony to the commission, described the situation:

When Carcajou was formed, we had to, to use a popular expression, quickly turn ourselves around on a dime. I had for months asked the Minister of Public Security for special funds to put together a squad comprised of all police agencies in Quebec to tackle outlaw bikers.

One afternoon, Saturday the 23rd of September, [public security minister Serge] Ménard showed up at my office at 4 o'clock. He had a meeting with the prime minister at 5 o'clock. He told me: "Mr. Barbeau, if you want something, this is the time because it's true things are not going well." We only have to read the newspapers from that time to see that, I think it had even become a political crisis. It had surpassed its criminal aspect.

We were ready. I asked Mr. André Dupré to bring me the plan we had thought out, that the investigators had put together, and Mr. Arcand, who is the Sûreté specialist, who was at that time specialist in the organized crime bureau, who already worked in conjunction with the Montreal police and the RCMP, but in a distinctive way in the battle against outlaw bikers, came to my office with Mr. Ménard. We looked at the plan, we came up with some idea, a scale of what we needed in terms of a budget, and, at ten to six that same day, Mr. Ménard called me and confirmed that the prime minister had just given me a special budget and I had to start the next morning.

The commission noted that the Sûreté was not ready to tackle the biker problem when approached by the minister, even though the war was by then already fifteen months old. The report offers a sobering assessment of police resources and response:

Carcajou was thus born through collaboration of the Montreal police, the Sûreté du Québec and the RCMP. In retrospect, we have to wonder if anyone foresaw this crisis in the sense that it was quite evident that in periods of budget restraint, only these kinds of situations [the death of Daniel Desrochers, the bombing of the Jokers' clubhouse, the taking over of Sorel by the Hells Angels during the funeral of Richard (Crow) Émond] would justify receiving budget money needed to intensify the war against outlaw bikers.

What is so striking in this episode is not only the quest for more money when the circumstances would warrant it, but also the veritable lack of medium- and long-term strategic planning, which we define as longer than one year. In effect, the biker war was not new. It was even on the list of prioritized goals submitted by the director general of the Sûreté du Québec to the Ministry of Public Security in the late fall of 1994. However, the managers in the criminal investigations bureau in the Sûreté du Québec were only pondering possible solutions that they must quickly adapt to circumstances in the fall of 1995.

By way of deception thou shalt do war
　　　　　　　　—*motto of the Israeli Mossad.*

When they weren't stabbing each other in the back, Quebec police continued to beat their brains against a wall in 1999 as they speculated about the "imminent" conversion of the Rock Machine into Bandidos and the subsequent bloodbath that would follow.

It's time I let you all in on a little secret. The Bandidos had no intention of taking the Rock Machine into their organization. The Bandidos, like true warriors, perpetrated the greatest deception of the biker war when they gave the impression they were interested in the Rock Machine.

The Swedish Bandidos were embroiled in their own war with the Hells Angels when wannabe Fred Faucher wrote Jan Jensen and asked that his gang take the Rock Machine into their organization. Jensen, a former Hells Angel who was kicked out of the gang and survived numerous assassination attempts, was a shrewd player. He knew the Scandinavian war, which I discuss at length in the next chapter, needed to end. He wanted to strengthen his hand so he had something to offer the Hells Angels at the bargaining table.

When Jensen read in Faucher's letter that the Rock Machine were involved in a much bloodier war with the Hells Angels, he saw his opportunity. Jensen decided to offer the Hells Angels the Rock Machine. He faked interest in the gang, and visited Canada frequently with other Bandidos from Europe and Australia; he even came with George Wegers, Bandidos vice-president who became president in September 1998. The Bandidos were seen in public with the Rock Machine. They sent them boxes of Bandidos knick-knacks, such as stickers and T-shirts. The Bandidos bought the Rock Machine's trust with trinkets and a show of friendship because Fred Faucher and his supporters were blinded by ambition.

The Rock Machine gave Jensen and the Bandidos all the tactical and strategic intelligence they needed to bargain with the Hells Angels and trade for favors and goodwill. The Bandidos used the Rock Machine as a pawn and a lever in their peace negotiations with the Hells Angels. In all wars, deals are made and allies are betrayed for the good of the country: in this case, the Bandidos Nation.

The Bandidos did not conspire to deceive the police. The police deceived themselves because they created entire scenarios from few facts. They let their wishful thinking, in-fighting, and cheap competitiveness with other law enforcement agencies blind them to the truth. The truth comes to all who are patient. The police tried to fit the meager facts they had into grandiose schemes they outlined to the media to portray themselves as experts. In doing so, they deceived the public and the public trust. Police agencies with multi-million-dollar intelligence budgets were no closer to the truth than the Rock Machine. How the Bandidos and the Hells Angels must have laughed.

The Bandidos and the Hells Angels started to negotiate a truce before the war in Quebec started and just as tensions were building in Scandinavia. I will quote from minutes of Hells Angels' meetings dating back to 1994 that show both gangs were working out their problems diplomatically while blood was shed on the battlefields. (Note that the Hells Angels always misspell the Bandidos name as Banditos.) I will quote more meeting minutes about Hells Angels-Bandidos meetings in a chapter devoted to the Hells Angels' documents.

Hells Angels United States Presidents Meeting
March 26, 1994

All United States Present. Mamoe, Sweden and Copanhegan, Denmark also present.

Banditos Meeting Guidelines

1) The date of the meeting with the "Banditos" is April 2nd at 12:00 non in Spokane, WA. Representatives should be there April 1st.

2) Our representatives from the East Coast are GREG, GLEN, KEVIN, and PAT, and from the West Coast are CISCO, MARK, CHICAGO JOE, and MIKE, to attend the meeting with the "Banditos".

3) We will back whatever decisions that our representatives make.

4) Washington prospects will wear a Washington bottom rocker.

5) No Banditos in Sweden.

* * *

West Coast Officers Meeting
October 19, 1996

General Business

GEORGE (Ventura) and BOBBY (Long Island) will go to Europe as soon as they can.

Motions

Motion made to allow a committee consisting of MIKE HURN (Alaska), GEORGE (VENTURA), WAYNE (BERDOO), CISCO (Oakland), DENNIS (Richmond), JEFF (Sacto), RICK (SPOKANE), BOBBY (Long Island), TEDDY (NYC) and Reps from Canada and Europe to deal with

the Bandito's. THIS IS TO BE A CALL-IN VOTE DUE BY SATURDAY,
OCTOBER 26, 1996 BY NOON

* * *

West Coast Officers Meeting
November 16, 1996
General Business

GEORGE (Ventura) and BOBBY (Long Island) discussed their trip to
Scandinavia.

Motions from Last Month

Motion made to allow a committee consisting of MIKE HURN (Alaska),
GEORGE (Ventura), WAYNE (Berdoo), CISCO (Oakland), DENNIS
(Richmond), JEFF (Sacto), RICK (Spokane), BOBBY (Long Island),
TEDDY (NYC) and Reps from Canada and Europe deal with the
Bandito's. Yes 314 No 69 PASSED

MOTION MADE BY: West Coast Officers

DATE: 11-16-96

PRESENTED TO: United States

1) Reason for Request: To allow GEORGE (Ventura) and BOBBY (Long
Island) meet with George (Banditos) for the purpose of telling the Banditos that if they stop taking in our ex members, ex prospects, and ex
hangarounds that would be a sign of good faith and we could possibly
have serious discussions (6 months to a year) in the future.

2) Motion or Request: To allow GEORGE (Ventura) and BOBBY (Long
Island) meet with George (Banditos).

* * *

West Coast Officer Meeting
January 18, 1997
Motions

To allow GEORGE (Ventura) and BOBBY (Long Island) meet with
George (Banditos). Yes 350 No 33 PASSED

* * *

West Coast Officers Meeting
March 15, 1997
General Business

BOBBY (Long Island) and GEORGE (Ventura) had a meeting with 2
Banditos (George and Lee).

* * *

West Coast Officers Meeting
April 12, 1997

General Business

GEORGE (Ventura) talked with George (Banditos) about several issues. They are upset that we copyrighted their name in New Zealand. JOHNNY A. will discuss this at the next EURO meeting.

* * *

West Coast Officers Meeting

May 17, 1997

General Business

GEORGE (Ventura) talked with George (Banditos) about several issues (copyrite, Sturgis, and Iron Lords M/C). The Banditos will not take any more ex Hells Angels into their club.

* * *

West Coast Officers Meeting

June 21, 1997

General Business

GEORGE (Ventura) talked with George (Banditos) he said that they want to resolve any problems we may have. They will meet in Sturgis.

* * *

West Coast Officers Meeting

July 19, 1997

General Business

Fritz Clapp will get a hold of New Zealand's lawyer to stop the copywrite of the Banditos name.

* * *

West Coast Officers Meeting

August 23, 1997

GEORGE met with George in Sturgis but, nothing was resolved.

* * *

Hells Angels United States Presidents Meeting

October 18, 1997

General Business

1. Our club and the Banditos in Europe have come to paceful agreements and there is a truce.
2. Ex member information that is sent out to charters must have a picture.
3. George (Ventura), Bobby (Long Island), and Canada will meet with the Banditos.

It is important to note that Hells Angel George (Gus) Christie of the Ventura chapter and Bandidos vice-president (later president) George Wegers met nearly every month in 1996 and 1997 while their gangs were at war in Scandinavia and while Swedish Bandido Jan Jensen supposedly courted the Rock Machine in Quebec.

More noteworthy is the fact the Quebec Hells Angels met with the Bandidos in 1997 while the former warred with the Rock Machine. Ten days after this Hells Angels presidents' meeting, Bandidos president George Wegers met with the Rock Machine in Quebec City. The Bandidos also accompanied the Rock Machine to Ottawa to meet with the Outlaws. Wegers scored a major intelligence coup through this ruse, as he learned the intimate details of the Outlaws and Rock Machine plans against the Hells Angels.

*　　*　　*

West Coast Officers Meeting
November 22, 1997
New Business

NOMADS, WA: We have a video of bandito George with the rock machine in Canada.

General Business

Discussed the continuing peace with the banditos. GEORGE (Ventura) will call bandito George one more time.

Although the Hells Angels and Bandidos talked, the gangs did not stop actively gathering intelligence on each other.

*　　*　　*

West Coast Officers Meeting
December 20, 1997
New Business

NOMADS, WA: George (Washington) is the new head of the Banditos.

General Business

GEORGE (Ventura) talked to George from the Banditos.

*　　*　　*

West Coast Officers Meeting
January 17, 1998
General Business

GEORGE (Ventura) talked to George from the Banditos.

*　　*　　*

West Coast Officers Meeting
February 14, 1998
General Business

GEORGE (Ventura) talked to George from the Banditos again.

*　　*　　*

West Coast Officers Meeting
March 7, 1998
General Business
GEORGE (Ventura) talked to George from the Banditos and things are working on a positive note. George (Banditos, Washington) moved to Texas.

It is unfortunate the Quebec police and the Rock Machine did not have the intelligence-gathering apparatus to make them privy to these documents. The police would have interpreted circumstances more accurately, rather than being wildly off-base with their wishful thinking and speculation. And the Rock Machine would not have been so cocky and careless. These minutes are just a taste of what's to come. Biker politics is much more intricate than the police would have the public believe. I will reveal more secret biker correspondence and information in the following chapters, to expose one of the greatest deceptions ever perpetrated in the criminal underworld—a deception with horrible ramifications, and not for whom you would expect.

Postscript

The Rock Machine announced on June 2, 1999, that they had become an official outlaw motorcycle gang with chapters in Montreal, Quebec City, and Sarnia, Ontario. Their colors have the gang name across the top, the stylized eagle head as center crest, the letters MC below and to the right of the crest to signify Motorcycle Club, and a bottom rocker that reads: Canada. They claimed to support the Bandidos.

Two Hells Angels hangarounds tried to assassinate Rock Machine leader Marcel Demers on Saturday, June 5. They emptied 30 rounds from an AK–47 into his car over a distance of one kilometer as the biker tried to outrun them along a street in Beauport, a suburb of Quebec City.

Chapter 2: Scandinavia
The Nordic War
Hells Angels vs. the Bandidos

"We shouldn't lose sight of the fact that behind the facade of brotherhood and motorcycles, their main enemy remains the state." Siv Persson, a Swedish member of parliament the Hells Angels and Bandidos plotted to kill because of her relentless fight to eliminate them in her country.

*   *   *

When the Hells Angels set up their first Scandinavian chapter in Copenhagen, Denmark, on December 31, 1980, they did so with the intent of taking over in the Nordic countries of Denmark, Norway, Sweden, and Finland. As I've said before, the Hells Angels are monopolistic. They have always been guided by their vision of being the only outlaw motorcycle gang in the world. The Hells Angels do not tolerate competition and find it easier to respect themselves if there is no one around to be compared to. The Hells Angels' clubhouse in Copenhagen has a sign that expresses the gang's attitude toward the world: "Let them hate as long as they fear." This motto has guided the Hells Angels from their inception.

Scandinavia was awash with outlaw motorcycle gangs in the early 1980s. The new Hells Angels were well-versed in the gang's traditional ways of winning them over. First they try diplomacy and hook them on the money from their drug networks. If that doesn't work, they con their enemies into fighting them, and then pick up the pieces to form a new chapter. And so the disease spreads. Violence begets violence.

The Hells Angels ordered Denmark's dominant outlaw motorcycle gang to submit and give up its colors in 1981. The Bullshit told the Hells Angels to stuff it. From 1981 to 1986, the Hells Angels waged a fierce war against the Bullshit, of which the public took little notice and retains little memory. Thirteen dead bikers later, Bullshit folded in 1986.

The remaining members would not be driven out of the biker underworld. They immediately formed the Undertakers. One of the first outsiders to join them was Michael Garcia Lerche Olsen, the former president of the Hells Angels' Copenhagen chapter who had been dishonorably kicked out of the gang shortly after the Undertakers were formed. His hatred for the Hells Angels made him the Undertakers' natural leader.

1989

Although thirteen bikers were killed in the six-year war between the Hells Angels and Bullshit, few Scandinavians understood the violence of outlaw motorcycle gang culture. Most people didn't see beyond the chrome-and-leather style into the horrid heart of the beast.

Scandinavian society was enthralled with biker culture. The British rockers' influence of the 1960s, with its oil-dripping Triumphs, bolting BSAs, Norton Commandos, Vincent Black Shadows, and Ariel Square Fours, gave way to the Harley-Davidson juggernaut in the late 1980s. American biker culture, with its violence, venom, and desecration of brotherhood for money became the norm. So much so, that a 28-year-old member of the Viking Motorcycle Club in Skien, Norway, legally changed his name to Harley Davidsen in 1993. Norwegian law prevented him from spelling the name "son," because that is a Swedish name.

The Harley-Davidson promotional machine revved its engine and the throb-throb-throb through glitter chrome pipes and the glare of lacquered paint and low-slung weight with jeans astride was all the rage in an age where style ruled over substance. Even furniture monster IKEA fell prey to the prevailing penchant for leather lust and hired two Canadian Hells Angels in 1989 for a television commercial—fifteen seconds of infamy—crafted to be cool. The idea, to promote IKEA's 1990 catalog, was conceived by a Vancouver advertising agency through virgin birth, as obviously no thought had soiled the process. IKEA's Quebec store manager, Ingemar Palmquist, stood sandwiched between two beefy Hells Angels and extolled "more color, more selection and more leather." And the Hells Angels' eyes lit up.

"Outrageous," the weekly trade tabloid *Marketing* called it. "What possessed them to show real bikers in a commercial—thereby showing television audiences who see it that a major advertiser considers them socially acceptable members of the business world—is completely beyond our understanding. The very idea of doing it is outrageous. The fact they implemented it is incredible. IKEA may be quite prepared to do business with 'bikers,' and others of their ilk, and accept them into the advertising and marketing fraternity. We definitely do not."

Although Scandinavia had hundreds of outlaw motorcycle gangs, these bikers knew little about the world's most powerful gangs, other than the Hells Angels. The Big Four gangs—the Hells Angels, Outlaws, Bandidos, and Pagans—dominated the biker underworld in North America where eight hundred outlaw gangs roamed the roads. The Hells Angels garnered most of the media attention. That was about to change as American gangs looked toward Europe to expand their power, networks, and markets in the 1980s. The Outlaws set up chapters in England. The Bandidos set their sights on France. The Outlaws and Hells Angels were deadly enemies in North America. The Hells Angels and Bandidos tolerated each other and had a non-aggression pact (as long as each gang stayed on its turf), but the pact said nothing about Europe, where the Hells Angels had set up chapters decades before the arrival of the Bandidos. The two gangs were destined to clash.

The Bandidos Nation was formed, not unlike other outlaw motorcycle gangs, by a bunch of guys who hung out together and wanted to make life a little more interesting. Former U.S. marine Donald Eugene Chambers and other dock workers who had served in the military partied hard in the Texas fishing village of San Leon in Galveston County during the summer of 1965. Chambers was fond of motorcycles and adored the Hells Angels, who were little more than a myth that crept over the continental divide and seeped into Texas through the national media that started giving the California gang attention in 1965 as the drug counter-culture of the hippies came to the forefront in San Francisco.

Chambers decided he wanted to start a motorcycle gang. He sat around watching television in March 1966 and was taken by the Frito Bandito cartoon figure that scooted across the screen to promote corn chips. Chambers called his gang the Bandidos. As an insult to Mexicans, he adopted the cartoon figure for the gang's colors and armed him with a sword and machete. The gang motto: We are the people our parents warned us about. Another motto: Our colors don't run.

The gang's criminal activities started with stealing motorcycles and selling the parts. They also rounded up the most beautiful and willing beach bunnies in San Leon and put them to work for the gang as prostitutes. The Bandidos became renowned as the best pimps in the biker underworld. They supplied women for brothels, strip clubs, and massage parlors.

The Bandidos' search for more women took them to the larger beach resort of Corpus Christi in 1968. Within two years, they had a twenty-member chapter in that town. The Long Island, New York, chapter of the Pagans visited the Bandidos in Corpus Christi in 1971 and taught them how to manufacture speed. The Bandidos, in return, showed them how to run prostitution networks. The gangs got so close that they had a brotherhood patch made up with Zutar, the devil on the Pagans' colors, and the fat Mexican from the Bandidos' colors. The friendship was short-lived. The Pagans ripped off the Bandidos for money and drugs when they returned north. The Bandidos subscribed to the Confederate philosophy that Yankees could not be trusted, and have hated the Pagans ever since. Two Bandidos murdered a Pagans prospect in 1977 because he wore that gang's colors.

Bandidos national president Donald Chambers, nicknamed "Mother" for having founded the gang, was a violent man. He proved it time and time again to anyone foolish enough to cross him. Two brothers sold the gang baking soda instead of speed in El Paso in 1972. Chambers, Bandido Jesse Fain Deal, and former Bandido Raymond Barriett abducted the two brothers and drove them into the desert north of El Paso. They forced the two men to dig their own graves, then they shot and burned them. The three Bandidos were jailed for the killing.

The Bandidos elected former U.S. marine Ronald Jerome Hodge as national president to replace Chambers. The gang named him "Step-mother." Hodge was a tough go-getter everyone called Mr. Prospect when he first came around because he so eagerly proved his worth that he earned his colors in one month. Hodge was the meanest biker in Texas, and scared anyone who met him. He stripped the Bandidos of all members he did not consider 100-percent devoted to the gang. He even shut down the Montana and Indiana chapters.

Hodge expanded the Bandidos' realm of influence and power in 1978 when he took the gang to Bike Week in Daytona Beach, Florida, for the first time. They befriended the Outlaws, and the gangs began a business partnership in which the Bandidos traded speed for Outlaws' cocaine.

The Bandidos were severely harmed by law enforcement in 1979 when they were falsely accused of assassinating federal Judge John J. (Maximum John) Wood in San Antonio on May 29, and of shooting at an assistant U. S. attorney. Wood was presiding over a Bandidos case when he was killed. A Bandido owned a van similar to that used by the men who shot at the U.S. attorney. Raids and investigations severely crippled the Bandidos and set back their expansion plans. Wood was killed by professional hit man Charles Harrelson, father of actor Woody Harrelson. Harrelson was sentenced to life in Marion, Illinois, federal prison on December 14, 1982. Wood had been scheduled to hear a case against Bandido Jimmy Chagra. Chagra was acquitted of charges in Wood's killing, though his wife and brother were convicted of plotting the judge's death.

The Bandidos, who had nearly seven hundred members at the peak of their power, never bounced back from the beating they took at the hands of law enforcement. They operated in near anonymity before Wood was murdered. Since then, they have been scrutinized by police, and their world membership is less than four hundred. The Bandidos moved their headquarters from Houston to Corpus Christi. Hodge stepped down as national president in 1980 after he was charged with aggravated assault and moved to Rapid City, South Dakota, where he ran a bar.

Alvin Frakes became the new national president. Donald Chambers retired from the Bandidos when he was released from prison in 1983 and had his tattoos covered. That year, the Bandidos became an international gang when the Comancheros Motorcycle Club in Australia split after a brief war and half the members joined the Bandidos, whom they had met in Albuquerque, New Mexico. Frakes died of cancer in 1985 and Hodge once again took control of the gang, but to avoid scrutiny by law enforcement, did not wear the El Presidente patch on his colors. Rather, he wore the president's patch for the Bandidos' Nomads chapter, the gang's enforcement arm. The Nomads, whose members were all hand-picked, old-time Bandidos, ran the gang.

Twenty-three Bandidos and former members were arrested on murder conspiracy charges in March 1988 after member Randy Hanson ratted out to the U.S. Drug Enforcement Administration a 1985 attempt by the Bandidos to kill two members of the Banshees Motorcycle Club with bombs. Eight Bandidos pleaded guilty, and seven were found guilty of conspiracy to murder. Hodge, who was the national president, as well as the national vice-president, both national secretaries, and two national sergeants-at-arms were sentenced to jail terms. After the arrest of the gang's leaders, Hodge held a meeting at his new home in Memphis, Tennessee, where new national officers were elected. James Edward (Sprocket) Lang, vice-president of the Northwest Houston chapter, became national president. Lawrence (Beaver) Borrego, a member of the Nomads chapter, became vice-president. Both men helped expand the Bandidos into Europe, where they would run into trouble with the Hells Angels. Lang also forced the gang to clean up its image and wear clean colors to improve public relations.

The Bandidos officially arrived in Europe in August 1989 when their probationary chapter in Marseille, France, was made an official member of the Bandido Nation at the Black Hills Motorcycle Classic rally in Sturgis, South Dakota. The Marseille chapter was set up to corner the lucrative used Harley-Davidson motorcycle market in Europe, where the bikes fetched more than three times their worth in the United States. American Bandidos bought motorcycles and rode them for six thousand miles before shipping them to France, to reduce duties.

I was in Sturgis in 1989 and took the first photographs of the nine French Bandidos and their colors in the pit area of the dragstrip where they gathered around their motorcycles. The pit area was protected by guards who carried concealed guns. Bandidos' national president James (Sprocket) Lang was hospitable to me, though he had no idea who I was. Lang and his officers posed with me for photographs. (See photo section.) Lang began a lengthy prison term early in 1999.

The Hells Angels did not wear their colors in Sturgis that year, but members wore red-and-white bandanas to identify themselves to the biker world. I sat in a bar on Sturgis's main street for two hours and counted seventy-five Hells Angels. By my third day in town, members of the Sons of Silence, close friends of the Hells Angels, recognized me as the author of *Hells Angels: Taking Care of Business*, which had been published in October 1987. I did not know this, but I knew I was pressing my luck as some biker security officers went out of their way to photograph me. I decided to buy a few Sturgis trinkets and hightail it out of town.

In a town with fifty thousand outlaw bikers and wannabes, it's difficult to tell if you are being followed. Sturgis is not a place for the paranoid. I went about my business and walked into a building to examine the wares at different booths. As I scoured the table farthest from the main entrance, nine Sons of Silence who had tailed me quietly surrounded me and started chuckling and making threatening noises, all the while pretending to look at the wares on the table. They closed in around me. I knew they would either shoot me, abduct me, or stab me. When I first walked in I noticed the light from a back door that had been opened to allow a breeze to waft through the room. I slammed into the left side of the biker who stood between me and the door, rolled off him, and hauled ass like a watermelon thief through parking lots and back streets. *Hasta la vista, baby.*

1991

Tension between the Bandidos and Hells Angels mounted in France. The two gangs flirted with war in August 1991 when four Hells Angels from Grenoble pulled up to the Bandidos' Marseille clubhouse on motorcycles, shot the gang vice-president dead, and wounded two other Bandidos. The Hells Angels and their puppet gang the Buccaneers wanted exclusive control of the market for used motorcycles and their parts. Gang leaders flew over from North America and ironed out differences at a sit-down. Neither side wanted to draw too much heat from authorities, who allowed them breathing space they did not get from police in America.

1993

The Hells Angels expanded quickly across Europe in the late 1960s, 1970s, and 1980s. Thirteen years after they opened their first chapter in Denmark, they set up their first Swedish chapter in the southern city of Malmö on February 27, 1993.

The Bandidos moved into Scandinavia in June 1993 when the Undertakers MC in Stenløse, Denmark, became a Bandidos' probationary chapter. (The Hells Angels use the word "prospect," the Bandidos prefer "probationary".) The Hells Angels were not amused. They considered Scandinavia their turf, and saw the Bandidos as dangerous rivals for that portion of the drug market that is controlled by outlaw bikers. They knew that a Bandidos chapter made up of Hells Angels enemies could not be won over and would fight viciously for drug turf. Despite their enmity, both gangs understood the need for good public relations. The Bandidos and Hells Angels, prompted by stories in the Danish press that described them as enemies, issued a joint press release in the summer of 1993 stating there was no animosity between the gangs. Using the media to deny hostility and dampen public furor and fear would become commonplace in the battle to come.

The Hells Angels targeted Scandinavia for strategic reasons. It has thousands of miles of unprotected shoreline for smugglers. Norway, Sweden, and Finland have isolated forests where smelly drug labs could be set up far from prying eyes and noses. Such sanctuary could not be found in continental Europe. And the countries were close to Russia and its eastern satellites, with which the Hells Angels could trade drugs for weapons. Sweden alone had 24,000 islands that could be used as bases for forays into eastern Europe and Russia, and as transshipment points for drugs and weapons.

The Bandidos understood the importance of quickly securing a power base in Denmark and made the Undertakers an official chapter—the Bandidos Northland—on December 17, 1993. The first Danish Bandidos were Hells Angels enemies, defectors, and expelled members. The two gangs had little in common except hatred for each other. Former Danish Hells Angels' president Michael Garcia Lerche Olsen became Bandidos president.

Sweden

While the Bandidos rushed to set up in Denmark as the worried and angry Hells Angels looked on, a scenario developed in Sweden that would soon engulf both gangs and allow them to vent their hatred for each other.

The first outlaw motorcycle gang in Sweden was White Trash, which introduced a new level of violence to the biker underworld in the mid-1980s. The gang had a lot of contact with the Hells Angels in Germany and Denmark before the police shut them down. However, White Trash was just the beginning of a new phenomenon that quickly spread across the country. Like many organized crime gangs, the public only got to hear about them once they were well established. The Hells Angels, on the other hand, followed their development with interest.

A detective inspector with the Swedish National Police, in an internal memorandum on September 3, 1993, outlined his concerns about the power the Hells Angels were gaining in the Swedish underworld:

> During the last year, or since we got our own Hells Angels chapter in Sweden in February this year, we have had a galloping development among the clubs ... where only a few members are suspected of being involved in crime or of having connections with criminal motorcycle gangs (and) clubs where a majority of the members are suspected of earning their living by committing crimes.
>
> Hells Angels MC Sweden is developing its organization continuously and it seems to go even easier than before. Today we have at least 20 gangs which are supporting them officially. After they got their promotion they have started a large number of business companies and their criminal activities seem to have increased. The police and other authorities have also noticed how the members of Hells Angels have the control over several criminals and also how they take the power when they are in prison.
>
> Since a month ago we can see the result of a couple of meetings during

the springtime between Hells Angels MC Sweden and three or four of the supporter-groups in the Stockholm area.

The 25 years old Choppers MC Floda, a well respected club which has become a Hells Angels supporter-group since more than a year ago, moved from Floda to Stockholm. The distance is about 150 kilometers and some of the members even brought their families along. Of course we must believe that this club will be the next prospect club in Sweden.

We have also noticed that several motorcycle gangs in Hells Angels nearness have started criminal activities and they do it with new self-confidence in their relations to other gangs and to the police.

The motorcycle gangs which are not supporting the Hells Angels are trying to "mind their own business" and at the moment will not take position. However, we have the information that Sweden and Norway will have Outlaws chapters in the near future.

* * *

The Hells Angels worried in the early 1990s about the independence and rebelliousness of many motorcycle gangs across Scandinavia, especially in Sweden, where punks did their best to emulate the Hollywood version of bikers and gangsters. These bikers not only shunned social norms, they didn't even want to be part of a bigger gang that was bound by strict rules and regulations. The Hells Angels, as far as they were concerned, were over 30. They might be powerful and rich, but they were just another establishment that liked to control biker society. There was no freedom where the Hells Angels roamed.

The Morbids MC Lowland in Sweden was a tough, criminal bike gang whose members had been convicted of manslaughter, extortion, kidnapping, armed robbery, and weapons theft from military depots. Like most other motorcycle gangs in Scandinavia, they were formed when the Harley-Davidson cult swept the land. Japan and Europe are prone to emulate the most current trends in American culture, which they believe to be the epitome of cool. The push by Harley-Davidson in the late 1980s to put an expensive, retro-style motorcycle made of antiquated technology in every yuppie's garage eventually had an effect in Europe, where anything with the Harley logo imparted to its millions of bearers a cachet that oozed a tough, sinister independence.

The Morbids MC stumbled into the real world of Hells Angels politics in 1992 when they became a support gang for the Hells Angels in Sweden. In the intricate web of biker machismo, mistrust and paranoia, it was the first step in a long initiation process used to screen out the weak of heart and those prone to honesty. The next steps are hangaround gang, prospect gang, and finally, full-fledged membership. The Morbids MC did not get along with another Hells Angels support gang, the Rebels MC. The Morbids were too independent to take orders from anyone, and they considered the Rebels to be Angel ass-kissers who lacked self-respect and pride in their colors.

Morbids MC member Marcus Sjoholm and Hells Angels prospect Rudaz Rodin served jail sentences in the same prison in 1993 and became friends as they developed plans to expand the Morbids MC criminal activities within the Hells Angels' empire. The plans were shelved in the fall of 1993 when once again the Morbids MC stubborn streak prevented them from taking orders from the Hells Angels. This created tension between the gangs, as the Hells Angels demand submission and servitude. With little notice, the Morbids MC informed the Hells Angels at the end of 1993 that they preferred the Bandidos' way of doing business, and had shifted their allegiance to their new Danish chapter.

1994

The Hells Angels fired the first shots in the Nordic war when they attacked the Helsingborg, Sweden, clubhouse of the Morbids MC, on January 22, 1994, the day they became Bandidos hangarounds. The Hells Angels attacked the Morbids' clubhouse again on January 26, and fired several shots at the building. The Morbids shot back. Morbids member Stefan Sjoholm opened the roof skylight to look out, and had a finger shot off.

The Bandidos granted a Danish biker gang hangaround status on January 28, setting in motion the process of testing and assimilating the gang that would become their East Coast chapter. The Bandidos were expanding quickly in Hells Angels' territory, something even the American Bandidos would not dare do.

The Swedish Hells Angels held a Defense Fund party in Malmö on January 29 to raise money. At the party, the Hells Angels made the Rebels MC West Side from Helsingborg, sixty kilometers north of Malmö, an official hangaround gang. This gave the Swedish Hells Angels muscle to do their dirty work, muscle they had hoped a year earlier that the Morbids would provide. The Swedish Hells Angels also indoctrinated two Stockholm gangs into their ways, and tasked them with recruiting support among area gangs. The Choppers MC Stockholm and Perkele MC Stockholm met in February with representatives of thirty motorcycle gangs from the Stockholm area, to instruct them in how to handle police and how to behave in restaurants and pubs, as the Hells Angels had shown them. The Sofia Hogs and the Plebs MC Choppers were not impressed by the long list of rules and said they didn't become bikers to follow rules. They wanted to maintain their independence. The Choppers MC Stockholm and Perkele MC Stockholm changed their names at the Hells Angels' request to Choppers MC North Side and Choppers MC South Side. It was a sign they were about to be taken into the lower levels of the Hells Angels organization.

Fifteen Danish Bandidos visited the Morbids in Sweden on February 12, 1994. The bikers partied at the illegal Roof Top Club in Helsingborg. Word quickly got to the Hells Angels and within an hour Swedish Hells Angels, backed by members of their support gangs, the Rebels MC West Side and Rednecks MC South Ridge (who later merged with the Rebels) showed up at the club to confront their enemies. One Morbid picked up a telephone to call for reinforcements, only to see it ripped from the wall. The Hells Angels locked the entrance and exit and positioned themselves inside the club to surround the Bandidos and Morbids. Several Hells Angels and supporters followed two Morbids members into the club kitchen, where the shooting started. Thirteen shots were fired. Rednecks member Joakim Boman, 23, was shot dead. Swedish Hells Angel Johnny (Sjoman) Larsen, Danish Bandidos MC Northland member Ben (Karate-Bent) Olsen, and a Rebels member suffered serious gunshot wounds.

Hells Angel Johnny Larsen's street name was "Seven bullets, no problem." He earned the moniker when he stole the motorcycle of a member the gang had kicked out in bad standing. When the Hells Angels expel someone from their organization, they take all he owns: often his woman, certainly his motorcycle. That's why prospective members are bound by gang rules to show up with their motorcycles the night their membership is voted on. The expelled biker didn't want to part with his motorcycle, and shot Larsen seven times. When police asked him in hospital about the shooting, Larsen responded, "I don't talk to pigs." He even wrote a letter to Sweden's largest newspaper during the biker war: "Ordinary people don't have to be afraid. This is something we do within the club. We take care of our problems." He signed it "Seven bullets, no problem." Mister lead-head took two more bullets in the kitchen of the Roof Top Club. The Hells Angels later realized his big mouth was bad for business, and expelled him in bad standing.

The Bandidos, who had no chapters in Sweden, realized they needed to protect their new hangaround gang in Helsingborg from the Hells

Angels and their allies. They transferred five Bandidos to Sweden to guard the Morbids' clubhouse. They put a Sweden bottom rocker on their colors, which further angered the Hells Angels.

This was the first Bandidos incursion into Sweden, and the Hells Angels were worried. The Hells Angels and Bandidos had a long-standing deal in the United States not to tread on each other's toes. The gangs didn't like each other, but the balance of power was too even for one gang to attack the other. The American Bandidos were not an aggressive gang. They did their own thing and subscribed to the old biker notion of live and let live—a notion long shed by the expansionist, controlling Hells Angels.

The Morbids and the Rebels waged an ongoing battle throughout the month of February. The Morbids had a clubhouse in Helsingborg and the Rebels had one in a small village nearby. The bikers couldn't keep out of each other's way. The Rebels started the bad blood between the gangs with a series of violent attacks on Morbids and visiting Danish Bandidos. They chased and shot at one Bandido from a car. He sought shelter at the Helsingborg police station. Another time, the Rebels shot at Bandidos and Morbids in a nightclub and beat them with baseball bats. The Bandidos and Morbids, in turn, planted bombs in two Rebel cars. Both failed to detonate. One car driven by a Rebel had three passengers not connected to the biker underworld, and would have exploded near children.

The Morbids stole twelve Carl Gustav shoulder-fired Light Anti-Tank Weapons (LAWs rockets) and grenades from a military weapons and munitions storage vault in Söderåsen, Sweden, on February 20. Hundreds of such vaults are hidden in the Swedish countryside in case the country is attacked. Military service is mandatory in Sweden, and in case of war, reservists must report to these vaults to be equipped. The location of the vaults is no secret, and the Morbids had a history of looting them.

The Hells Angels are sensitive to public criticism and the gang's American leaders were concerned about mounting tension in Sweden. They also wanted to ensure that the Swedish Hells Angels would maintain control of the territory and wouldn't lose face by allowing the Bandidos to set up a chapter in what the Hells Angels considered to be their exclusive turf. Members of the Hells Angels' Oakland, California, chapter, hand-picked from chapters across the United States, summoned the Swedish Hells Angels to a meeting in March 1994 and set down the rules. The Swedish Hells Angels were told that the Hells

Angels and Bandidos have a non-aggression agreement in the United States. European Hells Angels and Bandidos did not abide by the non-aggression agreement, since both gangs clashed in France in 1992. The Hells Angels consulted with the Bandidos in Houston and a deal was struck: the Bandidos agreed that in order to keep the peace, the Hells Angels would be allowed to retain exclusive rights to Sweden, because they had set up operations there first. The Swedish Hells Angels were told to return home and order the Morbids to cut their ties with the Bandidos and to keep the Bandidos out of Sweden at all costs.

While the Hells Angels were away, the Morbids moved their clubhouse to within two kilometers of the Rebels clubhouse. They told the returning Angels they would maintain their ties with the Bandidos and would not honor the American non-aggression deal.

Bandidos officers from the gang's headquarters in Houston visited Denmark and Sweden in May and participated in a large meeting of the gangs. The Hells Angels from Denmark and Sweden, the Bandidos from Houston and Denmark, and the Morbids sat down and discussed the situation. The Bandidos informed the Hells Angels they would do the right thing and stand up for their hangaround gang in Sweden. The Swedish Hells Angels president subsequently decided to declare war on the Morbids, but his own chapter and the Danish Hells Angels refused to support him. They knew war could be costly.

Despite opposition from the Morbids, the Swedish Hells Angels controlled the biker culture in their country, unlike their brothers in Denmark. Biker gang violence increased across Sweden as idiots trashed nightclubs and restaurants and assaulted policemen to boost their reputation as tough guys.

*   *   *

In southwest Sweden, another motorcycle gang terrorized the small village of Svenljunga and its police force for most of 1994. The Butchers Riders retaliated against police each time one of their members was arrested. They detonated a bomb in a police officer's garden after he cited a Butchers member for a traffic offense. They felled a tree—with a bomb—into the garden of a man who had an argument with a Butchers member. They vandalized police cars and the police station after members were arrested or the clubhouse raided. The president, shortly after his release for an arrest, shot at the police station. After another member was released, a retaliatory bomb which was to have been planted in the station was instead left on the front steps, where it blew up. Police had trouble investigating the gang because citizens were afraid to talk about the bikers.

The Butchers in Svenljunga were not the only bikers who threw their weight around. Outlaw bikers across Sweden assaulted and threatened police officers, prosecutors, and witnesses.

Members and associates of the Hippi Haggs MC West Bay, Choppers MC Stockholm, Bax MC Stockholm, and Road Riders MC Landskrona threatened and attacked police across Sweden in December 1993 and January 1994.

The sergeant-at-arms for the Choppers MC North Side knocked a police inspector to the ground with a punch to the face in February 1994.

Members of Hells Angels MC Sweden threatened and badgered a policeman scheduled to testify against a biker for assaulting a patron in a restaurant in March 1994.

An associate of the West Mountain MC in Stockholm tried to kill an undercover policeman with a Glock Model-18 9-mm pistol equipped with a silencer and a laser sight in May 1994. The policeman dodged bullets until the biker was overpowered.

A member of the Bros MC Stockholm hit a policeman in the face during a disturbance outside a restaurant in June 1994. Police encountered bikers often in restaurants and nightclubs, businesses from which each of five gangs tried to extort protection money. The high number of assaults on police by bikers prompted the formation of the bar squad, a group of physically fit, tough and well-armed policemen who patrol Stockholm's bars to control biker violence.

In April 1994, Swedish Hells Angels Dennis (Gogler) Jensen and Johnny (Sjoman) Larsen were arrested on marijuana charges. They were acquitted, while two women pleaded guilty and were sentenced to two-and-a-half years in prison. Jensen had been transferred to Sweden from Denmark in January. The Hells Angels were unhappy with the bad publicity the arrests gave the gang. For the third time in two years, Johnny (Sjoman) Larsen focused the media's attention on the dirty side of the Hells Angels. He twice lost gunfights with Bandidos. The Hells Angels suspended Larsen from the gang and later expelled him in bad standing.

It also became apparent in April that outlaw bikers had formed links with other organized crime groups. Members of the Gjutjarm MC testified on behalf of a local mafia leader at his gang's trial.

The Swedish Hells Angels bolstered their ranks in May and made the Choppers MC North Side and Choppers MC South Side official hangaround gangs in Stockholm.

The long-time owner of a restaurant/night club in Växjö, a small city in southern Sweden, got tired of being extorted by Makrellen Sorensen (the secretary/treasurer of the Bandidos MC Nyköping-Falster in Denmark) and another Bandidos member. The owner shot Sorensen three times in the back and once in the buttocks on August 21. His choice of weapon raised a few eyebrows: it was an unusual Hungarian Femaru-Fegyver-ES-Gepgyar RT 37M 9-mm pistol equipped with a silencer and a brass-catcher for the cartridge casings. Such a gun is believed to be used by some East European intelligence agencies. Sorensen said the extortion was his personal business and had nothing to do with the Bandidos. Both men were sentenced to jail terms. Danish Bandidos were upset by publicity given the incident because it showed the public that it was possible to fight back against bikers.

A jailed member of Bandidos MC Sweden killed a fellow prisoner in the fall of 1994 for giving police information on the biker's accomplice.

Two Rebels (HA) in Helsingborg found bombs in their cars in December, but removed them before they exploded.

*   *   *

Swedish police learned much about the burgeoning outlaw biker culture in 1994. The link between bikers and white supremacists worried them because both groups were prone to violence. A confidential 1994 report by the Swedish National Police expressed these concerns. It was titled "Swedish outlaw motorcycle gangs and affiliation to right wing extremist circles and football huligans."

Since about five years back, or since the outlaw culture started to spread out over Sweden, we have noticed that people from right wing extremist circles and the outlaw motorcycle gangs quite often are recruited from the same social group of people. Particular among them who are below 30 years old.

The people in these groups often know each other since long time and have a strong loyalty to each other even before they joined the different groups. It has led to cooperation and movements between the groups. They also have the searching after something different together – to live outside the society.

Another thing that attracts right wing extremists is obviously the history of the outlaw culture, its opinion of 'white power' and its use of nazism symbols as for example helmets, badges and medals.

In the following we will draw attention to some connections between outlaw motorcycle gangs and right wing extremist circles.

• The support group of HAMC Sweden, Hippi Haggs MC, celebrate Adolf Hitler's anniversary day. A couple of the members are former skinheads and right wing individuals.
• A group of very dangerous skinheads and new nazism supporters belong to the outlaw culture and stand in very close relation to HAMC Sweden.

Among other crimes, individuals in the group have committed assault, intimidated or in other ways put pressure to plaintiffs, witnesses, investigators, and prosecutors in conjunction to trials involving members of HAMC Sweden.

- Hildings MC, Gothenburg, consists of new nazism supporters. This political opinion is a provision for membership. Earlier this year Hilding MC was taken up in the former support group to HAMC Sweden, Hawks MC, Gothenburg.
- Nordsmen MC Stockholm consists to some parts of former skinheads.
- Choppers MC Stockholm, hang around club to HAMC, has recruited members from gangs of skinheads and football huligans. Absolut MC Agesta and Absolut MC Surahammar have a lot more nazism symbols in their clubhouses and on their clothes than what's usual in the culture.
- Butchers MC in Svenljunga has a close relation to skinheads in their neighborhood and the local police suspect them of having committed crimes together.
- Outsiders MC Norrland, a support club to HAMC Sweden, has a lot of nazism symbols and literature.

The connection: Outlaw Motorcycle Gangs— Football Huliganism

The connection and cooperation between an outlaw motorcycle gang and a group of football huligans is a phenomenon that appeared in Stockholm just a couple of weeks ago.

Black Army is the biggest and most famous (and even infamous) football support club in Sweden. The club supports AIK, one of the biggest football clubs in Sweden. Black Army has about 4,500 members. Among them there are quite a large group of football huligans. During the last five years they have committed countless acts of violence both in Sweden and abroad.

Today four members of Black Army have joined Choppers MC Stockholm. Two of them are the president and the former president of Black Army. Consequently, they have a strong influence over quite a number of the members of Black Army.

As a result of that we could see how Black Army and Hells Angels Defense Fund (through Choppers MC) shared a business tent at Stockholm Water Festival, which took place a couple of weeks ago.

The future

In Sweden we have to ask ourselves if the connections between outlaw motorcycle gangs and right wing extremist circles are dangerous for the society or if it can be in the future. We also have to ask ourselves if there is a possibility that the outlaw culture becomes politicized in the future.

1995

By July 1995, the Hells Angels and Bandidos had marked their territory and recruited enough supporters to guarantee that neither gang was going to be beaten by the other. The gangs were also well armed: the Bandidos with weapons stolen from military depots, the Hells Angels with weapons bought through a numbered company from former army depots in the Estonian Republic. There were two hundred outlaws motorcycle gangs in Scandinavia on July 1, 1995: one hundred in Denmark, fifty-five in Norway, thirty in Sweden, fifteen in Finland. These gangs controlled fifteen thousand members, prospects, hangarounds, associates, and sympathizers. And most of them supported the Hells Angels, who had five full-fledged chapters in Scandinavia, three prospect chapters, and three hangaround chapters. The Bandidos had five full-fledged chapters and two hangaround chapters.

Denmark

Denmark was by far the hottest spot for biker violence and turf wars. The 100 outlaw motorcycle gangs in the country had 1,100 members, prospects, and hangarounds, as well as 8,000 associates and sympathizers. Denmark had three Hells Angels chapters: Hells Angels Copenhagen—20 members, 4 prospects; Hells Angels South—17 members, 3 prospects; Hells Angels Århus—16 members, 2 prospects, 1 hangaround. MC Denmark Odense was an official prospect chapter until October 1994, when it was abolished and its seven members, prospects, and hangarounds were absorbed by existing Hells Angels chapters. Four Odense members became members of Hells Angels South and one became a hangaround. One member became a member of Hells Angels Århus and another became a prospect.

The Danish Hells Angels allowed five gangs to wear the Denmark bottom rocker on their colors to signify their close relations with the Hells Angels. The next step would be to become a hangaround gang. The five gangs were Highlanders MC Denmark, No-Name MC Denmark, Hog Riders MC Denmark, Avengers MC Denmark, and Gonzo MC Denmark.

The Bandidos had four chapters in Denmark: Bandidos MC Northland—seven members, two prospects, one hangaround; Bandidos MC

East Coast—seven members, one prospect; Bandidos MC South Island—seven members, one prospect; Bandidos MC South Side—five members. They had no probationary chapters.

Danish Hells Angels traveled extensively throughout Scandinavia and to the United States, Canada, South America, South Africa, Baltic countries, Russia, and many European countries. The Bandidos traveled within Scandinavia and to the United States and Europe. The Danish Hells Angels had contacts with the Chinese triads and Lebanese drug and gun smugglers. A Hells Angels associate was believed to arrange real estate deals as a front man for the triads, who in turn helped the Hells Angels launder their money in casinos.

Although the Danish Hells Angels were concerned about the Bandidos expanding into the other three Scandinavian countries, they refrained from using violence and worked hard to set up stronger drug networks to corner the markets in those countries, leaving the Bandidos little opportunity to make money. The Hells Angels also didn't want to attract police attention to their drug business with a war. After all, as in Quebec, there is no shortage of roads in Denmark that would justify bikers shooting each other.

Finland

The Hells Angels and Bandidos raced to control the wide-open Finnish drug market in 1995. The Bandidos made the Undertakers MC Finland an official hangaround chapter in January. The Hells Angels renamed Overkill MC and made it the prospect chapter MC Finland in February. The Undertakers publicly challenged MC Finland to compete for the status of most powerful gang in Finland. They warned that they would spare no effort to destroy MC Finland and prevent it from becoming a full-fledged Hells Angels chapter. In an act of defiance that harms egos only in the biker subculture, the Undertakers used the Finland bottom rocker on their colors. The Hells Angels forbid anyone in their territory from using the country, state, or provincial name on their rocker. They sometimes allow city names, which indicates the gang is small and of no consequence. The Finnish gangs first clashed in the fall of 1994 with no injuries. The second time they fought, in April, an Undertakers hangaround shot the vice-president of Cannonball MC, an MC Finland support gang, in the stomach as he sat in restaurant. As in most biker wars, the gophers did the dirty work.

Hells Angels from several countries voiced concern at the gang's European meeting in England in April about the rapid growth of the

Undertakers MC. They decided to speed up the timetable to make MC Finland an official chapter faster than gang rules allow. Before the meeting ended, the Hells Angels learned of the shooting of the Cannonball vice-president, and realized that MC Finland didn't have what it takes to become Hells Angels. They failed to immediately avenge the shooting, as good Hells Angels should. The issue of granting MC Finland full membership was withdrawn from the agenda until the fall meeting.

While the gang politicians debated, the bikers in the trenches filled their war chests with drug money, stockpiled weapons, and recruited sympathizers. MC Finland established connections with the Moscow biker gang, Night Wolves. MC Finland associates delivered stolen Harley-Davidson motorcycles to the gang in Moscow, where there are about five hundred bikers. The city's other large gang, the Cossacks, also had ties to the Hells Angels. The Russians had steroids and weapons to trade for drugs.

Norway

The Hells Angels and Bandidos also competed against each other in Norway to control the country's drug market. The Hells Angels had one official chapter established August 1, 1992: Hells Angels MC Norway Trondheim—fifteen members, one prospect, one hangaround. They granted the 22-member Shabby Ones MC West County, from Sandnes in southwest Norway, prospect status during the World Run in Amsterdam on June 4, 1995, and renamed them MC Norway. They appointed the Customizers MC Oslo (seven members, one prospect, one hangaround), thirty kilometers north-west of that city, a hangaround gang after the Bandidos made the Rabies MC Norway in Oslo a hangaround gang on June 17, 1994. The Hells Angels ordered the Customizers to move their clubhouse and activities to Oslo to compete with the Rabies.

The Hells Angels and Rabies fought their war of intimidation with restraint, for fear of arousing the authorities, who could shut down their drug and weapons smuggling operations. Most of the fifty-five outlaw motorcycle gangs in the country supported the Hells Angels. The Rabies had eleven members and two hangarounds. They were one of the oldest biker gangs in Norway, and told the Hells Angels they wanted to remain neutral and enjoy the businesses they ran. But the Hells Angels pressured them to take their side, and the Rabies reacted by contacting the Danish Bandidos. Former Rabies member Lars Harnes obtained Bandidos prospect status in Sweden. The Rabies knew they were outnumbered, so they invited members of the Outlaws MC Midlands in England to establish links with them.

Sweden

Swedish outlaw motorcycle gangs turned more violent in 1995, catching the public and police off guard. The Hells Angels had one chapter, Hells Angels MC Sweden Malmö—7 members, 3 hangarounds. They granted Rebels MC West Side prospect status on April 14 and changed their name to MC Sweden—11 members, 6 hangarounds. They had 2 Hells Angels MC World hangaround gangs: Choppers MC Northside in Stockholm—13 members; Choppers MC South Side—19 members.

The Bandidos MC Sweden Probationary chapter (formerly the Morbids) had 11 members. The Hells Angels and Bandidos controlled the so-called Harley-Davidson culture in Sweden, with 23 of the country's 30 outlaw motorcycle gangs supporting the Hells Angels.

Media attention garnered by the biker violence early in 1995 forced the Hells Angels to change their strategy to avoid a public outcry against them. By mid-year they exercised strict control over their supporters, and forced them to maintain a low profile. Swedish member of parliament Siv Persson pressured the minister of justice to take steps to curb biker gang violence. The bikers threatened to rape and kill her. Police found plans to assassinate her during a raid on a clubhouse. The increased number of bikers in prison (because of police investigations) resulted in an increased number of threats against prison officials. Police also noticed that bikers were dealing with other organized crime gangs such as the Yugoslavian mafia.

Guerrilla warfare

The war between the Hells Angels and Bandidos, which included all the gangs that supported them, was fought at a crazed, staccato pace that gave neither gang, nor the public or the police, breathing room. The violence was brisk, sometimes predictable, always public and spectacular. People didn't go missing. They were shot in public, sometimes with hundreds of witnesses. The war was fought with little subtlety or thought, as it was driven by anger and hatred. Retaliation was a given. And the escalation was so abrupt that the leaders of Scandinavia's four nations, who were paralyzed with surprise for nearly two years, were quick to admit that they had no solutions for outlaw motorcycle gangs other than banning them. Society will carry forever the burden of the bikers' reaction to this attempted solution.

*   *   *

Bandidos MC Probationary (Morbids) in Sweden became a full-fledged chapter of the Bandido Nation on July 7, 1995.

Police found a machine gun in the Swedish Hells Angels' clubhouse in Malmö on July 13.

The president of Bandidos MC Sweden, Michael (Joe) Ljunggren, was hit by four bullets, one through the heart, as he rode his motorcycle on highway E/4 near Markaryd, Sweden, on July 17. His assailants shot from a passing car. More than 230 people, including Bandidos and Outlaws, showed up at Ljunggren's funeral on July 25.

Two members of the Undertakers MC (Bandidos Probationary MC Finland) were shot at the MC Finland clubhouse in Helsinki at 2 a.m. on July 26 with a recoilless Swedish AT-4 rifle.

The Choppers MC Stockholm Northside and the Choppers MC Stockholm Southside were granted prospect status by the Hells Angels on July 28 and changed their names to MC Sweden Stockholm Northside and MC Sweden Stockholm Southside.

An anti-tank rocket traced to a February 1994 theft hit the MC Sweden clubhouse in Hasslarp, outside Helsingborg, on July 31. Another rocket missed its target. Police raided the Bandidos clubhouse that day and seized ammunition, explosives, and anabolic steroids.

The president of the Undertakers MC and two members assaulted the former president of MC Finland and stole his colors in August. Police later seized the colors from the Undertakers' MC clubhouse.

The Bandidos held their European meeting in Helsinki in August and promoted the Undertakers MC to the status of Bandidos probationary chapter.

Police arrested a member of MC Sweden Stockholm Southside for armed bank robbery on August 10.

Police seized a machine gun stolen from the Swedish army and drugs at the Bandidos clubhouse in Stockholm on August 17.

A hangaround of the Thunder HD Aaros in Olso, Norway, was caught with stolen Harley-Davidson motorcycles in a rented trailer stamped with the letters HD which he was hooking up to his car on September 8. Seven persons arrested by police admitted stealing twenty-four Harley-Davidson motorcycles in the Oslo area in 1994 and 1995.

After a shoot-out between the gangs on September 10, the car of a member of MC Sweden Stockholm Southside was found in Helsingborg with seven bullet holes and blood in it.

Members of MC Finland and MC Sweden assaulted the president of the Bandidos MC and a member in front of the Helsinki City Courthouse on September 27.

In October, Finnish and Danish Bandidos used baseball bats to wreck the inside of Tattoo Center in Helsinki, a business partially owned by the Hells Angels. The Hells Angels considered the attack an extremely serious insult to their gang and colors, and portrayed it as the Bandido Nation's attack on the entire Hells Angels organization.

Later in the month, Bandidos rushed into the Stardust restaurant in Copenhagen and attacked several Hells Angels having dinner. Two Hells Angels ran away, escaping through the women's toilet. The two bikers became the butt of many jokes among Copenhagen's tough bikers, who were well aware of the popular Bandidos patch, "Our colors don't run."

The Finnish government was ordered by court to pay $6,000 in compensation and trial costs to the Overkill MC (later to become Hells Angels) in November for damages caused to their clubhouse during a 1993 police raid.

On November 15, police seized a large stash of guns and explosives in the apartment of a Bandidos associate.

Shots were fired at the Outlaws' clubhouse in Oslo, Norway, on November 18. A former member of the South Florida chapter of the Outlaws had started the chapter, and sided with the Bandidos during the war.

Two Bandidos were arrested with weapons outside the MC Sweden clubhouse in Helsingborg on November 22.

Police in Djurslov, Sweden, arrested two MC Sweden prospects from the Malmö chapter outside the clubhouse on November 27 and found 81.6 kilos of Dynamex explosives and ten loaded guns in the car.

Members of MC Sweden Helsingborg and Bandidos MC Sweden shot at each other from their moving cars at a Helsingborg gas station on December 6. One MC Sweden Helsingborg member was hit in the leg.

Police raided the Hells Angels MC Norway clubhouse in Trondheim at 8 a.m. on December 17 and charged three members with the attempted murder of a member of MC Bronx 95.

The Swedish Hells Angels dissolved MC Sweden Stockholm Northside on December 23. Half the members were expelled in bad standing and the rest were transferred to MC Sweden Stockholm Southside.

Ten Bandidos stormed into a Copenhagen restaurant the Hells Angels used as a permanent meeting place on December 26 and severely beat a Hells Angel and his associate.

1996

To underline the importance of Denmark and the rest of Scandinavia in the Bandido Nation's scheme of things, the gang moved its European headquarters from Marseille to Copenhagen in 1996.

The Daily News in Ålborg, Denmark, reported under the headline "Hell's Angels Have a Heart" on January 18 that the Hells Angels in Ålborg had opened a fund-raising store where they sold Hells Angels' T-shirts, sunglasses, and marijuana pipes made by Hells Angels "newbies" (prospects). The store, run by "The Defense Fund Denmark" used the money to help Hells Angels who had been arrested. The gang planned to open similar stores in Copenhagen and Århus.

Police charged ten members of MC Norway in Oslo with the attempted murder of a member of the Outlaws MC who was shot in the shoulder in his car while parked outside the MC Norway clubhouse on January 26. The case against the ten persons was later dropped.

In February, grenades were thrown at a Helsinki bar owned by MC Finland and a Harley-Davidson repair shop linked to the gang.

A member of MC Sweden Stockholm Southside forced his way into a house in Stockholm on February 12, put a gun to a two-year-old boy's head, and forced the father to open a safe.

MC Sweden Helsingborg became a full-fledged Hells Angels chapter on February 27.

Two Danish bikers linked to MC Norway in Stavanger and five Norwegians were sentenced in Stavanger City Court in Norway on February 27 to seventeen years in jail for importing thirty kilos of hashish and one kilo of amphetamines from Denmark.

Police disarmed a grenade a Hells Angels MC Sweden prospect found rigged under the hood of his car in Helsingborg on February 29.

Two members of MC Finland attacked Bandidos' Finnish vice-president Jarkko Kokko and another member outside the Bandidos' clubhouse in Helsinki on March 1. Kokko died two weeks later.

MC Finland became a full-fledged Hells Angels chapter in Helsinki on March 23.

Police stopped a member of the Bandidos' South Island chapter in Denmark and found a bullet-proof vest, a balaclava, duct tape, and nunchuks in his car, as well as a loaded pistol in his belt on March 1.

Members of the Hells Angels and Bandidos drove into a downtown Helsingborg parking lot at lunch time and shot at each other on March 5. A Bandidos probationary member was injured.

Scandinavian Bandidos attended a party in Helsinki in early March while the Hells Angels attended a tattoo convention in the city. Members of both gangs were on flights from Fornebue airport (Oslo) and Kastrup airport (Copenhagen) on March 10. The Hells Angels called ahead to warn gang members to set up ambushes at both airports.

Bandido Uffe (Sir His) Larsen of the South Side chapter was shot and killed in the Kastrup parking lot. A Northland Bandidos chapter member was seriously injured. A probationary member and a hangaround were also injured. Six Hells Angels were later convicted in this shooting.

Swedish Bandido Lars Harnes survived a shot in the chest at Fornebue.

In the days following the shootings, police seized forty handguns from bikers in both countries.

Two Bandidos, most likely bodyguards for injured gang members, were arrested outside a Copenhagen hospital on March 11 with sawed-off shotguns.

Bandidos president Jim Tinndahn told a Danish newspaper in the spring of 1996 that the war with the Hells Angels was about respect. "This is about pride and honor. There will always be somebody ready to kill for that."

The Hells Angels MC South clubhouse in Snoldelev, twenty miles southwest of Copenhagen, was severely damaged by an anti-tank missile at 12:04 a.m. on April 11. Ninety miles away in Jutland, the clubhouse of the Danish Hells Angels' official hangaround gang, the Avengers MC in Ålborg, was severely damaged by an anti-tank missile at 4:20 a.m. Ten minutes later, the Hells Angels' clubhouse in Hasslarp outside Helsingborg was heavily damaged by two anti-tank rockets at 4:30 a.m.

Danish police found a loaded revolver on a member of the Heathens MC Roskilde as he left the Hells Angels South clubhouse on April 11. They raided the clubhouse and found eight pistols and a rifle.

Göteborg, Sweden, police searched the Gamlestan MC Göteborg clubhouse and found three illegal loaded handguns on April 12.

The Bandidos attacked two Danish Hells Angels' clubhouses simultaneously on April 17 with anti-tank rockets: HA South in Snoldelev, and the Avengers in Ålborg. The second missile did not detonate.

Stockholm police raided the MC Sweden Stockholm Southside clubhouse on April 22 and found a grenade, two homemade bombs, ammunition, and robbery tools.

Morten Borup (Traeben) Christiansen, 27, vice-president of the Bandidos' Southside chapter, was badly injured when a Hells Angel cut through a perimeter fence at Horserød prison north of Copenhagen on April 26 and tossed a grenade into his cell before spraying it with machine gun bullets. Christiansen's wooden leg, the legacy of a motorcycle accident, absorbed much of the grenade's impact. Police found an automatic rifle near a hole cut in the fence.

Two Bandidos threw Swedish grenades and shot at two Hells Angels and a woman as they left a house in the south Copenhagen suburb of Broenshoej on May 7. Hells Angel Brian (Bremse—The Brake) Jacobsen, 31, was saved by his body armor, but had one leg amputated below the knee.

The Swedish Hells Angels were aware by May 1996 that they had offended their countrymen's sensibilities by flaunting their racist attitudes with white-power tattoos and Nazi insignia worn on the colors in the way Hells Angels dressed in California in the 1960s. Sonny Barger had ordered the Hells Angels in 1969 to remove Nazi insignia and colored wings earned for the performance of sexual acts that included intercourse with a cadaver and oral sex on a menstruating woman. The Hells Angels cleaned up their image for fear of offending the public, who might turn to politicians and demand that they clean up the biker problem. Scandinavian bikers lived in a time warp. They still surrounded themselves with Nazi paraphernalia in the 1990s, and publicly voiced their racist beliefs. Orders from California forced them to tone down their image in 1996. The Hells Angels are avid internet surfers. Some of the more politically aware members noticed discussions in the Swedish media about banning Nazi insignia. Part of the German government's case against the Hells Angels in Hamburg that allowed them to seize their clubhouse and ban their colors in 1983 was the gang's use of swastikas and other Nazi emblems. To this day, German Hells Angels carry their colors in suitcases when they leave the country and don them only when they leave German airspace. The Hells Angels sergeant-at-arms for the Malmö chapter in southern Sweden sent a stern letter to all Hells Angels in May 1996: "All Nazi insignia and racist patches have to be removed immediately. That is an order."

* * *

A Danish Bandido wrote this letter to a Texas Bandido in June 1996. It illustrates how active the gang was at gathering intelligence on the enemy. Even though the man was in Denmark, he had information about the Hells Angels all over the world.

The HA chapter that closed on the small island in Denmark have some former members (not HA anymore). We have got contact with one of them. He have informed us about a lot of things.

Sons of Silence, and another club in Arizona, have been to a HA world-run and you only go there when you start probating in HA. Our source told us that they are wearing their own colors, to keep it secret.

The HA plan is to start up chapters in the southern states, wherever they can. They have supposed to have started a chapter in Chicago too (also undercover).

Info Europe

HA England, Germany, and Sweden wants trouble. They are afraid that Outlaws Midlands will become Bandidos. I will send some more info about that on a fax. HA Germany are afraid that Bones will become Bandidos, and even more afraid that they will become Outlaws.

HA Germany, England, and Sweden are trying to put pressure on HA Denmark, and France, to do something, because they didn't do anything in the start to avoid the Bandido problem, and now they get the blame. It's HA Denmark's opinion that Bandidos Denmark are the biggest organizers, starting up chapters everywhere, and therefore the biggest problem. But HA Denmark are not interested in any trouble, because they think that Bandidos Denmark are more organized than themselves, and they know very little about us, so they are very insecure, and the main problem for HA Denmark, are that we are so big now, that they can't close us down, and they desagree a lot how to deal with us. Some chapters are more afraid that Outlaws (USA) will spread in Europe, so they think that it would be better to co-operated with us instead.

The sources opinion is that we are in a strong position, because the HA are not on a friendly level with each other. England, Germany, and Holland, have split up, and have a lot of trouble inbetween.

I think we have to watch our backs all around the world, just in case.

All this is difficult to explain to people that never have been to Europe, but try to explain to our American brothers to be carefull about the southern territory, because this information is to be taken very seriously.

It's difficult for me to tell everything in a letter. I talked to this guy for 2 hours.

Is it possible to find an undercover address, for letters like this. If possible send the adress to: [me].

During a trip to Sweden in June 1996, I addressed law enforcement officials and politicians from every level in a lecture theater at the national police headquarters. Outlaw motorcycle gangs and their violence was a recent phenomenon for them, and I described their evolution and warned them what they could expect in the current war between the Hells Angels and Bandidos. Unlike their counterparts in North America, police administrators in Scandinavia were eager to tackle and end the biker problem. Their primary concern was not careers, but public safety and police honor. They took their job seriously.

The Nordic war was fueled not only by a sense of territoriality, but by men with the moral sensibilities of seven-year-olds and the egos of two-year-olds. The back-and-forth attacks and retributions reverberated in a senseless frenzy of bullets and bombs as each side soothed bruised egos and tried to instill fear and wear down the enemy.

*   *   *

An Uzi submachine gun, a sawed-off shotgun and a grenade were found in a Hells Angels' house on June 19.

Police arrested two Swedish Bandidos in a stolen car near the home of a Hells Angel in Helsingborg, Sweden, on July 8.

A Bandido found a bomb in a van parked near the clubhouse in Nykøbing, Denmark, on July 10.

Swedish Bandido Jan Krogh-Jensen, 37, was shot to death east of Drammen on July 15.

A Hells Angel was shot in downtown Oslo on July 20.

A Bandido threw a bomb that failed to explode at the Hells Angels' clubhouse in Titangade, Denmark, on July 21.

A Bandido was shot in the leg as he drove near the Hells Angels' clubhouse in Helsingborg on July 23.

Hells Angels spokesman and convicted murderer Jorn (Jonke) Nielsen was seriously shot in the stomach and chest in Denmark's Jyderup low-security prison on July 25 when someone fired a machine gun through the cell door.

Bandidos president Jim Tinndahn issued a statement to the Oslo newspaper *Aftenposten* on July 31 about police pressure on the bikers—raids, surveillance, evictions from clubhouses, deportations, and tax audits: "If the police continue this, we'll see a lot of violence in the streets. We will defy them."

Two men in a stolen car fired six bullets into a private bus on August 4 and hit Hells Angel Conny (Mummel) Wickman of the Malmö chapter in the stomach. Wickman was returning home from a drag-bike tournament.

Police found two assault rifles and a grenade believed to belong to the Bandidos in a bag in a field near the Hells Angels' clubhouse in Helsingborg on August 8.

Two probationary Bandidos were shot at—one was hit in the shoulder—in their car outside the clubhouse in Dalby, Sweden, on August 14.

A Bandido was arrested with a 9-mm semi-automatic pistol outside the Malmö courthouse where a Hells Angel was on trial on August 26.

The Hells Angels and the Bandidos shot at each other in downtown Helsingborg on August 27.

A member of the Hells Angels' Helsingborg chapter was shot in the legs and foot near his home in Helsingborg on August 28.

*   *   *

By September, the citizens of Copenhagen felt their city had become a war zone. People avoided neighborhoods which had biker clubhouses for fear of being shot or injured by an explosion. The mayor of Copenhagen ordered the Hells Angels to vacate their clubhouse in September 1996.

The Hells Angels refused to leave the building they rented from the city under a law that provides low-rent facilities to clubs and organizations.

*   *   *

A Danish Hells Angel was wounded in a drive-by shooting of the Hells Angels clubhouse in Alborg on September 2.

A car bomb exploded in a car driven by a Hells Angel in Ålborg on September 4. No one was injured.

Police arrested seventeen Hells Angels and found eight guns in a search of houses in Malmö and Helsingborg on September 10.

A car bomb exploded at the Hells Angels' clubhouse in Roskilde, Denmark, on September 12.

Police responding to a shooting in downtown Helsingborg on September 15 found a car with fifteen bullet holes. The next day, police found a machine gun with silencer, a shotgun, and two grenades in a stolen car driven by a Hells Angel.

Two snipers using a hunting rifle and a submachine gun fired more than 250 shots at the Danish Hells Angels' clubhouse in Roskilde on September 22. A member was slightly injured.

The Hells Angels' clubhouse outside Helsingborg was hit by an anti-tank rocket on September 24.

Four days later, another anti-tank rocket was fired at the Hells Angels' clubhouse in Helsingborg. It veered off course when it hit a wire and pierced a storage shed that held debris from the earlier rocket attack. Two grenades and a smoke grenade were also thrown at the building. Police found two more grenades on the roof of an adjoining house.

Danish prime minister Poul Rasmussen said in a speech to Parliament on October 1, "People are frightened of the motorcycle gangs, which are putting the lives of ordinary people at risk with their internecine rivalry. People are terrified of the violence and drugs, of open narcotics trading in the streets. We cannot accept this." Prime Minister Rasmussen discussed enacting emergency legislation to allow police to tap phones and search property without warrants. The legislation broadened police powers and doubled the maximum penalty for illegal possession of weapons to four years in prison. Police were also able to confiscate money or property if a suspect was unable to prove it was legally obtained.

A proposed new Hells Angels' clubhouse in Malmö was severely damaged by a heavy bomb that exploded at 3 a.m. on October 3. Four Hells Angels in the building were not hurt, but surrounding buildings were damaged and twenty people living across the street, including a four-month-old baby, were cut by flying glass. Later that day, Malmö police commissioner Hans

Wranghult evicted the Hells Angels from their clubhouses in Malmö and Hels-ingborg. The Hells Angels were subsequently prohibited from entering their clubhouses for one month. More than a hundred citizens protested against the Hells Angels the next day.

Legislation was tabled in the Danish parliament on October 4 to prevent bikers from setting up clubhouses in residential neighborhoods.

The Bandidos MC Downtown probationary chapter in Helsinki became an official chapter on October 5, 1996.

*   *   *

The Nordic war claimed its first innocent victim on Sunday, October 6, during the Hells Angels' annual Viking Party at their heavily-fortified Fort 1 clubhouse on Titangade in the popular Noerrebro district in central Copenhagen. About 150 police officers guarded the building as three hundred bikers celebrated the chapter's tenth anniversary. At 3:05 a.m., a Bandidos prospect aimed from the sloped roof of an adja-cent building and fired a Carl Gustav anti-tank rocket through the club-house's brick wall. Hells Angel prospect Louis Nielsen, 38, died, along with Janne Krohn, 29, a neighbor who had accepted the gang's invita-tion to party. Nineteen others were injured, some badly.

The violence stunned the Danish public, who had seen the Hells Angels as an integral part of their pop culture, warts and all. People knew the Hells Angels sold drugs and weren't to be messed with, but they figured they caused no harm to those outside the biker underworld. It was easy to avoid dealing with the problem when the problem lurked in the shadows. But the missile attack on the clubhouse punched a hole through the thin veil of naivete behind which the citizens of Copen-hagen hid. An innocent woman's death could not be dismissed as just one of those underworld settlings of accounts. Ignorant acceptance metamorphosed into a fear that spurred political action.

Bandidos president Jim Tinndahn said on Danish television on Octo-ber 7, "We want it stopped because it is hurting many innocent biker clubs and can hurt many innocent people as well. The Bandidos think this has gone far enough."

Detective Commander Per Larsen of Copenhagen said the following week that fear over the biker war was unfounded. "There is no danger from the gangs to anyone in Denmark. The groups are fighting one another, and no innocent bystander has yet been hurt. If two groups really want to kill each other, the police in a modern democracy can do little to prevent it happening."

The prime ministers from Sweden and Denmark met with the justice ministers from the four Scandinavian countries on October 11 to discuss new legislation, strict enforcement, and seizures of drug dealers' assets. Police from the four Scandinavian countries agreed to form a task force.

Police raided Bandidos clubhouses and fifty residences in Sweden on October 14.

The Danish parliament banned biker clubhouses in residential neighborhoods on October 16. Civil libertarians stood up for the bikers. "We are witnessing an unfortunate evolution in Danish society," said Morten Kjaerum, director of the Danish Center for Human Rights, "where specific minority groups have been targeted by particular laws which are susceptible to future use against other marginal interests." As always, the civil libertarians forgot about the most important minority group of all: the victims. The Hells Angels and Bandidos met discreetly at their homes and continued to wear their body armor. More than 150 police officers in Copenhagen alone followed the bikers twenty-four hours a day.

A Helsingborg police detective was arrested on October 23 for allegedly providing the Hells Angels with information about the Bandidos. He claimed he was innocent, but resigned. There were corrupt policemen all over Sweden, and the National Police were careful who they dealt with. During my trips to Sweden I was told who I could safely talk to outside the National Police: no one. Without jest, in the nearly twenty-five years I have been involved in this area, I have learned to not even speak to myself, as a precaution against listening devices.

*   *   *

A car bomb exploded at the Hells Angels' clubhouse in Oslo on October 30, the day the prospect gang became a full-fledged Hells Angels chapter.

Six Hells Angels and associates went on trial in a heavily secured Copenhagen courthouse on November 11 for the shooting and murder at Copenhagen airport. Two were convicted of manslaughter.

Thirty-one Swedish grenades and three kilos of military explosives were found near the Bandidos clubhouse on November 18.

Two Bandidos were shot in the legs outside a house in Horsens, Denmark, on November 22.

The Hells Angels and Bandidos had another shootout in downtown Copenhagen on December 1.

Two Bandidos hangarounds were shot, one in the arm and one in the leg, during a gunfight outside a restaurant in the Copenhagen suburb of Valby on December 5.

A Danish Bandido from the Ålborg chapter was seriously injured on December 9 when a car with four Hells Angels drove by and one of them fired ten shots from an M-75 machine gun into the Bandidos' car in downtown Ålborg.

*　　*　　*

The German Hells Angels contacted the German magazine *Biker News* in December 1996 and granted them an interview in which an unidentified German Hells Angel merged fact and fiction in an effort to sanitize the gang's image, tarnished in the Scandinavian war with the Bandidos. The interview was part of the Hells Angels' disinformation campaign to blame the Bandidos and police for starting the war. The article deals with many issues I raised in the Scandinavian media in an attempt to explain the origins of the war and ways to end it. The article also illustrates the time-honored Hells Angels' ploy of hinting at a subversive police conspiracy to undermine the gang. The Hells Angels have made such claims since the 1960s in California to rationalize the thousands of convictions against gang members. In the world of criminals and spies, the only answer when caught is deny, deny, deny. The Hells Angels would not give detailed interviews to other media, and it is the only in-depth view of the war from their distorted perspective. The December 20 article was translated by Hells Angel Django in Hamburg, and copies were sent to all Hells Angels around the world.

BN: For some months the biker scene and the press have speculated about the reasons for the troubles between the Hells Angels and the Bandidos in Scandinavia. Most newspaper and magazine reports, based on information supplied by the police, have published that it has something to do with the domination of drug markets, prostitution, and the expansion into new markets in the East, especially into the Baltic States. Others think it is a question of honor that started with a fight between members of both clubs. How did it really start?

HA: First of all, it has nothing to do with drug markets. The police especially, and all others who are informed, know which people really have control of these markets.

It all started in the late summer of 1993. The Bandidos wanted a meeting in Paris with Hells Angels Europe. They were represented by their National President—USA, their National Secretary—USA, and members of the future Bandidos club in Denmark, also Jim Tinndahn [who is today President of Bandidos Denmark].

The meeting was to establish guidelines so the Bandidos could exist in

Europe without any problems. This in itself shows we had nothing against the Bandidos at all. They were a good club with a very good reputation, and for a long time we had a good relationship with them in the USA. We wanted to have the same relationship with them in Europe. The agreement was, the Bandidos could do whatever they wanted to in Europe, but they were going to inform us about any new people they took on, just to make sure that the newcomers had not caused any problems for us in the past. This was a clear agreement. They could move into new areas, but not with people who caused problems. This agreement was broken a short time later by the Bandidos.

BN: Especially by Bandidos Denmark, or by European Bandidos?

HA: By Bandidos International, because the American Bandidos replaced their National President with a new man who declared the agreement was no longer binding. At the same time, Tinndahn started to move over into Sweden and recruited guys who had caused problems, not only with us but also within the whole biker scene. He filled his club, formerly the Morticians and later the Undertakers, a club with a good reputation, with this dirt. That's the bottom line of the whole story.

BN: Were there also former Bullshit members involved? [The Bullshit were a club who over a long time made serious problems for the Hells Angels that resulted in many killings.]

HA: That's right! Former Bullshit members and also members who had been dishonorably kicked out of other Danish clubs, and some EX-members of ours also kicked out dishonorably. Tinndahn recruited all that garbage, and it's clear that such a sick mixture produces more sick things. For example, one of these ex-members from HA Denmark was a right-wing extremist. It is not that we didn't see this in a democratic way, but this guy was 100% Nazi and we as Hells Angels do not identify ourselves with the right wing; our way of life doesn't fit in with Nazis. I personally hate those guys, and I don't want to be compared to those motherfuckers of the right-wing scene, like some newspapers have already published about us. So this guy was kicked out because of his extreme right-wing mind, and he was taken on by the Bandidos to keep active in it.

BN: Is there a specific political attitude for the Hells Angels?

HA: No. We are neutral as far as political parties are concerned. Every member has his individual political convictions. The limit comes when it starts to get extreme like that Nazi shit that is opposed to our philosophy of life.

BN: Back in Scandinavia, exactly what started the trouble?

HA: It started in Sweden when a hangaround for our applicant club in Helsingborg was shot in a bar by a Bandido.

BN: Were there Bandidos at that time? When were they officially founded in Denmark, or Scandinavia, for that matter?

HA: The foundation of the Bandidos in Scandinavia was a fact after the meeting in Paris in the late summer of 1993.

BN: To move a bit further forward, was it at that time that some rockets were stolen that were later used against Hells Angels' clubhouses in Scandinavia?

HA: Yes, ten bazookas were stolen at this time. Looking back from today's point of view, this is an important fact in the whole story. Something about this theft is very, very strange, and the police must have known very early on who had taken possession of the rockets. Later on it became clear that the initial peaceful co-existence between the clubs in Denmark was based on a deception from the very beginning, but at the Danish Super Rally, for example, both clubs were sitting together in the same tent. It was a deception by the Bandidos, because at that time they were secretly planning actions against us. We have recently received information that has confirmed our earlier suspicions. One-and-a-half to two years ago the Bandidos president, Tinndahn, got a phone call from the Danish police, and later on two Danish police met two Bandidos by the side of a freeway. The cops gave the Bandidos a detailed plan of Hells Angels' South clubhouse, which is due south from Copenhagen; they also gave them the security rota's [rotations] for our members looking after the clubhouse, plus the times when the police would not be doing any surveillance on the clubhouse. They also asked the Bandidos if they wanted to carry on taking action against the Hells Angels. This was a straight-forward offer of cooperation and Tinndahn accepted! The Bandidos made themselves tools for sections of the Danish police, and worked together with them. That is the background.

BN: Is there any proof of this accusation?

HA: Someone warned us early on, but we don't want to say who told us. But it comes full circle with Tinndahn's interview with a radio station a short while ago when he confirmed this himself. We believe he's scared for his own dirty life, because what would be easier for this particular police squad in Denmark than to liquidate him and put our people in the frame? He has covered his own arse with this interview.

BN: If you really believe that part of the Danish police force would liquidate someone, are you also insinuating that some of the attackers were not members of the biker scene?

HA: There are many curious things about this case. Possibly this police force has instigated these actions, and maybe they took part themselves, because in the years between the Paris meeting and the beginning of the well-organized attacks on us, a special police squad called the "Bravo Team" was formed in Copenhagen. Those guys attacked our people in a way never experienced before; even German clubs found it hard to believe what was happening. Our Danish lawyers counted every case of the "Bravo Team" against us, and believe it or not, it added up to a couple of thousand! Chargeable offenses were about 800 to 900. We don't know if the former "Bravo Team" or the "Secret Service" are behind all the cases, but if you saw how they worked and how they were not restrained when they broke the laws they were meant to be upholding, then you can easily imagine that they did more than just making tools out of the Bandidos. It would also explain much more of what has happened in Denmark. Everybody within the German and foreign club scene, also lawyers, friends and supporters, were asking how it could be possible to fire eight or nine rockets and yet nobody had been arrested. If you kept an eye on the details, it becomes clear from the information that the police force started and tolerated everything, and that they were responsible for it.

BN: But didn't the police throw a massive security cordon around your clubhouse in Copenhagen to prevent any attack?

HA: If I had gone to the Viking party where the attack caused two deaths, then I would have been subjected to total police control and would have probably had my vitamin pills confiscated as being drugs. They would have searched me three times! The clubhouse was surrounded by two circles of 150 cops. Nobody can tell me that somebody could have sneaked through with two five-foot bazookas, climbed up onto a roof and fired a rocket, and then disappeared without the police knowing; but I'm not saying they did it themselves. Everybody who was going to the party got searched. All guests, both male and female, were searched several times, but they sneaked through with the bazooka? And after the attack it took about fifteen minutes before the police started to make a search. While the burned guests were getting out of the clubhouse and then standing outside on the street, the cops were just lying down on the ground. A chaotic scene, but the attackers had fifteen, twenty minutes to escape. So the question is, did the cops really want to catch them, and did they know in advance about an attack?

BN: Hypothetically, if they knew in advance or were involved, how would it be to their advantage?

HA: On the weekend when the bazooka was fired at the clubhouse, everyone knew that on the following Wednesday the Danish parliament was to consider introducing a new law which should have no place in a constitutional state. Previously the vote from the Danish politicians was about 50% each way, but after the attack no politician was able to vote against it. Strangely, after the law was passed some Bandidos were arrested, one for another crime, and five here and some more there. It is clear that the police got exactly what they wanted. They now have a law that gives them the power to stop people from entering their own clubhouses (a contravention means two years in jail); they can also forbid our people from entering their own flats because their presence endangers people in the area; they can also forbid us from entering our own business premises. If someone considers themselves to be in danger due to the presence of a club member, even in a supermarket, the cops can throw him out. Furthermore, bugging rooms, and raids without a judge's approval have been approved. The police wanted these powers all along and now with the help of the Bandidos they have these powers. And after they got this power they gathered up their tools.

BN: Do you condemn the Bandidos for willingly working with the police to grow larger under their protective shield, or do we understand you correctly when we say you think the police just used the Bandidos to make their own plans become reality?

HA: The second. That's how we see it. For years we had very good, big, and popular bike shows in Scandinavia; we had shops, and all this was systematically destroyed by the police. For example, we never had serious problems at the showgrounds, but they were closed down. But the police couldn't achieve it by themselves, and so they searched for some helpers, the Bandidos. Every Bandido is a fucking tool of the police. They not only broke their word, given in Paris, but also became tools.

BN: To ask again, clearly: tools with complete knowledge or not full understanding about the case and the consequences?

HA: I don't know what I.Q. a cockroach has, but I'm sure they knew exactly what they were doing. They couldn't resist the temptation to secretly become bigger under the protection of the police. That's why Tinndahn did it. He was a nothing, a nobody, before the American Bandidos accepted him as a member. Because of the hierarchical structure of the Danish Bandidos, he has since then become the ultimate power above all others. The people he collected into his club are similar motherfuckers. That's the bottom line. Something happened in Denmark that should never have happened. They were all people who had been kicked out of the bike scene or their own clubs dishonorably, and they shouldn't have been allowed to come back. In Denmark they made it under the name of the Bandidos, and that's why everything escalated. That's why they made themselves into tools for the police. I cannot imagine that any club in Germany would be that stupid. If people don't believe that the Scandinavian police would commit such activities, then they should look at the parallels to the assassination of Olof Palme. [The former Swedish prime minister was killed in 1986 and the circumstances have never been cleared up.] Many things were hushed up by the police who were probably involved in the assault but they won't allow investigation within their own ranks.

BN: Today, there is no disputing that the fight between both clubs has caused very negative effects throughout the entire scene, not only in Denmark but also internationally. Meetings between Scandinavian and Hamburg officials are in progress because of the Hells Angels ban of 1983, but the escalation was caused by both sides' activities and because Bandidos members got killed. Could a peaceful solution have been found when the confrontation was not so serious?

HA: The answer is simple. We can only say that, as German Hells Angels, if someone opens fire on us, we don't go to the nearest police station. Anyway, how can you talk to someone that you had met officially three years before in Paris, only later to find out it was all for nothing, and when you finally realize what garbage they take into their club, you will also know that talking to them is a waste of time.

BN: You say, in your opinion, that talking peace makes no sense and you don't want to talk to them at all, yet on the other hand, isn't it a fact that in a TV interview the Bandido president made an offer of peace or armistice to you?

HA: We can't consider it because he's unbelievable. The Danish bikers don't believe him, and even the Danish police said they don't believe him. If you know the Bandido system and Tinndahn's influence within it, all you have to consider is that two days after his "peace offer" a car bomb exploded in front of our Oslo clubhouse and destroyed it.

BN: If you believe that the police are capable or directly involved, isn't it also possible that such an attack was done by somebody else to destroy any such peace talks?

HA: Maybe yes, but it's not our job to find out if Tinndahn organized it or not. Fortunately nobody was in the clubhouse and so nobody got hurt, but there were amazing similarities to many of the attacks in Denmark.

BN: Why do you think that so many of the attacks before the Viking party were not heard of? Was there the intention not to hurt or kill anybody, or was it just luck?

HA: We definitely believe that there was no such intention! First of all, it would indicate that professional soldiers had done the job, which these people definitely are not. Secondly, there was a lot of luck for us involved in most attacks. When firing at the South clubhouse for example, the rocket penetrated the outside wall, passed close by an old lady's face, broke through a thin wall, and then flew over a member who was lying down on his bed; it then exploded in the gym. It is impossible to control this from the outside. At that time fourteen members were living at the clubhouse. At another attack on the Helsingborg clubhouse the rocket probably hit a wooden beam at an angle and flew off over the clubhouse before exploding in a neighbor's pool. This was also very lucky as there was a party going on and the clubhouse was full. It is remarkable that on every occasion the attackers could disappear, even though the police knew about the potential danger at clubhouses. The attackers had prepared themselves; they had all the time they needed to do their thing and then to disappear. This is remarkable and not an accident!

It reminds us of the events in California in the late '70s when a special police squad called BET [bikers' enforcement team] tried to start a war between Hells Angels California and the Mongols California. Dynamite was found under a Mongols car; later on, one of these special squad cops, Barnes, admitted in court that the police had planted it. We suspect, although we have no proof, that the escalation and heavy hostility of the Scandinavian police was also started after FBI activities years ago across the whole of Europe, where they found accommodating partners in Denmark and Germany. There was an Interpol summit in Scandinavia shortly before the confrontations began.

BN: Was the Bravo Team also a special police squad like the BET team?

HA: Yes of course, but such activities not only happened in California but in Canada as well. The clubhouse in Montreal, for example, got filled with gas and exploded. The whole clubhouse exploded, but the police didn't plan it well enough and so other buildings in the neighborhood were destroyed as well. Fortunately it was possible to prove that the attack had been committed by the police, and therefore high-ranking police officers lost their jobs. For those people who cannot imagine that the police commit such crimes, they have already done it! They started such cases in the past, they are continuing to do it, and we are sure they will do more in the future. That's the point: we had decided not to comment to the public, as none of it made any sense. A part of the press in Denmark is fair, but others, especially the conservative boulevard press, just throw dirt and wallow in the blood at the scene. That's why we will definitely not do any more interviews in Denmark. Within the past two years the Danish Bandidos have been able to damage the whole of the Danish bike scene so badly that at the moment it is impossible to say if it is reparable or not. For many years many people combined to form this scene, filled it with life, and made it great with bike shows, Harley shops, and made good publicity; but this wild mixed Bandido scrapheap has set a heavy damage on it, with instructions and possibly active support from the Danish police! If anyone else maintains that we have given any other interviews on this subject, it is a lie.

BN: What are the opinions of the other Danish bike clubs on this confrontation?

HA: Except one or two clubs who sympathize with the Bandidos, all other clubs are definitely against them and what they are doing. It is also difficult to forcast how this will continue because many members from other clubs were wounded in the attack at Copenhagen. Nobody is able to say if or how this problem can be settled.

BN: Do your opinions apply to all Bandidos or are they limited to their Scandinavian chapters?

HA: It is regrettable that a club like the Bandidos USA, who had an excellent reputation in Europe, should agree with what has happened in Denmark. It's hard to understand because this reputation is gone now. Either the Texas Bandidos cannot yet see how much of their reputation and respect the Bandidos have lost, or they simply don't care about it. Both attitudes should be condemned.

BN: So do you think that the American Bandidos really support their Scandinavian chapters, or that possibly they don't know everything about these people's backgrounds, or they don't agree with what they're doing at all?

HA: If you understand what a solid club the Bandidos USA are and always have been—for instance, they kicked out four members right after the Paris meeting for making statements to the police—then there is only one explanation. They do back their Bandidos' patch and also their Danish brothers, but we cannot believe or imagine that this good, long-established U.S. club really knows who they've given their name to. That's why we also cannot believe that they know the true background and tolerate people in their club who are tools for the police.

BN: After a Danish commission visited Hamburg officials to learn about the ban on the Hamburg Hells Angels, it's possible that everything creates international consequences today, especially in Germany. How can the Scandinavian situation be stopped from spreading over into Germany?

HA: First of all, we want to explain briefly the facts about the Hamburg ban. In 1983 there was a big raid, but even before there were any charges the state secretary (minister of internal affairs) declared that the Hells Angels MC Hamburg Germany were illegal, but only the Hamburg chapter. The ban was never confirmed by the criminal court; Hells Angels Hamburg has never been banned by any criminal court. Today's ban is only based on an administrative law, which is normally never tolerated in a democratic state with a constitution, because this type of law needs no proof of guilt: it's enough that the court thinks that the suspects have done what's happened. This law would be difficult to transfer over to Scandinavia, but they may possibly try to introduce such a law.

BN: It sticks out in many newspaper articles that the Scandinavian situation and the "background" are similar, and that when German Hells Angels are mentioned the impression is given that the entire MC has been sentenced and banned for criminal conspiracy.

HA: It is important to explain that only Hells Angels Hamburg are banned and only because of suspected criminal activity, nothing else. But to return to your earlier question, it is difficult to say what it all means for Germany. We want it made clear for all the German clubs, that's why we have made an exception and given you this interview; if we have the same confrontations here in Germany it will be deadly for the entire bike scene. Deadly in the way that nobody can win. Such occurrences would damage the German scene so badly that every club would lose.

To make it clear, everybody in Germany who supports or joins the Bandidos would be the same as them, a cockroach. We are sure that not even a small club in Germany would make the mistake to open their doors for people who have been dishonorably kicked out of the scene, because if such a sick mixture should start growing here it would become a threat to our entire evolution here as well. This is why we have given this interview to the *Bikers News* and not to any newspapers, radio, or TV stations. We contacted the *Bikers News* to make the situation clear and we hope that from now on it will open people's eyes once and forever.

1997

Kim (Slim) Thrysoe, 26, a member of MC Denmark in Ålborg, was shot to death at 10:10 p.m. on January 10 in his car in downtown Ålborg. Police arrested seventeen Bandidos associates.

A Hells Angels' attempt to assassinate a Bandidos president on January 13 turned into a gunfight outside his house in Ödåkra, near Helsingborg, where he lived with the widow of murdered Bandidos president Joe Ljunggren. Later that night, a member of MC Sweden in Stockholm was treated in the emergency department of a nearby hospital for a bullet wound to the shoulder.

The Hells Angels used the first of a shipment of Russian-made anti-tank missiles they bought to counter Bandidos attacks against their clubhouses on February 2. They fired a missile into the cell of Bandido Poul Bjorn (Liller) Andersen in Køge, Denmark at 4:08 a.m. The heat generated by the rocket set part of the jail on fire, but Andersen was not injured because the walls were not resistant enough to detonate the explosive. Andersen was sentenced to eleven years in 1996 for killing Hells Angel Brian Paluden Jacobsen.

The Hells Angels and Bandidos shot it out once again in Copenhagen on February 2. One member from each gang was injured.

The Hells Angels fired an anti-tank rocket into the jail housing two Bandidos in Holbæk, Denmark, at 1:25 a.m. on February 18. The rocket passed through two cells before it hit a wall without detonating.

The Hells Angels fired an anti-tank rocket at the home of a Danish Bandido who wasn't there. His girlfriend was shaken.

*   *   *

MC Sweden in Stockholm became a full-fledged Hells Angels chapter on Thursday, February 27. I watched on a relatively warm winter day as the MC Sweden sign was replaced with a Hells Angels MC Stockholm sign with the gang's logo, the Death Head. I was in Stockholm to address police officers, prosecutors, and politicians who made up the four-country task force dedicated to ending the biker war. I had spoken to the media about the biker war and the Hells Angels often since my previous trip to Sweden in 1996. Media from the Scandinavian countries called frequently for interviews and a Danish television team traveled to Canada to interview me. Needless to say, my profile concerned security experts. Sweden's crack counter-terrorist unit did a threat assessment before my arrival and found out that the Hells Angels had branded me public enemy No. 1 and were actively seeking me out to kill me. Steps were taken to ensure that I had a pleasant and informative stay in the country. It is always a pleasure to deal with real professionals.

In an attempt to arm the Scandinavians with more intelligence, I arranged for conference organizers to invite Ted Baltas, head of tactical intelligence on bikers for the U.S. Treasury's Bureau of Alcohol, Tobacco, and Firearms. He brought along his boss, Ted Royster, chief of intelligence for the ATF. I had hoped to build better communications between law enforcement agencies in North America and Europe because both the Hells Angels and Bandidos traveled extensively between the continents.

I also wished to introduce Europeans to American agencies other than the Federal Bureau of Investigation, which courted the Danish justice minister aggressively in the fall of 1996. The FBI flew the justice minister to Washington to meet officials who promised to help the Danes fight the bikers if Denmark allowed the FBI to open a four-man bureau there to monitor them. The FBI had no intention of monitoring bikers in Europe—it hardly monitored them in the United States. The FBI has a tendency to think that once it wraps up a large operation, the problem disappears. At the end of Operation Cacus in 1987, the handful of FBI agents interested in outlaw bikers were assigned to other investigations. The only other major FBI biker investigation ended in 1985. Arrogant FBI administrators have repeatedly refused to accept outlaw bikers as an ongoing organized crime problem worthy of a permanent task force. Consequently, the agency uses its Washington clout to muscle its way into successful investigations by state and local authorities. The FBI tried to use the Danish justice minister's need of help to plant on Danish soil an economic espionage detection team. The FBI has no mandate to operate outside the United States, although it often resorts to subterfuge to do so. The FBI also approached authorities in New Zealand to set up a biker investigation office there. Its true purpose is unknown, but it certainly has nothing to do with bikers.

I saw evidence once again on Friday, February 28, that Americans think the world can't operate without them. I was invited to an afternoon reception at the U.S. Embassy in Stockholm. An hour after I arrived I was asked to step into the office of the media relations officer. He got The New York Times correspondent in London on the telephone and I was interviewed about the new Hells Angels chapter in Stockholm. I did not stay around to hear Ted Baltas's interview or listen to information given to the reporter by the media relations officer. Hundreds of police and intelligence officers blockaded the streets leading to the new Hells Angels clubhouse where three hundred bikers celebrated all weekend. It was strictly a Scandinavian operation, with police officers from the four countries. The ATF was there as an observer, at my request. *The New York Times* article appeared on the front page on March 3, with my name misspelled and quotes put into my mouth. That was the least of my concerns. The subhead pointed to a curious paragraph. "Aided by the U.S., Scandinavia leans on biker gangs."

> The police here and in Norway, Finland, and Denmark are operating with the United States Drug Enforcement Administration, and the Treasury's Bureau of Alcohol, Tobacco, and Firearms. Theodore C. Baltas II, an agent from the bureau who was here this weekend, said a joint task force had been set up. "It is the least we can do," Mr. Baltas said this afternoon. "After all, we exported the problem to them. Containing it has got to be a multinational effort."

Sweden is more than seven hundred years old. Its intelligence and law enforcement agencies have at least five hundred more years of experience and history than American agencies. The only help they need on their soil during tactical operations is information.

*   *   *

A Bandido was shot in the legs as he left his house on March 4.

A Bandidos motorcycle shop in Oslo was bombed on March 13.

The Hells Angels' clubhouse outside Helsingborg was hit for the fifth time with an anti-tank rocket on March 22. Again, it did not explode.

A grenade was thrown into a Bandido's house in Ålborg, Denmark, on March 23.

A Hells Angel was shot in the head on a Copenhagen street on April 1.

Three shots were fired into a Bandido's house in Horsens on April 4.

The war claimed its second innocent bystander as a bomb exploded outside a Bandido's house in downtown Drammen, Norway, on April 6 and killed one person and injured another in a passing car.

Bombs exploded simultaneously at the Aphuset, clubhouse and a garage used by the Bandidos on April 28. Some members of Aphuset patch over to Bandidos. The same garage was bombed again on May 1. That day, a jailed Bandido received (by mail) a bomb planted inside an electric razor. It failed to explode.

The Hells Angels and Bandidos shot at each other from two cars in downtown Ålborg on May 12. Two of three Bandidos hit by bullets are seriously injured.

*   *   *

A devastating car bomb flattened the Bandidos' clubhouse outside Drammen, at 11:45 p.m. Wednesday, June 4, and claimed the war's third innocent victim, a 51-year-old woman who drove by with her husband as the bomb exploded. The two-story building was reduced to rubble and three Bandidos sleeping on the second floor fell to the ground, unhurt, as the building collapsed. They ran away clad only in underwear. Irene Astrid Bekkevold was killed in the passenger seat of the family car. She was only feet from the bomb when it went off. Her husband and three neighbors were injured; windows shattered a mile away, and nearby buildings caught fire.

"These damned murderers," Norwegian prime minister Thorbjorn Jagland said as he visited the site in the morning. He promised legislation banning gangs from populated areas, and would not let the Bandidos open a new clubhouse until the law was passed.

"We will do everything we can to fight such criminality, which has now hurt innocent people," justice minister Gerd-Liv Valla said.

I was over the Atlantic Ocean *en route* to northern Sweden to speak at an international law enforcement conference at the time of the explosion. I was met by Norwegian media to whom I had predicted on camera in June 1996 that politicians would sit idly by in Norway until an innocent bystander was killed by a bomb, certainly within a year. "The politicians have been warned," I said in 1996. "They must take action to end this war or they will have the blood of innocent people on their hands. They can't claim they didn't know how dangerous the situation is." The prediction was so eerily accurate that the television station played the 1996 interview back-to-back with footage of the June 4 blast.

I met with the Swedish justice minister in June 1997 to discuss ways of ending the biker war. I suggested she deal with the problem once and for all and amend the constitution to outlaw biker gangs. Otherwise, the Hells Angels would haunt them forever. There are few occasions in the evolution of organized crime gangs when they can be destroyed, I said. The Nordic war had given authorities one of those rare opportunities. The public was sufficiently aware and frightened by the problem to support the banning of outlaw motorcycle gangs. People who a year earlier had supported the bikers' rights to exist and kill each other in a free society had been silenced by the deaths of innocent bystanders. Bombs had shattered complacency and muffled self-serving civil libertarianism. A window of opportunity had opened and the bright light of reality briefly showed the bikers for what they were: terrorists who cared little for the society they lived off and that sheltered them. I urged the justice minister to act where North American politicians had failed. Lead the way. Ban bikers, and give the rest of the world an example to follow.

* * *

Hells Angel Vagn (Krudt) Schmidt, 39, shot at five unarmed Bandidos and probationary members as well as a woman with a 9-mm machine pistol in front of two hundred witnesses as they left the Liseleje café twenty kilometers northwest of Copenhagen, Denmark, at 7:05 p.m. on June 7. He hit four of them. Probationary Bandido Bjorn Gudmand Gudmandsen of the Fredriksværk chapter was shot in the throat and killed. Another probationary member was hit in the back and paralyzed. The Hells Angel was convicted and sentenced to sixteen years in prison.

By June 1997, the growing public hatred of bikers frightened the Hells Angels and Bandidos. Public pressure forced politicians to deal with the issue the only way they could: with laws. The justice ministers of the four Scandinavian countries, after a series of meetings beginning in late 1996, decided that the magnitude of the problem, compounded by the arrogance and defiance of the bikers, required extreme measures. Four of the world's most liberal democracies, which have always believed that the freedom of association was sacrosanct, decided to amend their national constitutions to ban outlaw motorcycle gangs. Denmark would ban them first, and the others would follow as they watched the effects and repercussions in that country.

Danish lawyer Thorkild Hoeyer, past chairman of the National Association of Public Defenders, who acted on behalf of both Bandidos and Hells Angels members, tried to get the gangs to agree to a truce in October 1996, but the Hells Angels refused to talk. In June 1997, both gangs were more than willing to sit down with Hoeyer—separately at first—and agree on a plan that would stop politicians from banning them.

The gangs were pressured by their leaders in the United States to resolve the issue before it dissolved them. Leaders of the world's Big Four outlaw motorcycle gangs met in Colorado and Seattle, in the spring of 1997 to discuss ways to fight society without inciting society to fight back.

These unprecedented meetings of the leaders of the Hells Angels, Bandidos, Outlaws, and Pagans was testimony to their fear of extinction. Bikers who started out in the 1960s with little more than a few dollars in their pockets had amassed large fortunes and underworld empires that they could easily lose if public pressure forced politicians to pass anti-gang laws. And the public only complained if they felt at risk. People didn't care as long as bikers only fought bikers, even in the early days of the Nordic war and the Hells Angels/Rock Machine conflict in Quebec. The bikers decided to immediately halt the momentum of the public outcry against outlaw bikers before it snowballed out of control. Survival of the gangs came before pride and honor. Better to make distasteful deals than be dealt a death blow.

"Accommodation before extinction" could very well have been tattooed on all bikers in the summer of 1997.

*   *   *

Earlier in the spring, talks were held in Washington state between Hells Angel Thomas Muller of the Malmö chapter and also European head of the gang, and Bandido Michael Olsen, the former Hells Angel who spearheaded the Bandidos' expansion in Scandinavia. Bandidos' European president, Jim Tinndahn, 35, also attended with bodyguard Danish Bandido Ben (Karate Bent) Olsen. The talks were sponsored and hosted by Hells Angels leader Ralph (Sonny) Barger, as well as Texas Bandido Charles (Jaws) Johnson and Bandidos vice-president George Wegers, months from becoming the gang's international president.

Barger and Johnson wanted to avoid at all costs the banning of their gangs in Scandinavia. Such a precedent could spread around the world as desperate governments sought new measures to rid their countries of organized crime. Already, 150 bikers were jailed in Scandinavia and the 120 left on the streets were under 24-hour surveillance. No once could conduct business anymore. Muller and Olsen pointed out that a truce between the gangs could prove fruitless unless competing gangs went along with the scheme. The Outlaws could easily attack the Hells Angels if they found out the gang was reluctant to fight. And so a plan was worked out to get all gangs to agree.

*   *   *

As Hoeyer mediated the talks between the Hells Angels and the Bandidos, he continued his attempts to convince the public they were not a menace. He told media in August 1997 that the bikers were not organized crime and were not involved in the drug trade.

"This war is a matter of a very old-fashioned, very stupid question of pride and honor," he said. "It's like the old stories of the Vikings fighting about honor. If you can pick a single incident as the start of the war, it began with a fight in a pub."

Hoeyer warned against the proposed anti-biker law. "Instead of fighting each other, the risk is that they will turn around and find a mutual interest in taking on society. The problem can't be solved by banning the bikers."

Hells Angels lawyer Peter Hjorne explained the issue in typical biker rationale. "Too many incidents have taken place. If the Bandidos would disappear, the war would end. That's the only way of getting peace. Hells Angels can never be beaten."

* * *

On September 25, Danish television viewers witnessed a historic truce which was also the linchpin of a major public relations effort by the newly joined forces of the world's outlaw motorcycle gangs.

Hells Angel Bent (Blondie) Nielsen and Bandido Jim Tinndahn appeared live on the Danish television news program *TV-Avisen*, and declared curtly that they had agreed to stop fighting. The former enemies shook hands. Tinndahn warned that both gangs would not tolerate members who violated the agreement, the details of which were not revealed. Officers from both gangs began to meet regularly and the gangs began going on runs together to show they were not enemies. Ten people had died during the Nordic war and there had been seventy-four attempted murders.

Several weeks later, Bandidos vice-president George Wegers, weeks before his election as gang president, along with Bandidos from the U.S., Australia, Denmark, and Sweden, visited the Rock Machine in Quebec and both gangs met with the outlaws in Ottawa. Neither gang knew that the Bandidos had struck a deal with the Hells Angels.

Not all Hells Angels accepted the truce with the Bandidos. They did not possess the foresight or the self-control of their leaders. For them, war was everything, even if it led them to a dead end. The Hells Angels suffered the first palace revolt in their fifty-year history when eight members from three Swedish chapters left the gang in disgust over the truce in October and created their own gang: five Malmö Hells Angels, including former president and avowed Bandidos' enemy Zillen Westberg, two members of the Helsingborg chapter (which had fought a vicious war with the neighboring Bandidos' Nomads chapter of Jan (Clark) Jensen, the gang's Swedish vice-president), and one member of the Stockholm chapter.

Although there had been no fighting for months, a biker in Stockholm took no chances when he visited the Hells Angels' clubhouse in December. He rode there naked so the Hells Angels could see he was unarmed.

* * *

The appearance of the Danish Hells Angels and Bandidos leaders on television was an ominous sign, a portent of worse things to come for society. The handshake was one of the last steps in the fulfillment of one man's lifelong quest.

AGREEMENT OF CO-OPERATION
between
Hells Angels MC and Bandidos MC

We think, that all nessesary endeavours should be taken to keep the biker-milieu (environment). We also think, that a premise for that is, that there are no violent confrontations between people affiliated with the Hells Angels and Bandidos. We think, that a continuously closer co-operation between the two clubs can prevent frictions and confrontations. We consider it desirable, that such co-operation can leed to the merge of Bandidos and Hellls Angels, with HAs name and with Bandidos' colours (red and yellow) or any other way, wich can be accepted by both parts. In a more explicit formulation, that will not take place until the members of the two clubs have got to know each other better and carefully have discussed, how such a merging can happend, including wich organizationel adjustments both parts can agree upon. We agree, that the excisting structur and the rules of HA shall be changed, if possible in a way, so it will take form as a brand new club, as an example; with the name Hells Angels and with Bandidos colours (yellow and red), or in any other way, wich both parts can agree upon.

The duration of such a process can noone be sure about. It could take a few months or many month, maybe even a few years. We agree, that both parts wont drop their patches until the merge have taken place.

We also agree upon, that non of the two clubs in Scandinavia establish new chapters, as long as the (above) mentioned talks are taking place.

Both parts are commited to work for, that no confrontations in -and outside Scandinavia, will take place, between the two clubs members and supporters.

It is agreeable, that members and supporters, who do not respect this agreement, will be banned from the clubs.

This agreement so far includes Hells Angels and Bandidos in Denmark, Norway, Sweden, and Finland.

Copenhagen, september 25th. 1997.

On behalf of Hells Angels MC in Denmark, Norway, Sweden and Finland:

On behalf of Bandidos MC in Denmark, Norway, Sweden and Finland:

prepared by bannister Thorkild Høyer.

It has always been Sonny Barger's dream to unite all outlaw motor-cycle gangs into one formidable Big Red Machine, as the Hells Angels called themselves as they steamrolled toward the millennium. Barger said in 1987 he could foresee the day, in ten years, when there would be only four gangs in the United States, the eight hundred or so smaller gangs having been assimilated by the Hells Angels, the Outlaws, the Bandidos, and the Pagans. What Barger had not considered is that only the Hells Angels pursued an aggressive expansionist policy. The Hells Angels' rapid international growth in countries that had few motorcy-cle gangs to oppose them broadened their network and strengthened their leverage at the bargaining table.

With this leverage, the Hells Angels planned to entice the Bandidos into their fold. No one would have imagined that the Bandidos would ever bury their colors. But the Scandinavian war brought the gangs closer together as politicians threatened to legislate them out of exis-tence. Members of both gangs understood that they had one thing in common, and fighting for it could destroy them. So they called a truce.

Since neither side wanted competition, the Hells Angels used their political savvy and the lure of money to create a scenario that gave them total control: the European Bandidos would become Hells Angels and the animosity would disappear because all Hells Angels are brothers. Then everyone could make money because they would be on the same team. Then they would have only one enemy: the police and the public that pays them.

Assimilation of the European Bandidos is the first step toward taking over the whole gang. It would strip the Rock Machine in Quebec of its dream of getting into the big leagues by becoming Bandidos. They would have to continue their war with the Hells Angels, surrender and work for them, or give up the drug business. Even if they did, the other Alliance members such as the Dark Circle and their biker gang, the Palmers, would continue the battle.

The Hells Angels made the same sales pitch to the U.S. Bandidos. Initial talks were made over the telephone by Hells Angel George (Gus) Christie, president of the Ventura chapter. Then representatives of the Big Four U.S. gangs met face-to-face for peace talks and a truce. These are documented in the next chapter.

The international officers of the Hells Angels drafted a merger proposal they presented to their members and to the Bandidos in Denmark in the fall of 1997. It is a remarkable study in cunning, subversion, and arro-gance. (The spelling errors in this secret document are theirs.)

Attn: Members of Bandidos
     And Hells Angels MC

PROPOSAL
STRUCTURE AND TIME PROSPECTIVE IN
CONNECTION WITH BANDIDOS MC EUROPE
JOINING THE HELLS ANGELS MC WORLD

First of all it should be mentioned that this will be a very difficult process for both clubs nevertheless it is a necessary process to get the bike culture the way it used to be in Europe. Its important to get as many as possible (hopefully everybody) to support the idea and work hard to get it to become a reality. There will be a lot of new members joining in a shorter time than normal which may cause a big portion of mistrust between the old ones and the new ones. That's why everybody should know what's happening and why everybody should have a chance to voice their opinion.

Locally the acceptance might in a lot of ways appear as a fusion but that doesn't change the fact that they will be joining Hells Angels MC World. Therefore the international rules for HAMC World will be repeated for good order.

TIME SCHEDULE

In order to straighten things out and to ease the tension it is of great importance to more forward with the acceptance as quick and efficient as possible. We have worked out a time schedule which all parties should get familiar with and base their comments on. No decisions have been made yet but to make the acceptance process as smooth as possible it is necessary to develop a frame within which to work. Understandably there is a certain amount of mistrust between everybody involved in the process. This mistrust must be worked through and hopefully end in friendship and brotherhood.

PHASE 1
• Negotiations/truce/inform members
• Visits on OM for explanation (2 from each club)
• Final approval/All hostile intelligence stops
• Order patches (4-5 weeks delivery)
• Keep friends and associates in line

PHASE 2
• Cops supervisorvision of meetings is terminated
• Torkild Hoyer (Defense Attorney) is terminated from meetings and added to the Legal/Negotiating Group
• Meeting in newly established 14-Member Group Starts(OM)

- Prospects and Hangarounds get informed and is free to make their own decision
- Keep friends and associates in line
- Legal/Negotiating Group meets with attorneys and others
- Communications with authorities is established or expanded
- Communications between old and new members intensifies
- Patches get received and sewn on immediately
- All defensive intelligence stops/the acceptance is a reality
  PHASE 3
- The 14-Member Group is now Office Meetings (OM)
- More communication between old and new members
- Communication between Prospects and Hangarounds expands
- Legal/Negotiating Group begins contacts with authorities
- Individuals who still oppose to the process will not be tolerated
- Work Group is initiated/Expanded
  PHASE 4
- More communication to bring relationships between brothers back to the norm
- The media will be informed as needed
- Negotiations with authorities will continue pending their intentions and interests
- The Club is up and running and stronger than ever

We believe/hope that the rest of Scandinavia and France will adopt a similar process. But other than giving advice it must be solely their decision to create their own future. Remember that no one will lose face by this arrangement since we will all belong to the same club. We'll achieve piece so that we can enjoy our mutual interest in motorcycle riding and brotherhood. In short we can get on with our lives.

The Hells Angels' World Rules were included with this document. They appear in the chapter on the Hells Angels' documents later in this book.

For someone familiar with Hells Angels' documents for more than two decades, this proposal is both shocking and revealing. The Hells Angels have a cardinal rule about not talking to cops. THEY DON'T. So greed overrides even this primary gang law. They need—and will use—cops to ensure security at initial talks to assimilate the Bandidos. This underlines how desperate the Hells Angels are to take over that gang.

Danish Bandidos must have no pride or respect for their colors if they freely give them up and believe the Hells Angels' line that no one loses face. Of course the Hells Angels don't lose face, they're not giving anything up. Their arrogance leads them to think the Bandidos would be honored to become Hells Angels.

If the police and politicians participate in this scheme, they can be compared to Nazi collaborators during the Second World War. They will broker the sale of their society and its citizens to a unified and more powerful gang. They will sell out the public interest for the short-term goal of ending war. Lest they forget, the Hells Angels and Bandidos declared a truce for fear they would be outlawed. The public was about to win the war against outlaw motorcycle gangs. But the biker's clever truce strategy worked. Politicians retreated from a constitutional ban of outlaw motorcycle gangs once the war and the public outcry it created stopped. With one unified gang there will be no war. And the politicians will ignore the Hells Angels because there is no inter-gang violence to frighten and threaten the public. Out of sight, out of mind. The politicians snatched defeat from the jaws of victory.

*   *   *

While the Hells Angels connived to entrap the Bandidos in Europe, they continued their anti-Bandidos expansion in the United States. The following memorandum from the San Fernando Valley chapter to the West Coast Officers illustrates outlaw biker politics. It was drafted about the same time as the merger proposal, in the spring of 1997.

SUBJECT: RED DEVILS MOTORCYCLE CLUB

The following statements are reasons that we, in SFV, gave the Red Devil name to the club in Albuquerque and feel that they should be allowed to keep the name.

1. The original Red Devils in Orange County, Ca. were not at any time sanctioned or affiliated with the Hells Angels. The Red Devils were a guest club, not an official hang-around club before being absorbed by SFV. They were told from inception that they were on there own with no backing from the Hells Angels. If the Red Devils from Orange Co. would have made hang-around status before being folded up, the patch would have become a sanctioned patch. Some think that the Red Devils patch was sanctioned because we had it looked at by the club before they put it on, but the reason we brought the patch design to the O.M. was so Hells Angels could look at the design and colors before the patch was made and let them know if anyone objected to the design, or name.

2. We feel that because the patch was not sanctioned officially by the Hells Angels we had the right to let guys in Albuquerque use the name without approval by the rest of the club. Another reason was that we wouldn't need to go through the process of getting another patch design looked at before they put it on.

3. The Red Devils in New Mexico were told from inception that they are not sanctioned by the Hells Angels, or affiliated in any way. They were told that if they had any problems with any clubs they were on there own. They have had several meetings with the Bandidos in Albuquerque. They first time they talked to them they didnt even have their patches yet. At the meeting the Bandidos asked them if they are affiliated, or backed by the Hells Angels. The Red Devils president told them that they are not affiliated with the Hells Angels or backed by them. Ken, the Red Devils president told the Bandidos president that they are here to stay, that they would prefer to co-exist with the Bandidos in Albuquerque and that they wont put New Mexico bottom rockers on. But if the Bandidos move against them, the Red Devils will take the Albuquerque bottom rockers off and put on New Mexico bottom rockers. The Bandido presidents name is Cochise. He said that the problem isnt really with him but is with the Bandidos in Texas. Cochise said that if the Red Devils operate as a club without wearing patches they wont have a problem with the Bandidos, but as soon as they put on patches there will be a problem. Cochise said that if anyone comes to deal with Ken, it wont be him. Ken said that if I cant sleep at night you wont sleep at night and I know where you live.

4. No matter what name they put on in New Mexico they will still be the same guys. If they hadnt put the patches on already it would be easy to change the name, but to take them off looks weak.

5. The Bandidos have only one charter in the whole state of New Mexico, the Albuquerque charter. It had 3 to 4 members before the Red Devils came to town, they now have 6 to 7.

6. We told the Red Devils to quit wearing their patches until we resolve this problem one way or the other. One question is, if they change their name to something else can they still wear red and white supporter patches on their cutoffs? The answer should be yes. Another question is, can they still have support stickers on their bike? Anyone can have a support sticker on their bike, even a Bandido. So if they change their name, they are still the same people doing the same thing. When the Bandidos talked to one of our members about the guys in Albuquerque, they didnt even know their name. They only

knew that a new club had started in the area and they were concerned that they might be backed by the Hells Angels.

7. New Mexico is right next to Arizona. We will have charters in Arizona soon. The timing is right to start looking at people in New Mexico. If the people in New Mexico, whatever their name ends up being, end up having problems with the Bandidos it will be between them and the Bandidos. The Bandidos know these guys are on their own, and we dont back them. So whatever happens between them stays between them.

8. The Bandidos are friends with the Outlaws. The Bandidos are backing our enemies in Europe. They don't seem to care what we think, under the circumstances we dont feel they should have a problem with the Hells Angels because some of us have friends in New Mexico.

*   *   *

On October 18, 1997, five Dirty Dozen chapters in Arizona became Hells Angels chapters and Sonny Barger transferred from the Oakland chapter that he founded on April 1, 1957, to the Cave Creek chapter in Arizona. The Hells Angels also started a motorcycle company in Arizona called, what else, The Big Red Machine. The Hells Angels obviously have big plans for Arizona. Sonny Barger would not pull up roots, after forty years in the Bay Area, on a whim. Talks of his retirement are premature. His move to Arizona will allow Hells Angels' Ventura chapter president George (Gus) Christie to take over the political reins of the gang, but Barger will help legitimize the gang in the business world from the dry desert state. The Hells Angels Motorcycle Club is Sonny Barger's life. He will retire only when he dies. He has nothing else to live for.

*   *   *

The Nordic war pushed society's tolerance of outlaw bikers to the limits and forced them to adapt in a way that made them stronger and possibly invulnerable. Without the casualties and violence of war to upset the public, there will be little, if any, pressure on politicians to curb the criminal activities of bikers. The Hells Angels will get more powerful and entrenched.

The Nordic war offended sensibilities and forced a re-thinking of the sacrosanct belief in the right of free association, but did it change Scandinavians' attitudes toward their cherished Harley-Davidson culture?

Two days after his 86-year-old father died in late October 1998, Flemming Pedersen, 37, asked the staff at the Copenhagen morgue to be left alone with the corpse. He dressed his father in leather gear, hobbled to the parking lot with the body, strapped it to the passenger seat of his Harley-Davidson motorcycle and cruised around Copenhagen for three hours. Pedersen stopped at a bar and propped his father up in a booth. He bought two beers and stuck a lit cigar in his father's mouth. Then he talked to him for an hour.

Scandinavian society, in its failure to ban outlaw motorcycle gangs when given its once-in-a-lifetime chance to do so, has returned to its dormant, docile state, and relegated the reins of the underworld to the Hells Angels—not unlike the corpse being driven around on the back of a motorcycle.

*   *   *

Belgium showed more fortitude than Denmark and became the first country to ban the Hells Angels in April 1999. A court ruled that the Hells Angels are in effect a private militia "that wants to substitute itself for the state." The gang was under a 1930s statute that banned private militias at a time when Nazi support groups flourished across Europe. Hells Angels leaders were sentenced to jail terms ranging up to four years and police seized all members' motorcycles.

Police began to investigate the gang shortly after its first chapter was established in Ghent on July 15, 1997. A second chapter saw light in Antwerp on January 15, 1998. Police raided the clubhouses the following month and charged members with crimes that ranged from theft, uttering threats, assault, and drug trafficking. The arrests stemmed from an attack by the then prospective Hells Angels members on the Outlaws clubhouse in early 1996. Ten attackers were charged with attempted murder. Members were also blamed for the theft of forty-seven flame throwers from a military depot.

Because the court deemed the Hells Angels a private militia and convicted all members of this crime, the gang was outlawed and members were stripped of those items listed in their rules and by-laws as necessary for membership: their Harley-Davidsons and their colors. Belgian Hells Angels were seen wearing their colors in Rio de Janeiro, Brazil, in June 1999.

Chapter 3: Chicago
The Midwest Melee

Hells Angels vs. the Outlaws

The only conflict of consequence involving the Hells Angels in the United States in the 1990s occurred in the Midwest, where egos clashed and tempers flared as the Hells Angels and their perennial nemesis, the Outlaws, stepped into each other's territory.

The rivalry between the Hells Angels and Outlaws is the longest-standing feud in the biker underworld. It was sparked by the 1969 rape of the wife of a New York City chapter Hells Angel. The rapist was a former member of the Aliens motorcycle gang. The Aliens became a Hells Angels chapter on December 5, 1969, after being the only motorcycle gang allowed to prospect while wearing their own colors. The Hells Angels demand that gangs bury their colors and don partial Hells Angels' colors during the prospect period.

The husband put the word on the street that he wanted the rapist alive. The biker fled to the Midwest and joined the Outlaws, formally known as the American Outlaw Association. John Davis founded the Outlaws in Chicago, Illinois, in 1959. He modeled the gang's colors— a white grinning skull with crossed pistons affectionately called Charlie—on the crest worn by Marlon Brando's gang in Stanley Kramer's *The Wild One*, the 1954 movie based on the takeover of Hollister, California, by bikers during the Fourth-of-July weekend, 1947. Chicago remained the Outlaws' power base until the summer of 1984 when Henry Joseph (Taco) Bowman was elected national president and moved headquarters to Detroit. But Chicago remained the birthplace of the Outlaws, and their sentimental home.

The rapist had risen to the rank of officer for the Outlaws when he visited New York in early 1974. Two Satan's Soldiers recognized him. They informed Hells Angel Vincent (Big Vinnie) Girolamo, sergeant-at-arms for the Manhattan chapter, and he held the rapist until the husband arrived. He beat the Outlaw for twenty minutes in the street and left him for dead. The rapist dragged his sorry behind back to Outlaws' territory and cried that a dozen Hells Angels had beaten him. Word of the insult spread through the organization and many Outlaws plotted vengeance. The gang motto, which can be found on patches on their colors, is "God forgives, Outlaws don't."

Opportunity to avenge the slight came in April 1974, when two Hells Angels traveled to Florida to ensure that former member Albert (Oskie) Simmons, who skipped out of the Hells Angels' Lowell, Massachusetts, chapter with gang money in the early 1970s, had covered his gang tattoos as rules required. The Outlaws' South Florida chapter got wind that Hells Angels Edward Thomas (Riverboat) Riley, 34, and George F. (Whiskey George) Hartman, 28, were in town. They arranged to bump into them and invited them back to their clubhouse for a party. The Hells Angels explained they didn't wear their colors in Outlaws' territory out of respect. After enough beer had been consumed, one Outlaw proclaimed that no decent men should drink with scum like the Hells Angels. Members agreed. They tied up the two Hells Angels and Simmons, loaded them into a van, and drove them to a flooded rockpit near Andytown. They lined the men up facing the water, arms tied behind their backs with pink clothesline, and eight concrete blocks tied to their legs. They blew their brains from their skulls with a shotgun and dumped them into the water. The bodies were found on May 1, and the gangs have sought to kill each other's members ever since.

The last battle between the Hells Angels and the Outlaws was more of a skirmish than a war, mostly because the Hells Angels stuck to their game plan of taking over territory as quietly as possible, and refrained from striking back when the Outlaws attacked them. The Hells Angels had plotted for years to set up chapters in the American (and Outlaws') heartland. The Hells Angels controlled the west coast of North America from San Diego to Alaska and as far inland as Omaha, Nebraska; St. Paul, Minnesota; and Paducah, Kentucky. They controlled the northeast from the Carolinas to Quebec, and across all of Canada except for Ontario. From the Atlantic Ocean, they extended westward to Cleveland, Ohio.

The Midwest was the next logical territory for the Hells Angels to expand into, and Illinois and Indiana was ground they coveted. They pegged the Hells Henchmen as their takeover target in the late 1980s. The Hells Henchmen were formed in the 1970s and had three chapters: Rockford, Illinois (six members from a peak membership of fifty),

Chicago (twenty-two members), and South Bend, Indiana. Hells Angels tasked with orchestrating the takeover befriended Henchmen members at runs which both gangs attended. The Angels invited the Henchmen to attend an annual run to Myrtle Beach, South Carolina, with them in May 1992. The Henchmen were eager to impress the Hells Angels. "We're going to give you Chicago," they said. "Yeah," the Hells Angels replied, "but we're going to give you the world."

The Hells Angels picked the Henchmen because they were the kind of bikers they wanted in their organization in the 1990s. Their members were squeaky clean and free of criminal records. Law enforcement could never justify spending time and money investigating a bunch of bikers they had never caught committing crimes. In order to keep a low profile with the media and police, and to avoid incurring the wrath of neighboring Outlaws, the Hells Angels allowed the Henchmen to keep their colors during their prospect period. That kept everyone off guard. There was no physical proof that the Hells Angels were planning to move into the Midwest, and the media had no photos to publish. Only one other gang had been allowed the privilege of keeping its colors until it became a Hells Angels chapter: the Aliens in New York City.

Although they had no criminal records, the Hells Henchmen did have an interesting history. They fenced in the backyard of their Rockford clubhouse in the fall of 1984 to keep out vandals who cut the gas lines on their motorcycles, slashed seats, and pulled plug wires, Henchmen president Roger Feibrantz said. Hells Henchmen Peter J. Jacobson, 38, was killed with an auto jack by a man who defended himself when the bikers attacked a group of black people on April 6, 1986. By 1990, when it became known the Hells Henchmen had aligned themselves with the Hells Angels, the petty vandalism of the motorcycles stopped. Instead, the Rockford Hells Henchmen found an Outlaws' bomb at the back door of their clubhouse on November 13, 1990.

The Outlaws had been fighting the Hells Angels for sixteen years and were always prepared for war. Indiana chapter president Raymond L. (Shemp) Morgan Jr., 31, was arrested in Riverdale, Illinois (outside Chicago), on March 18, 1993, with Outlaw Alan Smick and the daughter of former Harvey police chief Nick Graves. Police found a gun in the car and a human fetus in a jar in the trunk.

Police in Illinois got their first clue that local gangs were preparing for war in July 1993 when agents for the U.S. Treasury Bureau of Alcohol, Tobacco and Firearms raided a storage facility in Round Lake Heights in Lake County rented by a Hells Henchmen from Oak Park and found 50 handguns, 10 machine guns, 10 silencers, 10 shotguns, 27 rifles, two grenades, and 32,000 rounds of ammunition.

Several weeks later, on August 6, Outlaws from the year-old Janesville, Wisconsin, chapter, beat two Hells Angels from Pittsfield, Massachusetts, outside a Janesville bar.

The Hells Angels threw two grenades into the Buffalo, New York, house of Outlaws leader Walter Posnjak on October 3. One grenade landed on the bed of Posnjak's ex-wife and her 12-year-old daughter, but they escaped without injury.

Longtime Hells Angel and former New York City Alien, James Lewis (Oats) Oldfield, former president of the Charleston, South Carolina, chapter, moved to Illinois in late 1993 to run the Rockford chapter of the Hells Henchmen.

ATF agents met with Chicago police who were concerned by the number of weapons seized and the tension between the gangs. Chicago's deputy chief asked the federal agency for a synopsis of the outlaw motorcycle gang problem in his city. His own intelligence department, which had volumes of information on the hundreds of street gangs that have plagued the city during the past three decades, had no information on the Hells Henchmen or other biker gangs. The Chicago police department assigned several officers to gather intelligence on area biker gangs in January 1994. By this time, however, the tensions between the Hells Henchmen and the Outlaws were primed to explode.

The Outlaws insulted the Hells Angels in the worst possible way in November 1993 when they opened a chapter in Brockton, Massachusetts, an area long controlled by the Hells Angels, who had long-standing chapters in Salem and Lowell. This was an affront the Hells Angels had to answer, or forever lose face in the outlaw biker underworld. They speeded up their plans to assimilate the Hells Henchmen. They also decided to take care of business. Peter (Greased Lightning) Rogers had come a long way since he left the Aliens in 1969. He was president of the Outlaws' Chicago chapter and the Hells Angels targeted him. They put two bullets into Rogers as he rode his motorcycle on Interstate 94—the Dan Ryan Expressway—in Chicago on June 25, 1994. Rogers survived.

Lamont (Monte) Mathias, 47, a nationally ranked drag racer, builder of fuel-injected motorcycle engines, and member of the Rockford, Illinois, chapter of the Hells Henchmen, was shot and bludgeoned to death in his MC Fabrication motorcycle shop in Rockford on June 28.

Mathias was targeted because he was easy to find and had a high profile that would attract media attention. The Outlaws would tell the world through the media that they, too, were taking care of business. The Hells Angels don't like seeing photographs of dead members in newspapers. It reminds the public that they are vulnerable. Nearly two hundred Hells Angels and other bikers from the United States, Canada, and Europe attended Mathias' funeral and he was posthumously made a gang member.

The Hells Angels and Outlaws wearing body armor and armed for battle clashed at the Lancaster National Speedway in Lancaster, New York, at 9:25 a.m. on September 25. Both sides lost a leader during a rumble where the bikers shot and stabbed each other. Parents shoved their children under cars to get them out of the way as more than a hundred bullets were fired. Outlaw Walter Posnjak, 44, the gang's northeastern regional president, died of a chest wound. Hells Angel Michael J. Quale, 44, of the Rochester chapter, bled to death from a stab wound to the neck. Fourteen people were injured and police seized twenty-five guns, four bullet-proof vests, three knives, two sets of brass knuckles, many ax handles, seven clubs, and pepper spray at roadblocks. The Hells Angels showed up at the race track near Buffalo to show they were not afraid to trespass on Outlaws' territory.

A bomb exploded beside a tattoo studio next to the Outlaws' clubhouse in Milwaukee on October 9. Two days later, Roger Fiebrantz, 41, president of the Hell's Henchmen Rockford chapter, suffered injuries to his right hand and leg when a bomb blew up under his flatbed truck. The Hells Henchmen soon learned to check under their vehicles and before getting in, and they started them through the open window. Caution paid off for Rockford Hells Henchman Michael Coyne, 37, who found a large bomb fastened to the driveshaft of his Chevy Blazer at 10 a.m. on November 7. Police detonated the bomb after failing to defuse it. At 5:50 p.m. that afternoon the third most powerful bomb used in the United States, after the bombs used at the World Trade Center in New York and the Murrah Federal Building in Oklahoma City, devastated the Hells Henchmen clubhouse in Chicago. "We have the whole thing on tape," a Chicago detective said in reference to a surveillance videotape from a camera aimed at the building. "You can see them pull up in the car and get out. There are cars and buses whizzing by. At first we thought they blocked off the street when they detonated the device a minute and a half later. But they didn't. They didn't care who they killed." The blast blew the tires off a passing car and shattered its windows. Amazingly, no one was hurt.

The Hells Henchmen chapters in Rockford and Chicago, Illinois, and in South Bend, Indiana, became official Hells Angels chapters on December 2, 1994. The Chicago chapter, run by Hells Angel Melvin (Road) Chancey, moved its clubhouse to a renovated bar at 15609 Halstead Street in Harvey, Illinois.

There was only one more killing in the war. Chicago Hells Angel Jack (4-By) Castle was shot nine times in the head in the city's Northwest side on March 3, 1995.

The Hells Angels and Outlaws in the Midwest have not fought since early 1995. Police investigated the shootings and bombings of the short-lived war and charged seventeen Outlaws with the crimes in 1997.

Outlaws international president Joseph (Taco) Bowman, 48, made the FBI's most-wanted list in March 1998 when he fled police who wanted to arrest him on charges of murdering two Outlaws in Florida and Indiana, as well as the president of a rival biker gang. Bowman was also suspected of being involved in several bombings and of running a nationwide speed network.

Truce

The minutes of the Hells Angels West Coast Officers Meeting on March 7, 1998, make an important reference to the Outlaws. "OAKLAND: The Outlaws contacted us for help. CISCO will talk to them and keep the East Coast notified. Everybody keep it off the phone."

The Outlaws and the Hells Angels began peace talks in 1998. Both gangs were fed up with investigations that jailed their members and put a damper on biker business. Gang leaders realized that law enforcement investigates them only when they go to war and upset the public with shootings and bombings. They decided that police would stop investigating them if they stopped fighting and kept a low profile.

The Hells Angels were not the only gang the Outlaws decided to make peace with. In March 1998, the Pagans and Outlaws, longtime enemies, buried their differences and for the first time ever, members of both gangs celebrated Bike Week together in Daytona, Florida. Pagans and Outlaws stood outside the Outlaws' clubhouse, arms around each other. Even the Sons of Silence, Hells Angels supporters likely to become part of that gang in the near future, partied with the Pagans and Outlaws in Florida.

Chicago Hells Angels chapter president Mel Chancey flew to California to discuss negotiating strategy with Sonny Barger in the spring of 1998. Then he set up a meeting with Edward (Shock) Anastas, president of the Outlaws' Milwaukee chapter. The Hells Angels and Outlaws met at the Angels-run Copacabana strip club on Cicero Avenue in Alsip, south of Harvey, Illinois, on Saturday, July 18, 1998.

Although Frank Wheeler from Indianapolis was the Outlaws national president, Shock Anastas was the gang's shrewdest negotiator. The Hells Angels and Outlaws set down certain rules as part of their deal to stop hostilities between the gangs. The Outlaws were allowed to keep Chicago, and the Hells Angels were given control over the city's suburbs, where they had a clubhouse. The gangs made similar deals in parts of the country where their territory overlapped. The Hells Angels and Outlaws agreed not to start any new chapters, but each existing chapter was allowed to take in new members.

The Hells Angels and Outlaws exchanged chapter and membership lists so they could keep track of each other to ensure the rules of the truce were adhered to. They arranged to update membership lists regularly, so both gangs could scan them to look for police informants. They also exchanged address and phone-number lists so members in distress while in the other gang's territory could ask for it. Once both sides had agreed to the elements of the peace agreement, the Hells Angels and Outlaws partied in Joliette, Illinois, at the end of July and attended motorcycle events, such as swap meets, together. Outlaws from Milwaukee, Chicago, Joliette, and Indianapolis flew to Oakland, California, with two Chicago Hells Angels for talks.

The Outlaws in Ontario and Quebec agreed not to forge ties with the Rock Machine, in return for peace with the Hells Angels. Any assistance to the Rock Machine would be seen as an attack on the Hells Angels. With the Bandidos and Outlaws on the Hells Angels' side, the future of the Rock Machine in Quebec became tenuous, although neither that gang or the police had a clue what was happening.

The truce was severely tested in November when the Hells Angels' Jimmy Cole, president of the South Bend, Indiana, chapter, tried to make the Avengers motorcycle gang in Michigan a new Hells Angels chapter. Shock Anastas complained to Mel Chancey and they met at the South Bend clubhouse on Sunday, November 22. Chancey threatened Cole with expulsion from the gang and said he would "clean up the chapter" in South Bend if they did anything to violate the truce.

The Hells Angels used the same reasoning with the Bandidos and the

Pagans, whom they had been talking with for several years. Members of the Big Four outlaw motorcycle gangs (the Hells Angels, the Outlaws, the Bandidos, and the Pagans) attended the National Coalition of Motorcyclists (NCOM) show in Columbus, Ohio, in November 1998, to show the world they had put all bad feeling aside and were now united in pursuit of a common goal. Bandidos president George Wegers spoke and the only tense people in the crowd were those who did not know the gangs had made peace.

The Hells Angels and Outlaws, joined by the Sons of Silence, held a final negotiating session from January 23 to 25, 1999, in Indianapolis, Indiana, where Sonny Barger and Shock Anastas decreed that any gang member who breached the truce would be "dealt with." The Hells Angels and Outlaws swapped copies of each other's by-laws and agreed that each gang could proceed with plans to establish web sites on the internet. The Outlaws officially invited the Hells Angels to visit them at Bike Week in Daytona Beach, Florida, in 1999 and to stay at their club-house.

The Hells Angels and Outlaws signed their truce in Indianapolis, Indiana, in February 1999. Outlaws members, who had never referred to the Hells Angels by name but called them "those guys," "them," or "maggots," now called them "the Hells Angels" in conversation.

Sixteen Hells Angels visited the Outlaws' clubhouse in Brockton, Massachusetts, on Tuesday, February 16, 1999, for a friendly meeting. Two weeks later, during the first week of March, Outlaws visited the Vallejo chapter clubhouse in California. Vallejo president George (Gus) Christie, the next leader of the Hells Angels, negotiated the truces with the Bandidos, Outlaws, and Pagans. Until the truce, Outlaws who showed their colors in California would have been killed.

About fifteen Massachusetts Hells Angels met with an equal number of Brocton Outlaws in a Somerville, Massachusetts, bar on Wednesday, April 14, for a friendly meeting. An Outlaw whose brother was murdered by two Hells Angels was present, though the killers tactfully stayed away.

The Hells Angels and their former enemies have put twenty-five years of bitter rivalry aside to fight the common enemy: society. Now that they are not battling each other, biker gangs will become wealthier and more powerful in the criminal underworld and will spread their tentacles into parts of our lives we never imagined would be soiled by organized crime.

PART II:
POLICE AT WAR

Chapter 4: Ontario
The Last Frontier

Nearly every year for the last two decades, police have predicted an imminent, bloody, all-out war between the Hells Angels and Ontario biker gangs for control of the province. Media have unquestionably given credence to these predictions and, for a few days every spring, people have cringed at the prospect of a long, hot summer.

All law enforcement agencies play games to secure funding and political support. Invariably, these predictions were made as administrators prepared police budgets. Without fail, the dire warnings were groundless. The public had been scared into exerting political pressure to loosen administrators' purse strings.

The Hells Angels and other bikers smirked at the heavy-handed displays of police deception. Every lie played into their hands. The false predictions were filed into their legal arsenal so they could remind the public during strategically timed press conferences that police records are tainted with false accusations—those who cried wolf were themselves wolves. Worse, the unfulfilled predictions undermined public trust and confidence. If the mighty intelligence-gathering apparatus of law enforcement could so consistently be wrong, how could anyone justify using the words intelligence and police in the same sentence?

I warned police to drop this tactic in a September 1988 speech to an annual conference of the International Outlaw Motorcycle Gang Investigators Association in Las Vegas. Instead of predicting war, all they had to do was tell the truth and attack existing Ontario gangs to weaken their hold on that portion of the drug market cornered by outlaw bikers.

The Hells Angels have indeed targeted Ontario for a takeover, but their strategy is more subtle than that of the police.

Ontario is the crown jewel in the Hells Angels' plan to control

Canada. It is the most desirable province because it contains one-third of the country's drug market in a concentrated area. But Ontario is also the best-defended province. An alliance of six major outlaw motorcycle gangs and half a dozen lesser gangs is determined to keep the Hells Angels out.

The Hells Angels, being monopolistic, won't share territory. Any Ontario gang prospecting to become a full-fledged Hells Angels chapter would have to eliminate or absorb all competing bikers before being granted a charter. There are more than five hundred outlaw bikers in the province.

Ontario's major gangs have ruled the province for nearly forty years. Although they have had skirmishes, they have a gentleman's agreement that recognizes the market is big enough for everyone to get rich. They don't step on each other's toes and they keep a low profile to avoid attracting police attention. This lulls the public into silent acceptance. The bikers know that unless they offend or frighten the public with displays of violence, politicians will direct police investigations toward problems that cause them more grief.

The Hells Angels first flew their colors in Canada on December 5, 1977, when the violent Popeyes became the gang's Montreal chapter after a two-year bloody war with the Satan's Choice and Devil's Disciples over drug turf. Their first priority was to wage war with the Outlaws motorcycle gang with whom the Hells Angels had a falling out in 1974, after the South Florida Outlaws killed two visiting Hells Angels and a former member and dumped their bodies in a flooded quarry. The Satan's Choice sided with the Joliette-based Outlaws. Ontario and American Outlaws frequently traveled to Quebec to help their brothers. (I documented these wars in *Hells Angels: Taking Care of Business* and will not repeat myself out of respect for readers who bought the book.)

Quebec's first Hells Angels also spent the late 1970s wooing, taming, and grooming a dozen gangs across the province to turn them into chapters or puppet gangs which would enable the Angels to consolidate their hold on the drug market.

So it was with great surprise that the Hells Angels read in *The Globe and Mail* on June 23, 1979, nineteen months after their arrival in Quebec, that they were supposed to invade Ontario. The story has become a template for countless similarly exaggerated tales in newspapers across the country during the past twenty years.

The story by Peter Moon ran under this headline across the top of the newspaper's front page: "OUTLAW BIKERS: War looms to control the new organized crime."

Police in Ontario are preparing for what they say could be a major war this summer between two "outlaw" motorcycle clubs for supremacy in the province.

At stake in the war would be not just territorial superiority in the brawn-and-bravado subculture of motorcycle renegades but control over a burgeoning criminal network that police rank next in power to the Mafia.

A senior police intelligence man in Montreal, whose bikers have links with the major clubs in Ontario, calls bikers "the new form of organized crime" and "more powerful than the traditional organized crime gangs . . . because of their use of violence and intimidation."

Specialists in biker intelligence in several Ontario police forces say bikers are arming themselves in preparation for war this summer. They say the clubs are stockpiling not only legal rifles and shotguns but illegal weapons such as pistols, automatic weapons, and even anti-tank rocket launchers and hand grenades stolen from Canadian Armed Forces bases at Borden and Petawawa.

The war is expected to be between two U.S. clubs—the Hells Angels and the Outlaws.

"I have to say the probability of open war between these two groups in Ontario this summer is a reality," said Commissioner Harold Graham of the Ontario Provincial Police in an interview.

"What's needed is a joint, concerted effort to control the situation by all of the province's police forces. We are giving it a very high priority and we are trying to contain it."

"If the war could be fought between the bikers there'd be no worry," said a police biker specialist. "If that's all it was, I'd say go to it and we'd probably direct traffic for them while they killed each other off. They'd be no loss.

"Unfortunately, it's not as simple as that. We know from experience that ordinary citizens get swept up in these things. They can be eliminated or intimidated as witnesses. They can be caught in the gunfire. We don't want that in Ontario.

"The publicity these people get when the killings start makes people, even the underworld, even more fearful of them. And then, whichever faction wins, it is held in such fear that they are a criminal force to be reckoned with. The bikers are bad enough without having that happen. . . ."

"We're trying to prevent what has happened in Montreal and in the United States from taking place in Ontario," said Staff Superintendent Bruno Dorigo, head of the OPP's criminal intelligence branch.

"The OPP is the central repository for all motorcycle gang information in the province. Based on the information we see coming in here, we foresee a hectic summer." He said many outlaw biker clubs in Ontario are forging alliances to resist the Angels' planned invasion, while others have entered into loose affiliations with the Angels. . . .

According to Detective-Captain Henri Marchesseault, head of the organized crime task force of the Montreal Urban Community Police, "We can say these motorcycle gangs are the new form of organized crime. They are more powerful than the traditional organized crime gangs, like our Italian Mafia and French-Canadian organized crime families, because of their use of violence and intimidation of witnesses.

"The problem is convincing our own men and our bosses that these people are a threat," the Montreal officer said. "We have to convince our bosses right now that we must have the manpower and the priorities to do something about motorcycle gangs. We have to follow through and get at them now, or in another two years it will be very hard to work on them; they will be invulnerable. . . ."

Inspector William Swanton, head of the Metro Toronto police intelligence bureau . . . said he thinks the possibility of a war between the Angels and Outlaws in Ontario is "a very serious concern."

He said Angels from various chapters in the United States and Quebec have been seen in Toronto. "I believe they have contacted some of the smaller clubs in Metro but the clubs don't want any part of them."

The reason is simple, he said.

"The biker gangs are just like the old Mafia. Here's another gang wanting to move in here and spoil a nice juicy criminal area for them."

*   *   *

The now-defunct *Montreal Star* was not to be outdone. Once the dust from the *Globe* story settled, they matched the tale on August 4, 1979. The headline across the front page read: "Police fear motorcycle gang war."

Today, two years after they muscled their way to supremacy in the Montreal biker underworld, the Angels are reported preparing to invade Ontario—where up to now they have been shut out of the lucrative drug trade by their arch-rivals the Outlaws, also U.S.-based.

In the last few weeks MUC police have been scrambling to prepare a dossier on the criminal activities of the gang, in a desperate attempt to prevent the outbreak of a major inter-provincial war.

But as one high-ranking MUC police officer told *The Montreal Star* last week, it may be a case of "Too little, too late."

"We missed the boat two years ago. They caught us with our pants down," the police officer admitted, "and we've been playing catch-up ball—without much success—ever since. . . ."

In Ontario the Outlaws heavily outnumber the Angels, having formed alliances with smaller clubs to protect their million-dollar drug franchise. Ontario police intelligence specialists say the gangs have been busy stockpiling all kinds of heavy weapons from submachine guns to grenades, preparing for a fight to the finish—a fight they confidently claim they can win.

But the invasion of a heavily-armed contingent of Hells Angels from Quebec, including a couple of professional hit men from the United States, could result in a major war.

And whatever the final result, police fear that many innocent citizens could be caught in the crossfire.

"An open war could break out at any minute and the result could be a bloodbath," an Ontario Provincial Police officer told *The Star* last week. "All we can hope for is that they kill each other off quietly without hurting anybody else. . . ."

In recent months the MUC police's anti-gang squad has been reduced from about 40 men to fewer than a dozen, after police district directors reported no problems with visible gang activity.

"They think that just because the gangs are no longer so visible, roaring up the street in their big bikes and scaring people, the problem has gone away," one MUC police detective said. "But in fact the problem is bigger that ever, and if we don't crack down now it may soon be too late.

"In a couple of years they could be too big to bust. . . ."

In Montreal, police hope the organized crime probe headed by Judge Denys Dionne, which is preparing a report on biker gang activities in the Montreal area, will focus public attention on the growing menace posed by the gangs—and lead to demands for stronger police action.

"I think it's our last hope to convince the public, if not our superiors, that what we're dealing with is something as dangerous, if not more dangerous than the Mafia itself," said one weary police veteran of the biker wars. "To convince them that if we don't take some form of concerted action now before they have a chance to spread into the rest of Canada, we'll never be able to put them out of business for good. . . ."

There are already indications that the Hells Angels are preparing to move the center of their Canadian operations from Quebec to Ontario, where several violent incidents involving the Angels' rival gang, the Outlaws, have occurred, said Pierre Fréchette of the Quebec Police Force.

An Ontario Provincial Police expert confirms this information and adds that the Outlaws, currently the strongest gang in Ontario, have made agreements with several other Ontario gangs to oppose the invasion of their territory by the Hells Angels.

But this situation is dependent, apparently, on how effective the Quebec crime probe will be when dealing with the Angels, North America's largest and most notorious motorcycle gang.

*   *   *

The following story was planted in *The Hamilton Spectator* on September 14, 1989, as the Canadian Association of Chiefs of Police held their annual convention in the city. Headline: "Cops brace for biker gang wars." Subhead: "Hells Angels member on local recruiting drive."

Police are bracing for an outbreak of violence between rival biker gangs over a move by Hells Angels to establish a Hamilton chapter.

According to regional police, a Hamilton-based Hells Angel, recognized as a member of the U.S.-based motorcycle gang, is recruiting people with the intention of setting up a chapter in the city.

"He is a *bona fide* Hells Angels member and he does have permission from the [gang's] national president to start a chapter," said Staff Inspector Bob Slack, who is head of the Hamilton-Wentworth police vice and drugs squads.

Police identified him as Walter Stadnick.

Police have been preparing for more than a year for a possible outbreak of hostilities between rival gangs and a new chapter, he said.

He was elaborating on a report on organized crime presented to Canada's police chiefs yesterday at their annual convention being held in Hamilton. The report, prepared by the Criminal Intelligence Service of Canada, warns "outlaw motorcycle gangs increasingly represent a major organized crime threat in Canada."

The report says although the Hells Angels do not have a chapter in Ontario, they have a foothold in Hamilton and are likely to attempt to establish a chapter in the city.

Statements in these articles are guesswork, assumption, speculation, and wishful thinking. The highest-ranking intelligence officers in

Ontario, with access to the most up-to-date intelligence, went out on a limb without a shred of substantive or corroborative proof and used circumstantial evidence and hearsay to create a scenario that would never come to pass. There were no professional repercussions for them. They were not held accountable. In the past two decades, newer generations of cops echoed the same old refrains in an effort to shape public opinion through fear.

Police, with some notable exceptions (such as the Ontario Provincial Police), put more emphasis on stopping bikers on runs than they do investigating their criminal businesses. That's because stopping a hundred bikers is a visible act which the public can witness. However, this does not constitute an investigation of organized crime. It is a public safety issue. It is also how police show bikers that their gang is bigger than the bikers'.

In an ever more complex age, we need more complex cops. Today's cops may understand the laws they enforce, but they can't grasp that the nature of the game is changing. Police departments and their members are too inflexible and rule-governed to adapt to a fast-changing world. The public they are supposed to serve and protect is well ahead of them. This explains the high level of frustration, displeasure, and job dissatisfaction among police, as voiced by their unions. The world is leaving them behind. Change is not easily discussed, let alone implemented among those comfortable with stringent rules. Criticism is less tolerated and taken as an affront, even if it is made within the law.

The 7,500-member Toronto Police Association is a case in point. Militant union president Craig Bromell announced in December 1998 that the union had budgeted a multi-million-dollar war chest to investigate, sue, or criticize in advertising campaigns anyone who brought "unnecessary hardship" on police officers. The police union said it would target politicians, journalists, government agencies, and especially the provincially appointed civilian Special Investigations Unit, tasked with investigating any police incidents which result in death or injury, from car chases to bank robberies.

Organized crime, on the other hand, lives by its wits. It survives and prospers because of its ability to adapt. Criminals are hustlers and schemers. They work the angles and look for ways to beat the system and get a piece of the action. Hoods are the epitome of change. They think and work twenty-four hours a day.

Cops, on the other hand, are clock punchers. Many of them are more concerned with overtime and pay duty shifts. In private conversations, they don't talk about righting social wrongs. They discuss second jobs, retirement, and pensions.

Police mindset contributes to the ever-threatening biker menace as well as other organized crime issues. Despite overwhelming evidence that biker gangs were becoming more sophisticated and powerful (and the same could be said of Asian gangs in the mid-1960s) police agencies were loath to tackle the problem until it got well out of hand. They could have curbed the growth of biker gangs in their infancy. They didn't, mostly because police administrators thought themselves superior and more intelligent than scum-bag bikers. How wrong they were. If given a performance evaluation, the bikers would score highly, the cops would fail.

Organized crime gangs have their foot soldiers and their brain power. Someone has the big picture and calls the shots. It works. Police agencies are mired in politics, rules, and regulations that hinder their ability to serve and protect. That is why police administrators have cried wolf about the Hells Angels for two decades. They could not and would not understand that brutal bikers don't always resort to brute force to attain their goals. They can cloak themselves in craft and cunning.

Police complain bitterly that bikers learn from every arrest and trial how the cops and court system works. They continually devise new ways to circumvent and foil the system. Instead of whining, police should emulate this adaptability and find ways to stay ahead of the gangs. They also need to learn and be innovative. But police are uncomfortable outside of their routine. They would much rather try to impose the old ways with more force.

For decades, police have been telling the public that bikers are just dumb white trash. The public believed this and wrote off bikers as belligerent losers. During that time, bikers took advantage of the lack of pressure to evolve. The Hells Angels evolved more quickly than other gangs. And when cops look into the eyes of the new breed of biker, they find no routine in their arsenal of rules and regulations to ease the panic of helplessness that grips them.

*   *   *

The Hells Angels had no intention of battling their way into Ontario in 1979. They consolidated their hold on Quebec and set their sights on British Columbia. Police knew the Hells Angels traveled frequently to Vancouver to party with the Satan's Angels. Instead of worrying about Ontario, police in Quebec should have tackled the Hells Angels while they tried to consolidate their hold on the province. The Angels went on a killing spree in Quebec in the late 1970s and early 1980s as they fought for drug turf. Yves (Apache) Trudeau alone killed at least forty-three people for the gang from 1978 to 1985.

The Quebec Hells Angels godfathered BC's Satan's Angels into their organization. They checked out their operations, drug networks—their mettle. They taught them how to be Hells Angels. By June 23, 1983, the west coast bikers had eliminated or tamed all other biker gangs in the province and were granted official chapter status. The Hells Angels took over British Columbia through diplomacy.

With both coasts secured, the Hells Angels drafted their takeover plan for the rest of Canada. They would court gangs in all remaining provinces and once they had control over the entire country, they would officially open chapters overnight. Such a dramatic show of force would give them immeasurable power and influence in the underworld. It was a plan they pursued for the next fourteen years, until they realized that Ontario would not capitulate easily.

The Hells Angels focused on the prairie provinces and the Maritimes. They traversed the country to wine, dine, seduce, and intimidate bike gangs into their way of thinking. It was easier to convince with money than with fists. They flaunted their wealth and got bikers to sell their drugs, to hook them on easy money as well as expand their own networks. Become Hells Angels, they said, and there will be no limit to your wealth.

To please the Hells Angels, these gangs did their dirty work. They got rid of competition. They coerced street dealers to sell Angel drugs. They intimidated bar owners into allowing only Angels' dealers to work in their establishments. Strip clubs were forced to hire only biker women.

All this work is an essential part of the Hells Angels' business plan. They never visibly move into an area until the groundwork has been laid: the drug networks have been established, criminal contacts have been made, money-laundering fronts set up, and a solid foundation has been poured for their operations. The Hells Angels don't officially start up a chapter and open a clubhouse until they have secured their domain. They never put themselves in a position to be usurped. Their preparations are so meticulous that no Hells Angels chapter has ever been dislodged in Canada or the United States.

The Hells Angels can be stopped before they officially establish themselves. They are most vulnerable in the preparatory stages of their takeovers. The gangs targeted by the Hells Angels don't have the resources or the sophistication to fend off police attacks. These are skills the Angels teach them. This is when police have a chance to shut them down and create a climate inhospitable to the Hells Angels. Unfortunately, police don't consider these other gangs a threat, and spend little time tracking them.

So police turn a blind eye to bike gangs when they are most vulnerable and deem them untouchable once those bikers become Hells Angels. All the world's Hells Angels have come from gangs that police made no effort to eliminate. They may arrest some members, but except for a few cases, mostly in Ontario, police have washed their hands of the biker problem. Yet police have no qualms about predicting biker wars to squeeze money from a frightened public.

Police inaction protects the bikers. Crying wolf serves the police. Who serves and protects the public?

The Hells Angels were unofficially present in all Canadian provinces except Ontario by the mid-1980s. That province was to become the special project of one of two English-speaking members of the Montreal chapter of the Hells Angels.

Walter (Nurget) Stadnick had been a member of the Red Devils motorcycle gang in Hamilton, south of Toronto, before he joined the Hells Angels. He kept a low profile and wielded enormous influence. He epitomized the Hells Angels' credo of not talking to police officers, and never failed to treat a cop or a judge with disdain when the opportunity arose. Stadnick is the most litigious of the Hells Angels, having sued police officers (and this writer) on behalf of the gang, as its national president.

Stadnick's early plans to take over Ontario were aided from 1985 to 1987 by the slaughter of the Hells Angels' Laval North chapter on March 24, 1985, by other Hells Angels who were tired of their heavy-handed ways. Police were all over the Hells Angels during those three years as several high-profile members targeted for death informed on the gang. Hells Angels found it difficult to do business in Quebec and spent more time on the road socializing with gangs they wished to take over.

Although the Satan's Choice was the most powerful gang in Ontario, the gang was an unlikely candidate for takeover because three of their Ontario chapters (along with the Joliette, Quebec, chapter) became Canada's first Outlaws chapters in June 1977. The remaining Choice members rebuffed the Hells Angels' overtures because they did not want to be a Canadian branch of an American gang. And no gang is more American than the Hells Angels.

The province's second most powerful gang, the Vagabonds, was the Hells Angels' first choice. Angels from British Columbia and Quebec visited Toronto regularly to strike drug deals with Vagabond members and feel them out. The Vagabonds were more suited temperamentally to becoming Hells Angels. They were a close-knit gang that operated much as the Hells Angels did—in isolated cells. The gang leaders did not instruct members to commit crimes and did not want to know what members did. Small groups of Vagabonds ran their own drug networks, truck hijacking rings, car and motorcycle theft operations, prostitution and strip businesses, debt collection agencies, and intimidation and extortion rackets. The gang endowed them with the ability to scare the daylights out of victims, intimidate witnesses, and muscle out competition.

The Vagabonds were also the smartest and canniest bikers in Ontario. They never tried to bully or out-macho the police. They were polite when stopped and never gave police a chance to arrest them or make them look bad in the media. Every year, the Vagabonds put up a huge sign on the front of their clubhouse at 1966 Gerrard Street East wishing everyone "Season's Greetings, Merry Christmas: Vagabonds MC." But underneath the veneer of civility was a controlled viciousness that exploded when necessary. The Vagabonds were not afraid to beat and kill anyone who got in their way.

The Vagabonds were on friendly terms with most Ontario biker gangs and had close ties with the Para-Dice Riders (who also had their clubhouse in Toronto's east end) and the Scorpions in Detroit. The Hells Angels hoped such a powerful chapter could easily sway other Ontario gangs to trade patches and become Angels without bloodshed.

Vagabonds president Donald Isaac (Snorkel) Melanson was targeted by the Hells Angels as the man to win over. The Vagabonds allowed members to deal with Hells Angels, but only on an individual basis. Members were responsible for all debts they incurred with the Angels, and the gang would not back them if they couldn't meet payments.

The Hells Angels courted Melanson to control his influence over the gang. They supplied him with a large quantity of high-quality cocaine at a cheap price. Any smart drug dealer would have turned a quick profit and gone back for more. But Melanson broke the cardinal rule of drug dealers—he stuffed most of the coke up his rather large nose.

By the first week of September 1987, Melanson had chalked up a large debt to the Hells Angels. He had also relinquished the Vagabonds presidency earlier that summer to Peter (Crow) Lordon because he was scheduled to begin a prison term during the second week of September.

The Hells Angels were angry that Melanson had not repaid his debt, and worried he would walk away from it. They didn't want other customers to think they were pushovers, so they took care of business. Melanson met someone in an eighteenth-floor room of the Novotel Hotel in northern Toronto on September 3. A professional killer shot him once in the head, walked across the street to a subway station, dumped the handgun into a garbage bin, and boarded a train. The Hells Angels sent flowers but no mourners to his funeral.

Melanson's death marked the end of relations between the Vagabonds and the Hells Angels. The Angels demanded that the Vagabonds cover Melanson's debt, believed to be over $10,000. The Vagabonds explained that individual members are responsible for their own business, and told the Hells Angels to fuck themselves. To this day, the Vagabonds look over their shoulders for Hells Angels, with whom they have no dealings. When Vagabonds attend events they don't control, and where they expect to encounter Hells Angels, they arrive *en masse* and leave together. For events such as funerals, one Vagabond goes alone as a show of respect for the deceased. A Vagabond showing up at a Hells Angels funeral doesn't mean the gangs are planning something, as some police repeatedly point out. It's just the way things are done in the biker underworld. Some places are considered neutral territory because of mutual interests. And funerals are a way bikers show force and solidarity to the public, even if it is tenuous.

Melanson's death coincided with a change of fortune for Hells Angel Walter Stadnick. Canadian president Réjean (Zig-Zag) Lessard was convicted with other gang members in the Laval North chapter murders of 1985. Stadnick ascended to the throne, a position he was to hold for eight years. Stadnick wasted no time continuing his diplomatic attempt to win over Ontario gangs. He set his sights, quite surprisingly, on the Satan's Choice, not only because it was the most powerful gang with chapters across the province, but because its legendary founder and leader Bernie (Frog) Guindon had charisma and the ability to charm the skin off a snake. Stadnick did not want to waste his time wooing someone without power. What Bernie said, people did.

But Bernie Guindon was no fool. Stadnick sorely misread the man and overestimated his own powers of persuasion. Guindon was a man of principle and could not be bought. It took Stadnick eight years to figure that out. Guindon was Canadian first and foremost. So was his gang. He took it as a personal affront when four chapters joined the Outlaws in 1977. He was proud of his colors and would never bury them to become a member of a punk American franchise. Whatever one might dislike about Guindon, his nationalism was to be admired.

Stadnick paid countless visits to Oshawa and strip clubs in north Toronto as he wined and dined Guindon. He would visit his parents on Hamilton mountain during the day and spend his evening flashing his colors in Toronto bars where servile kiss-ass hoods stroked his ego. Guindon played Stadnick along, and listened to his promises of power, wealth, and respect. Although Stadnick struck a high profile socially, he had absolutely no profile when it came to business. He was a slick operator whom police could not keep tabs on. No matter how hard they tried, police could not point to one illegal business deal Stadnick had been involved in. Stadnick would continually cruise a restaurant during a meal and converse with people at other tables, although he would conduct more serious conversations on walk-abouts along busy streets or down empty laneways, to avoid electronic eavesdropping.

By 1993, the Hells Angels had become impatient with Guindon. They pressed him for an answer. Guindon said there was no way he would allow the gang he had founded to become Hells Angels.

The Hells Angels, fed up with the slow progress of diplomacy, tried another approach. They recruited associates in Quebec and set up, overnight, a new motorcycle gang in Toronto called the Demon Keepers whose task was to establish drug networks with customers wooed away from the existing gangs. The Demon Keepers offered high-quality Hells Angels drugs at competitive prices, and promised efficient and safe delivery.

The Demon Keepers approached drug dealers in Toronto, Kingston, and in the Golden Horseshoe area extending south of Toronto to Niagara Falls. However, the Quebec bikers spoke broken English and could not converse smoothly with the drug dealers. They also had little intelligence to operate with, and no contacts. It was a rushed, heavy-handed infiltration attempt, a sign of desperation and arrogance. The Demon Keepers episode lasted several months, after which the bikers retreated to Quebec. The Hells Angels suffered a major loss of face in the Toronto underworld.

Over the next two years, the Hells Angels tried to take over drug dealers who were dissatisfied with Ontario gangs. The Angels offered better product and guaranteed delivery times. What seemed to be a superb opportunity to gain market control backfired when the Hells Angels learned these dealers were unreliable and had to be muscled into shape. To encourage business, the Angels fronted drugs to the dealers, who were expected to pay them back with the proceeds and buy more drugs with the profits. When Ontario bikers discovered the scheme, they threatened to kill the traitorous drug dealers if they repaid their debts to the Hells Angels. Then they protected the dealers when the Angels tried to collect.

The Hells Angels put more thought into their next assault on Ontario.

Ontario's major biker gangs are based in Toronto. It is the center of their universe. The Satan's Choice, with chapters in Sudbury and Thunder Bay, is the only gang to show interest in the province's vast northern region. The Hells Angels quickly grasped this fact and members of their rich and powerful Sherbrooke, Quebec, chapter, which hosted the slaughter of the North chapter in 1985, started to infiltrate northern Ontario towns with their strippers and drug dealers.

They started with Timmins, a gold mining town 450 miles north of Toronto, which at one time boasted more bars per capita than any other city in North America. Timmins is a two-hour drive from the Quebec border and an eight-hour drive from Toronto. The Hells Angels ran their strippers through area clubs for several years to gather intelligence on the drug markets and its major players. They wanted to know who to approach and who to eliminate. Quebec Hells Angels own many stripper agencies and control hundreds of women they use as spies, prostitutes, drug couriers, and set-up artists for hits.

Once the women had done their job, the Hells Angels moved in, secure in their knowledge of the area and armed with an informed plan based on greed. Local drug dealers were happy to get cheap drugs from the Hells Angels, who had the capital to undercut the independent suppliers then feeding the market. Dealers who chose to forgo profits rather than accede to the Hells Angels were dealt with brutally. Not one turned to police for help.

The Hells Angels showed a depth and breadth of thinking that police could never anticipate or fathom. Though police were quick to label the bikers as businessmen to the media, they had no idea how businessmen worked. (They were, after all, cops.)

The Hells Angels were after money: Ontario had it, and they wanted it. If they couldn't get into the primary market in Toronto, they would come through the back door which the big boys down south—both police and bikers—had left unlocked. When the time came, they planned to swoop down from the north and squeeze Toronto bikers into Lake Ontario.

Hells Angels prefer to set up clubhouses in small towns because police forces don't have the manpower or resources to deal with sophisticated organized-crime gangs. Northern Ontario was heaven for them. The Timmins Police Service intelligence unit was one man. He had to keep an eye on everything. He turned to the Ontario Provincial Police for help with the sudden influx of Hells Angels associates who did the dirty work for the gang. The OPP brushed him off. The citizens of Timmins had just become victims of inter-agency politics.

The OPP, not unlike the Hells Angels, for the past decade had pursued a policy of taking over small-town police forces to add to their jurisdiction. Shortly after the provincial government moved the OPP's headquarters from Toronto to Orillia in central Ontario, the OPP tried to take over the local police force. Local citizens and politicians told them to stuff their power play. The same thing happened in Timmins, where the sometimes arrogant attitude of some OPP officers earned them the nickname "Ontario Piss-Pots."

OPP administrators were pissed off that they couldn't take over Timmins, the largest police force in the north. But northerners are proud and don't want to be policed by a southern-based police force which rotates its officers from community to community. They want local cops they grew up with and who understand the local crime scene.

The OPP, which coordinates biker investigations across the province, abandoned Timmins to the Hells Angels. Individual police officers who did show an interest wanted a ready-made case they could plug into. But what Timmins needed was manpower and expertise to collect intelligence and deal with several dozen experienced criminals who assiduously laid the groundwork for the Hells Angels.

Timmins has no biker gangs, so the Hells Angels did not fear public exposure through warfare. Former Timmins native John (Turkey) Leblanc, a member of the Kitchener Satan's Choice chapter, tried in the early 1990s to start a gang in Timmins and was driven out of town by local dealers. The Hells Angels might learn a hard lesson if they try to open a chapter in Timmins. Although it is not the tough town it once was, true Timmins natives would not hesitate to shoot a peckerhead Hells Angel who pumped drugs into their children. In Timmins, hunters are well armed, and there are only three roads out of town.

While the Hells Angels quietly took over the drug trade in northern Ontario, biker life continued in the south with the not-so-subtle intricacies of gang politics leading to punch-ups, shoot-outs, and more dire predictions by police of an impending invasion by the Hells Angels. If they had looked over their shoulders, they would have seen that the Angels already had a hand on their asses.

In the middle of all this, one event underlined the sad acceptance of bikers into in everyday life. Canada Post contractors, determined to earn their salaries during a strike by postal employees, hired members of the Vagabonds to drive mail trucks in August 1991. The post office airlifted mail over picket lines at sorting stations with helicopters and loaded it into vans at the Toronto Island Airport. Bikers drove the vans onto the ferry to the mainland and delivered the mail. Although the post office could have hired anyone to drive the trucks, violent bikers suited their purpose. And so taxpayers paid bikers to do what they do best—intimidate. The mail must get through, rain, sleet, or shiner.

This tale illustrates the prevailing attitude among bureaucrats and politicians, both civilian and police: they are fully aware of the biker problem, but would rather use it than eliminate it. This was brought home in 1988 after 14-year-old Benji Hayward took LSD at a Pink Floyd concert at Toronto's Canadian National Exhibition stadium and drowned in Lake Ontario where he had chased a hallucination.

Hayward's parents had no idea their boy took drugs, and complained bitterly in the media about easy access to drugs. An inquest was held where it was determined most chemical drugs in Toronto are manufactured and distributed to street dealers by bikers. The jury recommended that $6 million be added to the Toronto police budget to hire ninety-nine more police officers. Not one penny or one cop went to the biker enforcement unit. Police targeted street-level dealers, who are as easy to bust as they are to replace.

This approach did not dent drug accessibility in Toronto, because the bikers who made them were not touched. It did create statistics, however, that police administrators and civilian politicians could flaunt as proof they were fighting against drugs.

During a Toronto radio talk show about drugs that I was on in 1992, a Satan's Choice biker called in. The issue of Benji Hayward came up, and I asked the biker what would happen to the drug scene in Toronto if all bikers disappeared overnight.

"There would be no drug scene," he replied candidly.

While the inquest may have given answers that appeased the boy's family, and provided recommendations that comforted other parents, the people we trust to apply these solutions served their own best interests rather than society's.

Police were so edgy in the early 1990s that any biker punch-up led to warnings of war. Biker brawls were a fact of life in the 1960s and 1970s. They were dealt with as common disturbances, and no one lost sleep over them. There are always paybacks in the criminal underworld. Intimidation only works if a person takes care of business. Respect is based on fear, not admiration.

It was a typical Sudbury Saturday night in early October 1992, and the local Satan's Choice bikers were not happy that members of Toronto's Black Diamond Riders were in town for a baseball tournament. Four cars full of Choice and their associates peeled into the parking lot of the Sorrento Motor Hotel where the Black Diamond Riders milled about. The Choice jumped out of the cars, shot one BDR, stabbed four others, and beat them all with splintered clubs. Then they raced away. Eight BDRs and two Choice were treated in hospital. Police told reporters they feared the fight would spread south, as the BDRs were from Toronto.

In the early to mid-1990s there were the six major outlaw motorcycle gangs in Toronto: Satan's Choice, 118 members in 5 chapters (they later added chapters in Owen Sound and Keswick); Para-Dice Riders, 61 members in 1 chapter (they later added 20 members assimilated from the Loners and a chapter north of Toronto); Vagabonds, 70 members; Outlaws, 68 members in 7 chapters; Loners, 62 members in 2 chapters; Last Chance, 20 members. Membership fluctuated throughout the decade as gangs bolstered their muscle and secured territory. Older members saw a need for fresh blood they could sacrifice if things got hot.

The Loners were the youngest of Ontario's six major outlaw motorcycle gangs in 1993. The gang was founded in 1984 by disgruntled Satan's Choice bikers, most of them Italians from north Toronto. They were brash, arrogant punks with a lot of attitude. By 1993 they had carved out a chunk of turf in the Woodbridge area north of Toronto and had connections in the Italian underworld. Of course, any self-respecting Italian hood says that. Despite their moderate success, they lacked what all bikers need: respect. Other bikers called them the Losers.

The Hells Angels, like all predators, are quick to sense weakness. The Loners' flaw was ego. The Angels were ready to stroke until the Loners did their bidding. The Hells Angels planned to suck the Loners into doing their dirty work in Toronto after hooking them into their drug network. They hoped the Loners would become their puppet gang, wage war against the other gangs, and eventually, after the weaker members were killed or kicked out, become the first Hells Angels chapter in Ontario.

The Angels gave the Loners much-needed attention. They invited a few of their members to events and introduced them to people to make them feel important. Then, on June 18, 1993, a hundred Hells Angels and associate gang members from Quebec rode through Ontario to Wasaga Beach where they rented the Allistonia Bar, cordoned it off, and held a meeting with the Loners.

The procession was stopped by police on Highway 401 near Bowmanville. Police once again jumped to conclusions. Durham Region police officer Bruce Townley, a member of the biker enforcement unit, told media there would be "turf wars" that summer.

"You can expect a pretty violent summer," another cop chipped in.

The show of force had several purposes. The Hells Angels wanted to prove they were not afraid to come into Ontario. They also wanted to draw attention to the fact they now had a pact with the Loners. They introduced the Loners to their Quebec business associates and working arrangements were made over the weekend. All of this was done in a strip club several blocks from the Wasaga OPP detachment.

Shaking Up the Neighborhood

Toronto's first biker war briefly spooked the city in 1995 and it had little to do with the Hells Angels. Rather, the blame can be pinned on tensions caused by that social butterfly of the biker underworld, the promiscuous Frank Lenti, who over twenty years wore the colors of nearly half a dozen Toronto gangs. The temperamental Lenti flitted from gang to gang when he didn't get his way. Mostly, the gangs wouldn't take him, so he started his own—three times.

Lenti belonged to the Rebels in the 1970s. In the same decade, he and several other bikers formed a new gang called the Loners. They used a Confederate (Rebel) flag on their colors. Lenti was accused of stealing money from the clubhouse kitty and moved to Italy while things cooled off in Toronto. The Loners disbanded in his absence.

Lenti joined the West Toronto chapter of the Satan's Choice when he returned in the early 1980s. He wasn't a very sociable or diplomatic man, even by biker standards, and his temper quickly flared up when he didn't get his way. He left the Choice in 1984 and formed a new Loners gang. This was the gang that the Hells Angels would target for takeover.

Even though he was Loners president, Lenti could not get along with fellow gang members and he threw another of his famous temper tantrums in 1994. They stripped him of his presidency and once again, he took the ball and went home. This time, home was half a block from the Loners' clubhouse on Kipling Avenue north of Highway 7 in Woodbridge. Lenti, who operated a towing business and supplied girls to strip clubs, never ventured far from his gangs. He started yet another gang called the Diablos at his house within insult range of the Loners, who did not like to see Diablo colors roaring by.

In July 1995, the Satan's Choice offered to absorb Lenti's nine-member Diablos to extend their influence in the Woodbridge area. Given Lenti's spotty record, they gave the Diablos prospect status until they proved themselves worthy of wearing Satan's Choice colors.

The Loners were furious that the rival Choice would dare move into their territory. They decided to take care of business. So did the Diablos. In late July, Diablos tossed a Molotov cocktail at a Loners' tow truck.

A few days later, Loners shot two Diablos as they sat in a car on Highway 7.

On July 29, several teenage girls poured gasoline over cars in a used-car lot on Caledonia owned by a man with connections to the Loners.

Police tried to convince the gangs that war was bad for business. The bikers agreed that public consternation would force an increase in police attention, but pride and fear overrode logic, and the battle was on.

The Loners bombed the heavy steel front door of the Satan's Choice fortified Toronto clubhouse on Kintyre Avenue in the city's east end at 11:40 p.m. on August 1. The explosives tore a large hole in the door and blew windows out of three neighboring houses, but did not injure five bikers inside the building. Three and a half hours later, at 3:25 a.m., the Choice tossed a firebomb through the front window of Pluto's Place tattoo parlor on Lake Shore Blvd. West, causing $50,000 damage. Pluto's was a Loners hangout.

The next day, at 4:30 a.m., August 3, three Molotov cocktails were thrown at Bazooka Jacks on Bayview Avenue in Markham, a Satan's Choice hangout north of the city. Later in the day, firebombs were tossed at the Diablos-linked Bullitt machine shop north-west of the city.

Sergeant Guy Ouellette, an investigator with the Sûreté du Québec who excels at planting information in the media, erroneously told a Toronto newspaper which unquestioningly publishes his comments that the Loners were opposed to any alliance with the Hells Angels. He said, again erroneously, that the Hells Angels had decided not to open chapters in Ontario, but had opted for an alliance with the Satan's Choice, the largest gang in Ontario.

The afternoon of August 16, Toronto City Council bowed to pressure from neighbors of the Satan's Choice clubhouse and declared legal war on the gang. Council struck a committee of police, fire, and building officials to scour by-laws and find ways to shut down the clubhouse.

City officials had failed to enforce an injunction granted in 1993 against the clubhouse on the grounds that the Choice violated city by-laws when they demolished the original clubhouse and rebuilt a heavily fortified single-family dwelling. The Choice bought the building in 1980 and were granted legal non-conforming designation to use it as a clubhouse because the area was re-zoned residential after they moved in. The renovations negated that designation, and the city obtained an injunction that prevented the Choice from using the building as a clubhouse.

*   *   *

Loners president Pietro Barilla, 38, and a gang member were charged with two other men on August 15 after police found two loaded .380-caliber semi-automatic pistols in their Lincoln when they stopped for burgers at Harvey's.

A Choice bomb blew a three-foot hole in the back wall of the Loners clubhouse on Denison Road in the city's west end on August 16. The next day politicians in that part of the city also began a legal war against the Loners' clubhouse. That afternoon, federal justice minister Allan Rock told the twenty-three-member Police Association of Ontario, which had asked for a new anti-gang law to fight bikers, that "we shouldn't assume that another federal law will solve the problem." The police association also asked for more money.

On August 23, someone tossed a Molotov cocktail into the house of the Kitchener Satan's Choice president, who wasn't home. Police and firemen saved a woman and baby.

The next morning, August 24, Frank Lenti opened the door of his Ford Explorer in his driveway at 10 a.m., put his right leg into the cab, and a Loners' hit man watching him detonated a bomb under the seat. Lenti lived to face charges after police found a loaded machine gun and handgun in his house. The Loners targeted Lenti because they feared he would use his new friends in the Choice to exact revenge on the gang that had stripped him of his presidency. With Lenti out of commission, the Loners had nothing to fear and the war ended.

*   *   *

The heavily fortified clubhouses of the Montreal and Vancouver Hells Angels chapters are testimony to how rich and powerful the gang has become.

Hells Angel leader Maurice (Mom) Boucher (*top right*), who looks more like a schoolteacher than a biker, is believed by police to be the driving force behind the gang's war with the Rock Machine.

The Quebec Hells Angels use their puppet gangs across the province to wage war against the Rock Machine. The Filthy Few symbol, worn as a patch on the colors or as a tattoo, indicates that a Hells Angel has killed for the gang.

(*Lower left*) The original Hells Angels colors in 1948 and the colors today. The first Death's Head was nicknamed the "bumblebee patch."

More than a decade after they were formed, the Rock Machine announced on June 2, 1999 that they had become an official motorcycle gang. They did so while attending a Bandidos function in Red River, New Mexico. Their red and gold patch mimics the Bandidos blue and gold color scheme. They also sport a patch indicating support for the Bandidos on the left breast of their colors.

Before they got colors, Rock Machine members wore rings (*lower left*) and tattoos (*lower right*) to identify themselves.

Two Grim Reapers pose with reporter Ralph Klein before he was elected Alberta Premier.

Years later, some Grim Reapers planned to black-mail Klein with the photo when he publicly objected to that gang becoming Hells Angels on July 23, 1997.

(*Left*) The Angels' Calgary colors.

Hells Angels Maurice (Mom) Boucher, Walter (Nurget) Stadnick and Tiny Richard signed this gang Christmas card.

Hells Angels pose with an Outlaw at a meeting of the National Coalition of Motorcyclists in April 1999 to show the gangs are no longer at war. Biker gangs are using NCOM money, contributed by millions of law-abiding motorcyclists to fund legal actions for their rights, to sue police officers who investigate them.

Springfield, Missouri police corporal Dave Zuhlke tests the wakefulness of Hells Angel prospect Dennis Lynch, who was assigned by the Durham, North Carolina, chapter to guard motorcycles while members slept in August 1992. Zuhlke is now a sergeant who teaches how to investigate bikers. Lynch is a Hells Angel.

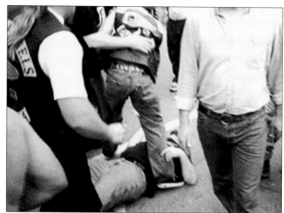

Hells Angels at the Loudon Classic "Motorcycle Weekend" in June, 1998, in Laconia, New Hampshire, demanded that members of the Wild Pigs police motorcycle club expel a member who called Angels criminals in a newspaper story. Two Wild Pigs met with Hells Angels contrary to the wishes of their club. This gave the Angels the impression they had beaten the police. To celebrate they pummeled an innocent bystander. When police came to the man's aid, Hells Angels attacked them with their own batons and pepper spray.

The bikers pleaded guilty to a variety of charges that stemmed from the incident after eight civilians anonymously gave police their photos of the altercation. They were given short jail terms.

The Hells Angels and the Bandidos in Scandinavia used anti-tank rockets in vain to destroy each other's clubhouses. Though the body count was much lower than in Quebec, the use of military weapons terrified the public.

Bandidos supporters from across Europe, such as the Outlaws from Wales, attended all funerals in a show of force against the Hells Angels.

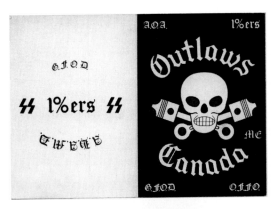

The Hells Angels and Outlaws have been at war since 1973. The Outlaws business card (*top left*) bears the upside-down inscription: "A.H.A.M.D." (All Hells Angels Must Die). The gangs fought a brief but violent battle most recently in Illinois and Indiana in 1994 and 1995 when the Hells Angels moved into Outlaws territory by taking over a local gang.

The public outcry caused by the biker wars in Quebec and Scandinavia prompted the Hells Angels to negotiate truces with the Outlaws and Bandidos in an effort to prevent politicians from banning outlaw motorcycle gangs because of their threat to public safety.

The author (*top photo, center*) poses with then-Bandidos national president James (Sprocket) Lang (*on author's right in top photo*) and three of the gang's top officers at the Black Hills Motorcycle Classic rally in Sturgis, South Dakota, in August 1989.

(*Top right and center photos*) The author took the first-ever photos of the colors of the new Bandidos France chapter. The colors were given out at a ceremony the previous night. (*Bottom photo*) Lang spots author photographing surreptitiously. He then granted permission to take photos and even posed.

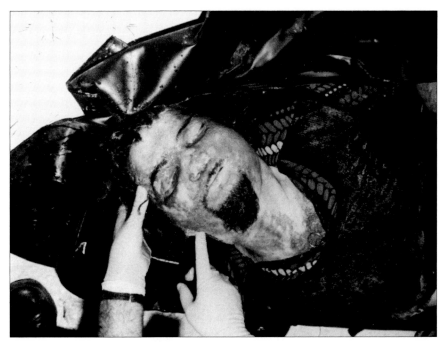

(*Opposite page*) The Bandidos and Hells Angels lobbied smaller gangs for support during their war in Scandinavia. The Hells Angels sold many more T-shirts than did the Bandidos.

(*This page*) Florida Outlaws lured two Hells Angels and a former member to a party at their clubhouse in April 1974. They drove them to a flooded quarry, bound their hands and feet with clothesline, weighted them with concrete blocks and blew their brains out with shotguns. Discovery of the bodies prompted all-out war between the Hells Angels and Outlaws.

The Hells Angels have registered their name and Death's Head logo and sue anyone who uses them. To reduce registration costs they decided in the early 1990s to use only one spelling of the word "Hells" and so they dropped the "Hell's" version.

They sued the author in 1988 for the artist's rendition of the Death's Head on the cover of his first book. They sued Marvel Comics for naming a new super heroine "Hell's Angel." Marvel changed her name to "Dark Angel" and donated a large sum of money to a children's charity on behalf of the Hells Angels.

OAKLAND

FORTY YEARS
Hells Angels MC Oakland
California
1 . 4 . 57 – 1 . 4 . 97

Charter Anniversary

Ralph "Sonny" Barger: 40 years
Gary Popkin: 30 years
Lee "Hamco" Staskunas: 25 years
Howie Weisbrod: 25 years
"Mouldy" Marvin Gilbert: 25 years
Rich "Spiderman" Grootendorst: 20 years
Eddie Shay: 18 years
Lil Gary Kunesh: 5 years

The British Hells Angels publish a magazine on behalf of the gang to promote events and sanitize their image. *The Big Red Machine* is synonymous with Hells Angels and is used for business ventures. A Hells Angel company by the same name in Arizona manufactures and sells custom motorcycles.

The Big Red Machine advertised Hells Angel Sonny Barger's fortieth anniversary with lavish color photos of the world's best-known outlaw biker.

The Big Red Machine

£3.00 No.3

WORLD

The Stories, The Clubs, The Bikes and more...

Outlaw motorcycle gangs are aware they must have the public on their side to keep law enforcement at bay. If the public does not complain to politicians about bikers, elected officials focus their attention and resources on other issues that can cost them votes.

(*Top*) Toronto's Para-Dice Riders painted their Internet address on the front of their clubhouse in 1998. They solicit donations on their web site to defray legal costs of their ongoing court battles with police.

(*Bottom*) Every December, Toronto's Vagabonds grace the front of their heavily-defended and monitored clubhouse with a festive billboard.

To heal wounds with the Choice, the Woodbridge Loners indulged in an intense ass-licking session where they hinted they would consider joining the Satan's Choice in the spring. The Choice wanted to beef up the organization in case they needed to fend off the Hells Angels, and accepted the Loners' olive branch.

Politicians and cops didn't know the war was over, and concern continued over another possible bombing of the Choice clubhouse in Toronto's east end. City officials met secretly with neighbors of the Choice clubhouse in September and were swayed by their fear and desperation to seek an expedient rather than effective solution to the problem. Such is the way of politicians—shut them up and move on. City council, at a closed-session meeting on Monday, September 18, 1995, authorized staff to negotiate with the Satan's Choice to buy their clubhouse.

Toronto mayor Barbara Hall learned during a talk with Choice lawyer Karl Jaffary that the owner, former Choice president Larry McIlroy, would sell. Politicians figured on a $300,000 price. Council decided to buy the building because it would take months for the Ontario Municipal Board to hear their complaint that the Choice had violated an injunction by using the residence as a clubhouse. The Choice, on the other hand, circumvented the issue by having a member live there full-time and accept visitors.

The idea of buying off the bikers angered the public and police. Neighbors were happy because it took care of their problem. But no one seemed to have considered that the Satan's Choice would buy a building elsewhere (because motorcycle gangs need clubhouses), and people in the area they moved into would put heat on their local politician.

The bikers realized the politicians were hungry for a quick fix, and decided to milk them. Within ten days, the Choice asked for $350,000 for the building, which city appraisers valued at $190,000. The media labeled left-leaning Mayor Hall "Biker Barb," and cartoonists portrayed her as a shakedown artist who capitalized on the public's fear on behalf of the bikers.

Toronto's acting chief of police, Bob Molyneaux, then made a curious remark. He refused to comment on whether the city should buy the clubhouse, a proposal that caused outrage among street-level investigators. "The truth of the matter is that clubhouse has been there for many years and there have not been that many complaints up until just recently," he said, illustrating the statistically oriented mindset of police administrators across the country.

The affair came to an end on October 20, when politicians pulled the plug on the deal after they failed to get a guarantee that the bikers wouldn't move down the street and buy a bigger building with the profits of the sale. Duh.

A week later, on October 27, police raided the Loners' clubhouse on Denison Road and wrecked the place. They found an AR-15 semi-automatic assault rifle and a Tec-9 machine gun, both loaded, along with 150 rounds of ammunition and a can of mace. The gang's Halloween party was canceled that night.

By early December, city council decided to give residents near the Satan's Choice clubhouse $10,000 to hire a lawyer and planner to fight the bikers at the Ontario Municipal Board hearing.

A fire in a wood stove ignited residue in the dirty chimney of the Loners clubhouse in Woodbridge on December 20. The Loners weren't lucky with holidays. It messed up their Christmas. They also lost their farm clubhouse in Milton, west of Toronto, when their landlord farmer read about their war with the Satan's Choice. The Woodbridge Loners moved their clubhouse to Rutherford Road at Highway 400.

1996

Early in 1996, police started to psych themselves out once again over the possibility of a Hells Angels' invasion that summer. The hysteria was prompted by the exchange of ideas between Sergeant Guy Ouellette of the Sûreté du Québec and Detective Jim Downs, head of Toronto's biker enforcement unit. The men met while preparing to testify at a civil case the Para-Dice Riders had launched against the Durham Regional Police, complaining that their rights under the Charter of Rights and Freedoms were abused by roadside stops of the gang en route to its summer clubhouse in Caesarea.

Sergeant Ouellette pumped up Detective Downs with tales of the new Hells Angels chapter Walter Stadnick had created on Saint-Jean-Baptiste Day, June 24, 1995. The elite Nomads chapter, made up of proven Hells Angels, had one goal: take over Ontario. Sergeant Ouellette called the chapter the Hells Angels' "dream team." Nomads sported a custom T-shirt that showed the Hells Angels' Death Head—the helmeted skull with wings—spread over the Toronto skyline. "Hells Angels Ontario—The first wave" the lettering announced.

The Quebec cop also attached significance to the presence of Loners at the September 1995 funeral of Richard (Crow) Émond, president of the Trois-Rivières chapter of the Hells Angels. Émond was the first full-fledged Hells Angel killed by the rival Rock Machine, who put six bullets in his back. His death took the war for drug turf in Quebec to another level. Until his death, the war's victims were gang associates, sympathizers, or members of puppet gangs such as the Rockers or Evil Ones.

Detective Downs mulled over his talk with Sergeant Ouellette. His conclusions were highlighted in a front-page story in *The Globe and Mail* on March 13, 1996, which echoed in many ways the 1979 *Globe* story that contained the first prediction by police of a Hells Angels' invasion of Ontario. The story, which started at the bottom of the front page and took two-thirds of an inside page, quoted two cops only. The headline read: "Toronto police brace for biker war in spring." The subhead warned: "Three major gangs bringing in serious muscle to stave off takeover bid by Quebec-based Hells Angels."

> Outlaw motorcycle gangs in Ontario are quietly adding muscle in anticipation of a widely expected takeover bid by the Quebec-based Hells Angels in the spring, police who monitor biker crime say.
>
> The recruiting is especially evident in the Metropolitan Toronto region, which has Canada's heaviest concentration of biker gangs.
>
> Three of Metro's biggest gangs have bolstered their ranks by 25 percent since last fall, one source said. "They're really getting some serious muscle in."
>
> "Short of some divine intervention, this city's in for a hell of an awakening," Detective Jim Downs, head of the Metro Toronto Police biker squad, said in an interview. "It has the potential to become worse than what's happening in Montreal." Guns and bombs have claimed two dozen victims, including an 11-year-old boy.
>
> Last summer's brief outbreak of hostilities around Toronto, marked by fire-bombings of several biker-owned businesses, were just a foretaste, Detective Downs said. "There'll be no more of these love taps. When they blow up a building, they'll take a block with it."

I spent two days on radio and television trying to calm the hysteria caused by Detective Downs's comments. A man paid to know the truth predicted death and destruction the likes of which Toronto had never seen. I politely attributed the statements to faulty analysis, and explained the different ways the Hells Angels had tried to infiltrate Ontario and how they would try in the future.

Detective Downs was under a lot of pressure. Although Toronto has the largest concentration of bikers in the world and the largest police force in the country, with 6,500 members, its vaunted biker unit consisted of two men who scrambled to keep tabs on nearly five hundred bikers and a possible 5,000 associates, as well as their women and the assorted hoods they dealt with. Downs desperately needed a larger budget. (Detective Downs was transferred to other duties shortly after he made the comments to the *Globe*. He now works as an investigator for the Toronto Police Association who gathers information on the backgrounds of police critics.)

Two months later, the crafty Hells Angels initiated the second leg of their current plan to take over Ontario.

The Memorial Run is the first event on the bikers' social calendar. Toronto gangs meet at the Para-Dice Riders' clubhouse on Eastern Avenue on the first convenient Saturday in May and spend the day parading from one cemetery to another along a 320-kilometer route in the Toronto area to pay respects at the graves of dead bikers. The night before the run, the Satan's Choice gloated at being able to announce the next morning to the gathered bikers that twenty members of the Woodbridge Loners would from that day prospect for the Choice. Such a show of force at the year's first event was good for status.

Although Toronto's six biker gangs had beefed up their membership since the previous summer's violence, the Satan's Choice had been most aggressive. On April 13, they convinced the five members of the Lost Souls in Milton to become Choice. Milton was booming with suburban yuppies and was a virgin drug market. The Lost Souls were a new gang, made up of disgruntled Black Diamond Riders who wanted to live the life of one-percenters—the one percent of motorcyclists who live outside society's laws, norms, and values. Black Diamond president and founder Johnny Sombrero, arguably one of the toughest bikers in Toronto in the 1960s and 1970s, kept a tight rein on his gang and shunned the outlaw image. He wanted to rebuild his gang with members who had no criminal records and didn't deal drugs.

The twenty Loners walked into the PDR clubhouse Saturday morning, May 4, and asked to be immediately accepted as PDR prospects. The PDR, who didn't like the Choice, jumped at the chance to bolster their ranks and pull a quick one on the devil. They didn't have enough prospect patches to go around, but the Loners who got them sewed them onto their colors immediately. The event shocked all bikers gathered outside, but none so much as the Choice, who nearly rumbled with the PDR three weeks later during a public demonstration at the provincial legislature against roadside stops of bikers.

The Loners successfully carried out the plan crafted by the Nomads chapter of the Hells Angels. They infiltrated the Para-Dice Riders, the gang the Angels had targeted for takeover. The Loners were the Hells Angels' Trojan horse. Their goal was to gather intelligence on PDR members who could be swayed and those who needed to be killed. They also needed to gain influence within the gang to get members to vote to become Hells Angels. The PDR's membership may have increased by twenty-five percent, but they failed to see the enemy within their ranks.

(Politicians unexpectedly scored a victory in the battle against club-houses at the end of August, when the Loners vacated their Toronto clubhouse on Denison Road East under a court order which had been sought by the city. Mr. Justice D.J. Cameron of Ontario Court, General Division, ruled that the clubhouse was not zoned for use as a private or commercial club. He told the gang to vacate by September 1. The victory raises a question: why haven't politicians or police objected to the presence of the Para-Dice Riders, Vagabonds, and Outlaws club-houses in residential areas?)

The Hells Angels' attempt to subvert the Para-Dice Riders will be the true test of brotherhood in Ontario. Everywhere they have gone, the Hells Angels have destroyed the mythical biker brotherhood with greed. This is their legacy to biker subculture. Bikers, who could once rely on a brother biker for help, can no longer trust the guy next to them. Toronto is the last bastion of biker brotherhood in the world. Nowhere else do so many gangs exist peacefully. A successful Hells Angels takeover would signal the demise of brotherhood as well as the last vestige of friendship. From then on, it's every man for himself. The Hells Angels have proven over and over that they kill their own when business warrants it. They choose the almighty dollar over a friend. That is why their passage is marked by blood.

The Hells Angels have bet everything on this operation. They have burned many bridges over the years, some which even money can't repair. Many Ontario drug dealers refused to deal with the Hells Angels after they killed David Boyko (past president of Winnipeg's Los Brovos motorcycle gang) in the Maritimes in May after a dispute with an Angel drug dealer. The Satan's Choice forbid its members from buying Hells Angels' drugs and will no longer party with them. The Los Brovos are destined to become the first Hells Angels chapter in Manitoba. If the Angels could kill their past president over a drug dispute, they could kill anyone.

Perhaps the most important event in Satan's Choice history since they were founded by Bernie Guindon in 1965 was their leader's retirement in June 1996. Nearly five hundred bikers showed up at a two-day field party on a forty-acre farm outside Port Perry at the end of June to bid the 53-year-old biker farewell. Guindon gave up his presidency in 1995 to mark his thirtieth anniversary with the gang, and now he was relinquishing his job as national secretary-treasurer. Although he spent many years in jail on drug charges in the 1970s and 1980s, Guindon always denied his gang was involved in crime.

Guindon's departure left the future of the Satan's Choice in doubt. His firm hand had kept the gang out of the Hells Angels' clutches. Younger, greedier members would be more susceptible to the Angels' tantalizing advances.

Former biker-gang presidents don't fare well. Rayne Doherty, who was president of the Lost Souls in Milton before they changed allegiance to the Satan's Choice, was confronted by two members outside the clubhouse in an industrial strip north of Highway 401 at 5:30 a.m. on October 2. They pumped five shots point-blank at Doherty as he got out of his car. They missed. Doherty hopped into his car and called police on his cell phone.

The Satan's Choice were not impressed. The Milton chapter had been under control of the Satan's Choice Kitchener chapter, whose church meetings—weekly meetings—members had to attend until the gang deemed them competent to run their own area. After the shooting screw-up, the Milton clubhouse was shut down and members were forced to answer to an associate gang of the Choice, the Royal City Riders, in nearby Guelph.

The Royal City Riders are a prime example of why the public should distrust motorcycle clubs who affect the outlaw biker lifestyle. There are millions of law-abiding motorcyclists in North America. Most ride alone, as one should, but many belong to clubs that socialize and tour. These range from mom-and-pop clubs to those which closely approximate outlaw bikers. Many of the fringe clubs present themselves as lobby groups for bikers' rights (mostly the right to ride without a helmet). Some organize fundraising and public-relations events. All of them welcome outlaw bikers, who use the events to sanitize their images. Often, outlaw bikers create and run the fringe groups behind the scenes. The Modified Motorcycle Association in California was created by the Hells Angels. Any event sanctioned by the MMA is sanctioned by the Hells Angels.

One of the fringe clubs is ABATE, Association of Bikers Aware Toward Education. Police do not consider this club to be a criminal gang, so it was a great surprise when the ABATE chapter in Guelph became the Royal City Riders early in 1996.

Wayne Greavette, 42, did not want to become an outlaw biker. He was an avid motorcyclist who liked to party, but he was not a criminal. He was the only ABATE member to walk away from the gang. He bought a hundred-acre farm in Puslinch Township for $600,000 in June and let bikers party there. Greavette walked out to the mailbox shortly before 1 p.m. on Thursday, December 12, and picked up a small parcel the postman dropped off. He chatted with his wife in his office as he opened it. The parcel exploded and killed Greavette.

The Choice, in what appeared to be an affront to Hells Angel Walter Stadnick, opened a chapter in his home town of Hamilton early in 1996. Most of its twenty members were beefy steroid monsters who gave the impression they were there to protect turf.

The Hamilton chapter didn't fare well. The Satan's Choice was targeted by the OPP, who set up Operation Dismantle to whittle down the criminal empire of Ontario's largest biker gang. On Thursday, December 19, cops arrested nearly a hundred Choice members and associates during raids on clubhouses and homes across the province. They seized an $11-million hydroponic pot farm, an Ecstasy-packaging lab, and a quarter-million dollars in other drugs, handguns, machine guns, and rifles.

The raids were part of an OPP plan to target a different gang each year and do as much damage to its criminal operations as possible. In 1996, 109 of the 125 Choice members were arrested. They nailed the Outlaws in Hamilton and St. Catharines in 1995.

Road Checks

The Para-Dice Riders, who had been stopped regularly by the Durham Regional Police east of Toronto on their way to their summer property in Caesarea, took the cops to court in 1996 in a civil action that alleged the road checks violated their rights under the Charter of Rights and Freedoms to not be arbitrarily detained. They claimed the police were high-handed and malicious in their treatment of the bikers, and that the roadblocks were designed to intimidate and harass them and their guests. PDR president Lorne Brown, past vice-president Donny Petersen, member Tero Rampanen, and 689571 Ontario Limited (operating as Sovereign Property Corporation) sued police; they were asking for $50,000 in general damages, $10,000 in exemplary damages, court costs, and the immediate halt of the road checks.

Although neither side knew it at the outset, by the trial's opening day they realized that despite decades of road checks of biker convoys around the world, no one had ever challenged this police tactic on legal grounds. The PDR had an opportunity to strike a blow for fellow bikers everywhere and set a precedent that would severely curb police powers. And all they had wanted initially was to be allowed to ride to their party grounds unhindered.

The police had to defend their use of roadside stops at all costs. A win by the PDR would allow bikers across North America to roam highways unchallenged while police stood by helplessly. But the case also presented police with the opportunity to set a precedent of their own. A court sanction of road checks based on the premise that biker gangs are criminal groups would mean open season on traveling bikers.

The PDRs talked themselves into the court action after being stopped four times in 1991 and 1992. They complained so much that other bikers egged them on until they were convinced they could beat the cops in court. It is ironic that a self-defined gang of outlaws, who call themselves one-percenters, should seek shelter behind one of those laws.

The PDR copied the Hells Angels and set up a legal defense fund to pay lawyers. They solicited money through biker-magazine ads, in bars, and at biker events. Other gangs and their associates contributed.

I was approached by Sergeant Tom Hart of the Durham Regional Police intelligence branch, the man who coordinated the force's legal defense. He needed expert witnesses and wanted a former Hells Angel informant to testify that the PDR had links with the Angels. I introduced him to the informant. My two books on the Hells Angels were also introduced into evidence to give the judge historical perspective and background information on the criminal activities of biker gangs. My first book had already been used as evidence against the Hells Angels in court by the New Hampshire State Police. During the raids which led to that court case, police found a copy of my book on a desk in the home office of a Hells Angel, with a pearl-handled, .45-caliber semi-automatic pistol lying on it. The book had been given to him by Fuki Fukishima of the San Francisco chapter, who signed it.

The Para-Dice Riders used a schoolhouse near Barrie, one hour north of Toronto, as their summer clubhouse until 1990. To protect their gatherings from the prying eyes of police, they cut down hundreds of trees and built a stockade.

Cops stopped them every time they traveled to the Vespra Township property during the 1970s and 1980s. The bikers' anger boiled over in 1989 and they retained Toronto lawyer Harry Kopyto, renowned for his toughness, to sue OPP Commissioner Archie Ferguson for alleged harassment and abuse by police over the decades. The suit was prompted by a September 1987 raid on the summer clubhouse. The case did not go to trial. One biker stubbed out his cigarette on Kopyto's conference table during their last meeting.

By 1990 they had tired of the intensive interest police, especially the OPP, showed in their holiday activities, and sought a property in a less-policed area where their reputation didn't precede them. They bought the Beacon Marina on an acre of land on the west shore of Lake Scugog, near Caesarea (population seven hundred), under power of sale. The place had a two-story hall, a storage building, a beach with two docks, and a large parking lot.

Bikers are a social lot, and a typical party at the marina attracted upward of three hundred people. The Durham Regional Police were quick to put a damper on the proceedings. They set up roadblocks on the two roads that led into the marina in May, July, August, and September 1991. The main roadblock on Regional Road 57 forced bikers to pull into the Scugog Firehall parking lot where their motor-cycles were checked for road worthiness, driver's licenses and insurance were verified, and their names were run through the Canadian Police Information Computer for possible parole or probation violations and arrest warrants. In fact, police already had CPIC printouts and knew who to look for.

The Para-Dice Riders made an application in Ontario Court, General Division in June 1991, for an injunction against the roadside stops because the police were violating their rights by arbitrarily detaining them. The police, who had been served papers, failed to attend the hearing and were shocked when the judge granted the PDR an interim injunction for one week. This allowed the bikers to travel unhindered. The police took the next court appearance more seriously, and showed up. At that hearing the PDR sought an interlocutory injunction to halt all road checks until their civil suit against the police was heard. They didn't get it, and police roadblocks continued until January 1996, when the suit finally went to court.

On the trial's first day, January 15, the police faced criminal charges when the judge learned they had illegally wired the courthouse with video cameras which they monitored from a room in the building. The law prohibits the taking of pictures, moving or still, of anyone who enters or leaves a courtroom. A police officer told the judge he had no idea he needed the court's permission to set up a surveillance operation in a courthouse. He said he did so with the best of intentions—to provide security for a former Hells Angel who would testify for police.

Police argued in court that the Para-Dice Riders are an outlaw motorcycle gang that threatens public safety. They said that as of January 3, 1996, there were 434 outlaw bikers in Ontario with 2,744 convictions, 422 of them for crimes of violence and 259 for crimes that involved weapons. Of 62 Para-Dice Riders, 40 had a total of 370 convictions, 67 of them for crimes of violence and 31 for crimes that involved violence.

Police said that in the interest of public safety they manned the roadblock with 1 staff-sergeant, 3 sergeants, 46 uniformed officers (8 of them at the little-used second road into the marina), 8 to 10 tactical support officers in full gear, an identification officer to photograph and videotape the bikers, and a police dog with its handler. Also present were 5 to 10 police intelligence officers from other police departments. Two police cruisers patrolled nearby Port Perry bars and waterfront. The police used a mobile command center, a paddy wagon, twelve marked cruisers with computers to run checks on bikers, gas generators, spot lights, and breathalizer machines. The tactical unit had a Brinks truck to be used as a battering ram, and a weapons truck.

Police stopped anyone who looked like a biker, checked his paperwork, motorcycle and helmet, and took his picture for their records. Few bikers were asked if they had been drinking. One biker was charged with trespassing when he tried to photograph police. A handful of driving and various unsafe motorcycle charges were laid. None ended up in court.

The judge did not pull punches in his scrutiny of police evidence, which included testimony, memoranda prepared before and after the stops, and videos showing police conduct at the roadblock. Judge Donald Ferguson's judgment shows that the purpose of the road checks was one of the principal issues in the case:

> The plaintiffs allege that the purpose was primarily intelligence-gathering and harassment. The police allege that there were multiple purposes, none of which can be identified as the main purpose.
>
> The issue is difficult because of the lapse of time, the potentially self-

serving nature of the explanations, the lack of specific evidence of discussions of purpose by the police, and the risk that the police have retrospectively tried to justify the operations.

There is also a subtle problem of distinguishing the purpose of the defendant [Durham Regional Police Service] from that of individual officers who planned or carried out the road checks.

Beginning in 1994, the defendant's officers began preparing briefing reports in advance in which they specifically set out multiple purposes of the road checks. The police memoranda created before the road checks at issue in this trial are much less specific. A memorandum of March 21, 1991, stated that the "requested equipment and manpower will be necessary to control the members and associates of the gang and to prevent any confrontations with members of the public." The same comment is made in memoranda dated June 25, 1991, and September 2, 1991. The following appears in a memorandum dated May 21, 1992:

> Because east coast gangs have been invited, it is anticipated that gang members will be arriving on Friday afternoon and evening and Saturday morning, as they have done in past years. Therefore our office feels it would be extremely beneficial for intelligence-gathering if a "spot check" was set up on Friday, June 12th in the evening hours as well as on Saturday, June 13th.

> Due to information received by the writer as well as from the O.P.P. Special Squad, it is verily believed that there will be some form of confrontation during the weekend.

> Informant information received is the Paradice [sic] Riders are still extremely upset at our Service for the situation that took place in Caesarea last September. Due to this possible "threat," as well as the number of gang members and their associate[s] that will be attending this function, the following equipment and manpower would be requested in order to institute a proper spot check program.

None of the reports prepared after the operations contains anything which clearly identifies the purposes or which measure whether they were achieved.

The defendant claims that the road checks were conducted for the following purposes:

a. to establish a police presence in the hamlet of Caesarea to reassure the local residents who were allegedly intimidated by the large numbers of bikers. [Author's note: The judge noted earlier in his judgment that not one member of the public had complained to the police about the bikers.]

b. to let the Paradise [sic] Riders know through the police presence that the peace will be maintained.

c. to investigate for contraventions of the Highway Traffic Act and the Compulsory Automobile Insurance Act.

d. to provide an opportunity to check for outstanding warrants for arrest.

e. to investigate any criminal or drug violations.

f. to identify all alleged biker gangs, members, associates, and persons allegedly known to be engaged in criminal activity in attendance at the function.

g. to identify stolen motorcycle parts. . . .

I reject the plaintiff's contention that there was a primary or dominant purpose. . . I also find that there were legitimate factual reasons for the police to wish to pursue these purposes. I also find the police acted in good faith in organizing the road checks and in stopping vehicles.

Having ruled that road checks are legal and that police had reasonable grounds to conduct them, Judge Ferguson mentioned the other issues brought forth by the Para-Dice Riders, although he was not required to rule on them. Before he did, however, he announced that a pre-trial deal agreed upon by the cops and bikers severely watered down the weight of the verdict.

While all parties originally intended this to be a test case concerning the legality of this type of road check, the case has some significant limitations in this regard. Because of the limited issues pleaded in the statement of claim, a number of issues which arose from the evidence cannot be pursued. There were lengthy submissions at trial concerning the scope of the claim. I made a ruling which would have allowed the plaintiffs to pursue a number of issues on terms including the plaintiffs bearing some expenses and costs. To avoid that financial expense the plaintiffs then agreed with the defendant to limit the issues. Consequently, I have not explored the allegations that the procedures at the road check were illegal on the ground that they allegedly breached the plaintiff's rights to security and rights to be free from unreasonable search and seizure under sections 7 and 8 of the Charter.

Also, because it was not pleaded, the issue of whether Rampanen had a claim in tort for assault was not pursued. Further, because the plaintiffs abandoned a tort claim relating to the photographing and videoing [sic], and never pleaded any tort claim based on the alternative possibility that the road checks were not a breach of the Charter but that the police were liable in tort for exceeding their authority during the check stops, the plaintiffs can obtain no relief on those grounds. The action was commenced outside the six-month limitation period applicable under the Public Authorities Protection Act and it appears that some common-law tort issues were not raised for this reason.

While no relief by way of damages or injunction can be awarded, I shall, nevertheless, make some findings about the legality of certain activity which was the object of evidence and submissions because otherwise the trial will be of very limited benefit to either side in terms of giving guidance in future situations. Also, the legality of the conduct is in my view a factor to be considered on the question of costs.

Judge Ferguson noted he did not need to rule on these issues because he had disposed of the matter on other grounds. He ruled that the bikers were not arbitrarily detained contrary to section 9 of the Charter, which states: "Everyone has the right not to be arbitrarily detained or imprisoned." The police had a right to stop and check them. He did, however, make findings against the police which could have caused them grief had the PDR's case been better structured. Judge Ferguson wrote:

> In this case the evidence showed that the police exceeded the scope of their authority under the Highway Traffic Act in several ways. They asked drivers questions such as where they were going or coming from; the video showed one officer surreptitiously looked in the saddlebag of a motorcycle; they asked questions of the passengers including asking for identification. . . .
>
> I conclude that the stops at the road checks were authorized by the Highway Traffic Act which has been held to justify a breach of s. 9. The fact that the police exceeded their authority under the Highway Traffic Act did not make them liable for a breach of s. 9.

Because of the restricted complaint agreed to by the Para-Dice Riders, their claim for relief on the grounds that police unlawfully took photographs and videos, unlawfully questioned drivers and passengers, assaulted PDR Tero Rampanen, and that police conduct warranted exemplary damages, could not be pursued because they failed to prove police had breached section 9 of the Charter.

Judge Ferguson highlighted questionable police behavior in his judgment to put it on the public record and send a warning to authorities that they should clean up their act, lest they give bikers ammunition to use against them in court.

The alleged assault on Rampanen was the subject of evidence called by both sides and of final submissions. Because it is important in the context of providing guidance to both sides in future road checks, and may be a consideration as to costs, I shall analyze the evidence about the incident.

Unlike the typical case facing the courts where there is only conflicting testimony about the event, here there was also a video which captured the event and most of the surrounding circumstances.

The video was taken on September 7, 1991, in daylight. It shows Rampanen at the road check, standing beside his motorcycle, facing a group of police officers. There are numerous officers in the background including one who is directly behind Rampanen and seems to be closely following the situation.

A uniformed officer repeatedly asks Rampanen to surrender his papers. There is a running dialogue between Rampanen and that officer during which Rampanen says, *inter alia*: "I don't give a fuck." "You are not taking my stuff." "I'll hold it and you fucking write it down." "I don't give a fuck what I'm supposed to do, you asshole."

During this dialogue Rampanen is pulling out his wallet and removing his papers. He eventually holds a paper up with a hand on each corner and holds it up in front of the officer. During these events there are at least four other officers, including tactical unit members, within six feet of Rampanen. Standing in the same group is Paul Braybrook, a member of the Paradise [sic] Riders, who appears to say nothing. He approached the group at the beginning of the conversation, greeted Rampanen, and then stood facing him. He testified that he was assigned by the club to attend the road checks to take videos and to encourage bikers to cooperate with the police. He appears to be quietly playing that role in this scene.

, Immediately after Rampanen holds up his papers and calls the officer an asshole, a very large officer walks around behind Rampanen and whispers in his ear, "You are under arrest for causing a disturbance." That officer immediately grabs Rampanen around the neck in an armlock and pulls him off-balance backwards and sideways. Simultaneously, at least three other officers, including two tactical officers, grab Rampanen by the arms and several more officers move close to assist. The officers drag Rampanen toward the firehall while the original officer keeps him in the armlock. As they reach the firehall the group falls to the ground on top of Rampanen. The arresting officer testified that they tripped over each other's feet. Rampanen is handcuffed, pulled to his feet, and taken into the firehall. Throughout these events Rampanen says nothing.

During the earlier dialogue at least three officers walk behind Rampanen but within hearing distance and appear to pay little attention, although one smiles. The other officers who are visible in the near background—perhaps 20 feet away—occasionally look toward Rampanen but do not seem to be disturbed. Those officers do not interrupt their conversations with each other.

Rampanen never raises his voice above loud conversation. He makes no threatening gestures. Both his hands are on his papers.

The officer who arrested Rampanen was a roving officer and not the one who was demanding his papers. The arresting officer said he thought Rampanen was highly agitated and was concerned that the incident would escalate if nothing were done. He testified that he put on the armlock and dragged him toward the firehall as he believed this was the safest and quickest way to diffuse the situation.

The officer said the disturbance consisted of Rampanen shouting and swearing. I find that there was no shouting. He agreed that the offense required the actual causing of a disturbance. I find there was no disturbance.

The only charge laid was causing a disturbance and this was not proceeded with because the officer was not given notice of the court date.

The behavior of Rampanen was rude, inappropriate, and obviously offensive, and I am sympathetic to police who have to endure this type of abuse during the course of their duties; however, this is not the issue here. Section 33(1) of the Highway Traffic Act requires a driver to "surrender the licence for reasonable inspection upon the demand of a police officer." Section 3(1) of the Compulsory Insurance Act contains the same requirement concerning an insurance card. I find that Rampanen was legally obliged to hand the officer the papers and not just show them. I also find that there were no reasonable and probable grounds for arresting Rampanen for the offense of causing a disturbance. I also find that the officers used excessive force. There is no evidence which would justify any force. The officers assaulted Rampanen.

Rampanen gave an exaggerated version of the event. I find that he suffered no significant injury.

The circumstances justified the original officer in charging Rampanen with failing to comply with s. 33, but there was no reason to arrest him. The officers knew Rampanen. I note that many charges were laid under this section during the road checks.

In view of the conclusions I have reached, I find that the road checks did not violate the plaintiff's rights under s. 9 of the Charter and, alternatively, that if they did then they were authorized by the provisions of the Highway Traffic Act which the courts have found to be justifiable under s. 1. I also find that the plaintiffs have not proved the tort of abuse of process. The action is therefore dismissed.

The decision told outlaw bikers they don't own the highways, and because of the criminal lifestyle they have chosen, they can expect to be stopped and questioned by police not only for the safety of the public, but to deter any criminally inclined bikers by having their presence noted and recorded.

The Para-Dice Riders appealed Judge Ferguson's decision. In the months before the decision was to be handed down, the bikers lobbied the left wing of the legal community intensively. The main complainant in the suit was Donny Petersen, past vice-president of the Para-Dice Riders who owns Heavy Duty Cycles on Kingston Road in Toronto.

Petersen met and courted Bay Street investment executive and Empire Club president Gareth Seltzer, who bought his first Harley in 1995. Petersen told Seltzer about the lawsuit and gave him Judge Ferguson's judgment to read. Seltzer passed it on to friend Peter Hogg, Canada's foremost constitutional law expert.

In the meantime, Seltzer was stopped by police with just cause. They treated him well and did not ticket him after he agreed to rectify the problem with his license plate. But he took the stop personally and started to see the world through Donny Petersen's eyes. Seltzer rode his Harley to a PDR party in Caesarea and was stopped by police at a road check. They treated him well. Seltzer invited Petersen to address the Empire Club with Mr. Hogg. The Empire Club has been addressed by heads of church, state, and industry.

The Para-Dice Riders heralded the event in a press release on their website:

The Empire Club of Canada which has provided a platform since 1903 to discuss relevant issues affecting society is situated in Toronto's Royal York Hotel and is widely covered by the television and print media.

Previous guests have included Ronald Reagan, the Dalai Lama, Billy Graham, Bill Gates and various prime ministers of Canada, Hungary, and Ireland.

Members of the Empire Club include the Governor General of Canada, the Lieutenant Governor of Ontario, as well as prominent members of the business, political, and judicial communities.

Peter Hogg, a law professor at York University and a recognized leading expert on the Constitution will Chair the luncheon meeting on Oct. 9, 1997.

Donny Petersen will address the meeting about a lawsuit that he, Lorne Brown, and Tero Rampanen have launched on behalf of the Para-Dice Riders Motorcycle Club of Toronto against The Durham Police Board.

At issue is the Para-Dice Rider contention that police blockades of their summer property northwest of Toronto are illegal and a breach of the Constitution.

Police Forces around North America are watching with great interest as this will be the first precedent-setting case involving such roadblocks which often masquerade as RIDE spot-checks whose sole purpose is to curb drinking and driving.

While the Para-Dice Riders insist that they are only looking for free access to their property, the outcome of the case will affect the way police forces conduct themselves in the stopping of motorists both here and in the United States.

The case has been progressing for the last four years and will probably be heard in the Ontario Court of Appeal early in 1998. After that, either side may appeal to the Supreme Court of Canada.

Canada's top constitutional lawyers and legal movers and shakers sat with ten Para-Dice Riders as Donny Petersen addressed the Empire Club:

While we were singing O Canada, I was thinking that to be born and/or to live in this country, that God has given each of us two aces in the poker hand of life from the getgo.

It is within this context that I wish you to view my ensuing comments.

By the way, I don't normally dress this way [in a suit]. But that will teach me, as I have left my speech in my black leather jacket at home.

I have been a Para-Dice Rider for 26 years and I must say that we are unlikely charter candidates. No one is going to feel sorry for a motorcycle club, gang, launching a suit against a police department. I mean this is the bad guys against the good guys.

But we have been painted into a corner. The only problem is that we are not holding the paint brush.

We only want access to a property that we own, but are denied free entry by the police.

This is all we want now and it's all we have wanted all along.

We do not want to hamstring the police in pursuing their legitimate duties. We are not interested in changing laws or setting case precedents. We had no intention of wanting to change the law here in Canada and in the United States.

All's we want is to get into our property without being blockaded.

Here is how this relates to you and the rest of North America.

There is no case law either here or in the USA dealing with how police are able to stop and monitor groups of people. Police departments everywhere use roadblocks to monitor and arbitrarily detain citizens including motorcyclists.

As this case winds its way into the Ontario Court of Appeal next spring and then on to the Supreme Court of Canada, new law is going to be enshrined on how police deal with different groups that thread their way through our society—how police deal with divergent groups such as Aboriginals, or what about congregating unionists such as the Queen's Park demonstrations last year. In any case, there are hundreds of examples that we could draw upon.

So, let's get to the heart of the case the Para-Dice Riders are involved in.

We, by that I mean the club members, purchased a power-of-sale marina on the southern shore of Lake Scugog in the tiny hamlet of Caesarea a few miles east of Port Perry in 1990. This marina was purchased to be a recreational spot for our club members, their families, and invited guests. It is not operated as a business.

There are only two roads that lead into the hamlet and dead-end there.

About 70 to 90 police officers will congregate here and operate roadblocks with the express purpose of stopping our membership and their guests. Overhead, sometimes a small police plane will circle above the marina. At other times it will be a police helicopter. On the lake, in front of our facility, two police boats, one from Durham, the other from the OPP will operate in order to stop everyone leaving or entering our marina. In Port Perry, at the local docks, one or two police cars will stop any sneaky bikers from attempting to gain access to the marina by water.

The roadblock, more correctly described as a blockade, is comprised of RCMP down to local departments. Officers from as far away as Sudbury and Hamilton have been observed, as well as visiting American police observers. There are uniformed officers with their patrol cars, there is a fully dressed SWAT team carrying weapons that range from four-foot truncheons to automatic weapons (as in machine guns). Plain-clothes officers seem to direct the actions of the rest. There is a ram vehicle which is an old Brinks truck fitted with a hydraulic ram. There are dogs and their handlers, paddy wagons, and a weapons truck.

All of this for such nefarious crimes as failure to sign your ownerships or having a scratch on your helmet.

You'll read ongoing items in the media, such as 130 Para-Dice Riders were charged last weekend with various offences. The media propagates this type of biker mythology and the legend of badness grows. I've told you the types of crimes, and now I'll let you know that the vast majority of these charges have been either withdrawn by the Crown prosecutor or have been put into limbo awaiting the outcome of our Constitutional Charter challenge.

Now! If you are riding a Harley-Davidson, you are pulled over into a vacant lot to be processed. Likewise if you are in a car or truck and affect biker-lifestyle dress. But if you are on a Yamaha motorcycle you are waved through, as you are if you appear to be normal in a four-wheeled vehicle.

So, you're pulled in. What happens next? After surrendering your documentation, you are processed for any perceived infractions. Your demeanor is written down, as is who you are hanging around with. And you are still photographed as well as videotaped.

During our trial, I realized that it is unlawful for police to photograph or videotape you while being arbitrarily detained.

We tried to roll this issue over into our trial with the able assistance of our lawyer Robert Girvan. I mean, the video evidence of the police was already there, as were our videotapes showing this unlawful behavior. Their witnesses were already there, as were ours and this was all the same evidence that would allow a decision on both issues: the arbitrary detainment and the picture-taking while being detained.

Well, Judge Ferguson ruled that a separate trial would have to be held to decide the picture-taking issue.

Our legal advice indicated that worst-case scenario, the cost would approach $300,000.

I know bikers are supposed to be rich, but the Para-Dice Riders do not have this much money.

We would lose our properties and more under this scenario.

So we were forced to drop it and continue with just the arbitrary detainment challenge.

Let's back up a bit.

We wanted to be accepted by the community and to coexist in a friendly way.

Before any thought of going to court, we arranged a meeting with the Durham police to conciliate our problems. It was attended by a superintendent and five or six other officers. I felt that we developed a rapport, and left confident that once the police addressed their concerns for public safety the roadblocks would come down. After all, the superintendent indicated if there was no trouble, the police resources would be utilized elsewhere.

Well, the roadblocks continued unabated.

We then went for an injunction to stop the roadblocks but this became a Constitutional challenge. The ante kept getting raised, and not by us.

We even tried to call it off, with the concession to give us uninterrupted access to our marina, at the beginning of the lower court trial.

No way, they said. So here we are, mired but determined to go on. Just as they are.

I've been restricted to the time I have here to speak. I mean, I could go on a long time about this subject and what has happened to us.

So, I'll end my talk by discussing whether there is justice in Canada.

If you have access to wealth, or a *pro bono* lawyer; if you are patient, like if you got seven years of your time to spend dealing with this instead of being out making a living; if you are stubborn; and if you have courage (going up against a powerful institution like the police can be detrimental to your future well-being): well, then, it is true, there is access to justice in Canada.

However, if you don't have three hundred grand to challenge unlawful photography while being detained, then in this case access to justice is denied.

Thank you very much for listening to me today. It has been very educational for me.

It can be very strange where you wind up in life.

The Ontario Court of Appeal dismissed in January 1999 the Para-Dice Riders' bid to have Judge Ferguson's ruling overturned. The ruling would have allowed them to pursue their claim of $60,000 in damages.

The court also turned down their appeal of the judge's order denying their request to have the police pay their $30,000 legal costs. The Para-Dice Riders got off easy. Judge Ferguson did not order them to pay the police's $200,000 legal bill, even though they initiated the case and lost. This was partly due to their beating of Rampanen, questionable police testimony, and failure to prove proper pre-set goals for road checks. The judge was doubtful enough of the police to stick them with a hefty tab that would prompt police administrators to ensure the mistakes don't happen again. Police appealed this decision.

The Para-Dice Riders devoted a large portion of the website to their Right To Ride campaign. They reproduced portions of Judge Ferguson's judgment with their own comments attached. After a gentle tug at the heart strings, they used their website to appeal for cash.

We are fighting for our rights—AND YOURS—all the way to the Supreme Court of Canada!!

We believe that the REASONS FOR JUDGMENT document by the Ontario Court is seriously flawed.

- That it dismisses the rights of motorcyclists.
- That it allows police to use excessive force.
- That it disagrees with precedent cases.
- That it contradicts witness evidence.

We need your support! [Author's note: The last sentence is prefaced with a cute smiley face and sits atop a piggy bank.]

This is a long, consuming process. Unfortunately, it's also a very expensive one, as lawyers don't come cheap! We were forced to severely restrict the scope of the initial test case claims due to a lack of sufficient legal funding. That's not the way to victory.

If you care to help us with this battle against injustice, we would be extremely grateful. We have established a fund with the sole purpose of accumulating all contributions which will be used exclusively to help cover our legal expenses.

Please make cheque or money order payable to:
Right to Ride Legal Fund. [The address is given.]
Please do not send cash in the mail.

NOTE: For those folks who donate $25 or more, we will send you a "'Right To Ride" sticker for you to display your own intolerance of police harassment.

1997–1998

Ontario police didn't rest on their laurels after the success of Operation Dismantle against the Satan's Choice in 1996. They continued their investigation of the gang and on June 25, 1997, arrested thirty-one more Choice across Ontario on drugs and weapons charges. Police understood that periodic raids don't hurt biker gangs, but constant pressure makes it difficult for them to do business. Six more Satan's Choice members from Hamilton and Sudbury were charged on December 15, 1997, for the bombing of the Sudbury police station on December 15, 1996. The blast caused $133,000 in damage to the station and the nearby bank. Police had no motive for the bombing.

Operation Dismantle took the fight against outlaw bikers to a new level on April 16, 1998, when police confiscated the Satan's Choice Lottridge Street clubhouse in Hamilton under the Proceeds of Crime legislation. Police installed new locks and video monitors to keep members out. Police alleged that Choice president John Croitoru, 34, known to wrestling fans as Johnny K-9, bought the restaurant in 1996 for $40,000. Croitoru faced charges in the bombing of the Sudbury police station and was convicted on April 24, 1997, of trafficking in marijuana and the steroids Depo and Deco Testosterone. Jerry Juretta, 30, was charged, along with his girlfriend, with delivering the bomb to Sudbury. He pleaded guilty in 1991 to bombing a Hamilton house for a local mobster in 1988.

On July 13, 1998, seventeen more Satan's Choice, Outlaws, and associates were arrested in the Toronto area on stolen-property and drug charges. Police seized twelve stolen 4×4 sports utility vehicles, a boat motor, and a trailer: goods worth $700,000.

*   *   *

The success of Carcajou in stopping the war between the Hells Angels and Rock Machine in Quebec for twelve months showed police that bikers could be fought and beaten. But the pressure must be relentless. Police have always been more comfortable with problems that have a start and end. That's partly because promotions are granted based on success in closing cases. Few cops want to get involved in long-term projects for fear they will be forgotten and passed over for cops with a higher profile.

Ontario police used the fear generated by the death of 11-year-old Daniel Desrochers in Quebec to lobby politicians for more money. Twenty years of fear-mongering had taught them which buttons to push.

The Canadian Association of Chiefs of Police formed a committee called the National Strategy to Combat Outlaw Motorcycle Gangs in February 1996. The announcement of the committee's formation appeared under the headline: "National Strategy. Police declare war on bikers."

> Canada's cops are getting tough on outlaw bikers with a new national strategy they hope will lead to special biker squads countrywide, a top officer says.
>
> "Now they're putting, for lack of better words, their money where their mouth is," said Staff Sgt. J.P. Lévesque of the Criminal Intelligence Service of Canada, which is coordinating the new strategy.

Police planned to designate ten provincial coordinators to keep tabs on biker activities and to educate police and public.

The first goal of this group was to unite cops across the country to lobby for laws and money so they could better share information and coordinate the fight against bikers. They were motivated by the success of Quebec cops who had pushed for and got a federal anti-gang law when war broke out again between the Hells Angels and Rock Machine in Quebec. But, as I documented, police and politicians allowed the war to start when they stopped doing their job.

The National Strategy reflected badly on the Criminal Intelligence Service of Canada, which is administered by the RCMP and is mandated by all major Canadian law enforcement agencies as the lead agency to gather, analyze, and disseminate criminal intelligence in order to "effectively combat the spread of organized crime and other significant criminal activity in Canada." For decades, provincial criminal intelligence services gathered and analyzed information from police agencies in their provinces under the direction of a police coordinator who met with his provincial counterparts and the coordinator of the CISC in Ottawa. For decades, cops across the country complained they never got out of the CISC in Ottawa what they put into it. The CISC was a black hole into which all information vanished. Laundered reports appeared every year, but these were vague and meant for media and public consumption.

In a crafty political sleight of hand, the new national strategy kept all the same players and agencies, but gave them new titles.

Police linked to the National Strategy committee use every opportunity to plant fear stories in the media. The two point men who became spokesmen for the drive to get more laws and funding were then-Police

Chief Julian Fantino of London, Ontario, and RCMP Sergeant Jean-Pierre Lévesque, head of the outlaw biker desk for the Criminal Intelligence Service of Canada.

Sergeant Lévesque used every Hells Angels event as a peg to which he attached dire warnings of worse things to come. He saw unwarranted significance in every move the Hells Angels made. No one questioned a cop who had access to the highest level of biker intelligence in the country. He continued the tradition of predicting how the Hells Angels would invade Ontario. The predictions made great headlines, but they were wrong. For the doomsayer with the sign that reads "The world ends tomorrow," there is always another tomorrow.

*   *   *

The following story ran in a Toronto newspaper on July 22, 1997, one day before Alberta's Grim Reapers became Hells Angels. The headline: "Hells Angels preparing for Ontario: Gang expert":

> Once the Hells Angels have marked their turf in the rest of Canada they'll set their sights on Ontario, says Canada's leading expert on outlaw gangs.
>
> And that takeover bid could come with all the violence associated with Quebec's biker wars, warned Sergeant Jean-Pierre Lévesque of the RCMP.
>
> "Their goal is to take over the drug distribution market in all of Canada," said Lévesque, who also works for the Criminal Intelligence Service of Canada.
>
> "Once they have Ontario surrounded on both sides, they will try and come in from each end.
>
> "And," he said, "they are very close to having the province surrounded."
>
> RCMP say a "patch over"—in which the Grim Reapers bike club of Red Deer, Alta., will doff their insignia in favor of the winged skull of the Angels—is set for today. The move will give the Hells Angels a foothold in Alberta.

Nine members and associates of the Sherbrooke, Quebec, chapter of the Hells Angels who drove to Toronto in a Cadillac and a 4×4 vehicle were escorted by a procession of Para-Dice Riders on Harleys to the gang's Eastern Avenue clubhouse for the weekly meeting on September 3, 1997. Police intercepted them half a mile from the clubhouse and arrested Hells Angel Sylvain Vachon on an outstanding assault warrant issued in Sudbury. The Hells Angels ordered half the bikers to wait outside the clubhouse while they talked business with the executive and several long-standing, influential members.

Here's how police interpretation of the event was reported in a Toronto newspaper under the headline "Hells Angels revving up to move here" on September 6:

Police believe a recent meeting between Sherbrooke's Hells Angels and Toronto's Para-Dice Riders may indicate the notorious gang has speeded up its timetable to enter Ontario. . . .

"That was obviously a meeting," said Det. Bob Lines of the OPP biker squad. The Hells Angels' "intention is to move into Ontario. It's coming down to the short strokes."

"You know something is in the works," another police source said. The meeting between the clubs "is significant for sure" because it comes at a time when gangs are clarifying alliances.

Last weekend, three rivals—the Outlaws, Montreal's Rock Machine and the Houston-based Banditos [sic]—met in Ottawa, possibly to forge a new pact to counter the Hells Angels.

The story below ran in another Toronto newspaper on October 12, 1997: "Police fear losing fight with bikers. Lack resources and political willpower":

Canadian police are starting to lose the war against outlaw motorcycle gangs, senior police officials say.

Investigators don't have the manpower and support from politicians and courts to win the fight against biker gangs, said Julian Fantino, chief of the London police.

Speaking at a news conference Friday after two days of meetings between American, Canadian, and European police officials, Fantino said police are being "nickled and dimed all over the place."

"We have not been able to keep up with them [the gangs] because of resource concerns and labor-intensive, bureaucratic laws," he said.

Fantino said many police officers waste their time in courthouse lobbies while cases are adjourned and delayed.

Motorcycle gangs have become "sophisticated" at manipulating the justice system to squander police resources, he said.

Jean-Pierre Lévesque, of the RCMP Criminal Intelligence Service, said the gang war in Quebec could spread to Ontario now that members of the Outlaws and Rock Machine gangs have formed an alliance in eastern Ontario.

"They've sent a message to the Hells Angels that they won't leave

Ontario without a fight. The Outlaws were decimated in Ontario by police tactics [a series of arrests in Toronto and Ottawa three years ago], but many of them are getting out of jail and back into business," Lévesque said. . . .

Fantino said anti-biker legislation passed by Ottawa earlier this year won't be a magic broom that sweeps gangs off the street. The legislation, passed in April, makes it a crime to participate in a criminal organization and gives police the power to seize the proceeds of organized crime.

"Just because we now have a law doesn't realize anything unless we have the support programs, which means resources for police and enhanced training," he said.

Predictions of war made the headlines in another Toronto newspaper on October 18, 1997: "Bloody biker wars feared. Expansion of gangs into Ontario could spark deadly violence, cops say."

Now police are intensifying their war against outlaw motorcycle gangs—particularly the Hells Angels—because of their growing threat.

The Rock Machine in Montreal, thought to have been an easy target for the powerful Hells Angels, is instead expanding, recruiting new members in their three-year war.

The Hells Angels are in Ontario, shopping for an ally, and have found one in the Toronto-based Para-Dice Riders.

The relationship only came to light by chance last month when Metro police arrested a member of the Hells Angels, and found themselves surrounded and challenged by more than two dozen bike-riding PDRs who were escorting the Hells Angels to a "church meeting"at the local club's Eastern Avenue bunker. . . .

The Hells Angels also have swallowed up the Grim Reapers in Alberta, have signed up Saskatchewan's Rebels as a prospect club—a move to annex the club into theirs—and appear to be siding up to the Los Bravos in Manitoba.

Meanwhile, the Outlaws and Rock Machine seem to have allied them-selves with the Houston-based Banditos [sic], a sworn enemy of the Hells. And if the Rock Machine get a Bandito's [sic] patch, they'll be able to open chapters in Canada as an international gang.

Police fear that could divide the country into two, with the Banditos [sic] and their allies on one side, and the Hells Angels and their pals on the other. The Banditos [sic] and the Hells Angels are also at war in Denmark and Sweden. . . .

The fear among anti-biker cops is that bloodshed will spread from Europe and Quebec into Ontario.

"I can see the bike gangs in Ontario that have been here for years not laying down and getting walked over" by the Hells Angels, and violence could erupt, said OPP Det.-Const. Joe Dorricott of Ontario's Criminal Intelligence Service.

"I don't know when, we don't want it to happen like in Quebec, 60 people killed in two, three years," he said.

"History speaks for itself," RCMP Insp. Jean-Pierre Lévesque adds.

"They have a trail of violence. That's their main tool."

Lévesque, with the Criminal Intelligence Service of Canada, is on a nationwide tour sponsored by *Reader's Digest* to get the public eye on the the nation's 40 gangs with 12,000 members. . . .

"We're not trying to be alarmists," Lévesque added. "Just because there are no bombs here or in other places in Canada, it doesn't mean they're not around."

"If there is no violence, chances are they are in complete control, they are doing exactly what they want to do," he said.

What police want is support. They want the public to pressure the provinces and Ottawa to keep police well-armed with money and the proper legislation.

Police also want the justice system to enforce the laws to the limit. Anti-biker cops are waiting to see how tough the new anti-gang law, enacted just before the last election, is in battling the gangs.

"We are not fighting street gangs," said Lévesque. "We are fighting transnational organized crime [groups] and it takes time to get results because they are so well entrenched, so well organized, so well structured."

Dorricott is quick to add that cops haven't been left out in the cold by governments, "but we need more."

"We can't blink now," adds London Chief Julian Fantino, who heads the national strategy against bikers. "We need to have a united front across the country."

Police took their roadshow to Hamilton where the local newspaper ran this story on December 20, 1997, under the headline "Police plead for cash to fight bikers":

Two Ontario police executives are calling on the federal government to put its money where its mouth is in combatting bikers across Canada.

Hamilton-Wentworth deputy chief Ken Robertson and London police chief Julian Fantino want the Liberal government to provide funds to help police mount lengthy joint-forces investigations against gangs of outlaw bikers across Ontario.

"We hear their verbal support, but the point I want to stress is that we're looking for resources to carry this out," Fantino, head of a Canadian Association of Chiefs of Police committee overseeing development of a nationwide anti-biker strategy, said yesterday.

"We're looking for the federal government to help us deal with this issue. I think the bottom line is that we've had a lot of commitments expressed, but we're still looking for tangible resources."

"You can't expect the provinces and municipalities to carry the ball alone," said Robertson.

"We're doing the best we can with the resources we have, but if the government infused us with more government support we could dedicate more officers and get involved in a more analytical and strategical [sic] approach against bikers."

The two made their comments as police involved in Operation Dismantle called for an extension of the 18-month crackdown on Satan's Choice or the creation of a permanent anti-biker unit. . . .

Biker expert Yves Lavigne, who has written three books on the Hells Angels, applauded such police efforts as Project Dismantle. But he denied police need money from senior government to tackle biker gangs. He said they can find the money within their own multi-million budgets by prioritizing resources.

Fantino and Robertson disagreed.

"This is an extra strain on police budgets," says Fantino. "I don't care who you are. Time and time again, we can't be effective as we want to be and we have to go looking for resources."

Police pressure to get funding to set up an anti-biker unit continued into 1998, according to a Toronto paper that ran this story on February 8; the teaser on the front page read: "Cops poised for biker war," and the headline on the inside story was "The first wave of Hells Angels. Police are gearing up to stop a notorious biker gang that has targeted Ontario as its next conquest."

Police agencies across Ontario are forming a special joint task force to slow down the dreaded Hells Angels' expansion into the province, which could lead to the kind of bloodshed that framed Quebec's vicious biker wars in recent years.

Although still in the planning stages and with few details available, the elite force, say police sources, is the only way to keep the Angels from gaining a complete stranglehold on Ontario's lucrative drug and prostitution trade.

It would also forestall violent confrontations with already-established biker gangs.

The new squad—using officers from the more than 40 police agencies that are part of the Criminal Intelligence Service of Ontario (CISO)—could be up and running within the next few months.

"We will put together a coordinated operational effort," confirmed Julian Fantino, London Police chief and chairman of the National Strategy on Outlaw Bikers.

"The fear of a repeat here of what happened in Quebec is more than justified. But we're optimistic that all levels of government will participate and help out. . . ."

Most anti-biker experts warn that Ontario—Toronto in particular—could very easily be the next battleground for an all-out biker war.

"The gangs in Quebec fought back vigorously and there was much bloodshed," says Det.-Const. Joe Dorricott of CISO.

"There are 500 gang members in Ontario and not all of them want to be Hells Angels. That means it could happen here the same as in Quebec. So we have to take a pro-active stance to avoid that kind of violence."

*   *   *

Ontario Solicitor General Bob Runciman told a meeting of the Police Association of Ontario on March 3, 1998, that he had been swayed by police arguments for more money and that the government was considering expanding anti-biker squads.

"We are hearing from police that they [biker gangs] are a real threat. Just how we are going to respond to it is what we are trying to come to grips with now," Runciman said.

Two weeks later, a contingent of Canadian cops traveled to California to watch the Hells Angels celebrate their fiftieth anniversary on March 17, 1998. Sergeant Guy Ouellette of the Sûreté du Québec was among them. He told reporters that Hells Angels associates and strippers make money for the organization in Ontario.

"They have Hells Angels controlling part of Ontario already," Sergeant Ouellette said, "Why have a chapter there? They don't need to. We won't see that before the year 2000, for sure."

Sergeant Ouellette then said that the Bandidos might set up a chapter in Ontario if the Hells Angels don't. He said the Bandidos have probationary chapters in Kingston, Quebec City, and Montreal. These chapters were originally the Rock Machine, and the Outlaws in Ottawa have aligned themselves with them, he said. "In Quebec, some Rock Machine members already are probate Bandidos. . . . Those Bandidos will represent in Canada an alternative for those who don't share Hells Angels goals."

*   *   *

The Ontario government said on May 8, 1998, that it would give police the money to fund a larger anti-biker squad:

> "There is a serious concern about the situation that exists in the province of Quebec, of efforts to import that situation into the province of Ontario," Solicitor General James Flaherty said. "And we certainly feel—and I know the police chiefs support the view—that we better take steps to ensure that we protect the people of Ontario from that menace. With this additional funding, our law enforcement agencies will be better equipped to combat the criminal activities of outlaw motorcycle gangs."
>
> Flaherty announced in London—a concession to Police Chief Julian Fantino, on May 11, that the province set aside $3.4 million to boost the OPP anti-biker squad from 7 to 20 members. The anti-biker squad would also get an additional $2.7 million every year and resources from 16 other police forces across the province.
>
> "We have to stop the expansion of new biker gangs in Ontario," Flaherty said. "We aim to stop them cold."
>
> The money would allow for 40 to 50 anti-biker cops, said Chief Superintendent Doug Scott, head of the OPP's investigative support bureau. "We certainly know how to do the job. All we are looking for are the tools to assist us in doing the job."
>
> Chief Fantino said the federal government should add to Ontario's contribution with tighter criminal laws and money seized under the Proceeds of Crime law.

By June 1998, the new Provincial Special Squad was formed with biker investigators from Toronto, the OPP, RCMP, Durham, York, Peel and Halton regions, Hamilton, Thunder Bay, and Ottawa.

The CISC's biker expert Sergeant J.P. Lévesque ended 1998 on a familiar note when he gave the media his 1999 predictions for the Hells Angels. This time his thoughts were prompted by the acquittal in November 1998 of Quebec Hells Angel Maurice (Mom) Boucher on charges of killing two prison guards.

"It's given them more aggressiveness," Sergeant Lévesque said. "They look at Mom Boucher and the others and say, 'They can't touch us.' In 1999, we'll definitely see more expansion of the Hells Angels across the country. They're going to finalize in Manitoba. Ontario is ripe now. I'm sure they'll be able to take it. The two main gangs there are the Para-Dice Riders and the Vagabonds, and both are friendly with the Hells Angels."

On January 23, 1999, the Criminal Intelligence Service of Canada once again predicted an impending biker war in Ontario and specified where the Hells Angels would set up chapters by year's end. The story below appeared in *The Standard* in St. Catharines, Ontario. I quote the text by reporter Grant LaFlèche in its entirety because it quotes me extensively and illustrates the extremes to which the RCMP is going to scare the public. The headline reads: "Biker war feared." The subhead is: "Police expert says Niagara ripe for bloody invasion."

An aggressive expansion into Niagara by the notorious Hells Angels motorcycle club could create the conditions for a bloody biker war within months, according to a leading police authority.

Jean-Pierre Lévesque, a specialist with the Criminal Intelligence Service of Canada, said the Hells Angels are on the verge of invading Ontario and will have clubhouses established by the end of the year. A local police source says Niagara is a prime candidate for expansion.

"Niagara is wide open to a criminal organization right now," said the specialist with Niagara Regional Police, who cannot be named because of his involvement in current investigations.

If that happens, established Ontario bikers, like the Outlaws of St. Catharines, would have little choice but to fight for their territory, he said.

After years of failed attempts to infiltrate Ontario, the Hells Angels have finally found favorable conditions to move in, said Lévesque, who is also a Royal Canadian Mounted Police sergeant.

Although not all police sources agree with Lévesque's theory, he cites three major factors that suggest the world's most powerful biker club will come to the province, and soon:

• The club has been emboldened by a recent court victory in Quebec. In November 1998, Maurice (Mom) Boucher, leader of the Montreal Hells Angels chapter known as the Nomads, was acquitted of the first-degree murder of two prison guards.

• The Hells Angels have expanded into Alberta, Saskatchewan, and Manitoba. Three major gangs, the Rebels in Saskatchewan, the Grim

Reapers in Alberta, and Los Brovos [Los Bravos] in Manitoba, have been absorbed by the Hells Angels. Ontario is the next logical step for the Angels, says Detective Sergeant Joe Dorricott, a member of the Ontario branch of CISC.

"I would be very surprised if by the Year 2000, the red-and-white flag of the Angels was not flying somewhere over southern Ontario."

• Ontario's other biker gangs are vulnerable. Niagara's dominant biker club, the Outlaws, based in a Merriton clubhouse on Oakdale Avenue, has been the target of police crackdowns since the late 1980s.

Although the club operates in relative obscurity, there have been several high-profile confrontations with police. The most notable incident was in June 1995 following a shooting at the clubhouse. Police arrested two men after a 10-hour siege and the evacuation of more than 40 nearby homes.

In June 1998, Richard Williams, the reputed international leader of the gang, was arrested outside the clubhouse for uttering a threat. Six months later, former Outlaw Thomas Culliton was convicted of attempted murder for trying to kill his ex-girlfriend in Thorold.

The Outlaws are one of the most powerful of Ontario's 13 biker gangs, but police have effectively eroded their power, leaving them with less than 70 members. By singling out the Outlaws, police may have inadvertently opened the door for other, more powerful gangs to expand.

"There is an almost natural balance of power established between the Ontario gangs," says Yves Lavigne, best-selling author of two books on Hells Angels and organized crime in Canada. "Taking out one gang is like taking a bucket of water out of a river. When you pull the bucket out, more water just rushes right in."

Although the Outlaws are considered weak, three other powerful gangs, Satan's Choice, the Para-Dice Riders, and the Vagabonds, could oppose the Angels if they were to move in.

"But, of these, the Vags and the Dice are friendly with the Angels," said Lévesque.

Lévesque believes members of the Para-Dice Riders will "patch over" and become Hells Angels, thereby giving them easy access to Ontario.

(A patch-over is a ceremony where, after a probationary period, an existing biker gang discards its own name and identifying logos and adopts those of the expanding club.)

Recent developments in the crime underworld in the Hamilton-Niagara district have contributed to the unstable conditions that could lead to a Hells Angels invasion, said the NRP biker specialist. One major factor is the murders of high-profile mob figures John (Pops) Papalia in Hamilton and Carmen Barillaro in Niagara Falls.

Such an environment is conducive to a gang like the Para-Dice Riders moving in, he said.

"What does Niagara have they would want?" he asked. "Is there easy access to the border? Yes. Are there elements, such as a casino or drugs, to attract them to money? Yes."

If the scenario Lévesque suggests plays out, the consequences for Niagara could be extreme.

The Outlaws have been bitter Angels rivals for more than 20 years, said Lavigne.

In Montreal, a five-year war between the Hells Angels and the Rock Machine has led to the deaths of more than 100 people, including children.

According to Lavigne, the Angels take war very seriously. In his 1987 book, *Hells Angels: Taking Care of Business*, Lavigne describes an outlaw biker club with experts in the art of war.

"The Angels never do anything half-assed. They set up intelligence teams to gather information. . . . They appoint security officers to protect the club. They equip hit men."

As violence in a biker war escalates, automatic weapons, along with fire and car bombs, become weapons of choice, and endanger anyone nearby.

Dorricott said he doesn't expect the Outlaws would last long in a war with the Hells Angels.

"I will be very surprised if [the Outlaws] just roll over, but I don't see how they could hold out. They just don't have the power," he said.

Police had predicted Rock Machine would not be able to slug it out with the Hells Angels, Dorricott said. But the Machine is still alive and kicking, largely due to support from the Texas-based Bandidos motorcycle club.

"It is hard to say what shadow players are out there," said Dorricott.

Lavigne said the major gangs in Ontario have learned to coexist with one another. The arrival of the extremely territorial and violent Hells Angels would disrupt this relative peace.

Lavigne adds he doesn't think Ontario is as open to the Angels as the police believe. If the established biker gangs are stronger than police estimate, he says, the Angels would have to negotiate, rather than batter their way in.

The critical question is how many Para-Dice Riders will voluntarily convert to the Hells Angels club. If, as Lévesque predicts, only a few patch over, a biker war is almost certain. The Angels do not accept rivals in their own territory and Dice members who patch over will be forced to kill their former comrades.

"This would not be the same as when the Grim Reapers patched over," said Lavigne. "That was a unanimous decision within Reapers to become Angels.

"It is not the case here. What we have got are elements of the Dice who want to be Angels, not the whole gang. I just don't see how they could not be put in a position to start shooting their buddies."

Inspector Ross Bingley of the Ontario Provincial Police special squad said he would not hazard a guess as to how the Angels plan to enter Ontario.

"That would be pure speculation on my part," he said. "The only people who know when and how the Angels will come to this province are the Hells Angels themselves."

Lavigne added he doesn't believe easy access to the border in Niagara Falls would influence the Angels.

"You don't smuggle drugs across the Peace Bridge," he said. "You do it in out-of-the-way border towns. You do it in the middle of nowhere or from the coast."

He also cautions that the CISC has had difficulty predicting with accuracy the movements of the Angels.

"They said the Angels were coming to Calgary in 1996, but the patch-over was in 1997," he said. "They have been predicting, for the past four years, that the Angels were going to break into Ontario, but it has yet to happen. You can't just make these predictions every year and then when it happens claim you are a genius."

But Lévesque says CISC's information is solid: "Mr. Lavigne is entitled to his opinion. He has been following the bikers for many years now, so it is good he is interested. But he just doesn't have the information we do."

Lévesque says the Angels are only interested in patching over "key members" of the Para-Dice Riders who will begin to build a power base. The remaining Dice would function as "business associates" of the Angels.

"The Hells Angels will not go to war with remaining Dice, unless those Dice get in their way," explained Lévesque. "It is going to happen."

Lévesque said law enforcement agencies across Ontario should ensure they are all working "under the same flag," with joint-forces operations, in order to combat the influence of the Angels.

When asked if he thought that police could keep the Angels out of Ontario, however, Lévesque said no.

For Lavigne, that answer is simply not good enough.

"The police have relegated themselves to being the handmaidens for the Hells Angels, prancing before them and announcing their arrival," said Lavigne. "Then they have the gall to go to the public, hat in hand, to ask for money to fight the gang while at the same time telling us they can do nothing to stop the Angels from coming."

*   *   *

Police once again raised the specter of war on February 22, 1999, in a Toronto newspaper under the headline: "Biker war feared—Hells Angels scouting Ontario." Police comments indicate they still haven't clued in that it's what bikers do privately, not publicly, that indicates their intentions:

About two dozen Hells Angels members from Quebec came to Toronto earlier this month in what police believe was a major step in the biker gang's bid to expand into Ontario.

A top intelligence cop said the visit by 22 bikers representing all Quebec chapters of the Hells Angels points to a looming struggle by gangs for more control of crime in Ontario.

Since 1993, about 60 people have been killed in clashes in Quebec between the Rock Machine and Hells Angels. A joint effort by Ontario and Quebec provincial police quashed a bid by the Hells Angels to open a chapter in this province in the early '90s.

"They arrived as businessmen, then ended up with their colors on," the source said. "Because they're an organized-crime group, we stopped them."

Wearing short hair and designer clothes, the Hells Angels didn't "look like bikers" when questioned by a task force made up of cops from several forces, the source said.

"And they were all polite, saying 'yes, sir; no sir.' They know how to stay out of trouble."

But by partying in their colors, "they want to show that they're the most powerful" and send a message to other gangs.

The CISC raised the specter of a Hells Angels invasion once more in the main front page story of *The Standard* in St. Catharines on Tuesday, April 13, under the headline: "Hells Angels show colors." The subhead: "Some authorities fear predicted biker invasion has begun in Niagara."

The appearance of a high-ranking member of the Hells Angels in Niagara Falls proves the biker gang is moving into Niagara, says a leading police authority.

Niagara Regional Police stopped a red-and-black truck off Portage Road near Stamford Green Park Sunday afternoon. One of the three men inside was wearing a leather jacket with a Hells Angels patch on the back. He identified himself as Walter Stadnick.

Stadnick is a member of the Quebec Hells Angels chapter known as the Nomads and the gang's former national president.

The other two men in the truck were not wearing Hells Angels jackets. No charges were laid against the three.

Jean-Pierre Lévesque, a specialist with Criminal Intelligence Service Canada, said Stadnick's appearance in Niagara confirms what he has been predicting for months: the Hells Angels are moving into Niagara.

"We have known before this that he was [in Niagara Falls] and all I can say at this point is that he was there taking care of business," said Lévesque.

Since December, Lévesque has said Niagara is ripe for an organized crime group to move into Niagara.

Lévesque and other police authorities have noted the rapid expansion of the Hells Angels across the country. The only province the gang hasn't moved into is Ontario.

In January, Mr. Lévesque said the Angels would move into Niagara through another biker gang called the Para-Dice Riders, thought to be active in Niagara Falls.

In an interview Monday, however, Lévesque said Stadnick is a likely candidate to establish the Angels in the region.

"He is part of a process of laying the groundwork to move in by the end of the year," he said.

Yves Lavigne, civilian biker expert and author, said Stadnick's presence in Ontario is not startling.

"He has lived here his entire life. It is nothing new," said Lavigne, who twelve years ago wrote, "[Stadnick is] the Hells Angels most important foothold in Hamilton."

Stadnick's real uniqueness, he said, is that he is one of the only Angels who lives in Ontario.

*   *   *

The Criminal Intelligence Service of Canada implemented an outlaw-biker telephone hotline as part of the national strategy on Monday, March 8, 1999. The police hope people will call the toll-free hotline with descriptions of outlaw bikers, their associates, and their criminal activities, as well as the location of stashes of drugs, weapons, explosives, and stolen goods. The hotline (1-877-660-4321) will be manned by police officers. "Once criminal groups become embedded within a society, organized crime ceases to be simply a criminal justice problem and becomes a public policy problem," said RCMP Commissioner Philip Murray, who is also CISC executive chairman. "We are 100-percent committed to the fight against organized crime, and this hotline is a step forward in the continuing national strategy to combat outlaw motorcycle gangs."

Commissioner Murray's words are frightening. He has admitted that the police will never be able to get rid of the Hells Angels and other outlaw motorcycle gangs. That's no surprise. The police have never tried to get rid of them. Now the police have carefully crafted a scenario where they are saying it's the public's job to help police manage the biker problem. Since when do police shape public policy in this country?

Commissioner Murray has confirmed that the police intelligence apparatus is too inept, lazy, or unwilling to investigate gangs. He has passed the buck to the public. Now when the public complains about outlaw bikers, the cops will say, "It's not our fault, no one has called our hotline to tell us about crimes."

Bikers will have a great time calling the hotline with fake tips ("There's a million kilos of biker coke stashed inside a mechanical whale in Rankin Inlet. Ask for Willie.") that will send police scrambling all over the country padding their expense accounts.

Canadian police have given up on fighting crime. The RCMP in Calgary in July 1997 asked that the people who run corner stores not sell milk or food to Hells Angels who were in town for the induction of the Grim Reapers into their organization. Some Mounties were so afraid of the Hells Angels they wore fake beards to disguise themselves. And they had the nerve to asked mom and pop at the corner store to put their lives on the line and turn away bikers? We pay our police to serve and protect, not to pass the buck.

The biker snitch line is just another brick in the bureaucracy that police are building on the public fear of bikers they have worked so hard to generate over the past twenty years. From now on, cops will fill the media with stories about how well they are doing. To get to the truth, ignore the talk and look at their actions. The bikers did not have to buy the cops to ensure their success in Canada. The police allowed them to take the country and gave us a play-by-play description as each province fell.

Twenty years ago, police administrators predicted biker wars in Ontario and left it up to Toronto gangs to keep the Hells Angels out.

In 1997, police administrators convinced governments to grant funds to create anti-biker squads in all provinces.

In 1998, all levels of police advised the country that the Hells Angels are so entrenched in our society, they can't get rid of them.

Canadian police failed to tackle bikers as a law enforcement problem when the gangs could be beaten. They waited until bikers became a management problem before taking action.

A top intelligence officer with a regional force outside Toronto who built a career dealing with outlaw bikers startled me with this comment in 1998 when I mentioned the possibility that some Para-Dice Riders would become Hells Angels: "Good. That means more work for us."

Chapter 5: Alberta
The Running of the Bull

The mid-1960s was a fertile period for social rebellion. Some youth traveled by thumb, tripped out on drugs, and rutted like rabbits. Others, no less secure, sought refuge in motorcycle gangs, sold drugs, and beat the crap out of each other. While the hippies faded into adulthood and conformity, the bikers grew into organized crime. Their world, though outwardly free-spirited, was no less constricted by laws and rules than that of any business. In fact, the biker world was more regimented and demanding. Paybacks are not a learning experience.

Albertans often seen themselves as isolated from the rest of the world, although they shouldn't complain—they chose the west, to leave their ails behind. One of their claims to fame is the hallowed rat patrol which keeps the province rat-free with its kill-on-sight border policy. If only the same policy had been applied to the vermin that migrated to Alberta in droves in the 1960s and 1970s to form biker gangs with local scum.

Thirty-five outlaw motorcycle gangs saw the light in Alberta between 1965 and 1975. One gang was born the most powerful, and fought the hardest to reduce its competition through violence or assimilation. By 1980 there were only three gangs in the province, one of them the deadliest underworld threat in the province.

The Grim Reapers were formed in Calgary in 1967. Within two years they had challenged all other gangs in the province and forced them to do their bidding. The Grim Reapers had the power to sanction or ban other biker gangs. They officially donned the 1% outlaw patch in 1970 after members beat a rival gang's president to death in Calgary. They set up their mother chapter in Red Deer after founding member Jim Glabais and his closest friends moved there to strategically position the gang midway between Calgary and Edmonton.

The Ghost Riders in Lethbridge were the last gang to stand up to the Grim Reapers. They did so only because they were the only international biker gang in Alberta and could call on support from members in Washington State and British Columbia. That support was quickly eroded by the Satan's Angels in British Columbia, as the Hells Angels from Quebec put them through their paces and trained them for assimilation into their organization. The Satan's Angels were forced to eliminate all the gangs in their province to show they were tough enough to control the entire drug market.

The Satan's Angels beat the Ghost Riders into submission during a rumble in Penticton, B.C., in July 1978 and the bikers disbanded. Some of them sought shelter in Alberta in December 1979. They didn't last long. The Grim Reapers ordered them (at gunpoint) to surrender their colors in November 1980.

That left two other gangs in the province besides the Grim Reapers: the Rebels and the King's Crew. The Satan's Angels, on the road to becoming Hells Angels on July 23, 1983, looked toward Alberta once they controlled British Columbia. They befriended the Rebels in 1981, which gave the gang enough courage and support to survive. The Grim Reapers respected that power and targeted the King's Crew in Calgary because they wanted to be the only gang in town. The war was brief and violent.

The Grim Reapers burst into the King's Crew clubhouse on March 16, 1983, and forced all Crew members to hand over their colors at gunpoint. Five days later, two Reapers delivered four sets of charred King's Crew colors to the media. They bombed the King's Crew clubhouse and a motorcycle shop on March 23. By August, the gangs had bombed each other eight times—a King's Crew biker died in his jeep, and a Grim Reaper motorcycle shop in Edmonton was damaged. The bikers beat and shot and abducted each other until the King's Crew retreated into the night.

The Satan's Angels in British Columbia served notice on the Grim Reapers that Alberta was no longer their exclusive domain. The Angels exercised a right they have always considered theirs in territory they own or want. They allowed the Rebels to wear an Alberta bottom rocker on their province to indicate they could roam the province at will. The Rebels offered a concession to the Reapers, to prevent war: they labeled the rockers Alberta North or Alberta South. Sensibilities are so fragile in the rough-and-tumble world of bikers. And the politics of war hinge on the smallest slight, real or perceived.

The Quebec Hells Angels godfathered the B.C. gang into their fold, and in the process got to know the Rebels and the Reapers. They supplied both gangs with drugs. The Reapers reveled in their independence, while the Rebels welcomed the Hells Angels' advances. They did the gang's dirty work and traveled to Quebec to party with them.

The Rebels used the backup of their new-found friends to change their bottom rocker to Alberta. But loyalties are fleeting in the underworld, and although the Hells Angels used the Rebels to do their dirty work and sell their drugs, they didn't show them how to deflect police attention. The Hells Angels informed the Rebels in May 1987 that they would not be granted prospect status, the last step before full-member status. The cops busted the eleven Calgary Rebels and their seventeen associates on drug charges on June 23, 1987.

The war between the Grim Reapers and King's Crew was rekindled. The Reapers kidnapped and buried a King's Crew biker. Police tried to stop the war with raids on fifty-one biker houses and businesses during which they seized 150 weapons on November 25. One week later, on October 3, the Alberta Court of Appeal ruled the search warrants invalid and the weapons were all returned.

By 1989, the Rebels were burdened with legal fees and drug debts to the Hells Angels. The Ghost Riders reappeared for one month, disappeared, and some members surfaced as Grim Reapers prospects in June 1990, two months after the Reapers opened a Lethbridge chapter. The Reapers asked the King's Crew on May 28, 1992, to surrender their colors. They refused. The British Columbia Hells Angels liked the Crew's attitude and took them on as associates. The Hells Angels succeeded where police couldn't: they stopped the biker war in Alberta.

* * *

Calgary police warned the public as early as 1980 that outlaw motorcycle gangs were the biggest organized crime problem in Alberta. This report appeared in a Calgary newspaper in October 1980:

> City police are warning that motorcycle gangs are trying to establish organized crime here. "When we talk about organized crime in Calgary, our biggest concern now is with bikers," Police Chief Brian Sawyer says.
>
> "Over the past 10 years, motorcycle gangs have changed the whole focus of organized crime across the country, and our information indicates their impact is being felt more and more here."
>
> Police say motorcycle gangs are behind successful and sophisticated forms of organized crime including drug trafficking, armed robbery, and

dealing in restricted weapons. They are also worried about warring among rival motorcycle groups.

Calgary police say they have information showing that gangs from Ontario, Quebec, British Columbia, and the United States are recruiting new members here and trying to persuade local gangs to align with them. They do not name the gangs, but police in other provinces say the Satan's Choice from Ontario and the Hells Angels from Quebec have been visiting Alberta. . . .

A report on organized crime by the Canadian Association of Chiefs of Police says that within the past two years, fifteen motorcycle gang members have died as a result of inter-gang warfare in Canada. "Highly organized, strictly regulated by club codes, well-connected both nationally and internationally, these gangs lend themselves well to a variety of criminal activities."

Alberta police knew in the 1980s that the Hells Angels had targeted Alberta. Provincial and federal police reports speculated every year about the Hells Angels taking over Alberta gangs. This story appeared in *The Calgary Herald* on Friday, August 26, 1994, under the headline: "Cops say bikers plotting takeover"; with the subhead "Hells Angels has taken Alberta gangs under its wing."

Hells Angels—the world's most notorious motorcycle club—is tightening its hold on Alberta, one of the last Canadian provinces it has yet to control, say police intelligence sources.

The club is poised for a takeover of Alberta' s clubs—the Grim Reapers, Rebels, and King's Crew, police say.

"Calgary's gangs have grown to prominence lately. They've gained the respect of the Hells Angels. They've been taken under their wing," said Det. Wayne Lauinger of the joint city police RCMP intelligence unit.

The takeover may be discussed privately in Calgary this weekend when the King's Crew plays host at its 25th anniversary party—a three-day blast that begins tonight and is expected to draw 100 bikers from clubs across Canada, including the Angels.

"That's police propaganda," commented a King's Crew spokesman.

"I don't want to comment about what's going on out there," said Fred Widdifield, spokesman for the Hells Angels Nanaimo, B.C. chapter, who suggested the *Herald* write about corrupt cops.

Over the years, the Angels have been attracted to Alberta's strong economy and the up-and-coming bright leadership of its clubs.

"They will take the best from each club and let the rest wither," said Det. Brad Robson, adding the recent drop in Alberta's biker violence is directly due to the Angels' demand for low-profile business.

Last month, police stopped 16 Hells Angels from Vancouver's East End chapter near Cochrane in a "routine check stop."

Claiming harassment, the angry bikers told reporters they were "vacationing" in Alberta. Police believe they were here to conduct business. Sitting quietly among the group was Walter Stadnick, the Hells Angels Canadian president. . . .

Young bikers see virtue in becoming Angels and evolving from the old-biker style to world-class bikerdom. But diehards don't want to give up control and profits, say police, who believe an Angel takeover here is virtually a *fait accompli*.

And when it is complete, Alberta's outlaw bikers—regarded by police as the province's "No. 1 crime force"—will be on-line with big-league organized crime.

In June 1996, Edmonton police Chief John Lindsay tried to pull a quick one on city council and the public with the help of RCMP sergeant J.P. Lévesque of the Criminal Intelligence Service of Canada. Edmonton City Council informed the chief in early June it would trim one percent, or $1.1 million from the force's $116 million annual budget.

Chief Lindsay responded one week later with the announcement that the Hells Angels would take over Alberta's Grim Reapers on June 23. He pleaded that politicians leave the $1.1 million in the budget so police could protect the people of Alberta from the Hells Angels menace. "At this time, I don't have the ability to respond to these types of outlaw motorcycle gangs in the way I think is appropriate or necessary."

Sergeant Lévesque confirmed Chief Lindsay's warning. Both men said the Grim Reapers would patch over to become Hells Angels. They cited unnamed intelligence sources and refused to give solid evidence, for what they described as security reasons. Chief Lindsay said a team of police officers from Calgary and Edmonton had been working with the RCMP gathering evidence for months. Politicians were not smart enough to ask for proof to back up a statement that had scared the population. The prediction had the desired effect on Calgary mayor Bill Smith. "I'm really now concerned with the violence, so we have to be very careful when we review that budget."

The media contacted me in early June for comment about the police predictions of a patch-over and I suggested that Chief Lindsay and

Sergeant Lévesque were frightening the people of Alberta in order to add money to police coffers. I said it was unconscionable for police officers to use fear and intimidation to extort money from the public purse in the same way outlaw bikers use these tactics.

There was to be no patch-over, I said. First and foremost, if either policeman had done his homework, he would have realized that no Alberta gang had yet been granted prospect status by the Hells Angels. Gang rules demand that a puppet gang prospect for at least a year before it is granted full charter. It seemed that the policemen had picked the June 23 date because the Hells Angels, who were close to the Grim Reapers, would make their yearly pilgrimage to Alberta on that date to party with local gangs. The anniversary of the British Columbia Hells Angels was June 23, 1983. But there was no logical reason to believe the Grim Reapers would become Hells Angels. That gang was not yet godfathering them, or indoctrinating them into the organization. Sergeant Lévesque is the highest-ranking police biker intelligence officer in Canada. He has access to every fact gathered around the world by all law enforcement agencies. His prediction in Alberta in 1996 was just one of many he has made over the years which have proven to be wrong. I told the media that police can't go on making unfounded predictions without seriously damaging their credibility. The day will come when they will ask the public for needed help, and no one will listen.

I also criticized police who had known for more than fifteen years that the Hells Angels had their sights set on Alberta, and yet did nothing about it. The police could have created in Alberta a climate inhospitable to the Hells Angels. They could have severely crippled (if not dismantled) Alberta biker gangs while they were in their infancy and before the Hells Angels taught them how to counter police and the justice system. Despite years of fear-mongering about the Hells Angels, during which the police stopped just short of warning parents to lock up their daughters, Alberta police, like police across Canada, did nothing to prevent the spread of the Hells Angels to their province.

"The police have reduced themselves to the status of being hand-maidens for the Hells Angels, prancing ahead of them and shrilly announcing their arrival," I told the media. "Then they have the nerve to hold out their caps and ask for money to protect the good citizens of Alberta. The people of Alberta deserve better police."

The Grim Reapers mocked the police in 1996 when asked about the predicted patch-over. "Next year," they said.

The police publicity machine went into overdrive to convince the public that the Hells Angels would shed blood in the province. This story ran in *The Calgary Herald* on Tuesday, July 16, under the headline "Biker invasion feared."

City police are braced for a turf war and bloodshed between rival motorcycle gangs when the notorious Hells Angels set up shop in the Calgary area.

"This concerns us and there are not many members of the public welcoming the Hells Angels with open arms," Supt. Jack Beaton said Monday.

"They take over another gang, then use intimidation and violence to take control of illicit actions—drugs, prostitution, extortion, firearms and explosives trafficking."

In Edmonton, members of the Rebels outlaw gang are planning to switch to Angel colors at a drag-race meet this weekend. Police fear the Angels will attempt to seize control of all other gang activity throughout the province.

Last week, Edmonton's police chief issued a warning that drugs, prostitution, money laundering, and weapons will flood into Alberta once the Angels move in.

Beaton urged Calgarians to report any sightings or activities of outlaw motorcycle gangs to enable police to keep track of them. . . .

"If they choose the Grim Reapers, for example, the King's Crew and Rebels couldn't exist because the [Angels] won't let them," Beaton said. . . .

One rival gang leader, who refused to be identified, declined comment on the Hells Angels' impending infiltration of the local market. He said police were just using it as an opportunity to seek more money.

Both the Rebels and Grim Reapers asked the Hells Angels for a charter in January 1995. The Reapers were granted prospect status in September 1996 in a manner seen only twice before in Hells Angels history. They were allowed to keep their colors during the prospect period instead of burying them and wearing partial Hells Angels colors with only the bottom rocker, as is the norm. That meant they would destroy their Grim Reaper colors the day they were granted their Hells Angel charter and colors. The only other gangs allowed to keep their colors until granted full membership were the Aliens from New York City, who became the infamous New York City Hells Angels chapter on

December 5, 1969, and the Hells Henchmen in Illinois and Indiana, who became Hells Angels on December 2, 1994.

The Grim Reapers sent out Christmas cards in 1996 that identified their prospect status. So did their phone lists and photographs. The Hells Angels circulate photographs of all prospects to the security officers in chapters around the world so members can scrutinize them for informants. The biker underworld is small.

The Hells Angels put the Grim Reapers through an intensive hands-on training program. They ordered them to take care of the Rock Machine in Kingston, Ontario, which is a stupid task for a bunch of Alberta boys. Two of them were stopped in Thunder Bay with a truck full of ammunition. The Reapers never did figure out the Rock Machine, a job more suited to Quebec bikers.

The RCMP and Alberta police dusted off their publicity machine again in the spring of 1997 and barraged the public with dire warnings of an impending invasion by the Hells Angels who were going to convert the province's presumably backwater bike gang into a multinational juggernaut that would bring hitherto unknown levels of organized crime to the province. Given the 1996 fiasco, I had hoped the RCMP would have rethought its strategy over the winter. No, the RCMP tried their best to scare the Alberta public into submission, and then asked them to open the provincial coffers so they could plunge their fists into the booty and subsidize police programs to protect the public against the bikers.

This time, the police pegged the patch-over date as July 23 in Red Deer. There was little doubt this year that the Hells Angels planned to conduct the ceremony on that date because in early May they reserved a hundred motel rooms in Red Deer under the name "Trust Me Racing" of Vancouver. Police started their media campaign in June and hyped the arrival of the Hells Angels until it became a national story.

Alberta police carefully crafted a media strategy to draw attention to the tactics they would use against the Hells Angels as they rode through the province. They began with the announcement in June that the Hells Angels were on their way. This story appeared in *The Calgary Herald* on Wednesday, June 18, under the headline "Hells Angels eye Alberta."

The notorious Hells Angels outlaw biker gang is poised to hit Alberta with a bang next month.

The Angels have apparently organized a series of celebration "rides" to mark their takeover of four Alberta chapters of the Grim Reapers motorcycle club, police say.

They are parties the Calgary force is awaiting with wariness and excitement.

"They do not like a high profile. They want to open a chapter without fanfare," said Calgary police Supt. Jack Beaton.

"For us, it's the same as last year: we do not want the Hells Angels opening a chapter in Alberta.

"With our zero-tolerance policy, when they come here they'll be stopped and arrested if they commit any offense or if any warrants are out for them."

Beaton said the gang has been recruiting actively in the province for two years, particularly among members of the Grim Reapers.

"Right now our information is that the Grim Reapers is probably the most lucrative one of the three [biker clubs] in Alberta, and they would be the likely candidates for a [takeover]." [Author's note: The Grim Reapers were the only gang in Alberta officially prospecting for the Hells Angels.]

Intelligence reports from Quebec, where the Angels' Canadian chapter is centered, suggest the gang's Montreal-based leaders have plans to set up a pair of chapters in Alberta, and will likely annex the Regina, Red Deer, Lethbridge, and Calgary Grim Reapers clubs. [Author's note: The British Columbia Hells Angels godfathered the Grim Reapers into the organization, not Quebec.]

Police busted a Red Deer prostitution ring linked to the Grim Reapers on Tuesday, June 24, in an attempt to keep the Hells Angels out of Alberta. Police tapped more than 30,000 phone calls to three escort agencies, videotaped 1,200 deals between escorts and customers in local hotels and 680 more in private homes during a four-month investigation called Operation Kitty Hawk.

Police dragged out their heavyweights to garner publicity and this story appeared in *The Calgary Herald* on Thursday, July 10, under the headline "Cops await Hells Angels' next move":

A showdown is looming in Red Deer where police believe the Hells Angels motorcycle gang will make its anticipated move into Alberta in the next couple of weeks.

Red Deer RCMP said Wednesday that Alberta's three outlaw motorcycle gangs—King's Crew, Rebels, and Grim Reapers—will patch-over, meaning they will start wearing Hells Angels colors in Red Deer.

"The patchover will take place in the next couple of weeks," said

Constable Dan Doyle of Red Deer RCMP. The date and location will be announced in the coming days, he added. "There will be a police presence at the event."

Calgary city police Supt. Jack Beaton said police are still trying to stop the event from happening.

"We are hoping the strong message through the media will have some effect," said Beaton.

Earlier in the day, senior officials from across the province emerged from a meeting with Premier Ralph Klein and Justice Minister Jon Havelock with tough talk for the Hells Angels.

"Our gang is bigger than your gang," said Calgary police chief Christine Silverberg. [Author's note: Stupid, stupid, stupid.] "We do not want anyone taking control of Alberta. We are going to keep them out."

To maintain press coverage and public interest, police fed reporters two-month-old information that appeared in *The Calgary Herald* under the headline "Warning fails to deter bikers" on Friday, July 11:

> The Hells Angels outlaw bike gang is apparently defying police warnings to stay out of Alberta.
>
> The notorious bikers have booked hotel space in Red Deer between July 21 and 23, when a merger with the Alberta-based Grim Reapers is expected to take place, police said Thursday.
>
> "We have information from reliable sources that they have booked approximately 100 rooms at the Red Deer Lodge," RCMP Const. Dan Doyle said.

Police spin doctors tantalized the media and garnered more coverage on Monday, July 14, by planting stories with reporters that major underworld celebrities would attend the ceremony in Red Deer. Police even dropped Sonny Barger's name as proof that the Alberta party was an event worthy of international attention. The truth is that Sonny Barger never shows up for these things. He also has a criminal record and police knew he would never be allowed across the border. But priming the public has nothing to do with the truth. Even though I told media there was no way Barger would attend, they went for sensationalism and celebrity worship in "Top California Hells Angels expected at Red Deer ride," which appeared in *The Calgary Herald* on Saturday, July 12.

Police sources said Friday they think a planned Hells Angels ride on Red Deer later this month will attract key underworld figures from the club's California headquarters.

"That is one of the good possibilities," said a senior police intelligence source.

Police biker unit members have received confirmation from a number of sources that high-ranking bikers from California, the birthplace of the outlaw biker club in 1948, might be headed for the Red Deer meeting on July 21, 22, and 23.

But he also cautioned that because of intense public scrutiny they may back off—and since they have to cross the border, authorities may bar them from entering the country.

The same story, but with more background information on Barger, appeared in the same newspaper on Tuesday, July 15, under the headline "SONNY: Hells Angels' feared leader may be headed for Red Deer":

He has starred with Jack Nicholson in a movie about his outlaw biker club.

He is also alleged to have ordered executions.

His name is Ralph Hubert "Sonny" Barger Jr. And as the recognized head of the world's most feared motorcycle club—the Hells Angels—he may soon be coming to Alberta.

Police sources confirm that a planned Hells Angels ride in Red Deer later this month is expected to attract top people from the club.

Hells Angels from British Columbia and eastern Canada assembled in Kelowna, B.C., on Saturday, July 19, to make the ride into Alberta. The eastern bikers had their bikes shipped by transport truck while they flew across the country. They don't have the time to ride cross-country like real bikers used to. The manager of a local hotel where the Hells Angels stayed put the issue in perspective as police asked the public on the radio not to cooperate with the bikers.

"We treat all our clients the same and we can't, by law, discriminate against anyone, especially the Hells Angels," Frank Fagel, general manager of the Grand Okanagan resort and hotel, said on Friday, July 18. "They've never done anything wrong in the years they've been here. But having said that, if the police can't control them, why should people expect the innkeeper to?"

Some Alberta RCMP officers lost their perspective on the event and treated the arrival of the Hells Angels like the eve of the apocalypse. "Some pastors were contacted by the RCMP and asked to cover them in prayer and just pray for the whole situation," Pastor Matt Kitchener of the First Baptist Church said on Sunday, July 20.

The day before the acceptance of the Grim Reapers into the Hells Angels organization, Vancouver Hells Angel Rick Ciarniello used his years of experience to toy with the media. Local reporters asked him on Tuesday, July 22, if the gang was going to establish a chapter in Red Deer. "We're here to celebrate the fourteenth anniversary of our B.C. chapters and have a party with the Grim Reapers," he said. "There's no patch-over—that's a police term. No members of our chapters are moving here anytime soon. So no, we're not going to set one up here, certainly not in the next few days."

He did not lie. The reporters failed to ask the right questions. They planned to set up chapters in Calgary and Edmonton, not Red Deer. "Patch-over" is indeed a police term. The Hells Angels never use it. They just accept a gang into their organization. No Hells Angels from outside the province transferred to Alberta. Only the Grim Reapers became Hells Angels in that province. And they did not plan to set up a chapter in Red Deer at that time. Ciarniello is a crafty biker. Some may view his statement as mere semantics, but it shows a grasp of the English language that mocked reporters. None had the wits or courage to ask the direct question: are any Alberta bikers to become Hells Angels?

Ciarniello mocked the police presence as the Hells Angels tanked up in a bar for two hours before heading down the highway toward the first roadblock. "We can't let them think they can scare us away, can we? This whole show for the media is unnecessary. It's a waste of time. This is a free country. I can go where I want, and the last time I checked, you don't need a passport to get into Alberta."

The Alberta media were not as gullible as the police had hoped. They approached me to put the scare stories in perspective. "It's a moot point whether the Angels move in or not," I said. "The Grim Reapers and the Rebels have been doing the Hells Angels' dirty work for years." The real story was the failure of police to act on more than fifteen years of information that indicated the Hells Angels had targeted Alberta. The police had chosen to play soothsayers rather than be crime fighters. And in the summer of 1997, they played traffic cop. Police invited the media to watch them throw the fear of god into the Hells Angels at blockades on Alberta highways.

As the big day approached, the police mounted the largest joint forces operation in the province in sixteen years. Police barricaded highways, stood hundreds of bikers on the hot asphalt and checked driver's licenses, helmets, and registration and insurance papers. Cops bullied bikers, who kept their cool and laughed. Cops bullied the media to vent their frustrations when the bikers didn't react. Cops bullied each other as they vied for power.

The public backlash against the police was so unexpected that it accomplished what the 1996 fiasco failed to do—it temporarily shattered their arrogance. The public mocked and ridiculed the police, whom they accused of violating the bikers' rights to ride through their communities. If the cops could stop with impunity a bunch of bikers who came to town to party, then they could abuse anyone's rights to be on the road, the public figured. Polls showed sixty-three per cent of Albertans supported the bikers.

Bystanders in Red Deer cheered and applauded when the Hells Angels arrived. The bikers posed for photographs and gave autographs. Police heavy-handedness made the Hells Angels counter-culture heroes again. Pogo had a phrase that explains the way police have dealt with the biker problem over the years: "We has met the enemy, and it is us."

Police from 15 agencies identified 193 bikers and associates, laid 205 traffic violation charges, and seized illegal helmets. Within weeks, 3 tickets were quashed for technicalities, 19 were withdrawn by the RCMP (who didn't know the helmet law had been amended), 4 were withdrawn for other reasons, 21 were paid, 46 accused were convicted *in absentia*, 2 pleaded guilty, and 108 bikers chose to fight the charges.

Ciarniello had a field day with the media. He mocked the police and challenged them to prove any of his Hells Angels were criminals. Police in B.C. have a dismal record against the Hells Angels. Corruption and incompetence have given the Hells Angels free rein of the province.

Calgary and Edmonton Grim Reapers became Canada's 13th and 14th Hells Angels chapters and the 109th and 110th in the world on July 23, 1997, adding twenty-three new members to the gang. The Rebels were granted prospect status and the King's Crew became a puppet gang, controlled by the Hells Angels. The Hells Angels would have two clubhouses only, in Calgary and Edmonton, with five members in Red Deer who belong to the Edmonton chapter and four in Lethbridge who belong to Calgary. "It's going to be the same people who were always here," Ciarniello said. "The only thing that's changed is that they belong to the world's largest and most notorious motorcy-cle club."

"I feel great," Critter, a newly minted Hells Angel, told a group of reporters as he showed off his colors. Each member sewed the $125 patches made in Vorarlberg, Austria, onto their vests themselves. "I need rocks in my pockets to keep my feet on the ground."

A Quebec Hells Angel yelled to reporters: "We came, we saw, we conquered, eh?"

Hours before the patch-over, police tried to convince the media they have always had the biker problem in Alberta under control. "Bikers in check, police say" appeared on Wednesday, July 23:

> A hard-line approach by police has kept outlaw biker gang criminal activity in check over the past 25 years, says a senior officer.
>
> As the Hells Angels—North America's most notorious outlaw biker gang—partied in Red Deer amid reports of a takeover of the Grim Reapers there, city police Supt. Jack Beaton confirmed Tuesday night that 34 bikers belong to three gangs in Calgary.
>
> Beaton told the Calgary Police Commission the Grim Reapers and King's Crew each have 14 members here. The Rebels have six members.
>
> He said the Grim Reapers also have two "hangers-on" while the Rebels and the King's Crew each have one prospect.
>
> "We have been successful in Calgary in keeping the numbers low," said Beaton.
>
> He said the biker gangs were a problem in the city in the 1970s when several bombings took place and one biker was killed. A task force was established about 25 years ago to deal with the problem.
>
> "We've been working on that for a good length of time," said Beaton. "Now we have to step up our efforts."

The Hells Angels did try to play dirty during their stay in Alberta. A police wiretap intercepted a scheme to embarrass and intimidate Alberta premier Ralph Klein with a ten-year-old photograph of him drinking beer with some Grim Reapers in Calgary's Cecil Hotel when he was city mayor. The photo hung on the wall of the Reapers' Red Deer clubhouse. "The police . . . had information that the Hells Angels from Vancouver wanted this picture to use against me," Premier Klein said.

The Hells Angels showed the photograph to media the week of the patch-over and called Klein a hypocrite for criticizing the arrival of the gang in Alberta and endorsing police tactics against the bikers. "It seems like we're the worst thing that has come to Alberta, but ten years ago the same people were good enough to have a drink with this man," Ciarniello said.

*   *   *

To put the 1997 road stops in perspective, the RCMP used them extensively in the early 1980s and they achieved nothing. They did not curb biker activity, criminal or social, although bikers learned to use other means to transport guns, booze and drugs to party sites. But they did boost police egos by allowing them to flex muscle.

Alberta bikers and their out-of-province guests have ridden to Coronation, 150 miles east of Red Deer, every Labor Day since 1973 to party in the middle of nowhere. The RCMP decided in 1981 to show them who was boss. They practiced their techniques in June when they stopped two groups of bikers—10 Grim Reapers and 19 King's Crew—on Highway 3 east of Pincher Creek and searched them. They laid eight criminal charges: possession of stolen property, two charges for possession of prohibited weapons, possession of a dangerous weapon, three charges of impersonation, and obstructing a police officer. RCMP Douglas Egan, head of criminal intelligence for Alberta, said the charges showed how criminally inclined the bikers were.

More than 200 police stopped 150 bikers on September 5, including Satan's Angels from British Columbia and Hells Angels from Quebec who arrived in limousines. The stop happened only because RCMP brass at "K" Division headquarters in Edmonton wanted to verify the efficiency of their emergency plans.

"We'd wanted to test our ability to move men and equipment to any operation," Corporal W. Brant Murdoch of the RCMP's crime prevention department said. "We seized the opportunity of the bikers, because we knew they were coming." The three-hour search led to the issuing of 112 traffic tickets and the seizure of six stolen motorcycles and five shotguns. Twelve liquor charges were laid and nine bikers were charged for small amounts of marijuana and cocaine.

Calgary police chief Christine Silverberg wrote a guest column in The Calgary Herald on Friday, August 1, 1997. She made no mention that her police department had allowed the Hells Angels to court local biker gangs for fifteen years and take control of the biker underworld through them during that period. She did not acknowledge that police inaction at that time allowed the Hells Angels to create the infrastructure which allowed them to officially set up in Alberta in July. Her column defends the police actions in July as an effective way to combat outlaw motorcycle gangs:

The assimilation of the Alberta chapter of the Grim Reapers motorcycle club into the notorious Hells Angels prompted a significant amount of debate in the media.

I do not believe, in some cases, that the views were fully informed. The recent initiatives undertaken by Alberta police agencies were part of a national strategy and are based on a strong foundation in Canadian case law.

Some argued that the initiative constituted harassment and a contravention of basic mobility rights as guaranteed under the Charter of Rights. Others asserted the program lacked any substantive community benefit.

The term "outlaw," ascribed to the Hells Angels and other similar motorcycle gangs, has been a part of the bike gang experience since 1948 when the chief of police in Riverside, Calif., coined the term. In 1997, the term possesses a greater validity since motorcycle gang members remain true to the belief that they are not bound by the law or basic values: standards that we as Canadians uphold to be essential to a free and democratic society.

The mere presence of the Hells Angels colors signifies an association to an internationally renowned group of violent individuals and access to immense criminal resources.

As their infrastructure grows in the Calgary area, I believe we will see an increase in tertiary crime such as thefts, break-and-enters, home invasions, and robberies. The Hells Angels will achieve a broader level of control over illicit drug distribution, prostitution and exotic entertainment, thus increasing the number of those indebted to the organization.

Innocent victims also suffer. Witness the tragic death so recently of the 11-year-old child in Montreal during the war between the Hells Angels and the Rock Machine. This is precisely the reason the Alberta justice community has taken such a strong stance on this issue.

From 1969 through to 1987, Calgary was the backdrop for a fierce and brutal display of gang violence as the Grim Reapers struggled to establish their pre-eminence. The peak year of violence, 1983, saw nine explosive devices detonated in Calgary and one in Edmonton. One person was killed.

During this period, the "zero tolerance" strategy was inaugurated by the Calgary Police Service. Outlaw motorcycle club members were checked and cited for violations whenever they became apparent.

The recent initiative is a component of a larger national strategy brought into force in May, 1996 thanks to the Canadian Association of

Chiefs of Police (CACP) in conjunction with the Criminal Intelligence Service of Canada. One important element of the plan is roadside check-stops which are not arbitrary acts of harassment. In the Ontario Court of Justice case *Brown et al. v. The Durham Regional Police Service*, Justice D.S. Ferguson found that "having the appearance of an outlaw biker raises reasonable grounds to be vigilant for highway traffic violations." The court accepted the view that outlaw motorcycle gangs are engaged in unlawful modifications to their motorcycles and often use stolen parts. Additionally, it was recognized that many members of these groups will attempt to avoid the judicial process by using false identification. Based on these factors, the court ruled the checkstops as a lawful police action.

Membership in these groups and the level of violence rapidly declined as a result of "zero tolerance." It became widely known that Calgarians cherished their sense of community and public safety, two important values. Contrary to one stated opinion, the recent police efforts are not the orchestration of an elaborate ruse toward the acquisition of more government funding. Community safety and a successful problem-solving approach are the primary motivating factors. Calgarians do not need, nor do they want, the recent experiences in Quebec. We have been down that road and do not wish to relive the mistakes of history.

Moreover, our legislature has now recognized the threat of criminal organizations to the people of Canada. With the recent enactment of Bill C-95, there has been a criminal offense created by participation in a criminal organization through the commission or furtherance of certain indictable offences for the benefit of the organization.

The provincial outlaw motorcycle gang strategy is the articulation and engagement of a coordinated and sincere belief that a strong message must be conveyed to those who wish to impose a criminal advantage over the prosperity and goodwill found in our province.

We know we must be diligent. My greatest fear is complacency. Targeting our organized criminals must continue to be a priority in Calgary; Calgarians deserve no less.

* * *

Thirteen months after the Grim Reapers became Hells Angels in Alberta, newly minted Angel Terry Malec from the Edmonton chapter won a landmark court decision to legally possess firearms. Malec applied for a Firearms Acquisition Certificate in the summer of 1997. Although Malec had no criminal record, RCMP Constable Joseph Coulombe in Leduc refused the request for the permit that would allow him to buy guns.

Police convinced the Crown to file an application to bar Malec, 41, from owning guns because of his membership in the Hells Angels. "If you give [an organization] like the Hells Angels the means to obtain firearms legally, that gives them the opportunity to legally arm themselves," Crown attorney David Marriott argued in court. Provincial Court judge Jeanne Burch denied the Crown's application because Canadian law forbids the courts from finding anyone guilty by association. Police had to grant Malec his Firearms Acquisition Certificate.

This was just another in a series of stupid failed police test cases that gave the Hells Angels a legal precedent they could use to defend themselves in courts across the country. The police hoped to create a loophole in the law that would allow them to smear innocent people because of the people they associate with. They wanted this power to attack bikers who either did not commit crimes or were too wily to be caught by police. Such a law caters only to lazy, untalented, and unprofessional cops. By trying to add a cheap trick to their arsenal, the police handed the Hells Angels another solid court decision to flaunt as proof that the police are just out to get them. The police can't afford to make errors like this. They are creating a file of legal precedents and arguments that will only hinder the fight against outlaw motorcycle gangs.

The Hells Angels launched three lawsuits under the Charter of Rights and Freedoms against Alberta police for the 1997 roadside stops. The cases in Red Deer and Edmonton were put on hold pending the outcome of the Calgary case, which went to trial on September 14, 1998.

The Hells Angels were prepared to be stopped because police had broadcast their intentions in the media for six weeks before the event. The Angels brought along Vancouver lawyer and constitutional expert Ken Westlake to witness the police stopping and videotaping them at roadblocks.

"The people of this province should be concerned," Westlake said. "The issue isn't whether they're Hells Angels or criminals. The issue is police misusing their powers."

I harshly criticized police tactics in Alberta in 1996 and 1997 because the police needed to be rudely jolted out of the time warp in which they were entrenched. Most of the police officers assigned to the operation, including those in charge, had never dealt with outlaw motorcycle gangs. Police officers who knew better didn't speak out. They wanted to seen as part of the team. Cops don't criticize or second-guess cops, even when they know they are wrong. I guess that's as good a definition as any for the word pigheaded.

In the end, they all looked like fools, not because of what the Hells Angels did, but because they went ahead with a flawed plan that failed to take into account counter-attacks by the Hells Angels. Sergeant Jean-Pierre Lévesque of the RCMP, who did much to prime the media about the coming of the Hells Angels into Alberta, never expected that the Hells Angels would fight back. Like other police officers, he expected them to be intimidated by the presence of so many police officers. A smaller contingent of police would have been more effective, because the Hells Angels would have perceived them as courageous and would not have spoken back for fear of being perceived as bullies. Instead, the police were given that label because of their overwhelming presence. Intimidation is an antiquated police tactic that modern police have yet to discard because it is so easy to use by cowards who have no proper game plan.

The police in Alberta felt that because an Ontario court had ruled in favor of roadside stops against the Para-Dice Riders, they could stop bikers with impunity. Law enforcement should not be about a show of force. Police have trapped themselves in the "my gang is bigger than your gang" mindset. The main tool in fighting organized crime is intelligence, both on paper and between the ears. Police take the easy route when they shadow and bully bikers in public. Their egos may benefit, but they gain little ground in the battle against crime and they harm their public image. You don't out-bully a bully; you bide your time, then knock him out.

The sad reality is the Hells Angels are much more intelligent and street-smart than the police. They adapt quickly in a rapidly changing world. They have learned to take advantage of police at roadside stops and turn the tables on them. The gangs have for nearly two decades ensured that their members cannot be arrested when stopped publicly. They don't carry drugs or guns on runs, and they behave themselves. They pay all their bills in cash, which pleases business owners, and they speak nicely to the elderly and children. This way they achieved the desired result: for the inconvenience of being stopped for several hours in the hot sun, they are able to portray the police as bullies who trample on their rights to freely use the roads. The public believes the bikers because decades of roadside stops and clubhouse raids have yielded few arrests, convictions, or proof of criminal activity.

Police have a false sense that they are investigating bikers when they shadow them at gang events such as parties and runs. They stop their processions and photograph them at funerals. Toronto police were in the habit of raiding the Vagabonds' Halloween parties in the 1980s and early 1990s. They smashed the clubhouse door, lined members up against the outside wall, and photographed them for their files. Occasionally, a liquor charge was laid.

An intelligence officer invited me to one bust in 1987 when I was a reporter with *The Globe and Mail*. The police officers involved, especially the members of the Emergency Task Force, were so wound up with fear that one ETF officer ordered me away from the building and into the crowd of biker supporters on the opposite side of the street. I showed him my newspaper identification and my camera, and told him I had been invited by the lead investigator. He put the muzzle of his Ruger Mini-14 .223-caliber rifle to my head and ordered me to move. This cop was so rigid with fear that he could not hear or think. ETF officers are trained not to point their guns at anything they don't intend to shoot. I melted into the crowd where the biker supporters attacked me.

Parties and runs are public club events that have little or nothing to do with the criminal business side of the gang. Police don't raid Italian social events attended by mafiosi. They don't raid restaurant parties of triad members. They don't raid dance halls packed with Jamaican posse members. The Hells Angels and other outlaw motorcycle gangs are the only form of organized crime that advertises itself. The club is their cover, their social reason for being together, their source of intimidation, and the lifeblood of the gang. They would never risk it by giving police the opportunity to shut down the gang.

Too many roadside stops with too few substantial charges will work against the police. They are giving bikers the opportunity to argue that police have no reasonable grounds to suspect bikers have guns or drugs during runs. The weight of evidence of two decades of roadside stops is in favor of the bikers. The police can't honestly justify the stops on the basis that they expect to find drugs and guns. The bikers wised up a long time ago. It's time for the police to do the same and stop giving bikers ammunition to use against them in courts of law and the court of public opinion.

Some police officers did a lot of soul-searching after the 1997 patch-over in Red Deer. The public sided with the Hells Angels and branded the police bad guys. Although police will never publicly admit they messed up the operation, internal documents expose their awareness and attempts to revise policy so they don't mess up again. Unfortunately, new policy is not based on better policing but more effective media control.

Detective Ron Robertson, a member of the Edmonton Police Integrated Intelligence Unit and coordinator for outlaw motorcycle gang investigations in northern Alberta, filed this report with the RCMP on April 8, 1998.

This report has been submitted as an objective overview of the police operation conducted during the patchover of the Grim Reapers M/C Gang to Hells Angels during July of 1997. It is not my intention to criticize any individual(s) involved in the planning or execution of this operation, but to instead make suggestions that will help ensure future successes.

1. As one of the Provincial Coordinators, I was surprised the Provincial Strategy was not adhered to in the planning phase of the noted operation. It is imperative to the success of any operation dealing with OMGs [Outlaw Motorcycle Gangs] that the Provincial Coordinators and OMG investigators within the province have the primary responsibility in drafting the operational plan. During the planning phase of the Red Deer operation, it seemed that very little input from the Provincial Coordinators or OMG investigators was requested or accepted.

2. The police personnel assigned to work in Red Deer were dispersed into teams. Originally these teams were to have a team leader assigned who was familiar with Red Deer and area. The team leaders chosen were all uniform members. Initially members from intelligence units in Alberta were assigned to work within specified teams. This didn't occur for a variety of reasons, some of which I shall touch on:

   a. Intelligence members should have been assigned as team leaders. The intelligence officers should have been responsible for all check stops and should have been the first police officers to have contact with either the president or road captain of each large group of OMGs that was stopped. The initial mistake of assigning uniform members as team leaders and giving them responsibility and control over intelligence officers lead [sic] to some unsettled feelings between uniform officers and plainclothes members.

   b. The uniform officers assigned as team leaders were unfamiliar in dealing with OMGs and I felt they were also uncertain about their responsibilities and reasons for even stopping the OMG rides as they entered Red Deer.

   c. The team leaders' unfamiliarity with OMGs caused some dissention [sic] between intelligence officers who were familiar with their own OMG members, and some uniform members who appeared very uncomfortable when the intelligence officers dealt with OMG members.

d. Intelligence officers from other provinces were not included in the operational plans and at the time felt their presence and assistance was not needed as well as unwanted.

In order to avoid these problems in the future, I would suggest team leaders be OMG investigators, not uniformed personnel who are unfamiliar in dealing with OMGs. Uniform members could act in the capacity of assistant team leaders. In this way, the OMG investigators would dictate what actions would be taken against the various OMG members, ultimately stopping uniform traffic personnel from becoming too overzealous in issuing tickets for minor infractions, which ultimately made this operation "look bad to the public."

3. I had occasion to be at two check stops where uniform personnel appeared to be uncertain of their responsibilities. Large groups of uniform members gathered in areas and appeared to have no clear purpose for being at the check stops. This was another problem that was noticed by experienced intelligence officers and looked bad in their eyes as well as the eyes of the media.

4. At some sites media members were treated poorly by team leaders. This poor treatment of media members no doubt resulted in some of the poor press reports of police actions against the OMGs. Complaints were heard from media members who stated there were no police officers assigned as spokesmen at checkstop locations.

5. The operational plan that was developed and implemented in Red Deer was not followed. Contingency plans were made wherein police resources would be redeployed anywhere in Alberta dependent upon the movement of the OMGs. This did not occur. Once the OMGs left enmasse [sic] for a run to Calgary, it was immediately assumed that this event was over and police personnel were immediately sent back to their respective jurisdictions with no thought of "where are the bikers going? Are they going to return to Red Deer? Are they changing venue to somewhere else in Alberta?" Had the bikers turned around in Calgary and returned to continue partying in Red Deer, police resources would have been dismal. Had the bikers changed their venue to another small Alberta community, resources would not have been available to deal with them. It is my understanding that police resources were sent back immediately to their jurisdictions

with the intention of saving some budget money. This action could have resulted in disaster. Fortunately for police, the bikers continued on to British Columbia.

6. I was present at the checkstop which occurred in Calgary when the bikers left Red Deer on July 24th. I learned upon returning to Red Deer later in the afternoon of the 24th, the command post for this operation had been shut down and was unmanned. I found it unbelievable that only two people were in the command post when I returned to Red Deer. These two people were civilian support staff from Edmonton. Both were answering phone calls from detachments around the province wanting to report OMG movements. It is my understanding the command post was shut down almost simultaneously with the departure of the OMGs to Calgary. This should never have happened. The command post for any operation is critical to its success. This command post should not have been shut down for several days after this event. In my opinion a 24-hr phone line should have been kept in operation for at least two days after this operation concluded to provide assistance to anyone in Alberta who wanted to report OMG movement problems.

It is my opinion for successful future operations that the Provincial OMG Coordinators take the lead role in determining the total manpower required, and the deployment of the manpower for any large scale OMG events. Police managers must ensure that "ALL" members under their commands understand what the Provincial OMG Strategy is and the purpose for following it in all locations in Alberta.

Detective Greg Park of the Calgary Police Criminal Intelligence Section and coordinator for outlaw motorcycle gang investigations in southern Alberta, filed this memo with the RCMP on March 26, 1998.

Since my appointment as Coordinator OMG Investigations (South) (Dec 1997) it has been an exercise in frustration. I will confine my comments however to the (July 1997) "Patch Over" in Red Deer, Alberta. Many things regarding this event went well. As a group (Police) we should learn from our mistakes. So often we don't.

I believe the Policing problem is properly the responsibility of the Field Operations or Uniform section and therefore the responsibilities for planning are there. I feel that if the police response is planned without the CIS or Intelligence OMG investigator in mind we are making a mistake.

This event was tailor-made for the direct involvement of both the

North and South coordinators. I can see in future operations appointing a planning group which includes the Coordinators who will represent other jurisdictions in their area of responsibility (North or South in the Province.)

Team leaders were uniform members who generally didn't know any of the OMG members. Team leaders should have been CIS members, or the teams could have had co-leadership, one CIS member and one uniform member. Jurisdiction is a consideration, one or both could be from the Police Service in the effected [sic] area. CIS was largely ignored at the beginning of this operation and them [sic] at the end of the operation.

A clear mandate should be communicated to the teams and team leaders. This mandate should reiterate the Federal "Zero Tolerance" policies.

Many jurisdictions committed time, money, and personnel to assist with policy, however, when the Hells Angels went to Banff to stay overnight we didn't provide assistance to the detachment there. Assistance to Calgary on the final day was sporadic. We could have done a better job there.

The de-brief became a back-slap session as opposed to a meeting of discovery to identify problems to fix these areas of concern. Let's then start to develop a plan that all can use.

Some police managers were stung by the adverse publicity police received for the 1997 road checks and they tried to ensure mistakes would not be repeated. One person was especially taken aback by the public outcry. London police chief Julian Fantino staked his police political career in 1996 on the fight against outlaw motorcycle gangs. The Canadian Association of Chiefs of Police made him chairman in February 1996 of their newly formed National Strategy to Combat Outlaw Motorcycle Gangs. Chief Fantino surrounded himself with the country's highest-profile police bureaucrats to draft policy to deal with bikers. He was quoted everywhere as an opponent to the spread of the Hells Angels across Canada. He courted media who would unquestioningly print his statements. He had built a powerful publicity machine and the Red Deer debacle did not sit well with him. Chief Fantino wrote this memo to Assistant Commisioner Donald McDermid of the RCMP, commanding officer for "K" Division (Alberta), on April 8, 1998. The memo referred to a workshop on outlaw motorcycle gangs held from March 29 to April 1 at the Canadian Police College in Ottawa.

In my capacity as Chairman of the National Strategy to Combat Outlaw Motorcycle Gangs I attended the captioned workshop along with 18 Tier 3 representatives. Overall, the issues, the presenters, and the interaction, from my point of view, resulted in a very significant outcome.

I will not cover the content of the workshop as a transcript of the dialogue will be forwarded to you by CISC. However, I do want to share with you my perspective on a number of issues and concerns that were raised by those in attendance and merit particular comment.

At the outset, I wish to thank Richard Philippe, Director of CISC, who, along with J.P. Lévesque, J. Lemieux, and other CISC staff, provided an excellent initiative that, I feel, will greatly enhance the cohesiveness and effectiveness of the National Strategy.

Significant Issues Raised that Require Our Attention:

1. A shift in tactics is required with respect to the "OMG roadblocks."
2. The "0 Tolerance" message must be replaced with more strategic commentary about the public safety threat posed by OMGs, their enterprise, Organized Crime endeavors, and the need for law enforcement to be vigilant and proactive in the interest of public safety. We need to unify the message.
3. The growing threat to law enforcement and the justice system posed by OMGs, including violence and intimidation tactics.
4. The need to develop a new and more effective public information and communications strategy. A consistent and proactive public awareness campaign is required.
5. The ongoing difficulties being experienced in some jurisdictions in securing personnel and resources dedicated to OMG enforcement.
6. The National Strategy seems to be driven from the bottom up, but does not seem to have "the support of top management" in some areas of the country.
7. Difficulties being experienced in some areas with respect to coordination and the full integration of law enforcement agencies.
8. Require local and national trained/qualified expert witnesses on OMG.
9. Require media training for designated spokespersons who have OMG expertise.
10. Require specialized crown attorneys dedicated to OMG investigations/prosecutions.
11. A critical need exists for a common information bank for data, setting out facts about OMG activities, their philosophy, their hierarchy, the degree and forms of criminal activity both nationally and internationally, the significance of patches and emblems, their habits, and any

other information which can assist law enforcement with factual information and profiles that can be used strategically to inform the courts and the public at large about OMG.

12. A national data base is also needed to document significant court decisions—jurisprudence bearing on OMG cases.

13. Enhanced specialized training for OMG investigators, especially intended to elevate their expertise and ability to more strategically apply the laws of the land in ways that will attain the best outcomes, resulting in fewer public confrontations with OMG (during the traditional roadblocks) in favor of covert operations, arrests, seizures, and criminal prosecutions.

Obviously, these issues and comments were raised in a spirit of positive and constructive debate by a group of people with remarkable commitment and dedication to the objectives of the National Strategy, and I am grateful to them for their important input. At some point in the near future, we will need to convene to formulate an appropriate response/strategy to address these issues.

Finally, I am very pleased with our progress overall. For example, three areas of the country are busy putting into place dedicated OMG investigative units; the Solicitor General of Canada and his counterparts in some of the provinces have expressed their support for our efforts—hopefully, the necessary resources will follow; and the media is fast becoming more aware and informed about the threat posed to public safety by OMG.

All in all, we have come a long way; however, a great deal of work remains. Accordingly, I thank you for your invaluable support and look forward to continued progress in our collective efforts to "disrupt and dismantle" OMG.

Some police managers took public criticism of road checks to heart, especially within the RCMP. They tried to ensure mistakes would not be repeated, especially those brought to their attention by high-ranking policemen like Chief Fantino. Sergeant R.H. McDonald, bureau manager of the Criminal Intelligence Service of Alberta, wrote this memorandum titled "Strategies to combat OMGs" to RCMP assistant commissioner Donald McDermid, Commanding Officer of "K" Division (Alberta) on April 24, 1998:

This memorandum is forwarded in response to your request for comments concerning Chief Fantino's letter to you outlining the results of a meeting of Tier 3 representatives in Ottawa between 98 Mar. 29 and 98 Apr. 01. Reference item number 2 of Chief Fantino's letter, I conversed with Cpl. Jacques Lemieux one of the CISC [author's note: Criminal Intelligence Service of Canada] OMG Coordinators to receive clarification on what the Tier 3 representatives meant by replacing the existing "zero tolerance" policy with a more strategic commentary. He informed me the Tier 3 representatives on the Committee feel police should be projecting the message that police will not tolerate tactics of threat or intimidation utilized by the OMGs and that we will implement "zero tolerance" to ensure public safety. Based on our own experience in Red Deer last year, applying the "zero tolerance" to traffic violations created a negative backlash of public and media support. In future, more discretion should be utilized by officers relevant traffic violations.

I have discussed this issue with D/Chief Wasylyshen of the EPS [Edmonton Police Service]. He agrees the Alberta "zero tolerance" strategy as outlined in the Provincial Strategy document should be revisited as it is too vague. On 98 May 30 the EPS is hosting a meeting of police personnel and crown counsel to discuss the withdrawal of OMG charges. I suggested we should surface this issue at that meeting for discussion. Apparently Gary McCuaig, Chief Crown Counsel, indicates they were never made aware of a "zero tolerance" policy by Alberta police even though Justice Minister Havelock publicly stated he supported the actions of police. The results of the 98 May 30 meeting at EPS could be provided to the CISA Executive Committee when it meets in Medicine Hat on 98 May 07. I will place that on the CISA Executive agenda as an item from you.

Also, I believe we mistakenly made the assumption our middle managers, detachment commanders, and other police managers were fully informed on and supported the unified approach Alberta police would take toward dealing with OMGs. Again, the Red Deer experience revealed the OMG Coordinator experts were not allowed to be part of the planning process for the patchover of the Grim Reapers. As we indicated to you in separate correspondence, I have asked for a meeting with C/Supt. MacKay to deal with this matter to assure it doesn't occur again. I must mention the OMG Coordinators inform me the RCMP is not the only agency at fault, however, we feel the issues are best addressed by individual forums with the involved agencies to alleviate the politics coming into play.

In attempts to inform middle management on this issue I have arranged with S/Sgt. Lou O'Reilly of the Medicine Hat PS [Police Service] for one or both of the OMG Coordinators to address the CID Managers in Medicine Hat on this issue on 98 May 07. After that I will be encouraging the OMG Coordinators to arrange information forums with officers commanding, officers in charge, detachment commanders, duty officers etc. to reinforce with them where we are coming from with the Provincial Strategy. We will ask that the OMG Coordinators stress to middle management that their purpose is not to interfere with the policing of their jurisdictions. They merely want to be involved in the planning of operations dealing with OMGs so the OMGs are treated in a consistent manner throughout the province and police maximize their efficiencies during those situations.

Some RCMP administrators refused to listen to complaints from seasoned intelligence officers—especially if they were from local police agencies—and brushed them aside as unworthy of their attention.

Chief Superintendent R.D. MacKay, RCMP officer in charge of Criminal Operations in "K" Division (Alberta) curtly dismissed the concerns of Detectives Robertson and Park in a terse memo on April 30, 1998. He played his politics at a different level and had yet to learn that his superiors thought differently.

Firstly, my recollection of the developed Province of Alberta OMG strategy involved the expertise of our OMG Coordinators in developing appropriate ops plans. If the OMG Coordinators did not form part of the planning process in Red Deer, they should have! Notwithstanding, the jurisdictional police agency is ultimately in charge of the operation site and the OMG Coordinators and CISA [Criminal Intelligence Service of Alberta] component should have the opportunity for input in the planning process.

At this juncture, I am not satisfied there is an operational requirement to re-hash operation "Kittyhawk" [Author's note: An investigation into a prostitution ring in which some Grim Reapers were allegedly involved] and two-bit it to death. There was an operational de-briefing following the aforementioned operation and many of the concerns raised here were not surfaced.

Please ensure that both OMG Coordinators are provided with a copy of this correspondence and that there is a clear understanding they will form part of any future operational planning involving outlaw motorcycle gangs enforcement strategies.

The Alberta and National Strategy to combat outlaw motorcycle gangs set out admirable goals and philosophies, but little or no thought was given to their implementation. They are vehicles crafted to ferry political aspirations. Politics and personal goals have always been an impediment to waging a successful war, as they are always put ahead of the final objective.

By June 23, 1998, Alberta police had drafted a plan to help them win over the media and public. It was a convenient diversion in the war against bikers, as it gave administrators the impression they were achieving something. It generated paperwork and ate up valuable time that could have been spent doing what police should do: investigate criminals. The best argument the police can use to sway the media and public is fact. They need to secure convictions and let the facts speak for themselves. People across Canada are tired of hearing the cops cry wolf. They want to see the hide draped over the fence. Instead, this was Alberta's public relations scheme, better known in political circles as a damage control plan:

Communication Plan
Outlaw Motorcycle Gang Provincial Strategy

Goal

To gain the public's support and assistance in the police community's attempts to combat the proliferation of outlaw motorcycle gang activity in the province of Alberta. Hereinafter, outlaw motorcycle gangs are referred to as OMG.

Target Audiences

1. Primary:
    a) News and Current Affairs Media
    b) General Public
2. Secondary:
    a) Business Community (including individual business owners; Chamber of Commerce; hotel and hospitality associations)
    b) Legally Mandated Stakeholders (including individual police officers; all CISA Regular, Associate and Affiliate-member Agencies; crown prosecutors and judges; Customs; Revenue Canada; Immigration; Gaming and Liquor Commission; provincial jails and federal prisons; other regulatory boards)
    c) Political Advocacy Groups (all levels of Government; School Boards; Police Commissions/Boards)
3. Tertiary:

a) Members of outlaw motorcycle gangs, along with their probationary members and associates.

Objectives

1. A unified public information strategy that encompasses the diverse nature of police investigations and public safety issues concerning OMGs.
2. Increase the number of people in the primary and secondary target audiences who:
   a) know about and understand the threat of OMGs to public safety;
   b) share information with police on activities and associates of OMGs.

Strategies

1. CISA Public Information Team approach (Appendix I–page 5).
2. Standard Operating Procedures for media releases specific to each type of OMG event or investigation (Appendix II–page 7).
3. Measure the number of people in the general public (primary target audience) who:
   a) have knowledge of the presence of OMGs in the province;
   b) believe or disbelieve that OMGs are involved in criminal activity;
      i) if yes, what types of crimes do they believe OMGs are involved in;
   c) feel threatened by the presence of OMGs in their community;
   d) support police activities relating to OMGs;
   e) have been victimized by OMGs (e.g. verbal intimidation, violence, extortion);
      i) if yes, did they report it?
      ii) if not, why?

This strategy will help determine the public's level of understanding on the issue of OMGs, which is needed to plan effective information releases.

4. Develop an education/information package on OMGs which includes:
   a) their history, structure and function;
   b) an historical time-line of documented cases of OMG criminal activities in Canada, the US, and other countries around the world;
   c) a database of the criminal records (minus names) of OMG members and their associates in Canada, the US, and other countries around the world;
   d) a database of law enforcement successes involving OMGs in Canada, the US, and other countries around the world;
   e) key phrases voiced by judges in court proceedings against OMGs;
   f) examples of the financial and personal impact of OMG criminal activities on the business community;

g) examples of the financial and personal impact of OMG criminal activities on private citizens;

h) action steps for community response (including private and corporate citizens).

5. Develop Key Messages:

a) which address public safety issues for use by all police personnel involved in policing OMG gatherings. Criminal charges and convictions against OMG members and associates are, in and of themselves, convincing key messages;

b) which incorporate elements of the information/education package.

6. Conduct presentations to news media executives and reporters (primary target audience) utilizing OMG experts and the information package.

By virtue of the transient nature of the news business, this strategy must be flexible and ongoing to ensure news executives and reporters, who are new to Alberta, are afforded the benefit of this educational tool.

7. Conduct presentations to all groups in the secondary target audiences using OMG experts and the information package. The turnover rate in these areas must also be monitored closely so the presentations can be repeated in a timely fashion.

8. Develop an internal communication process to keep everyone from front-line officers to Executive Officers updated on OMG-related issues.

9. Include OMG-related news releases and excerpts from the information/education package on all CISA Regular-member agencies' websites/list servers.

Evaluation

- Retain records of all OMG-related news stories (print and broadcast) for analysis:
- an informal analysis will be undertaken following each event that generates media coverage;
- the results of the informal analyses will be retained for a formal analysis on an annual basis.
- Retain records of direct feedback from people or groups in the target audiences for use in the informal and formal analyses.
- Public surveys (as outlined on page 2, *Strategies*, # 3) should be undertaken on a yearly basis to monitor the public's level of understanding concerning OMGs.

Within the Alberta Strategy to deal with bikers was a plan to control media and public access to information. It was prefaced with a confidential letter from R.H. McDonald, bureau manager for the Criminal Intelligence Service of Alberta, and analyst Jane Webster. The letter is dated September 9, 1998.

Re: Alberta Strategy on Outlaw Motorcycle Gangs (OMG's)

On June 23, 1998, the CISA Executive Committee formally accepted an OMG Media Strategy as an appendix to the Alberta Strategy on OMG's. Within the media strategy is a plan to gain support for law enforcement efforts from the general public, news media, business community, judiciary, and elected officials. Additionally, a "Public Information Team" has been established and is comprised of police media personnel in the Calgary, Edmonton, Lethbridge, and Medicine Hat Police Services and RCMP.

The Media Strategy also contains a guideline for police media releases concerning OMG occurrences under the heading "Standard Operating Procedures," a copy of which is attached. This format was used during the Hells Angels ride to Grande Prairie in June this year and will continue to be used whenever a multi-agency law enforcement response is required anywhere in Alberta.

An amendment to the "Standard Operating Procedures" since the CISA Executive Committee gave its approval pertains to conducting a media presentation at the commencement of a police operation rather than at every shift briefing with the provision that if the media strategy changes during the operation, a media briefing may be requested at that time.

APPENDIX II
CISA PUBLIC INFORMATION STRATEGY
Standard Operating Procedures

In keeping with the agreement by the partners in the OPERATIONS STRATEGY TO DEAL WITH OUTLAW MOTORCYCLE GANGS— PROVINCE OF ALBERTA, the following Standard Operating Procedures define the parameters for effective public dissemination of information on OMG activities.

Information releases to the public through the news media will be dictated by the type of event or incident at hand.

All news releases and internal advisories to stakeholders, regardless of the type of OMG event, will be constructed using letterhead that displays the crests of the five CISA Regular-member agencies (Attachment I–page 12).

1. Multi-jurisdictional Events

   A multi-jurisdictional event can include public gatherings of OMGs where two or more of the CISA regular member agencies are involved, such as anniversary parties, swapmeets, or drag races.

   Prior to the event:

   a) maintain a low-key approach – no media press releases will be generated from police;

   b) all media requests for information will be directed to the Coordinator, who, together with the Team, the North and South OMG Coordinators, and the Commanding Officer from the event location will decide what information, and by whom, it will be released;

   c) the Commanding Officer from the location of the event and other key personnel will be briefed on critical public information issues;

   d) Executive members queried by the media about police operational plans for the event will consult with the Coordinator prior to responding.

   During the event:

   e) the CISA Public Information Coordinator and each member of the Team will attend the location;

   f) the Team will:

   • provide input into the overall strategy for the event;

   • monitor media reports as the event unfolds and correct erroneous information;

   • develop ongoing, alternative communication strategies as needed;

   • issue internal advisories to stakeholders as the event unfolds;

   • conduct a media briefing to police personnel at the commencement of the operation to emphasize key messages which officers can relay to the public and media, if asked;

   • update and distribute fact sheets containing background on OMG criminal behavior at other similar events in the past, explaining the need for increased police presence;

   • collect media reports for analysis.

   g) while the Coordinator has the authority to speak with the media at these events, where possible, the local police media relations officer will conduct interviews and issue news releases as deemed necessary by the Team;

   h) with guidance from the Team, OMG experts and other key personnel will conduct interviews to add depth and detail to the information being released.

2. Joint-forces Investigations

a) after consulting with the North and South OMG Coordinators, when more than two of the CISA regular member agencies have concluded an investigation, the Coordinator and the Team will attend the location to prepare the announcement;

b) key police personnel will be selected to conduct a news conference to announce the results of the investigation;

c) the selected "spokespeople" will be briefed by the Team and guided through the media process to ensure an informed and credible image is maintained;

d) through consultation, the Team will compile speaking notes for the "spokespeople."

e) the Team will prepare a media kit which contains:

• a fact sheet containing brief information on the investigation and its results;

• a list of accused persons (if over 18 years), their age, hometown, and charges laid;

• speaking notes of the "spokespeople";

• a news release that includes quotes from the "spokespeople" which will be faxed out after the news conference.

f) the Team will prepare and distribute regular internal advisories to stakeholders;

g) the Team will monitor and collect all news reports surrounding the announcement in order to:

• correct erroneous information as quickly as possible;

• maintain records of all news reports for event-specific and yearly analysis.

3. Isolated Incidents

• It is the responsibility of each jurisdiction's Executive and media relations specialist to decide when and what information will be released to the public regarding an isolated incident or significant development connected to an OMG in their town or city.

• If other CISA Regular-member agencies receive media queries regarding such incidents, the caller will be referred back to the originating agency.

• The Coordinator and the Team will have no authority over news releases on OMG activities specific to one jurisdiction.

However, the Coordinator will be informed of any intended media releases, prior to distribution to the media, and will, in turn, advise other Team members and stakeholders.

Reporting Structure

• The CISA Public Information Coordinator will communicate with the OMG Provincial Coordinators (North and South) on a regular basis to keep up-to-date on developments and must clear with them any information intended for release to the media.

• In order to avoid compromising ongoing investigations, this protocol must also be followed by individual media relations specialists when releasing information on OMGs on behalf of their municipal police agency or RCM Police detachment.

Stakeholders

All media releases and internal advisories on OMG activity from any jurisdiction will be faxed to:

• CISA Executive Committee (Attention: Criminal Operations Officers)
• CISA Regular-member Agencies:
  • Calgary Police Service
  • Edmonton Police Service
  • Lethbridge Police Service
  • Medicine Hat Police Service
  • RCMP—K Division
  • Red Deer—Criminal Investigation Section
  • CCIS
  • EIIU
• CISA Associate-member Agencies:
  • Camrose Police Service
  • Coaldale Police Service
  • Lacombe Police Service
  • Taber Police Service
• Criminal Intelligence Service Alberta, Bureau Manager
• Alberta Justice Minister
• Director of Communications, Alberta Justice
• Chairman, National OMG Strategy
• Criminal Intelligence Service of Canada, OMG Coordinator
• RCMP Headquarters Ottawa, Media Relations Unit
• RCMP National Operations Center

The National Strategy held a "strategy meeting" in Ottawa on December 7–8, 1997. Here are excerpts from the meeting's "Executive Summary" prepared by the Criminal Intelligence Service of Canada:

The Canadian Association of Chiefs of Police (CACP) in February 1996 adopted a National Strategy to combat Outlaw Motorcycle Gangs (OMG). Chief Julian Fantino, London City Police, was appointed Chairman of a national strategy committee and subsequently a set of general principles were established along with a three-tier operational infrastructure to implement the strategy.

Previous meetings on the national strategy had involved senior members of the police community to develop the general strategy. On December 7/8 a meeting was held in Ottawa involving, for the first time, those members of the police community from across Canada involved in the front-line battle against organized motorcycle gangs. The meeting was chaired by S/Sgt. J.P. Lévesque, Criminal Intelligence Service of Canada, although there were several representatives of senior police management in attendance.

The intent of this meeting was to deal with all issues of importance affecting biker investigators and front-line police officers in their battle against criminal biker gangs. An important concept during the discussions was the development of common strategies for each issue, if this was at all possible. . . .

The following resolutions were agreed upon by the delegates: . . .

It was recognized that the police community must improve their relationship with the media in order to get their own messages to the public and also counter the media campaigns by outlaw biker gangs which attempt to present a positive slant to the biker image. All biker coordinators were requested to inform other coordinators across Canada on any take-down action in their area so that the event can be publicized on a national level. . . .

Chief Fantino promised to encourage senior police management to support their staff on biker enforcement issues including participating in the media campaign to publicize police actions and the danger of OMGangs.

Chief Fantino, as chairman of the National Strategy, wrote this morale-booster to all CISC member on January 5, 1998. (This small group of people spent a lot of time writing letters commending each other.)

February 17–18, 1998 will mark the two-year anniversary of the official birth of the National Strategy on Outlaw Motorcycle Gangs (OMG), intended to disrupt and dismantle the activities of OMG in Canada.

Although we face many daunting challenges, the law enforcement community can be justifiably proud of the progress that has been accomplished to date. Admittedly, a great deal more work must be undertaken to fully implement the strategies adopted by the many police leaders who are the driving force behind this unique law enforcement initiative, which is intended to combat the threat posed to Canadian society by Outlaw Motorcycle Gangs.

Ironically, even though the "heat" has been turned up on the OMG, they continue to pose a significant threat, not only to the public at large, but, more and more, to law enforcement officers. Over the past year, OMG members have been implicated in the murders of two prison guards, the bombing of a police facility, and countless incidents of threats and intimidation directed at police officers. Moreover, OMG have developed their own public relations strategy, obviously intended to deflect public attention away from their criminal enterprises.

Although the foregoing observations may sound depressing, I am constantly reminded of a remark made by a "converted hard-core outlaw biker" who stated: "If cops ever get their act together—we're finished." I am convinced that we can effectively co-ordinate our efforts to do exactly that: put outlaw bikers out of business. All we need to do is take notice of the excellent police work, in part sustained by provincial funding, unfolding in some provinces where coordinated OMG investigations are consistently achieving very impressive results, including the seizure of OMG wealth, clubhouses, and toys.

The Anti-Gang legislation (Bill C-95) has provided an added tool to be used by law enforcement; however, to date, the central government has done very little else. In fact, a funding proposal intended to support the work of the National Strategy that was specifically requested by then-Minister of Justice A. Rock, with copy to Minister Herb Gray, Solicitor General of Canada, submitted in April 1997, has since been summarily dismissed by the incumbent Ministers. In many respects, the Canadian government is paying lip service to the serious public safety threat posed by organized crime enterprises, of which OMG are the most notorious. One would think that the body count of 60+ murdered victims in Quebec in the past few years alone, including OMG members, an innocent 11-year-old boy, and more recently two prison guards, would cause Ottawa to take a meaningful leadership role in fulfilling its national public safety mandate by supporting, in a tangible way, the work of the National Strategy. . . .

Over the past year, we have been far more proactive with the media and public information about OMG; consistently casting them as ruth-less, organized criminal enterprises; that the public should not be fooled by the OMG's public rhetoric intended to portray themselves as "motor-cycle enthusiasts who get together for charitable causes, etc."—a tactic intended to divert attention away from who they really are and what they really do: murder, deal drugs, run prostitution networks, extort, etc. We cooperated with the author of the piece: "Biker Gangs: Getting Away with Murder"—*Reader's Digest*, November 1997. We also made a few strategic media releases, conducted countless interviews, and partici-pated in a Global Television documentary illustrating the ruthlessness of OMG. And in all, I believe the media strategy and the consistence of our message are beginning to be heard and believed.

On the 7–8 December, 1997, we were able to have a meeting of the Tier 2 representatives in Ottawa . . . The meeting proved to be very successful, with decisions taken with respect to a number of important issues: . . .

- Continue to inform and lobby governments at all levels for support
  - resources to sustain dedicated OMG enforcement initiatives; . . .
- Pursuit of a proactive media strategy, also highlighting the National Strategy at every opportunity;
- Promotion of enhanced support and involvement of senior police executives in OMG initiatives, including media interviews.

*   *   *

The National Strategy to Combat Outlaw Motorcycle Gangs held a Tier 1 meeting of Canada's top police officers on August 23, 1998, in Edmon-ton. The minutes of this meeting, stamped "Confidential" and "3rd PARTY RULE" on each page, are undeniable proof that the police are using the media to upset the public and extort money from governments.

In attendance were:

> RCMP   Commissioner Philip Murray
> Deputy Commissioner Larry Proke – "E" Division (British Columbia)
> Assistant Commissioner Don McDermid – "K" Division (Alberta)
> Sergeant Bob McDonald – Manager, CISA (Crimi-nal Intelligence Service of Alberta)
> C/M Jane Webster, analyst, CISA (Criminal Intelli-gence Service of Alberta)
>
> Quebec   Assistant Director Jean Bourdeau – Sûreté du Québec

Ontario Commissioner Gwen Boniface – OPP
         Chief Julian Fantino – Chairman, National Strategy
         Chief David Boothby – Toronto Police Service
British Columbia Chief Bruce Chambers – Vancouver Police
         Department
         CISC Richard Philippe – Director, CISC (Criminal Intelligence Service of Canada)
         J.P. Lévesque – National Coordinator for OMG

Chief Fantino welcomed everyone and outlined the Agenda for this meeting:
  • Current Status of the Strategy
  • Threat
  • Future of the Strategy
  • Roundtable discussion

Minutes

While a firm believer of the Strategy and its impact on the bikers, Chief Fantino reiterated the necessity for everyone present to support Tier 3 actions and for a united front.

Commissioner Murray briefly stated that the police community came a long way in its fight against organized crime and that the National Strategy was a must as the Hells Angels not only have a strategy in taking over the country but also are very quick in adjusting to new challenges by the police. This is why we must keep working together.

A brief discussion on the Wild Pigs followed where Chief Fantino reinforced that the CACP [Canadian Association of Chiefs of Police], despite a recent article in the magazine *Blueline*, stood by their decision to denounce any behavior improper with police code conduct. S/Sgt. Lévesque added that any action against the Canadian Wild Pigs had to be filtered by Tier 1 as not all Wild Pigs in the United States are contaminated. It was decided that the situation would be closely monitored.

Richard Philippe, Director of CISC, stated that we have to realize that some police officers and crown attorneys are intimidated by bikers and required full support from management.

S/Sgt. Lévesque gave a brief overview of the threat as, despite Carcajou and the opposition in Quebec and Ontario, the HA are expanding quickly. He also identified the need for two very important actions to be implemented in the near future:

- a Canadian team of hand-picked Crown Attorneys to support the operations/court cases/training/Immigration challenges and positively influence other Crown Attorneys to join forces against OMG;
- timely use of a media strategy to maximize its impact on the public which will, in turn, force the government to commit more resources to our cause.

The Director of CISC gave an update on future actions to be taken by CISC.

A 1-800 line which would be made available for the public and police officers on patrol. A proper feasibility study will be required.

A/D Jean Bourdeau stated that their 1-800 line was a success but that people taking the calls must have quick access to the proper data banks to be efficient.

He also added that the killing at random of prison guards by Maurice "Mom" Boucher, President of the Nomads, created a climate of fear among enforcement agencies in Quebec. It is very expensive to protect informants and even Boucher alone costs $1 Million a year. [Author's note: This is a reference to the cost of keeping Boucher jailed in a secure facility pending his trial for the murder of two prison guards.]

Other actions included, but are not limited to the following:

- Five-day training courses on expert witnesses and handling of informants
- Video conference for Tier 3
- Two-day workshop for Canadian team of prosecutors
- Booklet on police rights to detain and general information on OMG

A/C McDermid added that our training sessions should involve all levels of government from municipal to federal, but most important to have one in hand that, during major events, would entail all the latest criminal activities of the HA and their impact on our society.

It was agreed that ACIIS II [computer program used for intelligence purposes] was to be used not only to enter pictures and bio-data of bikers, but also to track their movements and other activities so it can be more useful to investigators in the field.

Chief Fantino pointed out that because of the HA challenging our road blocks in court, we should ensure that we are more selective and, at times, change our strategy when it comes to SSG [Special Services Group] actions.

On the topic of media strategy, the main goal is to stay away from the fear factor as it could easily turn against us.

D/C Proke congratulated Chief Chambers for the timing of their press release on the arrests of three HA members from BC, just before the Canadian Run.

Finally, it was agreed that Correctional Services/Customs/Immigration would be invited to sit on Tier 1.

Chief Fantino concluded this meeting by reminding the participants of the importance of their commitment/support and that only a united front will ensure the success of this strategy.

* * *

Eight Rebels became full-fledged Hells Angels on September 18, 1998. Two King's Crew members became Hells Angels prospects. That brought the total number of Angels in Alberta to 31, plus 11 prospects and 4 friends—a new term created by Alberta Hells Angels to replace the hangaround moniker given those who do gopher jobs for bikers. Friends wear a black-and-white patch on their left front vest with the city name of the chapter they deal with.

The Hells Angels were cautious with six Edmonton Rebels, including the president, a prospect, two hangarounds, and an associate who were charged in October 1997 with drug, weapon, and stolen-property offenses, as well as income tax evasion and money laundering. The proceeds of crime law was used to seize nearly $1 million in assets. The bikers are alleged to have not reported $1.5 million in income. The Hells Angels have made seven of these bikers "prospects on restrictions."

As the Hells Angels expanded, the RCMP respected their time-honored tradition of shooting themselves in the foot. It was revealed during the bail hearing of two alleged eco-terrorists in Alberta on January 28, 1999, that the RCMP blew up a gas company shack in October 1998 to legitimize an informant who tried to gain the confidence of two men being investigated by the force. In a February 2, 1999, memo to RCMP staff across Alberta, it was said the bombing of the shack was supported by Supreme Court decisions and was "absolutely essential in furthering the credibility of the agent." Chief Superintendent Rod MacKay of the RCMP "K" (Alberta) Division, also supported his officers. "This was an operation that we followed all of our rules and regulations and certainly the laws of the land."

Dirty tricks are not new to the RCMP. The force was stripped of its national security mandate in 1983 following the revelation by the 1981 Commission of Inquiry headed by Alberta justice David McDonald that

RCMP officers committed hundreds of illegal acts such as break-ins, thefts, an abduction, mail openings, forgery and arson, mostly to destabilize the independence movement in Quebec in the 1960s and 1970s.

The RCMP stole dynamite and burned a barn on May 8, 1972, because they thought Front de Libération du Québec terrorists were to meet American Black Panthers there. Mounties broke into the left-wing Agence Presse Libre du Québec. They staged Operation Ham and stole the Parti Québécois membership lists from a computer in January 1973.

The civilian Canadian Security Intelligence Service was created in 1984 to protect national security after the government deemed the RCMP too untrustworthy to handle such a critical task. The bombing in Alberta in 1998—the RCMP's 125th anniversary—was just another incident in a long list of embarrassing foibles that jeopardize a force which was at one time the pride of our country

Chapter 6: British Columbia
The Land the Cops Forgot

The ill-founded police public relations war against the Hells Angels swept Canada, eventually arriving in British Columbia, where the police ferociously manipulated the media in 1998 to spread word of the coming biker apocalypse.

Nowhere in the world do the police appear more ludicrous and insincere when they talk about the Hells Angels menace. The 1998 public relations war by the police is the only battle they have fought against the Hells Angels since the gang took over the Satan's Angels on June 23, 1983. Only a handful of the province's seventy-five Hells Angels have a criminal record. Police investigations of the gang have been aborted before charges could be laid. Key investigators were transferred to menial duties before they could harm the gang. Years of intelligence work yielded little more than grainy photographs with blurred license plates. Fearful prosecutors refused to proceed with charges against the Hells Angels. And yet the police had the gall to call the Hells Angels criminals. In doing so, they gave the Hells Angels the perfect opportunity to cry persecution, something they often do at press conferences where they demand that police support their allegations with evidence that gang members are criminals. The police never do.

The British Columbia Hells Angels are the world's richest (gang members were asked at the Sturgis Motorcycle Classic to stop hitting on the BC Angels for money) and have the cleanest criminal records. About eighty-five percent of the world's 1,700 Hells Angels have criminal records. That leaves 255 with clean slates, one-third of them in British Columbia. Hells Angels leader Rick Ciarniello takes great pride in regularly challenging the police to name specific Hells Angels who have committed crimes. They can't.

The Hells Angels have seven BC chapters as of July 1999: Nanaimo

(14 members), East End in Vancouver (13), Nomads in Burnaby (6) formed by members of the East End Chapter, Vancouver in Coquitlam (16), White Rock in Langley (14), Haney in Pitt Meadows (13) and Mission City, formed by members of the Vancouver and Nanaimo chapters on July 10, 1999. The Hells Angels also control puppet gangs across the province: The Tallismen in Smithers (8), The Tribesmen in Squamish (6), and gangs in Willams Lake, Kamloops, and Prince George (13).

The Hells Angels issued this press release in March 1995:

> In an article dated December 16, 1994, the police stated their intention is to use the media to change the public image of the Hells Angels motorcycle club. Trial by media would be a very convenient tool for them. They can use speculation and innuendo. None of their accusations would require the burden of proof.
>
> The police imply that the successful business interests of Hells Angels members must always be the product of criminal activity. The police are very careful not to name anyone when they release a statement like this to the press. Even a policeman can be charged with libel. It would go against police dogma to suppose that a Hells Angel could be a hard-working, dedicated entrepreneur.
>
> The Police Gazette, the RCMP bible, is careful to digitize out the faces of Hells Angels in the pictures they print. Some sources used to imply truth in The Police Gazette are laughable. Occasionally they quote an earlier edition of their own publication as a reliable source. Other times they quote Yves Lavigne, a self-professed expert on the club. Yves Lavigne knows nothing about the Hells Angels. He has done no more than read police reports and court transcripts. Again a source supporting itself. This is classic propaganda The police should support their allegations with charges or they should remain silent. The media should not allow itself to be used by the police.
>
> Police must justify their budgets every year. They take a very visible group of people. A group, of which, they think they public will believe anything. Accuse them of controlling all crime in the country. The end result is that they get to waste millions of Canadian taxpayer dollars again this year.

*   *   *

The police alleged in late 1997 and early 1998 that the Hells Angels and their associates had taken jobs in Vancouver and Halifax ports to facilitate the smuggling of drugs into Canada. The media ran with the story, which was actually planted by disgruntled Canada Ports Police after the federal government announced the 29-man Port of Vancouver unit would be disbanded and replaced by municipal police.

Police used a published 1995 RCMP report on Hells Angels working the docks to entice the short-memoried media to pay attention to their concerns. That report said ten Hells Angels and thirty associates belonged to the longshoremen's union. Many Hells Angels and associates have union cards and work the docks in Vancouver. But, more than three years after the original report, police biker investigators were hard-pressed to name any of them. They also were conducting no investigations into alleged drug smuggling by Hells Angels through the ports. Rather, they tried to help their fellow brothers, the Ports Police, keep their jobs by scaring the public into forcing the Government to change its mind.

The print media first ran the story in the fall of 1997 and January 1998. Then CBC radio did a series of reports on the issue in early March 1998. The reporter's apartment was broken into on March 2. His tape deck and video cassette recorder were stolen. The radio receiver was wrapped in plastic and put in the water-filled bathtub. Police told the frightened reporter this was a typical Hells Angels intimidation tactic to curb the network's week-long series of reports on the gang. The Hells Angels denied the charge and the culprit has never been identified.

The day that the CBC radio reporter found his radio in the bathtub, I appeared on sixteen CBC radio and television programs from Halifax to Vancouver to discuss the Hells Angels. I revealed on the CBC National News on Tuesday, March 4, that the police had serious problems in British Columbia. Police and prosecutors admitted earlier in the day that they were afraid of the Hells Angels and had curbed their investigative activities. I pointed out that this was normal, as only a handful of police officers in any department are psychologically equipped and motivated to deal with ongoing organized crime investigations. Police and prosecutors should not be ashamed of admitting their limitations, I said, as the presence of an unreliable cop on an investigation jeopardizes partners' lives. Some cops and prosecutors were never meant to deal with anything more serious than traffic offenses. That is not a bad thing, as long as these limits are acknowledged and taken into consideration when people are promoted and assigned to major investigations.

I also revealed on the newscast that it seemed the Hells Angels had a top-ranking informant within the RCMP who contributed to the sabotage of several major investigations of the gang. One money-laundering investigation in the early 1990s was aborted by higher-ups who transferred key investigators out of the jurisdiction. Vancouver Police Detective Constable Al Dalstrom, who investigated bikers for six years, confirmed this allegation when I repeated it the next morning on CTV's *Canada A.M.* with Valerie Pringle.

Detective Constable Dalstrom is responsible for implementing in British Columbia the public relations tactics of the National Strategy to combat outlaw motorcycle gangs. The province is one of the world's leading hydroponic marijuana producers, and illegal growers export between four and ten million dollars' worth of prime pot every year. Marijuana is the second largest cash crop after lumber in British Columbia. Vancouver police raided more than fifty grow operations in 1997. Every time they busted one that was run by Hells Angels associates, they brought along the media. After such a raid in February 1998, Detective Constable Dalstrom held a forty-five-minute press conference about the Hells Angels. He talked about the gang's use of violence and intimidation to protect its drug business, then asked that police be given more money to fight the Hells Angels. This comment came from a man who had already spent six years on the biker beat. He said the money was needed not to end the biker problem but to manage it:

> I can tell you right now that, as a police community, we fear that the problem has grown to the point in this country, and in this province, and in this city, where it may no longer be combatable. In other words, I don't think we're ever going to end the Hells Angels in Canada. We're long beyond that.
>
> I think now what we have to do is contain the damage and reduce the damage. And for us as a police community to be successful in that, we have to say to you, our employers (the public), that we can no longer do this with the resources that we've got. The problem has outstripped us.
>
> It's no longer acceptable for police agencies to operate in silence, in secrecy, as we've done for years. It's time to go to the public, and it's time to go to our political leaders, be honest about the extent of the problem, be honest that we are not properly resourced to fight this problem, and be straight-up about what we need to combat this.

The honesty should have begun a long time ago.

I put the police publicity tactic in context for the British Columbia media: "The fault of policing has not been with ground-level investigators, but with police administrations which have lacked the will to tackle the biker problem," I told a newspaper. "Police managers, who always thought themselves better or smarter than bikers, consistently underestimated the strength and intelligence of the Hells Angels. I believe that this strategy—to be more outspoken—was prompted by a certain feeling of impotence that traditional police tactics, encouraged by police administrators across the country, were failing. The publicity ploy is a last-ditch attempt."

The police publicity tricks emulate the Hells Angels' ongoing public relations schemes, which they have polished since they were first adopted in 1969. They participate in charity events such as Toys for Tots and the media complies by running photographs every year of the ugliest biker with a teddy bear on his Harley-Davidson. To this day, every Hells Angels spokesman repeats the famous words first spoken by Sonny Barger in 1964. "We're just into motorcycling. We're not a bunch of criminals. We're misunderstood, and we're being attacked by the police." The Hells Angels continue to refine their public relations strategies because they know that advertising works through repetition. Say something sincerely often enough and people believe it because they tell themselves they've heard that somewhere before, so it must be true.

British Columbia's attorney general Ujjal Dosanjh conceded in March 1998 that the Hells Angels had taken control of the province through inaction by police and prosecutors. "This started out as a very insignificant problem in the early 1970s. If we had been doing our job the problem wouldn't have grown to the extent it has." He decried the fact that the Hells Angels intimidate police, prosecutors, and journalists. "No attorney general, no police officer can function in that kind of environment. We want to make sure we win the battle."

Dosanjh was sufficiently concerned about the rapid growth of organized crime gangs in the province and the lack of successful prosecutions to appoint a three-member independent review committee on June 9, 1998, "to examine and assess the ability of law enforcement agencies in British Columbia to combat organized crime and outlaw motorcycle gangs."

The committee reported its findings on the Coordinated Law Enforcement Unit on September 15 and Dosanjh disbanded the 25-year-old agency on October 1, citing mistrust and internal feuding among police agencies that allowed organized crime to flourish. I quote from the 71-page report.

In British Columbia, the Coordinated Law Enforcement Unit (C.LE.U.) has, since 1974, brought together civilian criminal intelligence analysts and police officers from contributing independent police departments and from the R.C.M.P. to target organized crime groups and to undertake enforcement operations. Eight specialized units target the main organized crime groups and proceeds of crime, as well as monitoring air travel and B.C.'s international ports. A policy analysis unit provides tactical and strategic analysis, and policy advice to the Attorney General. Criminal Intelligence Service British Columbia (C.I.S.B.C.), the provincial bureau of the Criminal Intelligence Service of Canada (C.I.S.C.), housed within C.L.E.U., also collects, analyses, and disseminates organized crime intelligence . . .

In the Committee's view an essential first step in combatting organized crime is to develop an accurate picture of its size, the types of activities in which it is engaged, and the magnitude of those activities.

It is only with this quantification of the organized crime problem that law enforcement agencies can make informed targeting decisions, managers can measure the effectiveness of enforcement operations, and government can take legislative and regulatory action.

The Committee discovered that no detailed quantification of British Columbia's organized crime problem exists . . . . The material provided to the Committee on the magnitude of organized crime activity, especially in British Columbia, is regrettably general in nature. Either C.L.E.U. and the other law enforcement agencies do not possess detailed information or they were not prepared to share it with the Committee . . . . Until such fundamental information about organized crime is available, it would be difficult for the Committee to advance a credible argument that more public funds should be committed to the fight against organized crime. Bluntly put, we simply do not know how big the problem is or what it will cost to combat organized crime . . . .

Although C.L.E.U. has no legislative or corporate status, its Directory of Services states that its mandate is to develop and coordinate efforts to identify, prevent, and suppress organized crime and major criminal activities in British Columbia.

In the 1960s the increase in organized crime activities forced separate law enforcement agencies to form *ad hoc* joint forces operations to target organized crime groups that operated across policing jurisdictions. A key component in this strategy was the development of a criminal intelligence-gathering capability. In 1968 the Vancouver Police Department created its own Criminal Intelligence Unit. In 1971 the Criminal Intelligence Service of British Columbia (C.I.S.B.C.) was established, as the provincial bureau of Criminal Intelligence Service of Canada (C.I.S.C.), with a mandate to provide facilities for the collection, analysis, and dissemination of significant criminal intelligence to aid in combatting the spread of organized crime in Canada.

In 1974 the Provincial Government established C.L.E.U. as a permanent agency, based in Vancouver, to combat organized crime. Municipal police departments, R.C.M.P. municipal detachments, and the R.C.M.P.'s "E" Division agreed to assign officers to C.L.E.U. for fixed-term appointments in conjunction with the establishment of the provincial Sheriff's Service and the consequential release of police officers from Court duties. The Province agreed to fund the policy, analysis and prosecutorial components. C.L.E.U.'s initial goals and objectives were sweeping:

- gather information about organized crime, undertake strategic and tactical analysis and disseminate the resulting intelligence,
- undertake enforcement activities through joint-force operation groups,
- provide legal specialists to investigators and prosecutorial services,
- promote cooperation and information-sharing among local, national, and international law enforcement agencies, and
- undertake research into organized crime and provide policy advice to government.

C.L.E.U. was initially divided into an investigative division, a legal division, and a policy, planning, and analysis division, although the legal division was disbanded shortly thereafter because of concerns about prosecutorial independence.

C.L.E.U.'s activities were overseen by a Policy Board appointed by the Attorney General. In 1975 a Vancouver Island C.L.E.U. unit was established in Victoria.

At about this time the Vancouver Police Department's and the R.C.M.P.'s criminal intelligence units merged, to form the Vancouver Integrated Intelligence Unit (V.I.I.U.). Its function was to conduct intelligence investigations and forward enforcement projects to C.L.E.U.

In 1992 C.I.S.B.C., which until then had been housed at the R.C.M.P.'s "E" Division headquarters, moved into C.L.E.U.'s Vancouver facility, in order to achieve greater coordination of organized crime intelligence. It remained operationally independent from C.L.E.U. In 1994 V.I.I.U. was brought into C.L.E.U. and became C.L.E.U.'s Intelligence

Unit. In 1996 its officers were rolled into C.L.E.U.'s operational units.

C.L.E.U.'s enforcement activities are conducted out of facilities in Vancouver and Victoria. Their mission statement is to suppress the power and influence of organized and major crime in British Columbia and bring all those involved in organized crime activity before the courts . . . .

Many officers consider outlaw motorcycle gangs the most serious organized crime threat in B.C. The Hell's Angels, with clubs in Nanaimo, the Lower Mainland, and Kelowna, are reportedly in ultimate control of the hydroponic marijuana grow operations, much of which is transported to the U.S.A. on the I-5 corridor, where it is often exchanged pound-for-pound for cocaine. The Committee was told that the Hells Angels control Lower Mainland strip clubs, street prostitution, call girls, and massage parlors, as well as 5,000 to 10,000 illegal video lottery terminals. Some claim that the Hells Angels control the placement and movement of ship containers in the Port of Vancouver, and possibly also at Surrey Fraser Docks . . . .

Although C.L.E.U.'s official mandate is "to develop and coordinate efforts to identify, prevent and suppress organized and major criminal activities in British Columbia," it also takes on inter-jurisdictional criminal activities . . . . C.L.E.U. has spread itself too thin . . . . Even if C.L.E.U. focused exclusively on organized crime, the Committee was told that the C.L.E.U. organization:

- has failed to set priorities and allocate resources accordingly,
- is perceived as an extension of the Vancouver Police Department, and does not assist forces beyond the Lower Mainland and Greater Victoria,
- is hobbled by not being authorized to initiate narcotics investigations,
- is inadequately funded to provide the kinds of services that are essential in organized crime investigations and prosecutions, such as intercept, surveillance, informant payments, witness protection, and legal advisors to investigators . . . .

Many people told the Committee that C.L.E.U.'s lack of results was not because of inadequate funding but because of poor management and priority-setting . . . .

Almost everyone told the Committee that the lack of a comprehensive staffing agreement among all the law enforcement partners was a fundamental flaw. At present a small minority of municipal police departments and detachments contribute members to C.L.E.U.

Other departments and detachments told the Committee they are reluctant to contribute officers if they, or their police boards or municipal councils, do not see any direct benefit back to their communities . . . .

Several commanders conceded that they would never agree to contribute their most talented officers to another organization. C.L.E.U. has very little voice in which officers will be assigned, and there do not appear to be formal qualification criteria. The result is that some assigned officers are of questionable competence, and most do not have expertise in the investigative areas needed for organized crime cases. One officer described C.L.E.U. as an entry-level plainclothes operation.

The Committee was told that appropriate staffing has been a problem even at the highest levels. There are no qualification criteria for commanding officers and senior managers, no established screening and selection process, and no requirement that the candidate have a demonstrated aptitude for, expertise in, and commitment to combatting organized crime.

Officers who come to C.L.E.U. are frustrated by the inconsistent operational policies between the RCMP and municipal forces (e.g., informant handling and contacting foreign police agencies) and uneven benefit packages (e.g., overtime and reimbursement for meals while on surveillance duty.)

The Committee frequently heard that some municipal forces and R.C.M.P. detachments do not share intelligence with C.L.E.U. or work cooperatively on projects because of a lack of trust. Several prosecutors said they have a good working relationship with all police departments based on trust, but the same level of trust and integrity does not exist with C.L.E.U. In some cases, C.L.E.U. has been less than candid with Crown prosecutors. The Committee was told that C.L.E.U.'s Outlaw Motorcycle Gang unit refuses to use C.L.E.U.'s intercept services, because they were compromised years ago. In at least one case last year the Vancouver Police Department's OMG unit went to the Canadian Security Intelligence Service for intercept services, rather than rely on C.L.E.U.

The Committee was told that the effective investigation of organized crime requires special skills and training in areas such as intelligence-gathering and analysis, undercover investigation, surveillance, wiretap, and computer analysis. Many officers who are contributed to C.L.E.U., including police executives, do not bring any of this expertise with them. Indeed, some police forces contribute the personnel in the expectation that they will develop this expertise while at C.L.E.U. and take it back to their home force . . . .

We were told repeatedly that the presence of the Policy Analysis Division within C.L.E.U. heightens concerns that there will be leaks, and outside agencies will not share intelligence with C.L.E.U. for fear that it will be shared with the Ministry of the Attorney General. Others told the Committee that there has never been a breach of security within the Policy Analysis Division.

Several senior managers told the Committee that the Operations side at C.L.E.U. gets nothing of value from the Policy Analysis Division. However, many street-level officers contradicted this, commending the Open Sources Section for producing high-quality profiles about individual targets very promptly and the Division for providing helpful computer and support services.

Most Operational Unit officers spoke highly of the Policy Analysis Division tactical analysts who are seconded to their units. The analysts have impressive analytical skills and provided an essential service to enforcement. However, they were strongly critical of the requirement that the analysts meet once every two weeks with their Policy Analysis Division manager, fearing that there may be a leakage of operational intelligence to the Executive Branch. The Committee was told that these tactical analysts could provided an invaluable service as part of their teams doing post-operational debriefings, to identify new targets and important intelligence. However, they will never be permitted to perform this role as long as they have a reporting responsibility back to the Policy Analysis Division . . . .

The Committee's interviews with police officers and civilians within and outside C.L.E.U., criminal justice personnel, and other public servants painted a less-than-impressive picture of C.L.E.U. Operations. Some people told the Committee that it lacked strong leadership: avoidance of any risk-taking in project approval, lack of an enforcement vision and no accountability. The Vancouver Joint Management Team meets only when requested to do so and responds only to issues put before it by management. The Policy Board exercises no meaningful oversight of C.L.E.U. Operations.

The Committee was told that the quality of briefs prepared for Crown Counsel was poor, and that the evidence often did not live up to the officers' initial claims. Only one in ten requests for wiretap authorizations were approved by the Crown, contrasted to a seven-out-of-ten approval rate for the Vancouver Police Department.

The Committee heard that in its early days C.L.E.U. had a well-deserved reputation as a crack crime-fighting unit, but it is now little more than a surveillance unit. Some people described its enforcement results as "disappointing" and "ineffective," and thought that conversion to a project-specific Joint Forces Operation would yield better results.

Several municipal police departments and detachments said that C.L.E.U. provided quality assistance when requested. Others said that C.L.E.U. was often "too busy" to help them, and that C.L.E.U. never shared with them intelligence about organized crime activities in their municipalities.

Many people told the Committee that OMG groups are the most significant organized crime threat in B.C. but that the police are "pathetically ill-equipped" to target them. The OMG unit at C.L.E.U. includes some highly motivated and experienced officers, and yet the unit has had no significant arrests, prosecutions, or forfeitures. The Committee was told that it has become little more than an intelligence unit, but refuses to enter its intelligence into the C.L.E.U. system, citing security concerns. Conversely, other police agencies that target OMG refuse to share their intelligence with the C.L.E.U. OMG unit, claiming that the unit lacks credibility, expertise, and trust. C.L.E.U.'s OMG unit is not looked to for leadership, either in developing enforcement projects or responding to the Hells Angels annual rides. The result is that various police agencies tend to work independently of each other.

The Committee was told by many officers from different police agencies active in anti-OMG activities that B.C. needs a province-wide coordinated response to OMGs, autonomous of C.L.E.U., with a single commanding officer and satellite units in each locality that has a Hells Angels club. Proceeds of crime should be an integral part of this response . . . .

In the early 1980s Vancouver Police Department's Criminal Intelligence Unit and the R.C.M.P.'s National Regional Criminal Intelligence Service merged to form the Vancouver Integrated Intelligence Unit (V.I.I.U.). Initially housed at the R.C.M.P. "E" Division Headquarters, it later moved to C.L.E.U. and in 1994 V.I.I.U. became the C.L.E.U. Intelligence Unit. The Committee was told that, because of this history, the Vancouver Police Department now has no in-house intelligence unit, and "E" Division's federal organized crime intelligence unit has only three officers.

There was almost universal agreement that B.C.'s organized criminal intelligence "system" is in fact disorganized. To take OMG intelligence as an example, C.L.E.U.'s OMG unit refuses to enter its intelligence into C.L.E.U.'s S.I.U.S.S. (Special Investigative Unit Support System), citing security concerns. Rather, it uses R.O.C.O.R., a much less sophisticated program developed by an R.C.M.P officer after the force refused to spend the $4,000 necessary to purchase S.I.U.S.S. However, the R.C.M.P.'s Vancouver Drug Section enters its OMG intelligence into the National Criminal Data Base (N.C.D.B.), which communicates with neither S.I.U.S.S. nor R.O.C.O.R.

The Criminal Intelligence Service of British Columbia (C.I.S.B.C.) operates the Automated Criminal Intelligence Information System (A.C.I.I.S. II), but neither the R.C.M.P. nor the most important organized crime units currently enter their intelligence into A.C.I.I.S. II, and there are technical problems with and political objections to sharing intelligence between A.C.I.I.S. II and S.U.I.S.S.

Almost everyone the Committee interviewed is frustrated with the lack of coordination between and integration of the many intelligence databases. Each police agency places its own short-term interests above the collective long-term needs of them all, resulting in poor intelligence-sharing. Many people told the Committee that B.C. needs one organized criminal intelligence-gathering and analysis system that is effectively linked to other provincial and national intelligence systems.

The purpose of C.I.S.B.C. (Criminal Intelligence Service British Columbia) is to "provide facilities for the collection, analysis and dissemination of significant criminal intelligence to aid in combatting the spread of organized crime in Canada." C.I.S.B.C. moved into the C.L.E.U. premises in Vancouver in 1992 and, although it is technically a separate entity, the Committee was told that many people see it as part of C.L.E.U., and indeed C.L.E.U.'s promotional material fosters that perception. For this and other reasons, key intelligence units (e.g. C.L.E.U.'s OMG unit and the R.C.M.P's Vancouver Drug Section) do not enter their data into the C.I.S.B.C. system, and the R.C.M.P. has recently formed its own "E" Division Criminal Analysis Section (E.D.C.A.S.) rather than rely on C.I.S.B.C.

The Committee was told that C.I.S.B.C. is vastly underrated and underused in B.C., and that it should be the principal organized criminal intelligence-gathering and analysis entity in the Province. This is the role played by C.I.S.B.C.'s counterparts in most other provinces, which are organized under the Criminal Intelligence Service Canada (C.I.S.C.) national umbrella . . . .

There was almost universal agreement among officers in C.L.E.U. and the R.C.M.P. that organized crime enforcement units need access to specialized legal advice throughout the entire operation. Prosecutors with knowledge of organized crime groups and with expertise in the law and practice relating to search warrants, wiretap, conspiracies, proceeds of crime, informants, and Crown disclosure would be invaluable in assisting the police . . . .

There is a perception among the police that prosecutors are sometimes intimidated by organized criminals such as the Hells Angels, which affects the Crown's willingness to proceed with prosecutions. The provincial Crown disputes that, and told the Committee that there has never been a problem with organized criminals intimidating prosecutors. The federal Crown concedes that some staff prosecutors have declined to accept organized crime files out of fear that their children and spouses will be subjected to intimidation . . . .

Many police officers and prosecutors cited the Crown's disclosure obligations as a serious impediment to effective organized crime investigation and prosecution. Foreign police agencies are afraid to share intelligence with C.L.E.U., fearing that it will have to be disclosed. Informants frequently risk their lives assisting the police, and aggressive demands for disclosure from defense counsel representing numerous different accused can sometimes unintentionally reveal the identity of an informant. Important organized crime prosecutions are sometimes terminated, rather than risk disclosure of information that might identify an informant . . . .

This review has led the Committee to some strong conclusions. Despite many highly committed individuals and significant public funding, B.C.'s response to organized crime has, at least recently, been unimpressive. In this Chapter the Committee will set out what it considers to be the principal obstacles to an effective response to organized crime in British Columbia.

One of the greatest challenges the Committee faced was obtaining a quantification of the organized crime threat in B.C. The Committee acknowledges that the nature of organized crime activity precludes a precise statistical assessment. Although the Committee did review C.I.S.B.C.'s annual report, it was surprising that neither C.L.E.U., C.I.S.B.C., nor the R.C.M.P. in its capacity as the provincial police force produces a comprehensive annual State of Organized Crime in British Columbia. Without a regularly updated description, it is difficult for C.L.E.U. to set priorities, decide on investigative techniques, or determine the human and financial resources required.

A decision made five or six years ago that C.L.E.U. would not initiate investigations that were primarily drug-related has seriously undermined its effectiveness and the morale of its officers and staff. Every major organized crime group is involved in the drug trade, and almost every enforcement project will ultimately have a drug component. It makes no sense to give C.L.E.U. the mandate to fight organized crime, and simultaneously take back such a significant portion of its mandate.

Everyone agrees that a single repository for organized criminal intelligence, and an integrated system for analyzing it, is essential to effective enforcement. Yet municipal, provincial, and federal police agencies have deliberately developed stand-alone systems that are unable to communicate with each other, and agencies have refused to share intelligence with other agencies targeting the same groups and individuals. Teamwork has succumbed to territoriality.

Although the C.L.E.U. model was designed to overcome jurisdictional obstacles, C.L.E.U.'s recent decline in credibility has resulted in individual police agencies working alone or making bi-lateral arrangements with one another to combat organized crime. Few police agencies look to C.L.E.U. to perform this vital coordinating role.

C.L.E.U. is trying to do too much with too few resources. It has accepted the mandate of combatting organized crime, major crime, and inter-jurisdictional crime but, in doing so, has spread itself so thin it has limited effectiveness. However, its acceptance of this sweeping mandate is a principled and understandable response to numerous independent and uncoordinated police structures in the G.V.R.D. (Greater Vancouver Regional District) and the C.R.D. (Capital Regional District).

Most police departments and detachments are not willing to contribute offices to C.L.E.U. Given the staffing and financial pressures faced by all police agencies, there is no reason to believe that this problem will be resolved in the near future. The caliber of those who are assigned to C.L.E.U. is uneven, and many do not bring with them the training and expertise necessary for complex organized crime investigations.

The absence of eligibility criteria and the lack of transparency in the selection of police executives within C.L.E.U. have led, over time, to uneven leadership, with resulting loss of morale within all ranks. The Officer in Charge is not effectively accountable to the Joint Management Team or to the Policy Board, and there are equally vague lines of accountability from the Policy Analysis Division to the Policy Board and to the Ministry of the Attorney General.

Every working environment experiences personality clashes, but the situation in C.L.E.U. is far worse. The relationships between the Policy Analysis Division and Operations, and even within each division, are strained and possibly beyond repair. Internal feuding and distrust seriously undermine C.L.E.U.'s capacity to combat organized crime.

The absence of a comprehensive funding agreement among the law enforcement partners (even after 24 years), routine disagreements over who will pay for what, and a steady erosion of federal and provincial funding for anti-organized crime initiatives (such as informant payments, witness protection, and legal advisors to investigations) has meant that some C.L.E.U. teams are too small to conduct effective surveillance, wiretap, or enforcement activities. Funding cutbacks have also reduced the Policy Analysis Division's capacity to undertake empirical research . . . .

British Columbia must provide adequate police and civilian staff to achieve the intelligence and enforcement goals that the stakeholders set. All law enforcement partners must contribute human resources on an equitable basis. Once committed, human resources should not be withdrawn prematurely. Personnel should be competent to perform the specialized tasks involved in investigating and prosecuting organized criminals, or should receive appropriate training before taking on their assignment. All personnel should meet strict security standards, and should be subjected to ongoing security clearance . . . .

Policing activities must ultimately be accountable to civilian authority. The intelligence and enforcement components of B.C.'s response to organized crime must be accountable to an oversight body that has meaningful authority and an expertise in and commitment to combatting organized crime . . . .

British Columbia's fractured intelligence-gathering and analysis initiatives cannot be allowed to continue. The only beneficiary of the territoriality that has produced our three uncommunicative systems is organized crime. The original and progressive concept behind C.L.E.U. was to coordinate intelligence and enforcement efforts, but it has recently had the opposite effect. Well-intentioned efforts "to do it better" in British Columbia have regrettably isolated us from the rest of Canada . . . .

British Columbia needs an ongoing capacity to monitor the activities of identified organized crime groups and individuals . . . . It is clear that outlaw motorcycle gangs and Asian organized crime groups warrant the largest intelligence units.

* * *

British Columbia's attorney general, Ujjal Dosanjh, announced on Tuesday, March 23, 1999, that he had created the Organized Crime

Agency to replace C.L.E.U.; Saskatchewan RCMP officer Beverley Ann Busson was hired to become the agency's first chief in May. It's a good start, but the public in British Columbia has a right to know why law enforcement has failed so miserably against the Hells Angels in that province. What have the police done with the multi-millions of dollars supposedly spent fighting outlaw motorcycle gangs in the last twenty years? Police should not be given the increased budgets they demand to fight bikers. They have not effectively spent their money in the past, and there is no reason to believe they will do so in the future. Police are now embarked on a massive public relations scheme to terrorize and hoodwink the Canadian public into loosening the purse strings. Something stinks in British Columbia, and it's not only reefer smoke.

Chapter 7: Police Turf Wars
The Enemy Within

The pressure of the war against outlaw motorcycle gangs took its toll on Canada's two most visible police officers in the biker intelligence field in the 1990s. Both men, seasoned police officers committed to the fight against outlaw bikers, found themselves increasingly at odds with each other over matters that pertained more to their personalities than to crime.

Sergeant Guy Ouellette of the Sûreté du Québec intelligence section is a *bon vivant* Québecois, a gregarious joker who can regale an audience for hours with his sarcastic dark humor, all the while educating them. He was portly when he began work on the biker dossier, which he tackled with fanatical zeal. There seemed to be several Sergeant Ouellettes. He was everywhere at the same time. Quebec bikers knew that every time they appeared in public chances were that Sgt. Ouellette would approach them with a grin and shoot the breeze. His persistence and friendly demeanor made the bikers tolerate, though not like, him. By 1999, Sgt. Ouellette's work ethic had cost him two marriages and nearly as much weight off his gut. Investigators who saw him only yearly were taken aback by his now healthy, but thin, appearance. They thought he was dying. A Hells Angel rumor that he had AIDS worked to his advantage—no biker dared resist arrest.

RCMP sergeant Jean-Pierre Lévesque of the Criminal Intelligence Service of Canada is a taciturn man most often quoted in the media as the police biker expert. He has little investigative experience with bikers, but is one of those police officers endowed with bureaucratic abilities sought for in desk jobs that require cops to balance the needs and desires of a multitude of interests. Sergeant Lévesque is head of the RCMP's Criminal Intelligence Service of Canada two-man biker desk.

CISC is the central repository of information from police forces across Canada and can access intelligence files of law enforcement agencies around the world. Sergeant Lévesque has at his fingertips every fact gathered by police investigators. Sergeant Ouellette is bound by protocol to report his findings to the CISC so that the information can be analyzed and disseminated.

Both men seemed affected by the intense media coverage given the war between the Hells Angels and Rock Machine in Quebec. Sergeant Ouellette was well-known in Quebec where he fielded media questions. Sergeant Lévesque was the source of information for English-language media outside Quebec. The men gradually became competitive. Media interest started slowly in the summer of 1994. The bombing of the Rockers clubhouse in March 1995 and subsequent public panic sent the media into a feeding frenzy. I gave more interviews in Quebec that year than at any time in the past decade. The public had an insatiable need for fact and analysis. People wanted to know where the war was headed.

The first hint that all was not right were complaints from investigators who were tired of hearing each cop bash the other. Ontario police became aware of the feud first. Then investigators in western Canada were taken aback by the animosity the men showed for each other.

I visited Scandinavia three times in 1996 and 1997 and got to know investigators well. They confided to me, as did American investigators, that they were confused by the squabble between Canada's top biker cops. They were taken aback by rumors and criticisms made of each man and were reluctant to approach either in the course of their duties.

Members of the International Outlaw Motorcycle Gang Investigators Association steering committee, of which Sergeant Lévesque is Canadian representative, were upset and embarrassed when he brought up a concern about Sergeant Ouellette as a matter for the committee to deal with. The committee deemed the issue trivial.

Investigators also got an earful from Sergeant Ouellette, and the soap opera became a boring irritant within the closely knit community of biker investigators who wanted nothing to do with a clash of swollen, fragile egos.

Investigators across the country were tired of seeing Sergeant Lévesque speak to the media about their work without giving them credit. In their eyes, Sergeant Lévesque gave the impression it was hard-won knowledge. He would have made friends had he given credit where credit was due. Most biker investigators work in anonymity, and a pat on the back once in a while goes a long way, even if the officer isn't mentioned by name.

Sergeant Lévesque was more apt to be general in his statements to the media and liked to cryptically cite informants. He wrongly predicted by one year the arrival of the Hells Angels in Alberta. His predictions for the gang's arrival in Ontario are years old. More often than not, he ascribed unwarranted importance to specific events. His patellar tendon twitched at every report of a meeting between the Hells Angels and Ontario bikers, to which he tagged a prediction of war or biker invasion. Sergeant Ouellette gave the media very detailed, specific information (sometimes inaccurate), in which he couched his favorite theories.

During the investigators' association's annual meeting in Quebec City in September 1995, Sergeant Lévesque held a press conference so that local politicians could cash in on the presence of investigators from around the world to draw attention to the flaring war between the Hells Angels and Rock Machine. He did not ask permission of some investigators, most of whom do not want to be seen on camera. The conferences are heavily guarded and inaccessible to the media. Biker gangs continually try to infiltrate them with their spies, usually women. Startled investigators in Quebec scrambled out of sight of television cameras. Sergeant Lévesque didn't.

Sergeant Ouellette quickly learned to feed information on the Quebec biker scene to journalists first. He cultivated an impressive collection of unquestioning reporters in Quebec to whom he provided fact, fiction, and speculation on a regular basis. Sergeant Ouellette was quick to formulate scenarios and float trial balloons.

I met with Sergeant Ouellette in September 1998 and we discussed his ongoing battle with Sergeant Lévesque. I told Sergeant Ouellette the fight was an embarrassment to everyone and that I had been approached for information by Canadian, American, and European investigators who were flabbergasted that two high-profile cops would be allowed to attempt to outdo each other in public for so long.

By early October, I feared that left unchecked, the battle of egos between the two sergeants could cause irreparable damage to biker investigations, damage the international reputation of Canadian policing and jeopardize the free flow of information and intelligence between police agencies. I filed an informal complaint with the Criminal Intelligence Service of Canada.

Officers took my statement in my home. I emphasized that my first priority was that they put an end to the squabble between Sergeants Ouellette and Lévesque. I told them Canadian investigators dared not complain because cops don't do that to each other for fear of repercussions on their careers, especially those in the RCMP. I outlined the hazards I feared the feud posed to the intelligence community.

The CISC investigated these concerns. Sergeants Ouellette and Lévesque were made to sit down at a two-hour meeting organized by their superiors in November. Both men admitted they had personality problems with each other. They agreed to keep their egos in check and end the fight. Sergeant Lévesque agreed that he would comment only on national issues. Sergeant Ouellette said he would limit his comments in the media to Quebec issues.

At the start of his presentation to the annual conference of Canadian biker investigators in Toronto at the end of November, Sergeant Lévesque announced that both men had buried the hatchet, and he invited Sergeant Ouellette up on stage to share his presentation time. The move was welcomed by all.

Only a handful of people in the world are committed to fighting outlaw bikers. They cannot afford to fight among themselves, especially now that the bikers have ended their wars. Professional criticism is not a slight, it's a help. Anyone who needs their ego stroked should walk into a bar full of Hells Angels and tell them to piss off. That will set their priorities straight.

The Ill-fated Toronto Police Biker Intelligence Unit

Investigating outlaw motorcycle gangs is one of the toughest, most demanding, and least rewarding jobs in any police department. Only the most dedicated individuals can do the job well and achieve some success. More often than not, the job is an exercise in frustration, mainly because police administrators have always considered bikers unworthy of their attention.

In the decades I have been involved in this milieu, I have known a few great and honorable men and women, many hard-working admirable people, and only a handful of misfits (who can be found in any profession). Most large police departments across the world have only one or two persons working on bikers. Smaller police departments have intelligence units made up of only one police officer who has to keep track of all criminal gangs. There has been a trend across North America to reduce even this bare-essential level of staffing. The quieter the bikers get, the fewer investigators are assigned to track them. And one or two men can't gather enough intelligence to convince their superiors to fund a broader investigation. So a vicious cycle of frustration takes its toll.

Nowhere in the world has the stress of investigating bikers been more evident than in the ill-fated biker intelligence unit of the Toronto police. The unit has had its successes over the years, and has employed investigators who rank among the best in the field. But it has also been plagued by nervous breakdowns and corruption. The first tragedy to scar the unit was the suicide of its most popular officer with his service revolver at his desk in the 1980s. Some members of the unit at that time will never get over the death of the man they thought they knew.

The second blow to the biker intelligence unit came in April 1990. Detective Sergeant Gary Vincent DeFoe, a jovial, amiable man with a cast-iron grip, became unit leader in 1986. He was a demanding but fair boss who never asked his men to do anything he wouldn't do himself. In 1990 DeFoe, 55, had been on the force thirty-four years and could retire within the year.

Detective Sergeant DeFoe, as acting duty staff sergeant, signed in to work at the intelligence branch's Dias Road office at 3:25 p.m. on April 4. He left the office in the early evening and drove to the Bolton home of Constable Gerry Alexander Demidow, one of the five biker investigators who answered to Detective Sergeant DeFoe. Constable Demidow was on vacation. An off-duty policeman joined them. They ate barbecued steaks and drank 28 ounces of whiskey as they watched a hockey game and a pornographic video. Detective Sergeant DeFoe left between 12:30 and 1 a.m. without calling the office to book off duty.

As he drove along the highway in his unmarked police car, a van cut him off. Detective Sergeant DeFoe leapt across the thin barrier that sometimes separates reality from insanity and gave chase.

Mario Romano, a bakery employee, was on his way to work at the Central Bakery on Cawthra Avenue at 2:30 a.m. Romano, who was driving a small car, noticed a car that followed his every turn. He got scared. He raced to the bakery, in the Keele Street-St. Clair Avenue area in the city's west end, and hopped out of his car without turning off the ignition or the lights. He yelled to his co-workers to call the police. Fellow employee Zdzislaw (Gerry) Falkowski, 29, drove to the nearby police station to report a crazy man in the bakery parking lot. When he returned to the bakery, co-workers described how a man had parked his car behind Romano's and paced around the parking lot. Then they saw him open the trunk of his car, take out a .30-caliber rifle and load it. Falkowski heard shots outside the building.

Detective Sergeant DeFoe shot a van he believed had cut him off. He shot its engine to kill it. Then he walked into the bakery as workers ran for shelter. Falkowski answered the ringing phone. The 911 emergency communications officer called at 2:55 a.m. on April 5 to verify a call by another worker about a crazed man. Falkowski said he could not see the man with the gun and wouldn't chance going outside to check if he was still there: "I don't want to take any chances. Someone will get hurt. There's a guy outside there now, eh," Falkowski told the communications officer. "Send someone over on the double."

DeFoe saw Falkowski on the phone, aimed the gun through the office door window, and shot him in the chest. The bullet exited through his back and pierced the wall. Falkowski fell to the floor, stunned that he had been shot. DeFoe walked out of the building and drove away.

Bakery workers described DeFoe and his car to police. They ran a check on the license and were shocked to find out it was an unmarked police car. Several cruisers spotted DeFoe, but he eluded them. He called Demidow from his cellular phone. "There's no heat on you guys, it's on me. Someone took a shot at me last night." DeFoe continued to drive around then he called Demidow again. "Don't try to cover anything up."

Later, DeFoe called his staff inspector and told him he would surrender with a lawyer. He claimed someone had shot at him, and he returned fire in self-defense.

Detective Sergeant DeFoe pleaded not guilty on April 6 to charges of attempted murder, aggravated assault and discharge of a firearm with intent to wound in the commission of an indictable offence. He was released on $25,000 bail.

Detective Sergeant DeFoe testified at his trial that he had followed a van being driven by a suspect. He actually followed a small car driven by Romano. The deputy Crown counsel said the police officer breached the trust of his office by drinking on duty and by misusing a gun given to him to protect innocent people, not hurt them. He recommended he be sentenced to penitentiary for three to five years.

Detective Sergeant DeFoe was convicted on November 20, 1992, of wounding thereby causing aggravated assault, and sentenced to six months in jail. He was also ordered to do 250 hours of community service during his two-year probation and prohibited from owning firearms, ammunition, or explosives for ten years.

"I have no doubt he was suffering a psychotic disorder," Mr. Justice Hugh Locke of the Ontario Court, general division, said. Three expert forensic psychiatrists testified that Detective Sergeant DeFoe's condition was caused by overwork and job tension.

Gary DeFoe died of a large brain tumor two years later. It will never be known if the tumor caused him to lose his senses that night, or whether it was the product of the subsequent stress.

Constable Gerry (Fat Gerry) Demidow, who worked for Detective Sergeant DeFoe in the Toronto biker intelligence unit, had problems of his own. Constable Demidow, a 34-year-old 15-year police veteran, drove his personal car into a police gas station in 1990 and filled up his gas tank at a cost of less than $20.00. He told the new young attendant his vehicle was an undercover car. Two newly minted constables witnessed the transaction and asked Constable Demidow who he was, because he looked like a biker. Demidow flashed his badge and drove off. The young constables noted that he failed to run his undercover account billing slip through the pump. They took down his license plate and reported him.

That led to an internal fraud investigation that uncovered the police officer's criminal side. Constable Demidow stole marijuana from a hockey bag full of the drug he had transported from court during the trial of an outlaw biker charged with smuggling drugs. He gave one of his informants two ounces of marijuana worth $500 on June 24, 1990. Three days later he learned that an investigation had been launched into the missing marijuana. He asked his informant, a man with a lengthy criminal record, to lie about the stolen gas and the marijuana.

Constable Demidow was arrested on May 10, 1991, after an investigation triggered by a tip given to the Internal Affairs Department in January that a police officer was selling cocaine and marijuana in west Toronto. He was charged with conspiracy to traffic in hashish and cocaine, two counts of trafficking hashish, trafficking marijuana, possession of marijuana, and two counts of obstructing justice. Constable Demidow was released on $10,000 bail the next day and a publication ban was imposed on the trial.

Constable Demidow's informant ratted him out to external affairs because he was afraid the cop would kill him. He told internal affairs investigators that Demidow made him sell drugs. They wired the informant with a body pack and recorded a conversation between the men during which Demidow threatened the informant by firing an empty revolver at him under the table. The tape recorded the click, click, click as the hammer fell on empty cylinders.

Constable Demidow was convicted for drug trafficking and attempting to obstruct justice on May 28, 1992, and sentenced to two months in jail. "The only thing he cared about was being a policeman and he was desperate in trying to salvage his career," Mr. Justice Edward McNeely said during sentencing in reference to the police officer's attempts to obstruct the investigation of his gas theft and gift of drugs to an informant.

Several years later, a biker investigator who monitored a Friday-the-thirteenth biker run in Port Dover, Ontario, watched a bunch of Vagabonds roar up on their bikes. As they parked, a non-member who rode with the gang approached the cop and extended his hand. It was Fat Gerry Demidow. The investigator quickly withdrew his hand and told him they were no longer friends since he had decided to cross the line.

Other police forces in Ontario have had problems with officers selling information to outlaw bikers. Kitchener-Waterloo Regional Police had a bad track record with its biker investigations in the 1980s. They were never able to charge Satan's Choice bikers because their investigations always fell apart before they could get incriminating evidence. The only successful busts against the bikers were made by the RCMP when they worked independently from the local police force.

After a lengthy investigation, internal affairs officers charged a local policeman who worked on the force's biker intelligence unit with being a paid informant of the Satan's Choice motorcycle gang.

Constable Kevin Hawkins, 38, was called the best biker investigator in Ontario. He was charged in 1988 with unlawfully accepting $5,000 from Satan's Choice member Claude (Gooch) Morin to facilitate the trafficking of a controlled drug, revealing to Morin the details of an RCMP investigation into the Satan's Choice drug manufacturing operations, giving Morin information from the Canadian National Police Information Computer (CPIC) system, and revealing wiretap information to another man. He also faced fourteen charges under the Police Act.

All charges of conspiracy and obstructing justice were dropped against Hawkins and Morin in late December 1990 by Justice Patrick Lesage of the Ontario Court general division who ruled that the nearly three years it took to bring the charges to court constituted a "clearly unreasonable" delay in light of a Supreme Court of Canada ruling that set the wait period at approximately eight months. Justice Lesage said there was "absolutely no evidence either accused played the waiting game" to delay the trial and that the responsibility lay with the Crown.

The Hawkins case was one of hundreds dismissed because of the ruling.

Hawkins still faced fourteen charges under the Police Act which included allegations he was on the Satan's Choice payroll for years, that he was given the Harley-Davidson motorcycle of a murder victim, and that he set up marijuana dealers to be ripped off by the Satan's Choice by detaining them while the bikers raided their homes.

The previous examples were not intended to slight police officers, but to put in perspective this ungodly war against outlaw motorcycle gangs. Only the finest people should be allowed to fight this war. It is dirty, intense and at times terrifying. The enemy is filthy rich and will corrupt, subvert, or kill to achieve his ends. Law enforcement must admit that the Hells Angels are the best the criminal underworld has to offer. In turn, it must counter the Hells Angels with the best cops, analysts, prosecutors, and judges. To do anything less is tokenism. The Hells Angels are out to win. We have to beat them back into the primordial ooze out of which they crawled. We are locked in a death struggle with the most vibrant, powerful, and ruthless criminal force on the planet today.

Chapter 8: Wild Pigs
Cops in Drag

One of the most controversial issues in law enforcement across North America during the past decade is the emergence and rapid growth of police motorcycle clubs whose members dress, behave, and act like outlaw bikers. The most notorious of these clubs is the Wild Pigs, whose members affect the outlaw biker image, although they don't commit crimes. Many of these police officers are indistinguishable from outlaw bikers, and that's where the problem arises with their fellow police officers. Many investigators shield themselves behind the cliché, "If it walks like a duck and talks like a duck, it must be a duck," and accuse the members of these clubs of being criminals. It is an unprofessional and slanderous charge unbecoming of any police officer. But law enforcement officials at all levels have turned viciously against their fellow police officers for their choice of lifestyle. Rather than conduct proper investigations and act on facts and truth, they choose to repeat discredited rumors to support their high and mighty position. True outlaw bikers sit on the sidelines and relish watching cops bash cops for no reason other than outright bigotry and narrow-mindedness. Sometimes a war of words can cause more damage than one of violence.

There are more than nine hundred Wild Pigs in sixty chapters across North America. The club was formed in San Jose, California, in 1987 by police officers and firemen from San Jose and Santa Clara. As word spread among police officers that there was an alternative to the Blue Knights police motorcycle club, requests for authorization to start chapters poured in from across the United States. Canada has one chapter of eleven members in Mississauga, west of Toronto.

Police motorcycle clubs are just a reflection of the larger social phenomenon of the outlaw biker lifestyle. Although members of the Wild Pigs will dispute it, the way of life they have adopted was fashioned, espoused, and promulgated by the more than eight hundred outlaw motorcycle gangs that terrorize North American. The lifestyle, with its heavily tattooed look, black leather, and military nomenclature was crafted to distinguish its adherents from society. The Hells Angels adopted the one percenter (1%) patch in the early 1960s to distinguish themselves from the rest of motorcyclists who are not involved in criminal activities. While police motorcycle clubs such as the Wild Pigs do not affect the 1% patch, they do wear three-piece colors which offend outlaw motorcycle gang investigators as well as outlaw bikers. The patch on their backs has a top rocker with the name Wild Pigs. The bottom rocker has the name of the chapter's state. In between is the club logo, a wild pig smashing through an American flag. The club name is a pun chosen to mock its use as a slur against police officers. And although the three-piece patch is similar to that used by outlaw motorcycle gangs, investigators should have asked questions before making their allegations that the patch is an indication of links to outlaw gangs.

The original Wild Pigs patch was a one-piece oval. As new chapters joined the club in other states, members found it was too costly to have the entire patch made over just to change the state name on the bottom of the oval. They re-designed their patch in three pieces so only the bottom rocker needed to be made anew. So much for the outlaw theory.

Outlaw motorcycle gang investigators have circulated at conferences and training seminars unfounded rumors about links between the Wild Pigs and outlaw motorcycle gangs. Every one of these rumors is untrue and malicious. One rumor still circulated in both Canada and the United States by senior investigators is that a Wild Pig killed an undercover officer in Arizona. In fact, there is no Wild Pig chapter in Arizona, and state police officials have written to other law enforcement agencies telling them the rumor has no basis in fact. Police investigators who have read this denial continue to denigrate the Wild Pigs. Another rumor has the Wild Pigs being investigated along with the Pagans outlaw biker gang in Connecticut. Once again, state law enforcement officials have done their best to discredit the rumor by writing to other agencies and categorically denying that the Wild Pigs were investigated. This has not curbed the slander against the Wild Pigs.

One of the most substantial pieces of evidence offered by police investigators as proof that the Wild Pigs are linked to outlaw bikers is a photograph in the December 1993 issue of *Outlaw Biker* magazine of a Wild Pig with his arm around a New York City Hells Angel. That Wild

Pig is the Hells Angel's cousin. Although he has no criminal record, the Wild Pigs banned him from their organization for fraternizing with a Hells Angel. But detractors of the Wild Pigs choose to ignore this.

In September 1998, four Wild Pigs crashed the annual convention of the International Association of Outlaw Motorcycle Gang Investigators in New Hampshire, a truly stupid move. The instigator was the sergeant-at-arms of the Boston chapter of the Wild Pigs, who falsely convinced three members he had been authorized by the club's leaders to confront the investigators. The four Wild Pigs were quickly corralled and thrown out of the convention. Wild Pigs officers, who had warned the sergeant-at-arms not to proceed with his plan, were angry that he had put the club in jeopardy, and banned him forever from the organization.

I decided to delve into the Wild Pigs issue and separate the facts from the bull because these people are being seriously abused by their peers for no reason other than they look different. I would not dress like a Wild Pig, belong to a bike club, get tattooed, or ride in a pack. But I recognize their right to do so. There are millions of bikers who affect this lifestyle, however weird and derivative of the outlaw biker mentality it may be. I have ridden motorcycles for thirty-one years. I have never ridden behind, beside, or ahead of anyone. For me, motorcycling is an individualist's sport. Never have I considered becoming an outlaw biker. Yet I realized how sensitive and unaware police officers can be when the top biker investigator for the Ontario Provincial Police visited me at home in the 1980s and saw one of my motorcycles in the basement. He returned to the office and asked a fellow investigator if he knew I rode motorcycles. The investigator, who sported the longest beard in the country, replied: "Yeah, so do I." And his superior was even more surprised.

Over the past years I have been given erroneous information on the Wild Pigs by police officers I thought I knew. I never had reason to investigate the Wild Pigs because I always considered them a lifestyle phenomenon, not a criminal organization. I do have concerns that some members might sympathize with outlaw bikers they meet along the way, but this should only give rise to wariness, not accusations. I believe that these police officers are free to choose their lifestyle, but police departments are also obliged to ensure the security of their intelligence operations and are free to ban members who espouse the outlaw biker lifestyle from certain sensitive jobs, pending proper security checks. I have known too many corrupt police officers over the years to suspect anyone because of their looks.

On November 5, 1998, comments I made about the Wild Pigs on a Toronto radio talk show were out of line. I began the one-hour call-in program on CFRB with a brief yet powerful diatribe against the Wild Pigs. The outburst was based on my distaste for the outlaw biker look, which is crafted to scare and terrorize people. Although decades of experience allows me to distinguish between someone who affects the style as opposed to a true shithead, I still cannot comprehend why someone would want to look like an outlaw biker. Even the Hells Angels have cleaned up their image. I reproduce my comments here because I am a stickler for fact. I don't believe these comments do me or the Wild Pigs justice, and while I am not obliged to show the world what I consider to be my mistakes, my sense of honor and pride in my accuracy make it imperative that I show how errors can be made and rectified. To those Wild Pigs who may have been insulted by my comments, I learned from my mistake and I hope the law enforcement officers who persecute you can do the same.

LAV: The Wild Pigs are a total embarrassment to the badge. They're a total embarrassment to law enforcement. And when it comes to law enforcement, as far as I'm concerned, they're the bottom of the barrel and they should be turfed out. They don't deserve to have a badge. They don't deserve to have the right and privilege to enforce our laws, and the right and privilege to carry guns.

HOST: That's pretty strong language and I guess the issue of individual rights is going to come to bear. They've also sought legal advice, from what I understand, because a lot of their superiors are as upset as you obviously are about it. You've spoken to their superiors?

LAV: No, I haven't; this is something that has concerned me for years. The Wild Pigs are a fairly recent phenomenon up here. They've existed in the States for a while. So what you're seeing is an offshoot establishing itself in Canada—Canadian cops saying: "We want to be like these American idiots down there. Let's ride around in gangs and look like bikers and look rough and tough." That's just the gutless, backbone-less, spineless punk attitude that you find among certain people in our society.

HOST: And cops now are emulating that. And these are supposed to be stellar models for the rest of society: to serve and protect. Who are these guys?

LAV: First of all, they're a very small minority of the law enforcement people out there. They're all over North America, but the group in our area is based in the suburbs, in Mississauga. It's typical. It's like your yuppies out there buying Harleys, cruising on the weekends and trying to impress people. It's a big ego thing. I hope some of them call in, because I'd like to get their point of view.

These are the kinds of people who still see themselves through the eyes of others. That's how they run their life. "If I look cool, if people think I look cool, then I must be cool."

HOST: Why are they so dangerous? They carry guns? It's this posture, this pose they've affected. What's wrong with a cop in his spare time belonging to an association of guys who like to ride American-made bikes?

LAV: Because the Wild Pigs adopt the attitude of outlaw motorcycle gangs. There are out there all kinds of motorcyclists groups, organizations. They're called clubs. Within their ranks are people who call themselves one-percenters. These are those who have chosen to live outside the norms, values, and laws of our society. The Wild Pigs choose to emulate the bad guys. They hang out, they go to runs with the bad guys. They hang out in proximity to the Hells Angels, the Para-Dice Riders, the Vagabonds, all those guys. When they go to the states, there's eight hundred other outlaw gangs they hang out with. The danger is they become friends with these people. They side more with the bad guys than they do with the cops.

HOST: This compromises their ability to be full-value law enforcement officers.

LAV: Not only that, it compromises the intelligence networks of law enforcement. These guys have access to police computers, police files. They can find out if any one of their biker friends is being investigated.

HOST: Is it that serious in the GTA?

LAV: The problem is that these guys fraternize with the enemy. If Chief Boothby was found sitting in a restaurant with a top Italian mobster in the city, he'd lose his job. The same should apply to his officers if they're hanging out with bad guys. I don't hang out with bad guys. I write about them. I don't hang out with many good guys, either.

HOST: You're kind of a loner.

LAV: You have to be.

* * *

The police officers who make up the Canadian Association of Chiefs of Police National Strategy committee to combat outlaw motorcycle gangs are concerned about the public impression created by the Wild Pigs. They discussed the biker cops at a strategy meeting hosted by the Criminal Intelligence Service of Canada on December 7–8, 1997. The executive summary of the talks stated:

The question of the "Wild Pigs" was discussed by the delegates. The Wild Pigs is a motorcycle club/gang consisting of law enforcement members whose club structure mirrors OMG organizations and generally also adopts many of the 1% gang attitudes and lifestyle characteristics. While there are only a few (9) Canadian "Wild Pigs," all located in Ontario, it was stressed by Chief Fantino that membership in a group such as this is incompatible with being a police officer. Chief Fantino assured the delegates that a policy on this matter will be developed by the Canadian chiefs of police and a mission statement issued. As well, he will handle all media requests for information and comments on the "Wild Pigs."

In a related matter, Director (Richard) Philippe (CISC) promised to take up the matter of the "Booze Fighters" with senior military officials. The "Booze Fighters" is a motorcycle club/gang made up of military personnel but who model themselves on traditional biker gangs and have been observed at biker events.

*   *   *

The CISC held an outlaw motorcycle gang workshop titled "A Canadian core group to combat OMG" from March 29 to April 1, 1998, in Ottawa. Bruce Brown, of the London, Ontario, Police Service legal affairs department, made this comment, according to the meeting's executive summary: "The wearing of colors by the Wild Pigs, i.e. police officers who emulate bikers, could undermine the current legal strategy of connecting bikers with criminality through their use of gang colors, insignia, structure, and by-laws."

*   *   *

CISC director Richard Philippe sent this letter to all provincial criminal intelligence bureau managers on May 6, 1998:

I am enclosing a copy of a letter from Chief Fantino that outlines the CACP position on a Code of Conduct pertaining to standards of professional conduct, specifically with regard to law enforcement personnel and involvement with any organization that emulates the conduct and image of outlaw bikers.

CISC unequivocally supports this position. Please disseminate this information as appropriate within your area of purview.

Chief Fantino's letter, dated May 1, 1998:

Re: CACP Position—Code of Conduct

As you will recall, as part of our National Strategy on Outlaw Motorcycle Gangs, I have undertaken to pursue a number of issues that were raised by OMG investigators concerning standards of professional conduct expected of law enforcement personnel. Matters pertaining to the Wild Pigs are especially troubling.

The members of the CACP Board have supported our efforts to adopt a common position in this regard that is more comprehensive than a mere reference to the Wild Pigs, as follows:

• That involvement with any organization that emulates the conduct and image of outlaw bikers and/or any criminal element is incompatible with the standards of professional conduct expected of law enforcement personnel in Canada.

The CACP position will be communicated formally to all police chiefs across Canada, the provincial associations of chiefs of police, the Canadian Police Association, Correctional Services Canada, police services boards, and the International Association of Chiefs of Police.

*   *   *

One Wild Pig who has gained a high public profile is Sergeant Joe McCain of the Somerville Police Department in Massachusetts. Sergeant McCain co-founded the Boston chapter of the Wild Pigs in 1993 and has taken a lot of flack for it. Sergeant McCain is a cop's cop, the son of the state's most highly decorated police officer and beyond reproach as a law enforcement official. His integrity is beyond doubt and he dislikes all criminals, including the Hells Angels. Sergeant McCain's appearance raises eyebrows: his head is shaved and he sports as many tattoos as most bikers. He wears his Wild Pig colors proudly and his Harley-Davidson gas tank is emblazoned with the skull symbol of the vengeful comic book character The Punisher, the scourge of all evil-doers. Sergeant McCain is a decent family man, a former U.S. marine, an amateur jazz musician, and an outspoken supporter of cops who want to live the biker lifestyle, which he distinguishes from the criminal biker lifestyle.

I chose to speak to Sergeant McCain and get to know him because it was the only way I could get to understand the Wild Pigs. Sergeant McCain explained his choice of lifestyle in this unpublished letter submitted to *Iron Horse Magazine* in 1997. The magazine celebrates the outlaw biker lifestyle and often features photographs of the Hells Angels and articles that support the gang's legal battles. Here is Sergeant McCain's letter:

Greetings from Boston. I am writing you AGAIN, because I am continually amazed by the ignorance of some of my colleagues within the law enforcement community who just don't get it. Yes, I am a cop; but first and foremost, I am a biker. My entire lifestyle stems from the motorcycle. I live and breath it, day in, day out.

Three years ago, I attended a week-long seminar on "Outlaw Motorcycle Gangs" and the investigation of their illegal activities. I was introduced to many investigators in this field, some of them "Self-proclaimed experts." I do not have to name them; it is not necessary, for there are many within law enforcement like them; they know who they are. Because of my lifestyle, I have accepted the fact that some people tell me one thing to my face and then say something completely different when I turn my back. Sometimes, however, it really comes as a surprise.

I do not write this letter in a malicious attempt to embarrass any of my colleagues within law enforcement. I write this letter because I am angered and saddened by those who continue to hold themselves out as experts in a field they really do not UNDERSTAND. They may possess a great deal of intelligence regarding the activity of outlaw motorcycle gangs, but what they do not possess, however, is any true first-hand knowledge of what it means to be a BIKER, and live the lifestyle. I, like the rest of the biker community, am continually looked down upon by those who do not understand. I do not blame them, for they know not what they do.

About a year before I attended the seminar, I began to organize the first chapter of the Wild Pigs Motorcycle Club in the Boston area. A chapter made up of bike people who also happen to be full-time, arrest-powers, gun-carrying law enforcement personnel. No security guards, no associate members, no firefighters, just real cops; federal, state and local. From the very beginning I had to fight prejudice from all sides, cops and bikers alike. I was safe from neither side's prejudice.

I had heard from one of the state troopers within my club that there was a trooper from another state who was holding seminars on gangs. During these seminars he was informing those in attendance that the W.P.M.C. was a club made up of "Rogue" cops, cops on the fringe, cops who were associated with outlaws, and cops who were committing illegal acts themselves. I couldn't believe it. I was outraged. This guy didn't even know who I was or personally know any of the members of my club, yet here he was saying that I was a bad cop, a crooked cop, a cop on the edge; other cops were buying it. I was angry.

I set up a meeting and went to meet with him at a state police barracks in another state. We sat for almost two hours and talked about various issues, mainly law enforcement issues. After the small talk about who I was and what I did for a living, I tried to explain that there is a monumental difference between honest, hard-working, bike people and those who have chosen to be criminals in biker clothing. The question he asked that stands out in my mind the most was, "Why do you want to look like THEM?" I was puzzled for a moment, but then it clicked. I understood what he was asking me. He wanted to know why I would want to look like an outlaw biker? Why would I willingly choose to wear a three-piece patch on my back? I went on to explain that I DO NOT look like an outlaw biker. I look like a BIKER. Fortunately, because of this meeting and further contact, both business and pleasure, this investigator has since become a friend and trusted colleague. He understands that I can be both a biker and a cop.

Outlaw bikers call themselves 1%ers for a reason, they are just that. They are one percent of the motorcycling public. If anything, it is the one percenters who look like bikers. They are nothing more than organized crime figures in biker clothing. Criminals DISGUISED as bikers! How unfortunate, that all of us honest bikers are saddled with their reputation. Mafia dons wear $1,000.00 suits; using the logic of some of these investigators, it stands to reason that everyone in a $1,000.00 suit is a Mafia don.

As I stated in my previous letter, the majority of biker people are honest, hard-working family men, who break their backs at difficult jobs in an effort to support their families and keep their sleds on the road. End of story. Excuse the hell out of all of us because we are heavily tattooed and ride Harleys. These so-called investigators and outlaw club members actually have something in common. Neither believe that I should be wearing a three-piece patch on my back. Both, however, have different reasons for their beliefs. These law enforcement officials believe that cops shouldn't be tattooed or look like bikers, nor should they want to. The outlaws, on the other hand, think that they hold the copyright on three-piece patches, that only they should be allowed to wear them. They do not believe that cops are worthy of the patch, that we don't understand what it means to be part of a BROTHERHOOD. They could not be further from the truth.

I have brothers in 37 other states, and I do not use the term BROTHERS lightly. I have traveled over 56,000 miles in the last five years; many of those miles were to other states to support brothers who had been shot in the line of duty, or run over by drunk drivers while driving their sleds home from work. I recently RODE out to Chicago, Illinois, 1,072 miles out, 1,072 miles back, for a club function that raised a considerable amount of money for a school for handicapped children. I rode and partied with all kinds of people for five days. That's what we do. RIDE (not trailer) the hell out of our bikes, put them up, and then have a few cold ones and a few laughs. We do not steal bikes, run drugs, assault people, or knowingly associate with members of outlaw motorcycle clubs; aside from being heavily tattooed and riding Harley-Davidson motorcycles, we have ABSOLUTELY NOTHING in common. We are not, as some law enforcement personnel would like others to believe, a club organized to commit illegal acts.

I explained this to this investigator: that I make no apologies for the way I look. I look the way I do because it is who and what I am. I am a PROUD BIKER, and everyone knows it. My wife, my kids, my friends, and the cops I ride beside every night on patrol know who I am and what I am all about. I challenge any member of law enforcement to come forward with concrete evidence of wrongdoing on the part of any of my brothers: not rumors and innuendoes, EVIDENCE. I would come down like the hammer of THOR to take out a crooked cop. I do not tolerate cops who hide behind their badge to be brutal, unfair, or criminal. Those that do hide behind their badge are cowards and have no place in my world.

Unfortunately, there seems to be a "holier than thou" attitude on the part of many police officers. There are bad people in every field of endeavor, and we in law enforcement are certainly not immune. There are cops in almost every department who are less than honorable and I cannot say with complete certainty that there are none in my organization, but it is ludicrous to say that because I am a biker, I am therefore a criminal. Just as the investigator I met with cannot say that there are no bad cops within his organization. My lifestyle is right out there in the open for all to see. For those who want to come after me for some perceived wrongdoing on my part, "BRING IT ON." I have nothing to hide. "Judge not lest ye be judged yourself."

Several weeks ago, I was informed that at a recent seminar given on outlaw motorcycle gangs investigators once again told the crowd of police officers that the W.P.M.C. were a bunch of rogue cops who were tied to several outlaw motorcycle clubs and that some members were involved in wrongdoings . . . . When the majority of cops realize that we are not what the EXPERTS make us out to be, the validity of the information that they do provide at their seminars will certainly be doubted.

What I am guilty of, however, is being a good street cop, a good provider, a good father of three little boys, and a good husband. My family and my motorcycle are the center of my universe. Do not measure me by my appearance; measure me by my honesty and integrity. Measure me by the kind of father, husband, provider, friend, and cop I am. It disturbs me greatly that some within my profession want to judge me by how I look and not who I am. I have no room for those who do not understand.

There are three investigators I feel obligated to mention by name. They enjoy seeing their names in the printed media, so I will give them another opportunity to view it here. Never have I heard more uninformed ignorance come from law enforcement personnel. In nine years of law enforcement, I have learned many things, one of them being, don't try to talk about something you have no knowledge of.

The first investigator is Sergeant Steve Tretheway of the Arizona Department of Public Safety. In an article recently printed in Canada, Sgt. Tretheway said, "I just don't understand why cops want to look like these guys." Of course he doesn't understand. He is not a biker, I am. I have been since I was a little boy. What does the fact that I am heavily tattooed, ride a Harley-Davidson, and wear black leather have to do with being an honest, hardworking cop, is a mystery to me. He wouldn't be upset if I were one of the "Whackers" as I refer to them: cops who can't leave the uniform in the locker room at the station, cops who drive personal vehicles with blue lights in the rear window and front grill so that everybody knows that they are cops when they're off duty. Another conformist with no identity other than being a cop; how fascinating they must be to their friends. I do not have to conform to anyone's standard but my own. I will not compromise my values for anyone. No thank you. I take pride in being an individual with my own identity.

The second investigator is Peel Region Detective Peter Willets, who, according to this recent article, was "taken aback" when he went to a meeting between some of the members of the Boston chapter of the W.P.M.C. and the new chapter in Ontario. In this article, he said, "They [Wild Pigs] don't portray the image that I want to see for police officers, in fact, they are too close to the criminal element biker. When I saw these guys they looked and acted like every biker I've ever seen. They look exactly like an outlaw biker."

The third investigator is London Police Chief Julian Fantino, who also happens to be chairman of the Criminal Intelligence Service of Ontario. Chief Fantino believes that cops should think long and hard before joining a club like the Wild Pigs. He went on to say, "I would certainly not encourage police officers to engage in any activity that brings the profession into disrepute. I don't think the public is prepared in this country to believe that police officers should look like or behave like outlaw motorcycle types." The author of the article, Richard Brennan, comments, "With their black leather jackets, skull-and-crossbone earrings, a crest with a wild boar crashing through the American flag, and their rumbling Harley-Davidsons, they are indistinguishable from hard-core bikers."

If these investigators come away with one thing from this letter, I hope it is an understanding that the reason that I am indistinguishable from a HARD-CORE BIKER is that I am a HARD-CORE BIKER, make no bones about it. Get used to it, get over it, I am not going away. It has absolutely nothing to do with the type of cop I am. I encourage anyone of these investigators to contact my department personally, and find out what kind of cop I really am; they may be surprised. I will gladly provide to any one of them a copy of my personnel folder, and a copy of my arrest record. Since they call themselves expert investigators, they should try something different for a change; they should try to take the time to actually do some investigating.

(Signed) Sergeant Joseph E. McCain, Somerville Police Department, Wild Pigs Motorcycle Club, Boston Chapter, Sergeant-at-Arms.

* * *

The Hells Angels took offense to a comment Sergeant McCain made about the gang in a newspaper story published in *Foster's Sunday Citizen* on April 26, 1998. The Hells Angels were already angry at The Wild Pigs because their black-and-red colors too closely resemble the red-and-white color scheme of the Angels. The Boston Wild Pigs also wear the state name, Massachusetts, on the bottom rocker of their colors, despite a Hells Angels' edict that nobody in the world wears a bottom rocker that indicates they roam the entire area that the Hells Angels control. As far as the Hells Angels are concerned, only they can wear Massachusetts bottom rockers. Other gangs are allowed to wear an abbreviated state name or a city name on the bottom rocker. But this is not what upset the Hells Angels the most about Sergeant McCain. It was this comment he made to the reporter: "I don't like the Hells Angels. They're drug dealers and punks. I can't stand them."

The funny thing about the Hells Angels is that they really don't like to be called names. You can beat them with a crowbar, and they'll let bygones be bygones. But call one a bozo and you have an enemy for life.

The Hells sought out Sergeant McCain at Laconia Motorcycle Week in 1998. The New Hampshire rally draws thousands of motorcyclists, both one-percenter gangs and clubs who affect the biker lifestyle. Two

Hells Angels mistook a Wild Pig member who walked out of a bathroom in a bar for Sergeant McCain. They threatened to beat him with a ball-peen hammer, and backed off only after two Boston policemen drew their guns.

The Wild Pigs had no idea what the Hells Angels were talking about. Two Wild Pigs arranged to meet the Hells Angels in a Mobil Oil gas station parking lot to discuss the issue. Sergeant McCain advised them not to, as police officers should never bargain with Hells Angels. The officers met the Hells Angels who ordered the Wild Pigs to throw Sergeant McCain out of their club and to apologize to them for his comments about the gang. To their credit, the two Wild Pigs told the Hells Angels they would take no action against Sergeant McCain. The Hells Angels were so angry they tripped the next man who walked by and caved in his skull with a ball-peen hammer. Two police officers rushed to help the innocent man.

*   *   *

Massachusetts Hells Angel William (Billy) Italiano, 36, grabbed policeman Christopher Cost's baton and beat him in the head with it. Cost suffered a concussion and temporary loss of sight. San Francisco Hells Angel Guido Venezia attacked Sergeant Michael Moyer of the Laconia police from behind as he tried to break up the fight. Venezia stole Moyer's pepper spray and sprayed him in the face. Other Hells Angels circled the policemen and threatened other policemen who tried to stop the fight. San Francisco Hells Angel Mark Guardado rushed the police officers. He kicked one and hit a state trooper in the face. The fight ended when a policeman pulled his gun.

The nine Hells Angels charged with beating police officers during the melee pleaded guilty on Thursday, March 18, 1999, to avoid going to trial, where they could have received twenty-year prison sentences. The Hells Angels struck a plea bargain with the prosecutor. Three agreed to serve state prison terms and six will serve lesser terms in a house of corrections. The nine Hells Angels agreed to stay away from the Laconia Motorcycle Week rally in 1999 and 2000. The Hells Angels who ran T-shirt booths where bikers fought with police agreed not to seek vending licenses for two years.

Venezia pleaded guilty to riot, simple assault, and criminal use of pepper spray, for a prison sentence of one to three years.

Guardado pleaded guilty to riot and assault, for a prison sentence of one to three years.

Italiano, who wears a Filthy Few patch on his colors, pleaded guilty to riot, first-degree assault, and criminal threatening; he was sentenced to two to four years.

Police officers who investigated the beating by the Hells Angels reviewed photographs of the incident and noticed an on-duty police officer in the background who had failed to intervene to help fellow officers. They interviewed him and he admitted he witnessed the beating. When the Laconia police later approached him to take his statement, he denied he saw the beating. Rather, he lied and said he saw New Hampshire State Police officers demolish a Hells Angels' booth.

*   *   *

Outlaw bikers such as the Hells Angels are more offended than police administrators by cops who affect to biker lifestyle. Hells Angel Ralph (Sonny) Barger, the *de facto* leader of the gang since 1956, made this comment about the Wild Pigs in *Super Cycle* magazine in October 1990, long before law enforcement had become concerned with its members fraternizing with outlaw bikers.

> Like on the last Redwood Run. I ran into some members of the Wild Pigs. Their patch showed an American flag with a pig coming out of it. They came up, shook hands with me, started conversations about this and that and everything, and then walked away.
>
> So one of my friends came over and said, "Those guys are cops."
>
> I said, "They can't be." I couldn't believe that cops could run around like that and act like that and actually be cops. So we went over and asked them, and they said they were.
>
> Then they wanted to talk to us some more and we said we didn't want to talk to them, but they insisted on explaining themselves to us and kept going on until we decided we would rather fight than listen to any more shit. Then they tried to explain that they were out having fun and not acting like cops at that time.
>
> I couldn't believe they were just out there mingling with the people like that, looking nothing like cops, dressed just like everyone else at the run. They said they were mostly from the San Jose area, and I wanted to get a picture of them and run it in the San Jose papers with a headline saying, "Chief McNamara, do you really believe they're only out patrolling in their police cars?" That's like the line the chief laid on us when a couple of Hells Angels owned a catering business in the San Jose area: "Do you believe they're really selling burritos in those catering trucks?"

*   *   *

The Wild Pigs are in a tenuous position. They are on the brink of war with the Hells Angels because they refuse to submit to their authority, as do all gangs and clubs that affect the outlaw biker lifestyle. And they have alienated their brother police officers because of that lifestyle. The Wild Pigs, even though they are cops and appear to be tough, are no match for the Hells Angels, who know no limits when it comes to the exercise of power. The Wild Pigs are not the kind of bikers who will get involved in a war. They also cannot afford to fight the Hells Angels or their fellow police officers in court. A war of words with the police has left them isolated. A war with the Hells Angels will decimate them.

PART III:
HELLS ANGELS AT WAR
WITH THE TRUTH

Chapter 9:
The Intimidation of Justice

The Hells Angels fight society in many ways on many fronts. One of their most destructive forms of warfare involves the subversion of the justice system through witness and juror intimidation. In *Hells Angels: Taking Care of Business*, I devoted an entire chapter to the Hells Angels' attempts to bribe and corrupt judges and jurors. The Hells Angels have waged this war against justice so effectively and for so long. Volumes of examples have been compiled to help convince judges to provide special protection to witnesses and jurors. These examples are presented in pre-trial motions, and reporters pay little attention to them. To underline the impact the Hells Angels have had on the justice system with their attempts to skew its fairness and impartiality through fear and intimidation, and to illustrate the level at which they practice emotional terrorism in the courtroom, I refer to motions filed in one case against thirteen current and former Hells Angels and associates successfully prosecuted on drug charges in 1992.

The case focused on the drug network of Hells Angel Charles (Doc) Pasciuti, president of the Lowell, Massachusetts, chapter, and his body-guard Charles (Chuckie) Casella, the chapter's sergeant-at-arms. The prosecution asked the court in 1992 pre-trial motions to grant jurors anonymity to prevent reprisals and threats from the Hells Angels, and asked that rules be imposed for spectators to prevent mass shows of force by the gang aimed at intimidating jurors and witnesses. It was the first time in New Hampshire history that the prosecution took such drastic steps to protect jurors. The judge ruled that the threat to jurors was so overwhelming that he must accede to the demand to safeguard them and he granted the motions. The twenty-one defendants pleaded guilty one week before the September 1992 trial and received sentences that ranged from one to fifteen years (the latter for Pasciuti).

Most of the documents in the following pages have been abbreviated to eliminate repetition and reference to case law. Hells Angels lawyers described this material as exaggerated and distorted, but the court found it accurate.

Government's motion to impose rules governing spectators at trial:

A. All male spectators shall be suitably dressed in a shirt, appropriate necktie, and coat or jacket as a condition of admission to the court-room. All female spectators shall be suitably dressed in a manner so as not to undermine the dignity of the court.

B. No insignia identifying a spectator, male or female, with any club or organization shall be permitted. In particular, "colors" or other item of clothing identifying the spectator as a member, prospect, associate, or supporter of any motorcycle club are strictly prohibited.

C. All spectators must register with the U.S. Marshals Service by show-ing photographic identification before being admitted into the court-room.

D. No spectator shall be permitted to take notes during jury *voir dire*.

E. No spectator shall be permitted to bring into the courtroom briefcases, packages, magazines, newspaper, or notebooks unless the spectator is a member of the press.

F. No spectator shall be allowed to enter the courtroom other than during recesses.

In support thereof, the Government says:

1. The district court has broad discretion to take steps as may be neces-sary and appropriate to permit jurors to concentrate on the trial proceedings and evaluate evidence in an atmosphere free from appar-ent threat or danger as long as those steps do not violate the defen-dant's fundamental rights. Indeed, it is the responsibility of the trial judge to provide for the protection and safety of jurors, witnesses, and counsel.

2. In the present case, several of the Government witnesses are presently in the United States Marshals Witness Protection Program. A number of those same witnesses' families have been threatened and harassed as a result of their cooperation with the Government.

3. All the defendants in the present case are either members, former members, prospective members, or close associates of the Hells Angels Motorcycle Club (HAMC). Their reputation for criminal conduct and

propensity for violence have been judicially noted. That reputation is well founded. As noted in the Government's Affidavit, HAMC members have in other cases intentionally attempted to interfere with witnesses and jurors in the courtroom by creating an atmosphere of fear and intimidation.

In the present case, color-wearing HAMC members have been present at every court proceeding. Indeed, defendants Beaton and Caruso have testified while wearing the HAMC deathhead patch.

Furthermore, there is reason to believe that the HAMC is currently "at war" with the Outlaws Motorcycle Club and the Devil's Disciples Motorcycle Club. Thus, the defendants' own safety may also be in jeopardy when this case goes to trial.

4. The proposed rules in this case are adapted from two previous cases that involved HAMC members and were tried in the Eastern Division of the Northern District of Ohio.

Government's motion for anonymous jury:

Jeffrey R. Howard, the United States Attorney for the District of New Hampshire, respectfully moves that this Court order the following procedures to be followed to safeguard petit jurors in this case from tampering, intimidation, harassment, or violence and for the purpose of protecting their privacy:

A. *Voir dire* examination of prospective jurors shall be limited so that the venireman's name, address, or place of employment are not disclosed;

B. At trial, the United States Marshals Service shall keep the jurors together during recesses and arrange for the jury to go to lunch as a group with Deputy Marshals in attendance at all times;

C. At the beginning and end of each trial day, the United States Marshals Service shall transport the jurors as a group to and from an undisclosed central location. The jurors will be allowed to live at home during the trial, and travel to and from the central location each trial day.

In support thereof, the Government says:

1. The defendants in the present case are charged with serious drug trafficking and firearms offenses which mandate lengthy mandatory sentences upon conviction.

2. All of the defendants are members, former members, prospective members, or close associates of the Hells Angels Motorcycle Club

(HAMC). Defendant Charles "Doc" Pasciuti is a national officer of the HAMC. The HAMC is a notorious international organization, the reputation of which for violence and organized criminal activity is beyond peradventure.

3. The HAMC and its members have a long, well-documented history of intimidating witnesses, intimidating jurors, and interfering with the judicial process.

4. In the present case, government witnesses have been the victims of attempted intimidation and threats of violence to themselves and their families.

5. There has been a significant amount of pretrial publicity in the present case and there is likely to be substantial media coverage during the trial such as to enhance the possibility that jurors' identities might be publicized and thus expose them to interference and harassment by the public and the media.

6. Such procedures are also necessary to protect the defendants' rights to a fair trial. Organizations or individuals opposed to or in conflict with the HAMC may attempt to intimidate or harass jurors with the intention of insuring that the defendants are convicted.

Government's memorandum of law in support of motion for anonymous jury:

There are strong reasons to believe an anonymous jury is warranted in the present case.

A. Seriousness of the Offense: The seriousness of the charges currently pending against the defendants is beyond dispute. Charles "Doc" Pasciuti is charged with operating a "continuing criminal enterprise." Mr. Pasciuti faces a minimum mandatory twenty years in prison if convicted. In light of his present age (46) and his extensive criminal history, a conviction on this charge alone will be tantamount to a life sentence. All of the defendants are charged with conspiracy to distribute methamphetamine. The government has alleged, and will prove, that the conspiracy was allegedly involved in distributing more than 100 grams of methamphetamine or one kilogram of methamphetamine-containing substances. Thus, every defendant faces a ten-year minimum mandatory prison sentence without any reference to criminal history. Furthermore, the Indictment alleges that specific acts of violence and dangerous conduct were carried out in furtherance of the drug trafficking conspiracy. The fact that a jury will hear evidence at trial of the defendants' alleged violent acts, which might, if believed, cause them to be apprehensive for their own safety and for the safety of their families is further justification for the use of an anonymous jury.

B. The defendants and their associates' history of interference with the judicial process: In the present case, government witnesses and their families have been hunted, threatened, harassed, and intimidated. Those criminal acts, combined with the witnesses' fear of violent retribution at the hands of the Hells Angels or their associates, have caused some of the witnesses to require placement in the Witness Protection Program in order to ensure their physical safety. "Doc" Pasciuti's propensity for violence and brutality is well-documented and already before this court.

Defendants "Doc" Pasciuti, Casella, Courtois, Caruso, and Beaton are full members of the Hells Angels Motorcycle Club (HAMC). John Pasciuti is a prospective member of that organization. "Doc" Pasciuti, a twenty-year member of the HAMC, is a national officer in that organization and has brazenly referred to himself as the "Sonny Barger of the East Coast." One author has described the HAMC "as the prototype for every outlaw motorcycle gang in the world" and "the underside of the American dream."

This court has already heard expert testimony regarding the HAMC structure, its dedication to violence, and its willingness to interfere with the criminal justice system. Members and associates of HAMC have murdered witnesses, bribed jurors, and threatened law enforcement officials. Furthermore, HAMC members in the past have attempted to subjugate the judicial process by creating an atmosphere of fear and intimidation in courtrooms.

In the present cases, HAMC members or prospects have appeared in full regalia at nearly every hearing held to date before this court and the Magistrate. Defendants have testified wearing HAMC colors. An HAMC member has predicted that the courtroom will be filled with Hells Angels and supporters when the trial starts.

C. Publicity: There has been a significant amount of pretrial publicity in the present case. The defendants' notoriety, their connections with the HAMC and other outlaw motorcycle gangs, and the local media's history of attention to criminal trials, all suggest that media coverage will be extensive. It should further be noted that should the trial begin on May 12, 1991 [Author's note: a typo in the document; the date was

May 12, 1992] as scheduled, it will very likely be in process during the Loudon Classic "Motorcycle Weekend" (generally Father's Day weekend in early/mid June). The presence in New Hampshire of tens of thousands of motorcycle enthusiasts, many of whom are strong supporters or bitter enemies of the HAMC, while a jury is sitting should be taken into consideration in ruling on the Government's motion.

Government's affidavit in support of motion for anonymous jury and motion to impose rules governing spectators at trial:

A. Interference with the judicial process in the present case:

1. BATF (Bureau of Alcohol, Tobacco, and Firearms) Special Agent Thomas Crowley provided the following information regarding government witness Gaylen Blake:

On June 15, 1990, Gaylen Blake, former President of the Crazy Eights Motorcycle Club (CEMC) and his wife, Janet, were residing in a town in the southern section of the United States. They were both served with subpoenas to testify before the federal grand jury sitting in Concord, New Hampshire on June 21, 1990, regarding their knowledge of the Hells Angels Motorcycle Club (HAMC) Lowell Chapter, and the CEMC, and those organizations' connections to and involvement in methamphetamine trafficking.

On June 16, 1990, Glen Blake, who is Gaylen Blake's twin brother and who resided in the same town, was approached by two white males claiming to be FBI agents and who were looking for Gaylen Blake. Glen Blake refused to talk to them because of their manner and approach, and told them to leave.

The FBI has had no role in the investigation of the present case, although it has been involved in the investigation of the criminal activity of other Hells Angels members in other parts of the country.

On June 20, 1990, Gaylen and Janet Blake and their young child arrived in Concord, New Hampshire to answer the subpoenas. After meeting with investigators, Gaylen Blake agreed to cooperate in the investigation and testify regarding his knowledge of methamphetamine distribution by Charles "Doc" Pasciuti and others. The Blake family did not return home and were relocated and protected by federal agents. They subsequently entered the U.S. Marshals Service Witness Protection Program. Blake, who had already been severely beaten by members of the HAMC and CEMC, was extremely concerned for his safety once it became known that he was cooperating and his whereabouts were determined.

On June 27, 1990, Glen Blake contacted a federal agent in Concord, New Hampshire and related that the Blake's home had been broken into some time during the previous twenty-four hours. Nothing appeared to have been taken. However, notes by the Blakes referring to their grand jury appearances in Concord were in plain view.

On July 13, 1990, two white males described as "biker" types approached Gaylen Blake's father at his home in southeastern Massachusetts. One of the men asked the senior Mr. Blake where his son Gaylen was. Mr. Blake told the men that he would call the police if the men did not leave. One of the men replied, "What are you, a wise guy? You want a slap in the head?" The two men then left.

On the following day, July 14, 1990, Glen Blake reported that he was driving his vehicle in his hometown and was stopped at a stop sign when a brown van pulled up next to him. The van's passenger jumped out of the van and reached into Blake's vehicle. The passenger grabbed Blake by the neck and said, "Let's go look for your brother." Glen Blake had a firearm under the seat of his car which he grabbed and pointed at his assailant. The assailant jumped back and said, "You and your brother are both dead motherfuckers." Blake then noticed the butt of a revolver in his assailant's waistband. The man reentered the van and Blake backed his car away and fled. Glen Blake was able to observe a round white sticker on the passenger's vent window which said, "Bad Co. Lowell." (This is a well-known nickname for the Lowell Chapter of the Hells Angels. These stickers identify the possessor as an associate or supporter of the HAMC). The van had a license plate which he believed had a green background and white letters. Glen Blake described his assailant as a tall, heavy, white male with tattoos on his arms and a northeastern accent.

On July 15, 1990, Glen Blake reported that he arrived home at 10:00 p.m. He heard a noise coming from his garage and observed someone running from the rear.

On September 4, 1991, Gaylen Blake told S/A Crowley that two members of the CEMC had recently been to visit Blake's father and mother looking for Gaylen.

2. BATF S/A Crowley provided the following information regarding government witness Robin Golden:

In May 1990, Robin Golden, a former associate of "Doc" Pasciuti and the Lowell HAMC, agreed to cooperate with federal investigators. At the time she began cooperating, she was in extreme fear that she would be harmed by the HAMC as a result of her personal knowledge of criminal activity. She subsequently entered the Witness Protection Program.

In May 1990, a federal search warrant was executed at defendant Charles Pasciuti's home in Westford, Massachusetts, which resulted in the seizure of a firearm and other evidence. The search warrant was based, in part, on information provided by Robin Golden.

On July 2, 1990, a relative of Robin Golden's told investigators that on June 22, 1990 another relative had found a typewritten note on the front porch of their home in the southwestern section of the United States. The note read something to the effect, "We know that you know something and we will find out." The relative who discovered the note destroyed it and did not notify the police out of fear.

On June 13, 1990, a former truck-driving partner of Robin Golden's told an ATF agent that he had recently been parked in a rest area in Missouri to sleep. When he awoke, he found that his truck had been entered by someone who removed a small observation window on the lower part of the passenger-side cab door. A pair of western boots had been left in the truck which were not his. Inside one of the boots was a note which said something to the effect, "This is what the future holds in store for you and your lady." The witness believed this referred to Robin Golden.

3. S/A Thomas Crowley provided the following information regarding government witnesses David Machado and Larry Machado:

Both David and Larry Machado (who are unrelated) were formerly associated with the CEMC and defendants in the present case. On January 22, 1992, they both met with federal prosecutors and investigators. Later that day, both men testified before the federal grand jury and returned home. The following morning, January 23, 1992, Larry Machado discovered a message on his answering machine. The male voice stated they knew Machado was cooperating and that he would likely by harmed if he cooperated. (S/A Crowley advised the affiant that the statement was to the effect, "We know you're the rat and you're going to pay.")

Both David and Larry Machado are now federally protected witnesses.

4. BATF Resident Agent in Charge (RAC) Louis Tomasello provided the following information regarding government witness Gordon Tardiff:

Gordon Tardiff is a former member and president of the Die Hards Motorcycle Club. Tardiff received methamphetamine from defendant

Charles "Doc" Pasciuti and other defendants and distributed it in the Lakes Region of New Hampshire. In the fall of 1991, Tardiff agreed to cooperate with federal investigators.

On or about February 4, 1992, Tardiff advised RAC Tomasello that he had met with two old acquaintances from the motorcycle world. Those individuals told Tardiff that they had heard that Tardiff was cooperating with the police and that the Hells Angels were going to get him. Tardiff believed he would be harmed if the HAMC learned of his cooperation.

Mr. Tardiff is presently a federally protected witness.

5. BATF S/A Terrence Barry testified at defendants Charles "Doc" Pasciuti and Charles "Chuckie" Casella's detention hearing before Judge Magistrate William H. Barry, Jr. on October 15, 1991. Barry testified that following "Doc" Pasciuti's conviction in Massachusetts for the brutal beating of Joseph Myrozek in March 1980, Barry met with "Doc" Pasciuti in prison. Pasciuti told S/A Barry that "the only mistake he (Pasciuti) made was not finishing Mrozek off." Barry understood Pasciuti to mean he should have killed Myrozek.

6. BATF S/A Joseph K. Granatino testified at a detention hearing before Judge Stahl in *United States v. John Pasciuti* on January 14, 1992. Granatino indicated that defendant John Pasciuti, a prospective member of the HAMC and brother of HAMC Lowell Chapter president Charles "Doc" Pasciuti, was arrested by the Massachusetts State Police on October 29, 1991 after a loaded .22-caliber revolver was found in the truck in which John Pasciuti was a passenger. The driver was HAMC member Michael Gardner, and the truck belonged to HAMC prospective member Ken Anderson. The truck was southbound on Rte. 128 in Lexington, Massachusetts at the time it was stopped by the Trooper. Pasciuti was also charged with possessing a hypodermic needle and syringe found in his vicinity after he had been ordered to exit the vehicle.

B. Courtroom displays and other conduct in the present case:

1. The affiant has personally observed color-wearing members and prospects of the HAMC attending nearly all the public hearings to date in the present case. I have observed HAMC members and prospects loitering in the hallway before and after hearings in the present case, conspicuously displaying HAMC insignias. On February 12, 1992, during a hearing on the Government's conflict of interest motion before Judge Stahl in Courtroom 2, defendants George Caruso and David Beaton appeared and testified while wearing full HAMC "colors."

2. I was advised by U.S. Marshals CSO Ed Hubbard that at a bail revo-
   cation hearing for defendant John "C.J." Courtois held on December
   12, 1991 in Courtroom 2, he approached an individual believed to be
   Ronald Alward. (Alward, a prospect for the Lowell Chapter of the
   HAMC, has attended many of public court proceedings in this case).
   The CSO asked Alward to move to other seats in the spectator section.
   Hubbard heard Alward say to another HAMC associate that, "They're
   going to have to have an auditorium when this thing goes to trial."

3. Trooper Terrence Kinneen of the New Hampshire State Police Intelligence Unit has received information that T-shirts are being distributed
   emblazoned with "Free Doc" and "Free Chuck," as well as HAMC and
   Lowell Chapter insignias and symbols. These shirts refer to defendants
   and HAMC members Charles "Doc" Pasciuti and Charles "Chuckie"
   Casella. In addition, other memorabilia is allegedly being sold to rally
   support for the HAMC and the members and associates under indictment in the present case.

4. Trooper Kinneen has received information that the HAMC (and particularly the Massachusetts chapters) are "at war" with the Devil's Disciples Motorcycle Club (DDMC). Two HAMC members were stabbed in
   Revere on November 8, 1991, allegedly by DDMC members.
   The conflict between the HAMC and DDMC is longstanding and
   allegedly has its roots in the murder of an HAMC member in New
   Hampshire after the Laconia/Loudon "Motorcycle Weekend" of 1972.
   In addition, the HAMC has been in conflict with the Outlaws Motorcycle Club (another international motorcycle gang) since the mid-
   1970s when HAMC Lowell Chapter members were allegedly
   murdered by Outlaws in Florida. That "war" has since resulted in
   multiple murders and other acts of violence.

5. On August 7, 1991, Trooper Kinneen participated in a telephone
   interview of William Medeiros a/k/a "Wild Bill." Medeiros is a former
   member of the HAMC and was security officer for the New York City
   Chapter. After "Operation Rough Rider" resulted in the indictment of
   him and many other Hells Angels members on drug and racketeering
   charges in May 1985, Medeiros was a fugitive from justice until October 1985. He subsequently agreed to cooperate with the government
   and entered the Witness Protection Program. Medeiros said he had
   known "Doc" Pasciuti for many years. He said that the HAMC will
   make a concerted effort to identify all potential government witnesses.
   The Lowell Chapter is "notorious" for going after witnesses. The
   HAMC circulate copies of all police reports, particularly those

containing witness statements, to every HAMC chapter. If an HAMC member cooperates, the club will circulate photos of the individual as a "wanted" poster among all HAMC chapters and other outlaw motorcycle gangs associated with the HAMC. The security officer in each HAMC chapter maintains security files on each member, including photographs and information about the member's family, as insurance that members will not cooperate with police. If a member cooperates, he is put in the "hit file" and will be killed if located.

Medeiros believes that the HAMC is still searching for him and is certain he would be killed if found because of the assistance he has provided to law enforcement and because he testified against the HAMC.

6. I have reviewed a report by Westford (Massachusetts) Police Department Patrolman Hervey P. Cote. That report indicates that he spoke with Charles "Doc" Pasciuti on September 1, 1990. During that interview, Pasciuti confirmed that he was an officer of the East Coast chapters (including Canadian chapters in Quebec) of the HAMC. When asked by Cote if he was considered an important member of the club, Pasciuti stated that some people in the HAMC call him the "East Coast Sonny Barger." During that interview, "Doc" Pasciuti confirmed that the HAMC was at war with the Outlaws Motorcycle Club, and that it began when two members of the Lowell Chapter were killed in Florida.

The government also filed in the Pasciuti case supplemental affidavits from other Hells Angels cases where anonymity was sought to protect jurors and witnesses from intimidation and violence.

*　　*　　*

From the case against Paul Francis Casey and Brendan Manning, two New York City Hells Angels, in the United States District Court Southern District of New York:

1. July 27, 1969, Carol Lane was forcibly raped by four members of the San Diego Chapter of the Hells Angels. After filing charges against those members, she was subjected to threats and intimidated into leaving the San Diego area, and she refused to testify in court.

2. On February 7, 1975, Officer John McGee stopped a member of the Bridgeport, Connecticut Chapter of the Hells Angels for speeding, and issued him a citation. The club member threatened Officer McGee with physical harm because the citation was issued. While returning to his residence at the end of his shift, Officer McGee observed a stalled vehicle. He stopped to assist the occupants. At that time he was

attacked by three members of the Bridgeport, Connecticut Chapter of the Hells Angels and beaten with a baseball bat. He was hospitalized in critical condition.

3. In November 1976, then Deputy District Attorney J. Leslie Duchnick received confidential information from a local defense attorney that members of the Hells Angels wanted to kill Mr. Duchnick. Mr. Duchnick was then assigned to the Special Operations Division of the District Attorney's Office and was prosecuting several cases filed against members of the San Diego Chapter of the Hells Angels.

4. During February 1977, a bomb exploded near the car of San Jose Police Sergeant John Kracht. Sergeant Kracht was in charge of all motorcycle gang investigations for the San Jose Police Department. He had been involved in arresting several members of the Hells Angels, and he had testified against club members on several occasions.

5. On August 8, 1977, Margo Compton, her twin 6-year-old daughters, and a 19-year-old boy, who was a friend of the family, were found murdered in Ms. Compton's home in Oregon. All four people had been executed by gunshot. Shortly prior to her murder, Ms. Compton had testified against Buck Garrett, a member of the Oakland Chapter of the Hells Angels, in a criminal trial in the San Francisco area. Law enforcement has learned that Ms. Compton was murdered by an associate of the Hells Angels, because she testified against Mr. Garrett.

6. In late 1977, Robert Provau jumped bail causing the Hells Angels Motorcycle Club to forfeit more than $30,000 in bonds. Also, when Mr. Provau left San Diego, he owed a personal debt to the San Diego Chapter's president, Thomas Renzulli. Both these offenses are considered capital offenses within the Hells Angels club. The club was afraid that Mr. Provau, if apprehended, would cooperate with law enforcement officers rather than go to prison where he would be killed because of his transgressions against the club. Consequently, a "contract" was put out for Mr. Provau. In fact, on several occasions members of the San Diego Chapter of the Hells Angels went to New York to search for Mr. Provau. James Brett Eaton, a Hells Angel who was then in New York, personally spoke to Larry Ditmars, aka "Dexter," a former member of the San Diego Chapter of the Hells Angels and a present member of the Vallejo Chapter of the club, Raymond Piltz, aka "Fat Ray," a former member of the San Diego Chapter of the Hells Angels, now deceased, and one David Harbridge about their searching for Mr. Provau to kill him. Also, Paul Vaudhelet, aka "Tattoo Paul," a member of the San Diego Chapter of the Hells

Angels, was assigned by the club to work with the bondsman in an attempt to locate Mr. Provau, so he could be killed by the club.

7. On the morning of January 10, 1978, Solano County Deputy Sheriff William Zerbe was leaving his residence *en route* to court to testify against members of the Oakland Chapter of the Hells Angels. As Deputy Zerbe entered his car, a bomb was detonated by remote control. Deputy Zerbe received severe injuries to his back, legs, and ears. He has retired from law enforcement because of medical disability.

8. In February 1978, two prospects in the San Diego Chapter of the Hells Angels Robert Johnson, aka "Mexican Mike," and William Peters, aka "Filthy Bill," were arrested while surveilling the residence of District Attorney Investigator Ray Morgan. Mr. Morgan had been investigating several crimes, including the instant charges, which had been committed by members of the Hells Angels. Mr. Morgan had arrested and testified against many Hells Angels. Search warrants were issued for the residences of Johnson and Peters. In Johnson's residence a "hit kit" containing a .45-caliber machine gun, a .22-caliber semi-automatic pistol with a silencer, ammunition for both guns, rubber gloves, a camouflage-type poncho, and a hand-drawn map to Mr. Morgan's house was found. An electronic eavesdropping device—a parabolic microphone—was found in Peters's residence. Mr. Morgan retired from law enforcement. He is presently in hiding in another part of the country.

9. In March 1982, Robin Waugh was walking her dog in Ocean Beach, California. When her dog began fighting with another dog belonging to Michael Rush, aka Mickey Canyon, a member of the San Diego Chapter of the Hells Angels, an argument started. Mr. Rush severely beat Miss Waugh, breaking her nose and cracking her ribs. Mr. Rush then told her that if she called the police she would be killed. Later that month Miss Waugh again saw Mr. Rush in the beach area. She told her boyfriend, who confronted Mr. Rush. Both men had weapons, but Ms. Waugh's boyfriend, Douglas Pittman, turned and ran away. Mr. Rush chased him and beat Mr. Pittman with a hammer, causing severe head injuries. Two days later Mr. Rush, accompanied by Ronald "Dirt" Liquori, another member of the San Diego chapter of the Hells Angels, and Roland Eddy, a club associate, approached Miss Waugh and Mr. Pittman near their Ocean Beach home. They threatened to kill Miss Waugh and Mr. Pittman if they told the police or testified against Mr. Rush. Both Mr. Rush and Mr. Liquori have been convicted of felony witness intimidation, and Mr. Eddy pled no

contest to misdemeanor witness intimidation. Mr. Rush was also convicted of assault with a deadly weapon.

10. In May 1982, the Akron, Ohio Police Department conducted a search at the Akron Clubhouse of the Hells Angels. Akron Police Captain Jerry Foys was involved in the search. Thereafter, the Akron Chapter of the Hells Angels attempted to hire a man to kill Captain Foys.

11. In October of 1982, Jack Gentry a member of the Cleveland, Ohio chapter of the Hells Angels, was tried in Ohio for the murder of a rival motorcycle club member. Hells Angels from all over the country showed up at the trial. Sonny Barger, then president of the Oakland Chapter, and Sandy Alexander, President of the New York Chapter, were both present. During the trial, the son of one juror was approached and told that if his mother returned a verdict of guilty, she would have "lots of problems." The person who contacted the juror's son described the juror and what she had worn to court that day. The juror became so frightened that she had to be excused from the trial.

12. In late 1982, law enforcement officers received information that the Cleveland, Ohio Chapter of the Hells Angels had issued a "contract" for the murder of a Cleveland Alcohol, Tobacco, and Firearms agent, who had been involved in the investigation of several murders committed by members of the club. The information came from a confidential source in great detail, including where the killing would take place. The people planning these events knew the agent was going to fly to a particular location and then drive from that location to a law enforcement seminar in a nearby locality. Contact was made with the ATF agent involved, and it was confirmed that he was going to go to the law enforcement seminar on the dates specified by the informant via the route specified by the informant. This information was not public knowledge.

13. Numerous informants have advised law enforcement officers that it is a *modus operandi* of the Hells Angels to threaten and/or kill witnesses to prevent them from testifying in court and to try to intimidate or influence jurors. According to these sources, the Hells Angels do not always carefully discriminate between targets of intimidation, preferring to do what is necessary to secure the desired results. As the other materials on file with the Court indicate, these practices have continued up to and including recent times. Moreover, this case may result in very extensive disclosure about the club's activities and could engender general discomfort and ill-feeling among its members.

*   *   *

From the case against Hells Angels Timothy Jay (Tiny) Blackwell, Harold Dean Cheek, Otis Buck Garrett, Eldon Bernard McCann, and William (Hangtown Bill) Sanders in the United States District Court for the Middle District of North Carolina, Winston-Salem Division:

1. The defendants are members of different chapters of the Hells Angels Motorcycle Club ("HAMC"), an organization proved to be involved in numerous types of criminal activity on a nationwide basis with a propensity for violence. The defendants are charged with serious drug offenses involving the distribution of methamphetamine and could receive lengthy prison sentences.

2. From observations of trials involving HAMC members in Kentucky and elsewhere, (*United States v. Barger, et al.*) it is standard for the HAMC to direct members to attend trial *en masse* in order to intimidate jurors. Each member is directed to wear his HAMC insignia, sit in the courtroom during the trial, and congregate in public areas during recesses in order to be observed by government witnesses and jurors. A deliberate effort is made to cause jurors to be apprehensive for their own safety and the safety of their families.

3. Accordingly, the government requests the selection of jurors without disclosure of their names and addresses. Anonymous juries are warranted in cases such as this one involving organized crime and are not unconstitutional. Despite anonymity, appropriate *voir dire* can eliminate any "risk that providing jurors with anonymity would cast unfair aspersions" on the defendants.

4. There is a very substantial risk in the present case that HAMC members from other areas and other chapters will be present throughout the trial and attempt to intimidate and harass jurors.

June 1, 1990, affidavit from the same case:

I, Charles Norman, hereby affirm that the following is a true and accurate statement provided by me voluntarily:

1. I was a member of the Hell's Angels Motorcycle Club ("HAMC") between 1979 and 1989 and was associated with the Winston-Salem, North Carolina chapter.

2. During 1988, the East and West Coast Officers of the HAMC directed that every club throughout the United States send members to Louisville, Kentucky for trial of *United States v. Barger, et al.*

3. Members were directed to wear their colors and sit in the courtroom

during trial to intimidate jurors and government witnesses. Members
were directed to congregate in public areas of the courthouse during
breaks in trial and to be seen around Louisville during the evening.
Additional motorcycles were brought in by trailer to be parked near
the courthouse to give the impression that there were even more
members than actually were present. Every effort was also made to
attract the attention of the media and warn the public that the HAMC
was present in force.

4. All members of the Durham and Winston-Salem, North Carolina
   chapters of the HAMC traveled to Louisville and participated in intimidating jurors and witnesses.

5. This proecedure has also been used to influence verdicts in other
   federal and state trials involving HAMC members.

*   *   *

The following November 26, 1991, letter from the assistant United
States attorney for the District of South Carolina to that for New Hampshire reveals another reason juror identities and addresses need to be
kept secret during Hells Angel trials.

Enclosed please find a copy of the pamphlet that was distributed to all
members of the jury panel in the case in which a Hells Angel, Timothy
"Tiny" Blackwell, was a defendant. The jury for this case was selected in
October of 1990 and the case was tried shortly thereafter. The FBI
attempted to investigate the mailings of these pamphlets, but could not
come up with a case for prosecution. This is the only case of which I am
aware that pamphlets were mailed out to prospective jurors in this
district in the past three to four years. Obviously, it is our belief that the
Hells Angels were responsible for the mailing of this pamphlet.

The pamphlet, with its militia-type rhetoric and elliptical thinking,
neglects to mention that courts of law are where the law is applied:

> Fully informed jury amendment.
> True or false? When you are asked to sit on a jury, you have a right
> to vote according to your conscience.
> TRUE . . . BUT it's very unlikely the judge will tell you this, because
> he doesn't have to.
> Instead, the judge is likely to say that you may consider "only the
> facts" of the case, and may not let your opinion of the law or the
> motives of the defendant affect your decision.

This is a serious problem. How can anyone expect to get a truly fair trial if the jurors aren't told of their right to judge the law as well as the facts of the case?

A lot of people don't get fair trials. Too often, jurors end up apologizing to people they've voted to convict, just because they thought they "had to" vote for a guilty verdict based upon the facts alone.

"BUT IF THIS IS TRUE," YOU ASK, "WHY DOESN'T THE JUDGE SIMPLY TELL THE JURY ABOUT IT?"

Obviously, an uninformed jury is something which should never occur in a country whose state and federal constitutions all guarantee every accused person the right to a fair trial by jury of his peers.

But it's a sad fact of life that judges generally don't want ordinary citizens making decisions about the law, even if it is their country. So they deliberately don't tell jurors their full range of rights and powers.

This lack of information undermines the whole idea of judgment by a jury of one's own peers, whereby a cross section of ordinary people from the community is supposed to consider both the law and its own standards of right and wrong in order to reach a just verdict.

Most Americans are aware of their right to trial by jury, but few know that the jury always has the power to judge according to conscience, regardless of the law and the facts of the case. Why don't we know this? Because we were never told—in school, in movies or television shows about trials, or even in most law schools!

The FULLY INFORMED JURY AMENDMENT (FIJA) is a way to tell EVERYBODY about jurors' rights, where it counts—in the courtroom.

The idea of FIJA is to revitalize the plan for America developed by its founders. They saw jurors as the key to our continuing freedom, because the jury was to have the final say on any law American citizens were expected to obey.

Our third president, Thomas Jefferson, put it this way: "I consider trial by jury as the only anchor yet imagined by man, by which a government can be held to the principles of its constitution."

John Adams, our second president, had this to say about the juror: "It is not only his right, but his duty . . . to find the verdict according to his own best understanding, judgment, and conscience, though in direct opposition to the direction of the court."

"SO WHAT BECAME OF THIS RIGHT?"

From colonial times until just less than a hundred years ago, it was routine for the judge to inform jurors of their full range of rights. But during the late 1800s, special-interest pressure inspired a series of judicial decisions which sought to limit the jurors' right to judge the law, by refusing to allow discussion of the issue in the courtroom.

While no court has dared deny that jurors have the power to acquit despite the evidence or the law, judges still regularly contend that jurors must be kept in the dark, and may not be told they have this power. Defense attorneys who know about it still occasionally manage to have it included in the instructions given the jury, but risk being cited for contempt of court if they bring it up without the judge's approval.

Still, this power of the jury continues to be recognized, as in 1972, when the D.C. District Court of Appeals held that the jury has an "unreviewable and irreversible power . . . to acquit in disregard of the instruction on the law given by the trial judge . . . the pages of history shine on instances of the jury's exercise of its prerogative to disregard instructions of the judge; for example, acquittals under the fugitive slave law." Other federal courts have recently affirmed the right of jury veto power.

"IN OTHER WORDS, JURORS STILL RETAIN THE RIGHT TO REFUSE TO CONVICT A DEFENDANT OR BREAKING WHAT THEY FEEL IS A BAD LAW, BUT THEY'RE NO LONGER TOLD ABOUT IT."

FIJA—The "FULLY INFORMED JURY AMENDMENT" is both a political and an educational campaign to inform American citizens about their rights as jurors.

Many states permit passage of laws or amendments to their constitutions by direct votes of the people (the initiative process). In these states, FIJA will be a ballot-issue campaign to require judges to inform every juror that he may base his verdict upon the facts of the case, the merits of the law, and his own sense of right and wrong.

As an organization, FIJA will sponsor educational media campaigns, encourage lobbying efforts aimed at persuading state lawmakers to reform court procedures, and assist grass root efforts to inform jurors of their rights.

WE WANT EVERY POTENTIAL JUROR IN AMERICA TO KNOW THE TRUTH!

YOU CAN HELP! Just contact FIJA's National Headquarters, Box 59, Helmville, Montana 59843. Phone (406) 793-5550. Or contact your state's FIJA organization: PO 7814, Columbia, SC 29202. 803-798-2278.

*   *   *

This motion to prevent the disclosure of juror identities is from a 1983 case against two Hells Angels in the United States District Court Northern District of Ohio, Eastern Division:

1. The defendants are both acknowledged members of the Hells Angels Motorcycle Club, an internationally organized group with local chapters in Cleveland and Akron. Since late 1982, members of the Hells Angels have been defendants in several state trials in various local jurisdictions within the confines of the Northern District of Ohio. While the subject matter of the trials is not relevant to this motion, the conduct and tactics employed by the Hells Angels should be viewed with grave concern by anyone interested in the fair administration of justice.

It is the contention of the government that a consistent pattern of subtle jury intimidation has been practiced by members of the Hells Angels who are associated with defendants in criminal trials in this district. This intimidation, regardless of how subtle it may appear, has a direct impact on the ability of petit jurors to assess the evidence in an impartial manner.

The tactics utilized by the Hells Angels in a state trial in Toledo, Ohio, in October, 1982, best illustrate the pattern which has emerged. There, a member of the Cleveland chapter of the Hells Angels was on trial for an offense that occurred in the Toledo area, which is a stronghold of the Hells Angels arch-rival Outlaw Motorcycle Club. During the course of the trial, members of the Hells Angels wearing colors constantly packed the courtroom and mingled in the hallways of the Courthouse. And, in addition to Hells Angels from Cleveland and Akron, members from all over the United States were present at the trial. Hells Angels also stationed themselves at the exits from the Courthouse, prompting several jurors to request that security personnel accompany them as they left for the day.

Also during the trial, the son of one juror was approached in a bar and was told that if his mother returned a verdict of guilty she would have "lots of problems." The person who contacted the juror's son described the juror and what she wore to court that day. The juror in question was so frightened that she requested to be dismissed from the panel, a request that was granted by the trial judge. The final incident in this trial occurred after the case concluded with the acquittal of the defendant. Each juror was contacted at home and invited to a luncheon given by the Hells Angels at the Sheraton-Westgate Hotel in Toledo.

During the fall of 1982, a member of the Akron chapter of the Hells Angels was tried in that city. Again, Hells Angels from various parts of the country were present, displaying their colors and constantly maintaining a large presence in the courtroom.

In early 1983, a trial occurred in Cleveland in which a member of the Cleveland chapter was the defendant. The courtroom scenario described above was repeated once again and additionally, members of the Hells Angels made it a point to constantly stare at the members of the jury.

Finally, in October, 1983, another state trial took place in Akron in which a Cleveland Hells Angel was the defendant. On September 28, 1983, in preparation for that trial, a list of the prospective jurors in that case was provided to attorneys for the defense and the state. That same evening a suspicious car was observed driving up and down a street in Akron where two of the prospective jurors lived. The car contained two bearded individuals and was found to be registered to an Akron Hells Angel.

Significantly, in three of the four instances alluded to above, Alan P. Caplan, the attorney for Mr. Wortman, represented the defendants. In at least one of those cases, Gary Eisner, the attorney for Mr. Ribich, was also counsel of record.

The government has placed the Court on notice that jurors sitting on cases in this district which involved Hells Angels have been subjected to various forms of harassment, however subtle, that can only be construed as deliberate attempts to intimidate. The sole purpose of such tactics can only be to inject fear into the jury deliberation process so that the jury's ultimate decision is based not just on the evidence but also on jurors' thoughts of retaliation.

And, while such fear may not permeate all of the jurors, it need only affect one to achieve the desired result.

Here the pattern established in other cases suggests that disruption of the integrity of the jury system is manifest, and that precautionary measures should be taken to insure the anonymity of the jurors selected herein. Such an action would serve to minimize the element of fear in the minds of the jurors, for they would feel secure in knowing that the defendants and their associates would not know who they are.

*   *   *

Connecticut State Police detective Nick Barone testified in an October 1991 pre-trial hearing of Hells Angels Charles Pasciuti and Charles

Casella. These are excerpts from his testimony while he was being questioned by the prosecutor:

Q. What role does violence play within the club?

A. The Hells Angels as an organization thrive on violence and they make it very clear to people outside of that organization who do business with them that that is the ultimate price you will pay for crossing a Hells Angel for doing anything that's going to question the integrity of the club itself, the way they look at it, and to bring any problems that bear on the Hells Angels organization or individual, that's usually attended to by violence perpetrated by a member, as far as that individual.

Q. Does this include any particular category of persons?

A. They would perpetrate the violence against some of their own members if the case, if it was necessary.

Q. Would this violence extend to a situation where a person's providing evidence against individual Hells Angels?

A. Yes.

Q. To what extent would the violence be taken, in your opinion?

A. It depends. If a person were to become a possible witness against a Hells Angel in the prosecution, for instance, then the Hells Angels would make every effort, first of all, to identify this individual and, if possible, to make sure in their way that this person did not testify or certainly had a change of heart, and if he was insistent upon it, other than the fact that this individual being in some type of protective custody situation, they would make sure physically that this individual would not be able to testify, if they had the ability to do so.

Q. Do you have an opinion about their ability to identify and take care of informants and witnesses?

A. They have the ability. Their problem in a lot of cases is the inability to identify some of these people. I think that if they were able to do that, they certainly would be carrying these acts out more frequently. But the fact of the matter is they do have a difficult time in some cases identifying people who are about to testify. If it gets into a trial situation, it's probably too late for them.

Q. What sort of means or standard procedure might be taken to identify and take care of witnesses?

A. If someone is going to testify against the organization or an individual in the organization, they are testifying against the Hells Angels. That's the way they look at things. When a person is going to testify against an individual Hells Angel, as far as the Angels are concerned, they view that as testifying against the organization as a whole. It's an affront to the organization, not just the individual member.

Q. When you say affront, what do you mean?

A. Generally they have an understanding when they do business with the club that this kind of behavior does not occur. You do not testify against the Hells Angels. This is the way they deal with people, and if someone has the audacity to turn around and decide to cooperate and to testify against them, then they will handle this matter in their own particular way.

Q. And what would that way be, in your experience?

A. Generally through violence or intimidation to the point where they would convince this individual not to testify.

Q. What if they could not convince the individual not to testify?

A. Then they would make every effort to silence the individual. If it meant killing the individual, they would make every effort to do so.

Q. Detective Barone, do you make a distinction between witnesses who provide information inculpating Hells Angels members or associates and witnesses who provide testimony that's harmless or amounts to nothing?

A. Yes.

Q. Which type of witness is in danger?

A. The type of witness who testifies about any kind of activity, criminal activity, that a member of the Hells Angels may be involved in or may have committed over a period of time. Somebody who has witnessed a particular Hells Angel committing a particular crime, who's been a part of the drug distribution network where the Hells Angels participate. Could be he participated in a robbery or a drug transaction or stealing a car, a burglary or something like that, where a person physically either witnessed the act or participated with the Hells Angels in a particular act. These types of witnesses are the ones I'm referring to.

Q. In your opinion, what efforts would be made to find out [which witnesses provided inculpatory testimony]?

A. They would make an effort to determine who said what to whom. That's generally what they want to do. They want to find out, for instance, if they were able to determine, who provided the most damaging testimony to their particular operation. They would certainly zero in on this person or persons who were going to hurt them the most. If somebody was just providing general information, I doubt very much they'd even be considered. They may make an effort to just have their presence known to this individual. Take it a step further beyond that, to an individual who could really create some problems legally for the club, that individual could really have some problems.

* * *

Here are excerpts from District Court Judge Fuste's written reasons on August 22, 1992, for the court's decision on July 17 to grant the government's request for an anonymous jury. Hells Angels lawyers did not oppose the request. After the ruling, they asked the court to reconsider its decision. The court considered and dismissed this request.

Having again reviewed the parties' submissions, we reaffirm our holding that, given the circumstances of this case, the empanelling of an anonymous jury is in order.

First of all, the government's motion and affidavit detail attempts at interference or coercion of government witnesses in the present case. In addition, the facts support the government's contention that members of HAMC are prone to the use of intimidation and threats to obstruct the functioning of the judicial process.

Second, the government has also come forward with affidavits and filings from previous cases in which claims were made that HAMC members attempted to influence government witnesses, jurors and other facets of the legal process. The supporting material confirms the known fact that the HAMC has historically demonstrated its willingness to corrupt and obstruct justice and that those associated with the organization are capable of doing so in the present case.

Third, we feel it would be irresponsible on our part not to take these measures. According to our independent assessment as the Article III judge assigned to this case, the potential for jury intimidation, violence, retaliation of tampering is indeed present. During these times of major drug trafficking and other similar criminal conduct, federal judges are exposed to a variety of criminal cases where dangerousness, jury tampering, threats against witnesses, and even violence have occurred. We have been exposed to these problems and to the solutions crafted by other courts in dealing with such situations. Anonymous juries and at times jury sequestration are tools available to minimize the impact that certain unique criminal cases have on jurors, witnesses, and parties . . . .

If an incident affecting jury integrity occurs, the presiding judge may not get to know of the details until it is too late to take corrective measures. When jurors are exposed to prying into their personal affairs, with the potential for intimidation, it is only logical to expect that the incident will distort and distract the quality of attention needed for a trier of fact to function properly. Under the circumstances, the Article III judge is afforded U.S. Marshal protection to deal with the adverse pressures and the risks involved. It is only logical to assume that a juror will also be affected by the potential intimidation in any of its forms. The effect on a juror, without a doubt, is more severe than on the Article III judge, who deals with these problems on a frequent basis. We think that this case is one of those unique cases where the potential damage of interference with jury service merits preventive action.

Defense counsel seem to believe that the government's motion and affidavits in support of its request for anonymous jury . . . represent exaggeration and fact distortion. We disagree . . . .

Furthermore, as part of sealed proceedings held by this court on August 5, 1992, the subject of the threats to relatives or friends of persons thought of as becoming government witnesses came up. Less than an hour after the sealed proceedings concluded, court personnel received a telephone call from what appeared to be a person related to this case, inquiring about the identities of those who participated in the proceedings. The spectre of retaliation was present. In addition, court security personnel spotted an individual taking photos of persons arriving at and departing from the courthouse on that occasion. Preliminary investigations point to a person with criminal record who poses as an investigator.

*   *   *

Witnesses and jurors are not the only persons in the justice system who are targeted and attacked by the Hells Angels. Spokane, Washington, prosecutor Dave Hearrean's life was turned upside down in April 1996 on the eve of the trial of a Hells Angel charged with murder. Hearrean was the deputy prosecutor in charge of the gang unit. He was an outspoken opponent of gangs, from street gangs to outlaw motorcycle gangs.

Hells Angel Timothy Myers, 42, was charged with shooting a rival biker to death and wounding another during a brawl outside a bar in Hillyard, Washington, in December 1995. His trial started May 1. On April 30, two bikers, one a Hells Angel, followed Hearrean's wife as she drove to a supermarket. They stared at her through the plate-glass window as she shopped. As the woman drove home on U.S. Highway 2, they roared along-side her on their motorcycles.

On May 1, someone called in a bomb threat to LDDS-World Com, the Spokane telecommunications company on the fifteenth floor of the U.S. Bank Building where Hearrean's wife worked. When she showed up to work the next day with two armed deputies as bodyguards, she was told not to return to work, and the company manager said she would be given a job at another location once the trial was over. "People got very, very nervous after the bomb scare and seeing her with body-guards and stuff," company manager Ira Amstadter said. "They're afraid, and I understand. [The Hells Angels] are not pleasant people."

The daycare center their son had attended for six years would no longer accept the boy because workers feared the Hells Angels would attack the building.

"Because of me, my entire family is at risk," Hearrean said. "We don't have a life anymore. I'm just furious that gang members can get away with intimidating everyone like this. It's absolutely not fair at all. Because I'm doing my job, she's [Mrs. Hearrean] losing one. I've even given a speech at [the daycare center] before, to teach the children about gangs. We have to stand up to these people collectively and say we won't tolerate it. If we don't they will always win."

The Hells Angels Legal Fund

The Hells Angels help defray their legal costs with money they solicit through advertisements in magazines and on the internet. They created the Hells Angels Legal Fund in the 1960s, although today's version has been refined by lawyers and financial experts. The Hells Angels sell T-shirts, bumper stickers, and a wide range of paraphernalia to raise money for the fund. Individual members also contribute hundreds of thousands of dollars to the fund. The Hells Angels Legal Fund has always been a bit of a mystery. Since it is not a charity and contribu-tions are not tax-deductible, there was no public documentation on the fund. Until now. The following is the Hells Angels' description of the fund, circulated to chapters around the world to help members under-stand its function and purpose.

It is noteworthy that despite the Hells Angels' continual denials that they are a criminal organization, they spend a lot of time and money defending themselves against criminal charges in court. Members of the public who choose to donate to the fund should be aware they are help-ing to strengthen an organization that considers itself an outlaw gang not bound by society's rules, norms, and values. However, its members will use and abuse society's welfare nets, its free legal aid, and its justice system to protect themselves and their crime networks, and to further their criminal goals. Every dollar you give a Hells Angels is a slap in society's face.

HELLS ANGELS LEGAL FUND

Purpose of the Fund: The Hells Angels Legal Fund is a national fund which has been established to help provide financial assistance for the payment of legal fees and costs incurred by Club members and their families who are being treated unfairly by the judicial system due to their membership in the organization. Additionally, the fund will be used to offset legal expenses in cases where the Club itself is under attack by wrongful accusations made against its members that they belong to a criminal enterprise. The fund, however, is not limited to providing financial aid in criminal cases but shall also be used to help finance appropriate civil actions for the advancement of the constitutional rights of Hells Angels. As an example of this, lawsuits are being contemplated against the owners of several San Francisco-Bay Area biker-oriented bars who refuse to allow Hells Angels colors to be worn in their establishments while, in fact, in some cases, letting members of other motorcycle clubs wear their insignia on the premises.

Structure of the Fund: The Hells Angels Legal Fund has been set up as a long-term trust fund with an administrator who has the responsibility for disbursing payments and receiving the funds and a five (5) member Board of Trustees made up of Club members from various chapters who will decide how the funds are to be applied based upon the guidelines of the trust. The fund differs from other previous defense funds in that, first, it is a national fund and not limited to providing aid to only a limited geographical area or to one or two chapters of the Club. Secondly, unlike previous funds, the Hells Angels Legal Fund does not exist merely to provide financial assistance for one particular round of prosecutions or for a few individual defendants. It is hoped and contemplated that this fund will be a permanent fixture and will be able to function for years to come. Thirdly, the fund is designed to be utilized for affirmative civil litigation and is not confined merely to helping with the defense of criminal cases.

Operation of the Fund and Qualifying for Aid: The fund is designed as a limited-purpose fund and is not a general criminal defense fund. The philosophy behind the fund is that it will not be used to provide financial assistance for the [defense against charges of] individual crimes which may be committed by members, but only for [defense against] prosecutions which are either brought or enhanced due to the persons' affiliation with the Hells Angels Motorcycle Club. Examples of both of these instances would be as follows: Member "A" is arrested for making a hand-to-hand sale of a controlled substance to a police officer. Member

"B" is prosecuted because a search of his residence produces a stolen motorcycle in his possession. Member "C" is riding his motorcycle while intoxicated, gets into an accident and kills his passenger. Of these three (3) examples given, all would be considered individual beefs and would not qualify for fund proceeds. Examples of the type of situations which would qualify for fund proceeds are the following:

1. Fifteen (15) members of a Hells Angels Chapter are indicted under a R.I.C.O. Act and it is alleged that the Club itself is a criminal enterprise.
2. A Hells Angels clubhouse is attacked by another club and a member of the other club is killed or injured by a Hells Angel who was defending his own life or the lives of other Hells Angels or persons present in the Clubhouse at the time. That Hells Angel is subsequently prosecuted for the killing or injury to that other person.
3. A Club member being prosecuted for something which would ordinarily be considered an individual beef is being treated extra harshly or in an unduly unfair fashion because of his membership in the motorcycle club. An example of this would be Member "A" is arrested for possession of a small amount of marijuana and in the particular jurisdiction most other people under the same circumstance would receive thirty (30) days in jail; however, the prosecution is going to great lengths to try to send Member "A" to prison because of his membership in the Hells Angels Motorcycle Club.

In the event that a particular member or chapter feels that they have a case or cases which qualifies for fund money, that Chapter, through its designated officers, should apply to the trustees of the fund and explain the facts of the case and why they believe the situation qualifies for fund money. The trustees will then review the matter and determine whether either all or a portion of the legal fees and expenses will be paid by the fund. This decision shall be at the sole discretion of the trustees. When the trustees determine that fund money is appropriate they will then direct the administrator of the trust to pay appropriate amounts directly to the appropriate attorneys. In no event shall the individual defendants receive any funds directly. Application for fund money would also work the same way when a Chapter is applying for financial assistance for the prosecution of civil actions. Examples of situations where the fund might provide proceeds for civil cases would be:

1. A national magazine prints an article which implies that all Hells Angels' wives are sexually promiscuous.

2. An unauthorized company starts making and selling T-shirts with the Hells Angels' insignia on them.
3. A Hells Angels member is beaten up by police or has evidence planted on him because he is a Hells Angel.
4. A Hells Angels' Clubhouse is ransacked and severely damaged by police officers.
5. This would be the instance outlined in the previous paragraph involving the situation where biker bars are discriminating against members of the Hells Angels by not allowing them to wear their patches on the premises.

These preceding examples merely point out possible civil applications and there certainly may be numerous other instances where fund money would be appropriate.

Fundraising and Donations to the Fund: The success of the fund is dependent entirely on how much money is available to it at any given time. It is, therefore, essential that chapters around the country render their best efforts in conducting fundraising activities or soliciting personal contributions from their members. It is contemplated at this time that there will be three (3) main sources of revenue for the fund:

1. Donations made by individuals throughout the country in response to national magazine ads.
2. Donations by individual Hells Angels members.
3. Proceeds derived from fundraising activities, such as concerts, T-Shirt sales, raffles, etc.

A post-office box has been obtained by the fund to allow for the receipt of mailed donations made by the general public as a result of national magazine solicitation and to receive funds sent by Hells Angels members or chapters throughout the country. Donations to the fund by Hells Angels members can be made either through the individual chapters or by members sending money directly to the fund at the post-office box. Please be advised that federal laws allow the government to seize any money which was obtained from illegal activities and were any such money traced to the fund it could be seized directly from the fund by the federal government and the entire fund could possibly be jeopardized. Therefore, no illegally obtained money should ever be donated to the fund nor will it be accepted by the fund. Mailed donations to the fund from members, chapters, or the general public should be in the form of personal checks, cashier's checks, or money orders. Please do not send cash through the mail. With regards to proceeds derived from fundraising activities such as concerts, raffles, etc., full documentation of the particular fundraising activities must accompany all proceeds sent to the fund. For instance, where raffles are held, sales receipts should be provided if possible as well as a ledger showing what the total receipts from ticket sales were and accompanying information about the raffle. Likewise, with concerts: accompanying information and records should be provided to the fund along with any proceeds.

It is undeniably a tremendous inconvenience that the fund must require such elaborate documentation; however, it may just prove to be the deciding difference between whether the proceeds are used as intended or end up in the hands of the government.

Miscellaneous Considerations: Please be advised that various state and local laws may apply to particular kinds of fundraising activities and prior to holding such activities each chapter should consult competent legal counsel to be sure that they are being conducted within the letter of the law. As an example, in California under California law, raffles are legal fundraising activities; however, the law states that a person must not be required to purchase a ticket in order for a chance at winning the prize. If someone does not want to make a donation, they still must be given a ticket anyway, upon request. If payment of money is required for a chance at winning the prize, the legal raffle then becomes an illegal lottery subjecting all proceeds and the prize to immediate impoundment by the state or county. This, in fact, happened in 1984 in Hayward, California, in that a couple of non-club member individuals who were selling raffle tickets to a raffle held by the Oakland Chapter were not aware of the requirement for giving away tickets upon request and, in fact, undercover vice squad officers did ask for free tickets and were refused. Within the days that followed, the business where the prize was located was raided, all tickets and proceeds were seized, and the prize was impounded and took some time and considerable expense to get back. Therefore, it is imperative that all persons engaged in fundraising activities be aware of all applicable laws in their state or jurisdiction which may pertain to the activity.

Also, it will be the responsibility of each individual chapter to be sure that all applicable state or local tax liabilities which may have been incurred as a result of the fundraising activities are paid.

Further, it should not be represented to any potential donors that donations are tax-deductible, because they are not. The fund is not a tax-deductible, charitable organization. Additionally, when holding fundraisers or soliciting money there may be instances where the particular chapter chooses to solicit money on behalf of a particular individual member as well as the fund. In these instances care should be taken so that the donors understand that the money they are contributing may be used for the general fund as well as the individual member.

Conclusion: In the preceding paragraphs I have attempted to explain the structure and workings of the Hells Angels Legal Fund. There may undoubtedly be, from time to time, other questions which might arise. Should that be the case, the trustees should be available for this purpose as well as the administrator of the fund. Finally, the effectiveness of the fund and how it will be able to contribute to any individual criminal defense or civil litigation will entirely depend upon the availability of funds. Therefore, the more money continuously provided and fed into the fund, the greater will be its success and effectiveness.

Chapter 10:

The Hells Angels
in Their Own Words

Police documents revealed in previous chapters gave us insight into the thoughts and motives behind their actions. The Hells Angels documents in this chapter, acquired over the past fifteen years, show how the gang's thinking evolved as they acquired experience. At times I have added notes for context, but discerning readers of my three books on the gang will easily figure out what the Hells Angels are talking about. Some of the documents included here are Hells Angels rules and by-laws, as well as minutes from chapter meetings, west coast officers meetings, east coast officers meetings, U.S. Presidents meetings, European meetings, and World meetings, where the issues range from mundane, to legal, to business, and include references to my books. I have tried to retain the character of these documents—spelling, phraseology, and all.

The first document is a summary of major events in the Hells Angels organization:

Actions pertaining to club: 1966 to 1981
    June 26, 1966 • Started to get ready for incorporating the Hells Angels
    July 31, 1966 • Each new charter to decide on what deathhead they want
                to use
               • California bottom rocker passed by unanimous vote
               • Name of city to be worn on right side, above pocket
    Aug 6, 1966 • Sonny voted as Chairman of the Board
               • Hells Angels MC California, a non-profit organization
               • Seven members will be on the board
    Sept 18, 1966 • Nothing on back of colors except Hells Angels, Deathhead
               and California, to be an unwritten law

- Keep control of H.A. colors, an unwritten law

Feb 5, 1968 • On all rules and desicions [sic], officers take back to club, come back and cast votes.

Mar 31, 1968 • All Presidents signed a contract with Mike Zalk and Barry Stern to be agents for us.

Sept 29, 1968 • Decided that Ed Roth will give up $1200.00 @ $300.00 per month for putting Tommy Thomas Oakland picture in his magazine. Money split to go to each clubs Calif treasury

- Case of the Big Brother album and things like that, 50% goes to the club that set it up, and the rest split among Calif. Clubs, Calif treasury for California runs

Oct. 26, 1968 • Any money made by members for movie guest appearances etc. will be split 50\50 with him and the Calif treasury.

- All deals for money will be voted on first. Subsidiary corp. will be set up for this.

- A prospects patch will not be anything like a Hells Angels patch, No one wears a patch like ours.

- Property patches on girls was brought up as it could be mistaken for ours

- Sonny gave a rundown on corporations and how they should work.

Nov 30, 1968 • Bob Roberts is having our Large and Small deathheads patented.

- All activities concerning the corporation will take 8 yes votes. One no vote will cancel it.

- Every June 30, elect new officers to the board, each president is a board once, eight in all.

- If holidays fall on the week of the officers meeting, move the meeting one week, one way or the other.

- Rundown on the movie and party, will be paid.

Dec 21, 1968 • If a charter gets below six members, it has to dissolve.

- California votes are by majority on all trips except corporation issues which are 100%

- For a new charter, run club under another name for one year bring it to an officers meeting and run it down, then vote on it.

Feb. 27, 1969 • 25% of all club money trips in the state go to the Calif Treasury.

March 29, 1969 • Deal with Ed Roth on book, $2700.00 plus 15% after 10,000.00

- Patent started on H.A. deathheads by Bob Roberts.
- New York Vultures are Hells Angels. Denny is President

May 24, 1969
- All new charters require a 100% California vote.
- Presidents only at the June 30 Corp meeting.

June 28, 1969
- Try for a USA patent
- All charters have to vote on any new charters, 100% vote
- No inactive members are to wear patches.

Aug 23, 1969
- Bob Roberts signed for Englands' Small deathhead, Sonny signed for the Large deathhead, All clubs to sign at the next run.
- Charters are limited only by towns.
- Tatoos's are left up to the individual charters

Sept 27, 1969
- Decided that bumper stickers are OK.
- Signed papers for England charters, all 8 presidents signed.

Jan 31, 1970
- LACO folded, two members transfered to Berdoo.
- All agreed that a member transfering should bring a letter signed by his President
- Gave San Jose LACO's movie money.
- Hells Angels money trips 50/50, movie 25%
- California meetings, one month 2 officers next month just presidents.

Feb 28, 1970
- Optional one or two officers at California Meetings.

Mar 28, 1970
- Movie money, $250.00 of each $1000.00 goes to the Calif Treasury

April 25, 1970
- All new charters have a choice of deathheads

Jun 20, 1970
- If anyone is using our name (non member), give info to an officer and he will take it to a lawyer. If no retraction in ten days, then it is eligible for a lawsuit.
- Other people can use our name until we patent it.
- Only $100.00 will come from the Calif Treasury, the rest will come from each club's treasury.

Dec 12, 1970
- Sonny says there can be a corporation inside of a corporation if there is no objection.
- Agree to change corporation statue to non-profit
- Voted and passed, No more COURTESY CARDS.

Sep 13, 1980
- Suggestion: That brothers in prison help design posters for the World Runs. Decide which one to use at the presidents meeting.

Oct 4, 1980
- Motion, Oakland: That we make Support your Local Hells Angels T-shirts West Coast voted NO

To be taken back to ECOM on Dec, 1980

- Europe's independance was granted by California, To be brought up at the next ECOM.

Feb 14, 1981
- CALIFORNIA RULE, Must have six members for a new charter. If charter falls under six members, it is up to California to decide whether to keep the charter or to freeze it.
- Dale (Sonoma co.) won law suit against a bar who refused to serve him while wearing his patch. Won $500.00 in punitive damages plus all lawyers fee's.

March 7, 1981
- Motion, Oakland: That the Satans Angels can ride and wear their patches in California and the USA. PASSED
- 30 day notice regarding voting on prospects. PASSED

April 04, 1981
- Losers M.C. voted in as Monterey Hells Angels

May 09, 1981
- Tatoo's are to be completely covered if member is kicked out

Jun 07, 1981
- Motion: Sponsor must know person for 1 year, then he must be brought up for hangaround for a period of one year before being voted on for prospectship in all clubs. Also hangaround must have his name brought up by his charter at the OM, and dated when he starts the one year period. DID NOT PASS AS A RULE BUT AGREED UPON FOR GUIDELINE
- Motion: No man can be voted in the club as a prospect or a member while he is in prison or jail, EXCEPT when a prospective charter gets voted in as a charter and the man is in prison, he becomes a member with the rest of his charter. PASSED
- Unless a prospect rides his motorcycle to a meeting, he can not be voted in as a member. Deal with exceptions when they come up.

Oct 03, 1981
- Motion, Oakland: For the name of the corporation to be changed from Hells Angels Frisco to the Hells Angels United States, with Sonny as Chairman, Fu as Secretary and the Oakland clubhouse as address. PASSED

*   *   *

These rules and by-laws are entered in chronological order, although many are not dated. Earlier rules and by-laws, from the 1960s, are handwritten. More recent regulations are written on computer. They are presented in order, from chapter rules and by-laws to organization rules and by-laws.

Chapter rules

From Frisco [handwritten]
Rules
1. Must be 21
2. Running motorcycle
3. No niggers, no cops, or ex cops
4. No hypes
5. Nothing on our back patch except out H.A. name, logo, MC, state
6. Must have 6 members in charter
7. males only
8. Weekly charter meetings.

*   *   *

More recent and elaborate chapter rules drafted by the Oakland chapter. They are handwritten.

1. Meetings will be held once a week at a predesignated location
2. No member will show up drunk or high
3. There will be a $2 fine for disrupting meeting
   a. specify open discussion
   b. included out of charter guest members
   c. late to church fines
   d. fines for not riding motorcycle to a meeting
4. Three year membership in the club before you may get full back patch tatoo
   a. Tatoos will be blacked OUT or OUT DATE tatooed aplied to Hells Angels tatoos
5. Any member quitting will have a one year minimum time period to come back to their original charter.
6. Elections: Will be held each January or as deemed necessary by the charter
   a. Nominees must be seconded by another member
   b. Two week period between nominations and voting
   c. Voting by show of hands
   d. President votes last
   e. Election of officers to be determined by a MAJORITY VOTE
   f. All other subjects will be by 2/3 majority vote except original membership
   g. Al members must vote
7. Original Membership: 1 week waiting period before vote
   a. Prospects sponcer will notify all members before the vote, or there will be no vote taken

    b. Vote will be by a 100 % of the membership present

     * Be there or your vote wont count

     * NO ABSTAINS

8. Patch Box Rule:

    a. Lose your patch and right to vote for 30 days

    b. All club insignias, belt buckles, T-shirts etc will not be worn. No exceptions

    c. Your office will be forfeited if you are an officer

    d. Discussion of collateral will be at this time if need be

    e. Said member will be expected to get his act together within 30 days or will be up for revote

    f. Member in patch box mandatory to attend all club functions

    g. A patch in the box will remain there for 30 days

9. Revote Rule

    a. Any Member may bring up another member for revote if motion is seconded

    b. One week period between motion and revote—or immediately if necessary

    c. Presence of accusors and accusees mandatory depending upon circumstances. Example: accused up for revote for non attendance still not present at revote

10. Fuck ups:

    a. Any Member who violates known club rules or standards written or unwritten will be dealt with at next meeting or immediately if need be

    b. Fines, patch box or revote will be decide by a majority vote of Members present

    c. Past fuck ups will be reviewed

11. Lying to the club will not be tolerated and said member will be out automatically upon verification of lies

12. Phones:

    a. Every Member and prospects will be required to have a phone, pager or immediate phone contact

    b. Members will have two week grace period to new phone hookup when moving or lose of phone services—failure may result in patch box

13. Responsibilities:

    a. [one line intelligible] club assignments without seeking help or advice will be up for fine, patch box or revote

Participation Rules:

1. Meeting Nights

     a. fines levied for not riding to meeting. Exceptions: health, bike down

     b. fines for being late

     c. fines for not wearing your patch to meeting

2. Missing 3 meetings in a row without prior approval or good reason is eligible for revote

3. Members not required to do anything to violate his parole - if member on parole chooses to participate all fines will be in effect

4. Bike down

     a. Down time is noted

     • 6 weeks maximum down time allowed per year

     • summertime, get bike up ASAP

5. Mandatory Runs: Determined by charter

     a. $100.00 fine missing mandatory run exceptions: hospital or jail

     b. $25.00 fine not riding your bike pending health/weather

     c. $25.00 fine not leaving with pack without prior approval (work)

     d. $25.00 fine being late at departure location

     e. Mising 2 mandatory runs in one year will be patch box or revote pending special circumstances

CHAIN OF COMMAND

President

Vice president

Treasure

Sgt at Arms

Secretary

Road Captain

Treasury Rules

1. Dues collected each week

2. Prospects pay same as members

3. 3 weeks behind on dues—patch box if not paid in full by 4th week

4. Collateral to be discussed at 4th meeting including debts owed to individual members

5. Fines:

     • one week grace period to pay all fines

     • 10 % each additional week for maximum of 3 weeks

     • after 30 days fines not paid—revote [. . .]

11. Loans

     • unanimous vote to members for club loans over $100.00

     • collateral discussed at this time

• 10 % of loan due minimum first meeting of every month . . .

13. Bail loans
  • Charter will post bail when affordable to charter and to be reimbursed according to agreements of charter and member or prospect
  • Charter will have a flat rate of 10 % interest paid back
  • Courtesy loans of $100.00 or less will be paid in 30 days or 10 % added

14. Inventory:
  • all club inditia weather charter property or in possession of members to be documented, videotaped and witnessed by member responsible for inventory list
  • updated annually/include reason articles not in possession; gifts or destroyed
  • $100.00 fine for losing any club item
  • include photos of club tatoos/bike tanks
  • Prospects will pay for full back patch after receiving prospect rocker, no refunds if they don't make member
  • No fire works or discharging firearms at club functions
  • No spiking of food or beverages at club functions without consumers knowledge
  • No kicking members, prospects or hangarounds

*   *   *

Hells Angels California By-Laws [handwritten]

1. All patches will be the same on the back. Large or small deathhead will be the only exception. Now changed to large deathhead only. Nothing will show on the back except Hells Angels patch. City patch will be worn on left front about where top pocket is on a levi jacket. City patch is optional for each charter. 1 patch only per member and 1 member ship card only per member. Prospects will wear California rocker on back and prospect patch left front above top of pocket. Fine 100.00 for breaking any above law.

2. No hypes. Anyone using a needle for any reason other than having a doctor use it on you will be considered a hype. Fine automatic kick out of club.

3. No explosives will be thrown into the fire where there is a group of Hells Angels in the area. Fine ass wipping and/or subject to Calif. President's decisions.

4. Guns on California runs will not be displayed after 6 p.m. They will be fired from dawn to 6 p.m. in a predetermined area only. Rule does not apply to anyone with that as seen by another member if it is not being displayed or shot. Fine: 100.00 for breaking above by-law.

5. When any Hells Angels fight another Hells Angels it is one on one. Prospects same as members. Fine 100.00 for breaking above by-law.

6. No narcotics burns. When making deals, persons get what they are promised or the deal is called off. Fine: automatic kick out of club.

7. All Hells Angels fines will be paid within 30 days. Fines will be paid to that members club treasurer to be held for the next Ca. run. Fine: kick-out after 30 days.

8. No persons, other than active Hells Angels should wear the Hells Angels patch. Fine: will lose patch.

9. One vote per charter at Calif. Officers meeting.

*   *   *

Hells Angels California Secondary Rules [handwritten]

1. Don't fuck up the guys in the other charters unless they need it.

2. no inactive member will wear a patch at any time.

3. all new charter will have the big skull.

4. if kick out, must stay out 1 year then back to original charter. Hells Angel tatoos will have an in-date and out date when a member quits. If a member is kicked out, Hells Angel tatoos will be completely covered. Not X out.

5. Each charter may keep 1 original patch. For Calif. votes, 2 votes instead of majority. 2 no votes will kill a new charter.

6. 25.00 fine for being late or missing officers meeting.

7. Runs are on holidays. 3 mandatory runs are Memorial day, Junly 4th, and labor day. For Calif. New Years party mandatory for north charters only.

8. if a charter ever goes below 6 members it must dissolve.

*   *   *

West Coast rules. [handwritten. Though the wording seems illiterate and archaic, the Washington State chapter referred to was formed on July 16, 1994. These are notes for a new draft of West Coast rules.]

Prospect club to member voting procedure. One man vote divide by total members one of charters 2 charters don't pass

No ammunition in fire

No interviews with media about H.A. or press without club approval

Pay for % airfare for Washington and southern charters to attend O.M.

Clubs being invited to a run must be brung up to charter for approval

Procedure for motion

No H.A. on anything sold to public unless approved by ?

All prospect hangarounds pay for all runs and partys

No taking patches with westcoast approval

U.S.A $ due by Jan 1st
Inviteing Clubs to U.S.A.

*   *   *

(West coast) Prospect Rules and Guidelines or expected [handwritten]
Pay Dues. World Runs. USA Runs. Westcoast runs. Westcoast parties.
Able to grow as a club.
Fax machine and mailing address.
Monthly reports from a representative for Q&A.
Profile on each member.
Able to send greeting cards to all charters.
World phone and address list.
Fighting is one on one always fight back.
No needles or using herion.
Able to go to all H.A. functions in the world.
Club photo to all charters in H.A. World.
Must attend U.S.A. and World Run and all Westcoast Runs and parties.
Must visit all charters on motorcycles.

*   *   *

U.S. rules. [handwritten. Notes for new U.S. rules.]
New state prospect and member voted on by whole U.S. One man one vote
2/3 majority to pass
  U.S.A. $ Due by Jan 1st 50.00 a man
  Coast putting on run has to have location by pryor U.S.A.
  All motions to world must be voted on in U.S. first
  Other clubs attending U.S.A. must be brung up to charter for approval.
  Procedure for motion

*   *   *

IDEAS [handwritten]
Member thrown out in jail should be charter discretion
  Prospect can't make member while in jail
  Procedure to bring up motion to all levels U.S. Westcoast World
  No H.A. on anything sold to public unless approved by ?
  Need to list cost of a run and party
  All members prospects hangarounds should have to pay for U.S.A. attending or not
  Tatoo covering and procedure to be discussed for quitting or kicked out
  If charter splits must have approval from what ever level W.C. U.S. World they are at first
  Need to make prospect rules and guildelines for Calif. U.S. World
  Profile on membership?

All Charters must speak English before making membership?

Allow are prospects to sell support items bring to [two indistinguisable words]

Will for all charters in World to have one

List of all Clubs in U.S. area also

* * *

PROPOSED UNITED STATES RULES UPDATE [typed on computer]

1. Only one patch per member, unless otherwise approved at an officers meeting:
2. No explosives will be thrown into any fire where there are any Hells Angels in the area.
3. Guns on Hells Angels runs will not be displayed unnecessarily after 6:00 pm They will be fired from until 6:00 pm in a predetermined area only.
4. Any fighting between members, prospects, or hangarounds is one on one.
5. No weapons will be used when fighting another member, prospect, or hangaround. Suggested penalty: Kick-out
6. Only Hells Angels will wear Hells Angels paraphernalia.
7. If kicked out must stay out 1 year, if quit must stay out 6 months, then must go back to original charter. No exceptions.
8. Hells Angels tatoos, each one, will have an out-date with the same size letters as corresponding tatoo if member quits. If a member is kicked out all Hells Angels tatoos will be covered or X'd out, the X will be as thick as the letters are tall on each corresponding tatoo.
9. A member cannot be kicked out of the club while he is in jail unless it is proved by his charter that he is not in good standing and it is first brought to an officers meeting.
10. Nothing other than patch to be worn on back.
11. A person cannot be made a member or a prospect while in jail.
12. Prospect charters must attend at least 1 USA run.
13. A person must be 21 to be voted in as a member.
14. Before voted into club, must have a running Harley Davidson motorcycle.
15. Each charter must have a weekly meeting.
16. A member must be in the club at least 1 year before he can attend officers meetings, except for new charters.
17. A member must be in the club at least 5 years before he can become an East or West coast officer.
18. All Hells Angels must own and ride a Harley Davidson motorcycles.
19. A member may keep his original patch for display purposes only in a manner so that it cannot be worn.

20. Each member must have an inventory list of all his club property.
21. Must have one year as member in good standing before transfer to another charter.
22. $100.00 fine for loss of any club property.
23. No transfers allowed from a charter with 6 members or less.
24. No one (member, prospect, or hangaround) will use needles to inject street drugs. Penalty: Kick-out.
25. No niggers in the club. Cops or x cops.

*   *   *

Hells Angels European Rules [typed on computer]
1. all members will pay 100.00 swiss francs per year to the european treasury, except if in jail or hospital for a long time.
2. members are not to use anabolic steroids <by injection>.
3. members have to pay a contribution to the costs for clubruns members are not to send club foto,s or club patches by mail, they must be handed over personaly [. . .]
1. all charters must attend euro meetings, a fine of 500,00$ to the euro treasury is payable for not attending.
2. there will be 4 euro meetings a year, 2 in england and 2 on the continent. Allways on Saturday 15.00 hour.
3. members must attend european runs on motorcycles.
4. when friendly clubs are invited to h.a. party,s they should not be forced to work, but are allowed to work behind the bar or elsewhere if they wish to help.
5. voting at euro meetings will be on the one man, one vote principle and a two thirds majority is required to carry a motion.
6. a two thirds majority vote applies when voting a hang a round club to prospect club.
7. at euro meetings the first point on the agenda is club events.
8. the voting system for clubs is as follows;
a. >for a club to become a hangaround club, two thirds mayority.
b. > for a club to bacome a prospect club, two thirds mayority.
b. > for a club to become foll patch, 100 % [. . .]
12. the costs of european & world runs is not to exceed 200,00 swiss francs. every member & prospect on the street pays, if they attend the run or not.
13. if the country who host the world run has border problems, the charters concerned can claim lawyers expenses from the euro,treasury.
14. the european secretary is responsible for giving a copy of the european prospect rules to prospect chapters in new european countries.

15. the country secretary must supply a copy of the european rules to new h.a. chapters in their country.

16. when a member is discharged from the club, good or bad standig, the info must be sended through europe immediately.

17. the europe run must be given on a steady date every year <first week of june>

18. hangarounds and hangaround clubs are welcom on anniversary,s &euro&worldruns.

19. o.m. must be given on anniversary,s or runs.

20. o.m. must be given in countries without border problems. if the country which host the euro run have border problems, than should the O.M. be given in an other country without border problems.

21. when members of a h.a.club want to form a new club and split from their own club and have less than 6 members, then they have to ask permission to chapters in their own country, also they have to ask permission in the euro O.M.

22. to let sponsoring countries, help new h.a. chapter in new country to organize their first euro/worldrun.

23. when there is a worldrun and euro-run at the same time in europe, first have a euro-o.m. before the world-o.m.

24. A emergency euro-meeting must always been hold in Amsterdam.

*   *   *

Hells Angels Canadian bylaws

1- All member must own a Harley-Davidson motorcycle.

2- No member may be of African decent.

3- All contact or use of heroin is strictly forbidden.

4- Use of needles is strictly forbidden

5- No burns or dealings of any kind that will reflect badly on the club.

6- No rapes.

7- Going from official hangaround to prospect or prospect to member requires 100% vote of the charter's membership.

8- New chapter or prospect charters in a province require a province vote only. New charters or prospect charters in a new province require a Canada vote.

9- There is a one year probation on all new charters or members.

10- Charter splits require approval of all charters in the province or 66% majority if deadlocked.

11- Changes to the Canada rules require approval of all charters or 66% majority if deadlocked.

12- All charters are required to have a road date.

13- 86 rule. [automatic probation for infringement of a gang rule.]

14- A member may only have one set of patches.

15- Six members (on the street) are required for a charter or prospect charter.

16- After road date, a member is allowed 30 days without a running motorcycle during the riding season.

17- At club functions there is to be no shooting of firearms or setting off of fireworks.

18- After 5 years a member may get his back patch tattoo.

19- After 1 year a member may get a Hells Angels tattoo.

20- A member retired in good standing must get his Hells Angels tattoo dated.

21- A member retired in bad standing or kicked out must get his tattoos covered or removed.

22- Any member or prospect who retires or quits must go back to his original charter before he can transfer to any other charter, and they must have each others blessing. A prospect must become a member in his original charter before transfering.

*　　　*　　　*

bylaws, world prospects & prospect clubs [typed on computer. Other versions ban the use or sale of ecstasy, crack cocaine and heroin.]

1. prospects are not allowed to be on official h.a. club foto,s.

2. prospects are not allowed to attend H.A. meetings.

3. prospects are prospects for every full member and not only for the chapter or country they are prospecting for.

4. prospects ride at the rear of the pack on runs.

5. prospects must prospect for a minimum period of one year.

6. if a prospect is voted in while he is in jail, he receives his colours when he is released on home leave or at the end of his sentence.

7. all prospect clubs must attend the world meeting, the fine for missing a worldmeeting is 2000,00$. the fine is appealable and if the appeal is successful, the fine is cancelled.

8. all prospect clubs must have a stable postal adress i.e. p.o.box#or a clubhouse. any change must be notified immediately.

9. every prospect club must visit every country in europe that has a H.A. chapter, before they can be voted in as full patch.

10. all prospects have to pay 100.00 swiss francs per year to the european treasury, except if in jail or hospital for a long time.

11. prospects are not to use anabolc steroids by injection.

12. prospects have to pay a contribution to the costs of euro-runs, even if they do not attend.

13. prospects are not allowed to send clubfoto,s or clubpathes by mail, they must be handed over personally.

14. all prospects must attend euro/worldruns, they are not admitted to the meeting itself but must be in attendance. the details of the location of the meeting will be given out by the local h.a.chapters. or in case of a new country, the euro-sec will inform them. a 500.00$ fine is payable for non attendance.

15. prospects must pay into all treasury and run-funds.

16. all european prospects must speak the english language before they can be voted in as full-members.

17. prospects can only give presents with death heads on it, after they asked permission to their sponsoring H.a. club.

18. prospects may not use the words hells angels prospect club on presents or cards.

19. when a hangaround club becomes prospect club they must wear, a prospect front patch, a city or country front patch & country bottom rocker, with MC patch.

20. prospects are not to wear any shirts or any other items with the word hells angels or hamc on them.

21. prospects are not allowed to become drunk or stoned at parties, runs or meetings. [. . .]

43. prospects must attend the euro/world run on motorcycles in europe.

*   *   *

World rules [typed on a computer.]

1. if a prospect is voted in while he is in jail, he receives his colours when he is released on home leave or at the end of his sentence.

2. if a member is in jail and is dishonourably discharged from the club, it is at the charter discretion if the member concerned is thrown out while in jail or on release from jail.

3. all charters must attend the world meeting. the fine for missing a world meeting is $2000,00 american. the fine is appealable and if the appeal is succesful the fine is canceled.

4. the vote at world meetings is one man one vote.

5. a charter representative must be present in order for there vote to be counted.

6. all charters must have a stable postal adress i.e. a po box # or a clubhouse. any change of postal adress must be notified immediately.

7. any fights between members will be stricktly one onto one, no rings are to be worn, no weapons to be used, no kicking when a guy is down. this rule also applied to prospect on prospect, and member on prospect. a 100.00$ fine if rule is broken.

8. there must be 100 % vote in favour from the world meeting for a hang a round club from a new continent to become prospect club.

9. the vote for a prospect club to become full patch also must be 100% of charters.

10. member cards are given only to members.

11. by producing from h.a. posters and h.a. support stickers and support items is a registration print compulsary .mandatory.

12. when a motion is brought up at the world run, it has to be brought back to the clubs for voting. after that the vote must be send to the europe or east-west secretary or the country who organize the world run.<within 4 weeks> patent funds money u.s.a. must be paid before march every year, 20$each member. if this is not paid by a h.a. chapter on time, a fine will follow <double payment> in europe the chapters send money to herman, <kent>.

13. if a prospect-chapter in a new country becomes h.a. they have to send a faz to guinea <oakland> with the request for trademark. Guinea will send that chapter back a confirmation and a official paper. <to be filled in> which must be sended back to guinea. after that the new h.a. chapter can arrange the trademark in their own country.

*　　*　　*

HELLS ANGELS WORLD RULES
Revised March 11, 1998
[written on a computer with a title page adorned with the Death's Head.]
August 24, 1985 by Essex England: No more t-shirts with Hells or Angels on it.
August 24, 1985 by Haarlem Holland: Must have one representative from every country to be at world meetings. Fine for missing World Meeting will be two thousand dollars, three months time to pay fine or appeal.
A valid reason will be taken into consideration.
October 12, 1985 – England will adhere to our tradition of 10 year members and older having the privilege and retaining the right exclusively to wear belt buckles portraying both the name HELLS ANGELS and the DEATH HEAD.
April 16, 1986 – One officer per charter for the World meeting.
August 3, 1986 – by Daly City: The World meeting to be held on Tuesday before the start of the run.
August 3, 1986 – No cops or ex-cops in the club.
August 3, 1986 – No niggers in the club.
August 3, 1986 – No snitches in the club.
November 29, 1986 – One man—One vote.

November 14, 1987 – To pay $20.00 per member worldwide to cover the cost of the Trademark bill. The $20.00 would be due March 1st every year. If more monies are needed a special request would be made.

Penalty for not paying by March 1st every year would be a 100% penalty of the original amount.

July, 1988 - That world issues be settled by one man one vote system. A ^{2}/$_3$rd's majority is needed to pass a motion.

May 19, 1990 – Every member have the same style patch by the next World meeting. (August 2, 1990)

April 4, 1992 – That we have world runs held in countries that are accessible to all members, such as Europe and the U.S.A.

October 17, 1992 by California: All world votes are on a 90-day answer system.

October 17, 1992 by California: Not to have 2 consecutive world meetings in countries not accessible by all charters.

October 17, 1992 by California: If there are immigration problems and only a few charters are represented at world meetings, each charter should be notified of issues to be voted on and have 90 days to respond.

November 2, 1996 – Each country to have at least 2 representatives at the World meeting.

November 2, 1996 – To have two World Officer's Meetings per year.

November 2, 1996 – To adopt a Hells Angels' property agreement.

November 2, 1996 – To adopt a standard motion form.

November 2, 1996 – To extend the appeal time for missing a world O.M.

November 2, 1996 – To have the 1997 World Run in South Africa.

* * *

Outlaws' Rules

For comparison, here are the Outlaws' national constitution and the European Outlaws' rules.

NATIONAL CONSTITUTION
OUTLAWS MOTORCYCLE CLUB OF NORTH AMERICA
All members must be 21 years of age and own his own motorcycle at all times. 30 day grace period is allowed. Chapter decision.

All motorcycles must be American made.

You have to have 100% vote from the membership. The sponsoring Chapter may bring a new member up for a vote after he has probated for a minimum of six months, has attended at least one National, attend all funerals, bills paid to date, and 100% vote of sponsoring Chapter. You may only bring up a new member for a vote three times.

A probate will not be told to do something, that a member himself would not do. Patch pulling offense for instructing a probate to commit a felony.

No needle law, patch pulling offense and expulsion in bad standing from Club.

No PCP, crack, heron, no bullshit dealings involving Club. Expulsion in bad standing from Club.

Club Houses to remain clean, and members are responsible for their guest. If you can't eat it, don't bring it.

No practical jokes that may alter the state of mind of your Brother or guest. Patch pulling offense.

Members must be in Club for one year before being allowed to have a Club tatoo. Club tatoos are Charlie, Outlaws, American Outlaw Association, or any abbreviations. Members must have five full years in before having a back patch. A member leaving in good standing will have his tatoo dated.

When changing Chapters you must clear through both Presidents and have a 100% vote by new Chapter. Must have one year in before you can request a change.

All new Chapters are to have a 100% vote by all Presidents. New Chapters must make Two Nationals. Attend all funerals. All probates in a prospective Club will wear a probationary rocker on back and the A.O.A. prospective patch on front.

Any Outlaw leaving Club in good standing is to be respected as such and any Brother not honoring this will immediately have his patch pulled. Any disrespect to your patch or stealing from Brothers is forbidden and is an automatic patch pulling offense.

OUTLAWS MC
MIDLANDS AND WALES
REVISED RULES (August 1994)

1/ Hands off rule; no member shall strike another member whatsoever. Any problems should be sorted at meetings. Punishment is to be dismissed from club unless a good explanation is given.

2/ All cutoffs must be of either black leather, or a Levi style black or blue denim, and must be kept in good condition. No other badges to be worn on it unless agreed to at an officers meeting.

Punishment is a fine of up to £100 and will be given to members chapter.

3/ A strict no comment policy to be aherd to. No statements to be given to the police whatsoever if to do with the club. Punishment is dismissal from club.

Statements may only be made if it only relates to yourself or your business. Discretion must be used at all times.

4/ No statements to the media.

5/ All members must have a motorcycle that falls into one of the following catagories: Chopper, Lowrider, Harley.

A non standard motorcycle of 500cc and over to be ridden on major runs per year.

A standard bike may be used as a second bike.

6/ No member shall live or set up a buisness in another chapters area without permission of the host chapter.

7/ No member to fly patches abroad unless agreed at an officers meeting.

8/ Two officers minimum per club must attend officer meetings. One soldier per chapter may sit in at meeting. The host club can be present but are also responsible for security.

Chapters late at an officers meeting results in a fine of £25 paid in cash to central fines officer.

9/ If a man is to be accused of any offenses, the complaintant and the accused are to be present at the next officers meeting to give both parties a chance to put there case forward.

10/ Members attending officers meetings must present there chapters views and not there own personal views.

11/ When riding together the host club will be responsible for the safety of the journey. Members will keep at a sensible pace.

12/ Petty crimes on runs will not be tolerated, or skulldugery in any chapters area.

The security of your men may be put at risk.

13/ Prospects will stay sober at all official functions.

14/ 100% attendances must be attended by all members. Only hospital or prison is a good enough excuse. Offenders will be dealt with by individual chapters.

15/ A/ Half the club to hold cumpulseries in 1994. The other half in 1995.

B/ Rock and blues to be compulsory.

C/ Aniversary to be compulsary.

D/ Two runs per year. First at Easter or May bank holliday. The second to be the last weekend in September.

16/ Members will seek permission from there chapter sergent if wishing to leave 100% do or run early.

Host sergent at 100% do's or runs will be informed of absentes or people leaving early.

17/ All club paraphinalia must be brought to a central officers meeting to be approved or rejected. The officers decision is final. There is no recourse for appeal.

18/ "Misuse of equipment" for a public display. A member will be reduced to prospect for a minimum of 12 months. If offender is a officer he will be barred from holding this rank for life. For directly endangering another member, dismisal from the club. All the above pending inquiry.

19/ Liberty takers at 100% do's i.e. people not sticking to relevent times, people vanderlising equipment marquees etc, will face concequences at officer meetings. There own chapters will be responsible for damages and costs.

*   *   *

Sonny Barger, who markets himself as an American legend on T-shirts, hats, and other paraphernalia, made his reputation on land. But once he dies, he wants nothing to do with dirt or motorcycles. In a pang of angst in 1996, he hand-wrote this letter telling the Hells Angels what to do with his remains.

March 4, 1996.

To the Oakland Hells Angels & to whom else it may concern:

In the event of my death I do not (double underlined) want to be buried. I want to be cremated & my ashes dumped at sea.

C.P. Bannon [the Oakland funeral home that buries Hells Angels] has paper work that says different, but in the event I die before I change the paper work at C.P. Bannon's this paper should be the one that is used!

3-7-96 Ralph Sonny Barger [Signed and printed]

3-7-96 witness John Palomar [Signed and printed]

*   *   *

Minutes of Meetings

The Hells Angels spend as much time in meetings as do corporate executives. Hells Angels' meetings are well organized, and the secretary keeps meticulous notes. Meetings are held at all levels of the organization: corporate, world officers, European officers, U.S. presidents, west coast officers, east coast officers, and chapters. The Hells Angels discuss club, not gang, business at the meetings. Criminal activities are never brought up, unless in reference to a member who has been arrested or jailed, or during discussions of fundraising activities to pay lawyers.

The following are excerpts of minutes of Hells Angels meetings at all these levels during the past decade. At times I have added comments or background information in brackets to add perspective and understanding.

Corporation Meeting

September 19, 1989.

George said that attorney advised that we merchandise out trademark. Fuki faxed all the paper work they attorneys wanted to show that we were protecting our trademark.

Hells Hotest Angels. A bill was sent to Flying Man Posters for $4,000.00 Figure charged at .25 per poster that they sold. [Author's note: The Hells Angels have copyrighted their name and will not let anyone use it unless they get money from the deal. Although the name has been in the public domain since at least the First World War and was even the title of a Howard Hughes movie in 1927, the Hells Angels have laid claim to the name and no one has had enough money to challenge them on it.]

Application for trademark in South Africa has been filed.

New Zealand has filed for the Deathhead. We are going to find out what they filed it under. They want credit for $800.00 they spent for their trademark. To be applied to their $20.00 per member donation.

Can we do anything about the words Hells Angels in various dictionaries.

Record album from England. A Attorney is going to listen to the album to see if the lyrics or music is a infrignment.

Copies of book TCB have been received in the United States by club members. Attorneys are looking into this matter. [Author's note: This is a reference to my 1987 book, *Hells Angels: Taking Care of Business*. The Hells Angels sued me, the English-language publisher in Canada, and the French-language publisher in Quebec for alleged trademark infringement for using an artist's rendition of the Death's Head on the cover. I explained this lawsuit in *Hells Angels: Into the Abyss* (1996). Briefly, the English-language publisher declared bankruptcy to get out of the lawsuit. The French language publisher decided it didn't want to spend the money to defend itself, although its lawyer believed he would win the suit, and settled out of court. It agreed to stop publishing the book, gave the Hells Angels an undisclosed sum of money plus all the books in the warehouse, and promised to never again publish a book about the Hells Angels. I have never settled with the Hells Angels and the matter has not been pursued for two reasons: the author is not responsible for the cover of the book, which is a publisher's decision, and the Hells Angels had achieved their goal—they got the book off the shelves in Quebec.]

Trademark reg. for all Canada have been received and are in the book. [Author's note: The Hells Angels registered their name and Death's Head in Canada after *Taking Care of Business* came out.]

Papers given to Canada to sign for TCB. [Author's note: These are the papers pertaining to the Hells Angels lawsuit against me.]

Rio would like to file for "Filthy Few" and Big Red Machine. Their attorneys wanted to file for (12) different trademarks. They should just take care of the basics.

US Deathhead was filed again in July.

Hells Angels trademark in Italy has been filed. [Author's note: This is an extremely important piece of information. This meeting was held in 1989. The Hells Angels chapter in Milan was not formed until December 16, 1995. Most police officers don't read these minutes because they bore them. But police could have used the knowledge that the Hells Angels were interested in Italy to make the climate in that country inhospitable to outlaw motorcycle gangs. I got these minutes in 1990.]

WORLD OFFICERS MEETING
June 2, 3, 4, 1995: Amsterdam, Holland

Nomads, Australia: 11 members—1 pros. Had problems with Bandido's. Took there patches.

Loners MC Australia hand a round for Bandido's Australia. There are rumours that Loners MC Australia plan to visit Loners MC in Canada.

Haney [British Columbia] 12 members 1 pros. Ther's a big case against immigration. All foreign bro's who come to visit must not have any criminal record and must be prepared to sit in jail at least a few days. Also; don't sign any papers, it can destroy the whole case against immigration.

Kent [England]; 13 members 1 pros. Herman trademark is refused in Germany, we make courtcase against gouvernement more info follows, a lawyer is on the case, also a European lawyer, try to get AU European trademark for 35 country's also country's without H.A. chapters.

Windsor [England]; 7 members 1 pros Proposal; to make a international Big Red Machine magazine + video. Send material to Windsor. [Author's note: The English Hells Angels now publish a slick magazine about the Hells Angels called *The Big Red Machine* that can be bought on newsstands.]

Paris; 8 members 3 pros. Doc out good standing, <if a member is kicked out good or bad standing send a fax around with picture>

Berlin; 6 members 4 pros. 15 Feb pigs raided clubhouse, confiscated t,shits and other stuff with Nazi-insignia,s please be aware that all goods with SS or swastca,s are illegal and the piggs use this against our club in court.

Amsterdam; 25 member 2 pros. Question about Neuwied <Germany>; was answered by Hamburg, Neuwied was hang a round for H.A. Germany, They got sended down the road and 2 weeks later became probationary Bandido.s.

Wanguanui [New Zealand]; 5 members 1 pros. About sending support shirts to the public in New Zealand, first contact out brothers. <They don,t want dickheads make profit on these T,shirts, or wearing them.>

Trondheim; 15 members 1 prospect club <Shabby Ones> since 29 May MC Norway. Proposal; asked to change the rule about selling T,shirts with the lettrs H.A. or with 81 on it.

August 2, 1996: Steamboat Springs, Colorado

BERDOO: We would like to remind everyone that all World meeting business is conducted in English.

RIO DE JANIERO: Motion made to exclude anyone from membership in the HAMC that has previously held political office and it is attached.

HALIFAX: We feel that HAMC should stay off the internet. [Author's note: Someone was thinking. The internet is the least private place on the planet. Although the Hells Angels sell items on their websites to raise money, they don't discuss business via computer. Some police officers, however, believe they have discovered the motherlode in the Hells Angels Helsingborg website.]

COPENHAGEN: New prospect charter Aalborg, 60 miles from Aarus. A bomb was placed at our clubhouse and the clubhouse was confiscated by the government. YOUNGER was shot 3 times in jail but, is O.K.

*   *   *

Motions are made on pre-printed motion forms, discussed, and voted on at all meetings. The following were made at this meeting.

MOTION MADE BY – CANADA
DATE – AUGUST 1, 1996

MOTION- Approval for Hells Angels projects such as movies, videos, books, or anything using the Hells Angels name or logo, must be passed at world level by a two thirds majority.

REASON FOR MOTION: Canada feels all such items about the Hells Angels club, as a whole, or it's individual members, regardless of where they are intended to be distributed, effect all Hells Angels world wide. Such projects, created about us, by non Hells Angels, can be discredited as hearsay or the fabrication of the author. Those created and or endorsed, by us, could be misconceived and used against us.

In the six minute video from New York, the narrator, obviously a Hells Angel, makes the comment of how proud he is that a brother would rather go to jail than to roll over. All Hells Angels know this. To those outside the club that statement begs the question, roll over on whom, about what. There are other quotes in that video that, we feel, are nothing more than a pep talk to Hells Angels. A made for Hells Angels, by Hells Angels film. The B.B.C,

Denmark tape speaks for itself. The public should NOT know what we think about such things.

It is Canada's opinion that projects such as these concern all Hells Angels and should be discussed and voted on at a world level.

MOTION MADE BY: Dago
DATE: July 2, 1996
PRESENTED TO: HAMC World

1) Problem or reason: In the past we have had numerous and prolonged problems recovering club property that has fallen into the wrong hands. Be it either through police actions, court ordered seizures, or the untimely death of a brother, leaving property that was in his keeping in the possession of surviving heirs.
   Even though it is a well known fact that all property bearing the name Hells Angels and/or the Death Head insignia, belongs not to the individual in question, but to H.A.M.C., Inc. the problem of "missing property" continues to exist. Due mainly to a wide variety of dubious arguments (particularly by law enforcement.)

2) Solution: To have every member in good standing, present and future, sign and notarize the previously submitted Hells Angels property agreement.

3) Motion: For the World to approve the adoption of the previously submitted Hells Angels property agreement. This property agreement to be signed and notarized by every member in good standing, present and future. With the responsibility of maintaining these documents on file, resting with the secretaries of each respective charter in the World.

4) Penalty: If passed, any person not having this property agreement signed and on file with his respective charter, will NOT be recognized as a member in good standing of HAMC, until at which time the document is signed and filed.

5) Exceptions: Any member who, due to court ordered non-association, imprisonment or serious hospitalization, is physically unable to sign this agreement. This exception will remain in effect only up until the time the member is free and able to comply with this motion. At which time he too shall be required to sign the agreement.

[Author's note: Here is a copy of the proposed property agreement submitted with the motion. Sign on the dotted line and ride free and wild, guys. But don't stray beyond the rules.]

HELLS ANGELS MOTORCYCLE CORPORATION
4021 FOOTHILL BLVD.
OAKLAND, CA. 94601

I, _____ do hereby acknowledge and agree with the standard, long standing policy of the HELLS ANGELS MOTORCYCLE CORPORATION, hereinafter referred to as HAMC, and it's Licensed Charters hereinafter referred to as "LICENSEES," which states that any and all articles bearing the name "HELLS ANGELS" and/or the winged skull insignia/logo known as a "DEATH HEAD" (which are registered with the United States Patent Office, the numbers being listed below in this document, but not limited to) are the sole and legal property of HAMC. These articles constitute, but are not limited to, the HELLS ANGELS vest/jacket commonly referred to as "colors," belt buckles, jewelry, T-shirts, hats and/or any other material item(s) bearing the afore-mentioned name and/or insignia/logos.

It is further agreed that possession by me, of any above mentioned article does not in any way, shape or form constitutes legal ownership of the item(s) in question, but merely identifies me as a member in good standing of HAMC and it's licensees.

I further agree to grant Power of Attorney to a duly appointed representative of HAMC, to sign, correspond or engage in an necessary action to retrieve any and all of the aforementioned items, seized by any law enforcement agency and/or their representatives.

It is also understood and agreed, that in the event of my death, or at any point in time at which I am no longer a member in good standing of HAMC and it's licensees, all articles in my possession and control, which are designated by this agreement to be the legal property of HAMC, shall immediately be relinquished to a duly appointed representative of the HAMC, by either myself or my surviving heirs.

United States Registrations	Foreign Registrations	Foreign Registrations	Foreign Applications
1,136,494	85,916 Austria	A-1305 Hong Kong	58-063290 Japan
1,213,647	85,962 Austria	2337/1985 Hong Kong	
1,214,476	A384,045 Australia	233761 Taiwan	
1,243,951	A384,046 Australia	300301 Taiwan	
1,294,586	A384,047 Australia	2056292 Japan	
1,301,050	A384,048 Australia	2056293 Japan	
1,582,050	A384,049 Australia	354,187 Canada	
	A394,453 Australia	356,389 Canada	

United States Registrations	Foreign Registrations	Foreign Registrations	Foreign Applications
	1,200,008 Great Britain	356,390 Canada	
	1,241,283 France	356,391 Canada	
	812870468 Brazil		

EXECUTED this _____day of _____, 19_____,
at _____, County of _____,
in the State of _____,

MOTION MADE BY: Rio de Janeiro
DATE: 8-2-96
PRESENTED TO: World

1) Problem or reason: Police and Guards cannot have membership in the HAMC. Because politicians make the laws for police, we feel that politicians should not be allowed membership in HAMC.
2) Solution: Pass a World rule excluding politicians or ex-politicians from membership in the HAMC.
3) Motion: No politicians (elected officials) or ex-politicians allowed membership in the Hells Angels Motorcycle club.
4) Penalty: Soon as it becomes known the person would be kicked out.

MOTION MADE BY: Malmoe
DATE: Aug. 3:rd 1996
PRESENTED TO: HA World

1) Problem or reason: The main reason for this motion is to show the world an objective picture of our organization, and maybe try to effect the authorities from using more special rules against us, like they do for example in Canada and Australia. Now a lot of people are talking about Yves Lavinges latest book, into the abyss, and everybody believe all the bullshit he is writing. So this is our chance to show the citizens in each and every country the truth. . . . We'll show the whole world that we are worldwide and that we stick together as brothers. Reason number two is that the club probably will make a lot of money on this deal. And it's better that we make them, instead of somebody who is whriting a lot of bullshit about us. [. . .]
4) Motion: To make a series of docomentary TV-segments about Hells Angels MC world. And side by side make a book on about 400–500 pages

containing mostly pictures. The whole project will be under total control
of HA as we have Thomas from SFV [San Fernando Valley] and Jensen
from Malmoe as projectleaders. We will also make a sort of group with 1
member from W.C. USA, and 1 from E.C. USA, 1 from W.C. Canada, 1
from E.C. and one from every other country, who will get together and
discuss the contents of the project, before we start working on it.

[Author's note: The following is the project proposal.]

AFFA

the story within. . .

1. DESCRIPTION OF PROJECT: We want to make 4-6 documentary TV-
   programs about Hells Angels MC World. We also want to make a book on
   about 400 pages containing mostly pictures, but also som little writing
   about history.
2. PROJECT LEADERS: As we are standing now we have Thomas from SFV
   and also Jensen from Malmoe as project leaders inside HA. We have also
   talked to Mike from Halifax and so far it looks like he is gonna be involved
   as well. (All project leaders will get payed for their work) Out principal
   job will be to travel together with the team and make all the contacts
   between the team and the charters.
3. PRODUCING TEAM: We have a team from a Swedish TV-producing
   company wich is: one producer, one photographer and one researcher.
   We also have a book team wich is one producer and one photographer.
   So this means that only 4–5 people will be travelling around to different
   charters. Except for our own projectleaders who will be two.
4. CONTENTS: If we get the permission to make this project, we will have
   a meet, probably in Sweden, with a small group containing representatives
   from US W.C. and E.C, Canada W.C. and E.C. and every other country,
   to decide the contents of the TV-programs and the book.
5. EDITION: When it comes to the edition, we have the right to look at
   material and sort out things that we think are wrong. We also have the
   right to pick out members, wives and other people who don't want to be
   in picture.
6. ECONOMY: As far as we have been calculating, we guess that the whole
   project will cost around $2 milj to make. Probably the incomes from the
   TV-programs will cover this and nothing more. But then we have the
   book, wich will be a real exclusive one. This will be sold in all potential
   countries for about $40-50, depending on taxes and stuff like that. From
   this income we will get 30 SEK [Swedish kronor] wich is around $4,50 for
   every sold book. No matter if only 100.000 books are sold, we will still

get the money even if the company looses a lot and no profit will be made for them.

It was written in the report that HA's profit should be divided between all charters. But that was only a suggestion, and of course we must think about Trademark funds and Defence funds as well. That is a later question.

1. A properly contract will be written by layers, after the meeting with the representatives from HA and the producing company.
2. AMENDMENTS: The team wich is handpicked by the producers are very good at what they are doing. They are making this project for a much lower salary than they are used to. They see it as a challenge, and they like to work with unusual stuff. So they are not making a lot of money on it. The photographer and the producer of the book has made one book about another swedish bikeclub before. But this is of course the ultimate thing for them. The producer and the photographer of the tv-programs has also made documentaries before. They have among other things been filming in Bosnia during the war.

Now everybody must notice that his project is not about making money and selling the club. If it was, we would not be working on TV-programs. But if we work on TV-programs a lot of citizens will be watching the programs for free. If we had been working on a movie people would have to pay money to see what they love, or hate, or whatever. And only the people who already know us, support us, or fight for us would spend the money. The main purpose is to show the world that we don't excist just to fight the society. That we feel happines when we are togther and when we ride our bikes. That we have normal jobs and don't finance our living on narcotic sales. And that we take care of each other, even though we are not "Gods best children."

* * *

March 13, 1998: Berdoo, California
United States: Discussion about the Internet. We feel that anyone that wants to use another charters name on the Internet should first ask that charters permission. This would also apply to calendars, ask any charter before you put out any information about their charter on any future calendars. Discussed using/borrowing corporate money to fight gang enhancement charges on a World level. Take this back to your charter and come back with ideas. USA will borrow money from the corporation and pay it back through donations.

Canada: We want to remind everyone not to be faxing sensitive club information.

Germany: We will be celebrating 25 years of Germany and 50 years of Hells

Angels World in at the end of summer with dates to follow. When sending any mail to Hamburg address it to HAMCHG only. Danny and Norman are out in bad standing.

New Zealand: We would like a summary of any RICO cases that were ruled in our favor ASAP.

General Business:

1. The "World" will voluntarily stop wearing lightening bolts and swastikas on a World level until we vote on a motion to stop completely.

Motions from 1997:

Motion by Brasil regarding "Support" stickers. It was felt that this did not have to be voted on by the World and should be dealt with the way Brasil wants. In Canada and the USA we have agreed not to sell "Support your Local Hells Angels" stickers but we can give them to prospects, hangarounds, and close friends.

The 1999 World Run will be hosted by Brasil.

Motions for 1998:

To stop manufacturing and wearing any items with SS Lightening bolts or Swastikas immediately.

MOTION MADE BY: Germany and Italy

DATE: 3-13-98

PRESENTED TO: World

1) Problem or reason: We have been having a continuing problem with our government because it is illegal to wear or display Nazi items such as SS Lightning bolts or Swastikas. This is especially a problem for Germany, Italy, Belgium, Holland and the European community in general. These Lightning bolts and Swastikas were emblems of the German Special Police and we do not understand why anyone would want to wear insignias of any police. We have tried to stop this problem for over 2 years on a voluntary basis through different proposals and motions and not everyone has taken this issue seriously

2) Solution: To immediately stop wearing or manufacturing any items with "Lightning bolts or Swastikas" such as shirts, jewelry, plaques, pictures, drawings, etc. This would also include members signatures (no lightning bolts).

3) (same as above)

4) Penalty: $500.00 fine and member must come to an Officer meeting to explain. A charter would be responsible for a prospect breaking this rule.

5) Exceptions: Existing headstones and tattoos and plaques (no new ones). If you already have a tattoo and are coming to Germany it must be covered.

Officers attending the meeting were given a new standardized membership application form to be filled out by prospective members.

HELLS ANGELS MOTORCYCLE CLUB INFORMATION
OAKLAND, CA

Date: _____

Full name: _____

Address: _____

City: _____ State: _____ Zip: _____

D.O.B.: _____ SS# _____ DL# _____

Place of Birth: _____

Single/Married/Divorced: _____ Spouse: _____

Names of Children, if any: _____

Military Service ID#: _____ Branch: _____ Rank: _____

Dates of Service: _____ to _____

Health Insurance: _____ Blood Type: _____

Have you ever been convicted of a felony? _____

Have you ever been incarcerated? _____ If yes, where and when:

_____

Inmate/prison I.D.#: _____

Are you currently on parole or probation? _____

Have you ever been AN INFORMANT or WORKED for LAW ENFORCE-
    MENT IN ANY CAPACITY? (jailer, guard, MP etc) _____ If so, explain

_____

Have you ever belonged to any other MOTORCYCLE CLUBS in the past? ___
    If yes, name the club, location & last year of membership.

_____

Identifiable Tattoo's or Scars, state location on body: _____

attach passport photo here

Signature: _____ Date: _____

HAMCIF94—use separate sheet if necessary for answers or tattoo photos

EURO MEETING
December 6, 1996

MC Lichtenstein to become a full H.A. charter (340 yes 58 no) as from 6th December 1996 Hells Angels MC Lichtenstein.

Meeting told of some new clubs in Denmark and people visiting Thailand.

It was said Thailand was a good place for a holiday and more members should try going there. Some Swiss members regarded Thailand as ther second home.

FINLAND: From 8th October new hangaround club "Backwoods" MC from north Finland (550 km north of Helsinki).

ENGLAND: England understands the difficulties of learning languages, but world and Euro meetings are held in English, so members prospects and hangarounds must try to learn English. Come and stay in England for a while and we will help you!

GERMANY: Gave interview with biker news concerning other clubs working with the police against H.A. to be published soon. If possible they would like to print and distribute the interview in magasines in England, United States, rest of Europe etc.

Want to register and trademark B.R.M. [Big Red Machine.]

Trial in Hamburg—Leal expert says we have a strong case against the govt. As the law stands, no company, organisation or club can be banned for life.

SWEDEN: Malmoe has split into 2 charters, Malmoe and Nomads. Goyler had his house broken into and had some T-shirts and sweatshirts stolen so they are in the wrong hands somewhere.

TRADEMARK: Asked for information on Italian video that infringes trademark. Copies to be given to East and West Coast U.S.A.

E.U. trademark lodged on 1st April.

HELLS ANGELS UNITED STATES PRESIDENTS MEETING
March 26, 1994

OAKLAND CA: Motion brought up to change out bottom rocker to United States, seconded by Minneapolis and is attached. Motion to change prospect patches to Hells Angels with a bottom rocker and a prospect patch instead of a deathhead seconded by S.F.V. will be presented at the next officers meeting.

S.F.V. CA: The Pagans that are living in California are no longer allowed in California as of April 26th.

Banditos Meeting Guidelines

1) The date of the meeting with the "Banditos" is April 2nd at 12:00 noon in Spokane, WA. Representatives should be there April 1st.

2) Our representatives from the East Coast are GREG, GLEN, KEVIN, and PAT, and from the West Coast are CISCO, MARK, CHICAGO JOE, and MIKE, to attend the meeting with the "Banditos."

3) We will back whatever decisions that our representatives make.

4) Washington prospects will wear a Washington bottom rocker.

5) No Banditos in Sweden.

* * *

EAST COAST BUSINESS

1) Regarding Mayor Gullianni wearing our patch. He has sovereign immunity from being sued. [Author's note: This is a reference to New York City mayor Rudolph Giuliani, who, when he was District Attorney in New York, wore the colors of a Hells Angels informant at a press conference in May 1985 to announce the arrest of more than 100 Hells Angels and associates in the FBI's Operation Roughrider. Giuliani, always a showboat, borrowed the colors without permission from the office of a police officer entrusted with their safekeeping, as they were evidence in the trial against the Hells Angels.]

October 18, 1997: Oakland, California

CAPE COD MA: We will be sending information on Terry Kineen (a local HA expert) to all charters. [Author's note: Sergeant Terry Kinneen of the New Hampshire State Police Special Investigations Unit is chairman of the board of the International Outlaw Motorcycle Gang Investigators' Association and has put quite a few Hells Angels behind bars.]

GENERAL BUSINESS

1. We have 5 new charters in Arizona, the final vote was—377 Yes—10 No.

2. Our club and the Banditos in Europe have come to peaceful agreements and there is a truce.

3. George (Ventura). Bobby (Long Island), and Canada will meet with the Banditos.

* * *

REQUEST FOR APPROVAL

MOTION MADE BY: Hells Angels Nomads, New York

DATE: October 18, 1997

PRESENTED TO: HELLS ANGELS UNITED STATES

1) Reason For Request: To generate money for all charters in the United States.

2) Motion or Request: To be able to use the name "Hells Angels" and "Death-head" of our choice for products to be sold to the public mostly kids from the age of 3-12.

i..e.: Action Figure Toys

Motorized Motorcycle Toy

Motorcycle Rockers

Computerized Games

School Backpacks

Coloring Books

Lunch Boxes

Halloween Costumes

Pinball Machines

Puzzles

Wind up Motorcycle and Figure

All Types of Toys in General

50 % of the profits going to be split equally with all Hells Angels charters in the United States to be used however they feel fit, for their clubhouse, lawyer fees, members in jail, etc.

3) Amendments: We can use the name and "Deathheads" of our choice. See samples attached.

COMMENTS: For years everyone and their mother has been making money off of our name and logo. From books, films, postcards, decals, toys, skate boards, etc. AND MAKING A LOT MONEY DOING IT!

It's time Hells Angels Profit From It!

ESPECIALLY the members that have built this Club from Sonny on down who have 30-40 years in the Club. THEY SHOULD BE REWARDED.

MOTION MADE BY: Hells Angels New York State
DATE: 10/15/97
PRESENTED TO: Hells Angels United States

1) REASON FOR REQUEST: The HAMC Calendar has proven to be a success. It is a product that strengthens our trademark and also a financial success. We have a large number of pictures that we have compiled over the last 4 years. The Hells Angels New York State would like to put together a book using these photos. It also would include old photos of Hells Angels and their bikes. 50 % of the profits would go the Corporation and 50% would go to the State.

2) MOTION OR REQUEST: The Hells Angels Motorcycle Club give the Hells Angels New York State approval to print, advertise, and sell this photo

album to the public. It would include the use of the name Hells Angels and the Death Head logo.

WEST COAST OFFICERS MEETINGS
October 19, 1996, Oakland
NEW BUSINESS
BERDOO: Toy Run is December 8th.

OAKLAND: Motion to allow Sonny to use HAMC name in his autobiography and it is attached.

MONTEREY: Pictures of George passed out, he went to the cops and the ATF kicked in our doors looking for stolen property.
SHASTA CO: We were raided last week for stolen property.

GENERAL BUSINESS
George (Ventura) and Bobby (Long Island) will go to Europe as soon as they can.

MOTIONS
Motion made to allow a committee consisting of MIKE HURN (Alaska), GEORGE (Ventura), WAYNE (BERDOO), CISCO (Oakland), DENNIS (Richmond), JEFF (Sacto), RICK (Spokane), BOBBY (Long Island), TEDDY (NYC) and Reps from Canada and Europe deal with Bandito's. THIS IS TO BE A CALL IN VOTE DUE BY SATURDAY, OCTOBER 26, 1996, BY NOON.

Motion made to allow Sonny to use HAMC name in his autobiography.
MOTION MADE BY: Oakland
DATE: 10-4-96
Presented to: United States

1) Reason for Request: Sonny wants to write a story about his life and he wants to use the name "Hells Angels". He would have complete editorial control of this book.

    For the use of the name "Hells Angels Motorcycle Club" Sonny would pay the club $100,000.00 (before taxes) and would try to negotiate $50,000.00 up front and $50,000.00 when the book is published. The split would be 25% to the West Coast treasury, 25% to the East Coast treasury, 25% to the Corporation treasury, and 25% to the Oakland treasury.

    There have been at least 5 books written in the past that used out name and we never got a cent. Also anyone could do an unauthorized biography about Sonny and we couldn't do anything to stop them.

2) Motion or Request: To allow Sonny to use the name "Hells Angels" for his autobiography and sales.

WORLD MOTIONS

To exclude politicians from membership in the club.   Yes 111   No 311 Failed.

To allow Malmoe to make a series of documentaries on the Hells Angels. Yes 163   No 333   Failed.

MOTION MADE BY: United States
DATE: 11-8-96
PRESENTED TO: United States

1) Problem or reason: To make members responsible for their club property and keep non members from wearing or possessing club property. Club property must be kept under strict control to prevent unathorized persons from possessing Hells Angels paraphanalia.

2) Solution: Apply a stiff penalty to any members letting non members wear or possess club property.

3) Motion: Only Hells Angels will wear Hells Angels paraphanalia.

4) Penalty: Put on carpet with penalty of dollar amount to getting kicked out.

MOTION MADE BY: United States
DATE: 11-8-96
PRESENTED TO: United States

1) Problem or reason: To keep members and/or prospects from endangering each others lives.

2) Solution: No weapons will be used when fighting another member or prospect.

3) Motion: No weapons will be used when fighting another member or prospect.

4) Penalty: Put on carpet with penalty of a dollar amount to getting kicked out.

5) Exceptions: Rings, if no time for removal.

MOTION MADE BY: United States
DATE: 11-8-96
PRESENTED TO: United States

1) Problem or reason: To prevent unfair fights between members and/or prospects. Occasionally disputes arise between members and or prospects. It is understood that members and or prospects have a right to one on one regardless of chapter.

2) Solution: Any fighting between members or prospects is one on one.

3) Motion: Any fighting between members or prospects is one on one.

4) Penalty: $100.00 fine.

MOTION MADE BY: United States
DATE: 12-8-96
PRESENTED TO: United States

1) Problem or reason: Irresponsible actions around campfires or campsites such as throwing explosive items in fires can cause injury or uncontrolled wildfires and unnecessary Red Alert situations.
2) Solution: Make a rule that keeps members from throwing any fireworks, paint cans, bullets or anything that may explode into any fire.
3) Motion: No potential explosives will be thrown into any fire at a Hells Angels function.
4) Penalty: $500.00 fine and put on carpet.

MOTION MADE BY: United States
DATE: 11-8-96
PRESENTED TO: United States

1) Problem or reason: To control guns and their use at runs and club functions. On occasion we have runs that are located in places that have good target ranges. To prevent unsafe use of guns we should have a designated time and place for the comfort and safety of all concerned.
2) Solution: Set a time and place for using guns.
3) Motion: Guns on Hells Angels predetermined gun runs will not be displayed unnecessarily after 6:00 pm. They will be fired from dawn to 6:00 pm in a predetermined area only.
4) Penalty: $500.00 fine and put on carpet.

*   *   *

November 16, 1996, Oakland
NEW BUSINESS
OAKLAND: We will celebrate SONNY'S 40, GARY P. 30, LEE's 25, HOWIE's 25, RICH's 20, EDDIE's 18, and LITTLE GARY's 5 year anniversaries at our charte's 40 anniversary party on April 5, 1997. Sonny wants only ONE plaque.

GENERAL BUSINESS

1) GEORGE (Ventura) and BOBBY (Long Island) discussed their trip to Scandinavia.

MOTIONS FROM LAST MONTH
Motion made to allow a committee consisting of MIKE HURN (Alaska), GEORGE (Ventura), WAYNE (Berdoo), CISCO (Oakland), DENNIS (Richmond), JEFF (Sacto), RICK (Spokane), BOBBY (Long Island), TEDDY (NYC)

and Reps from Canada to Europe to deal with the Bandito's. Yes 314 No 69 PASSED

Motion made to allow Sonny to use HAMC name in his autobiography. Yes 327 No 18 PASSED

MOTION MADE BY: West Coast Officers
DATE: 11-16-96
PRESENTED TO: United States

1) Reason for Request: To allow GEORGE (Ventura) and BOBBY (Long Island) meet with George (Banditos) for the purpose of telling the Banditos that if they stop taking in our ex members, ex prospects, and ex hangarounds that would be a sign of good faith and we could possibly have serious discussions (6 months to a year) in the future.

2) Motion or Request: To allow GEORGE (Ventura) and BOBBY (Long Island) meet with George (Banditos).

* * *

December 14, 1996, Oakland
NEW BUSINESS

OAKLAND: Out entire charter has completed our Property Agreement, all other charters should get theirs done, too.

SACTO: Toy Run pack leaves our clubhouse at 11:00 am.

MONTEREY: Toy Run December 22nd.

MOTIONS from Last Month

1) To allow GEORGE (Ventura) and BOBBY (Long Island) meet with George (Banditos). Yes 208 No 4

* * *

January 18, 1997, Oakland.

OAKLAND: We feel that we should not respond to anything directed to us on the Internet. Mike Lessard was kicked out for breaking 86 and lying. [86 is the Hells Angels numeric code for HF, an abbreviation of Hells Angels Forever. It means that once a Hells Angel, always a Hells Angel. And anyone who does something a Hells Angel is not supposed to do, like talk to the police or rat someone out, is no longer a Hells Angel.]

MOTIONS

To allow GEORGE (Ventura) and BOBBY (Long Island) meet with George (Banditos). Yes 350 No 33 PASSED

* * *

February 15, 1997, Oakland

BERDOO: 50 year anniversary party is March, 1998. We will raffle a new bike to help fund the party.

S.F.V.: The people in New Mexico are wearing "Red Devils—New Mexico" patches. Their empty clubhouse was shot at after they started wearing their patches. "Red Devils" pictures and phone lists were passed out.

SHASTA CO: We were raided by the BNE [California Bureau of Narcotics Enforcement] on January 23rd. and they confiscated lots of club property. TOM was charged with felon in possession of a firearm.

GENERAL BUSINESS

Chicago was raided and ROAD was arrested and charged with cocaine and steroids.

The West Coast officers decided that we will stop using "Lightning Bolts" or "Swastikas" on any "Support" items in the future without voting on the motion by Germany. The East Coast will decide at their OM next week.

*   *   *

March 15, 1997, Oakland

NEW BUSINESS

OAKLAND: CHICO is in a halfway house. [Charles (Chico) Manganiello was sentenced to forty years in jail on drug charges in the late 1980s.]

We have decided that Gregg Baker is an informant and is cooperating with law enforcement and we will not patronize his establishment, The Byron Station. We have the paperwork that we base it on.

Someone has set up an Oakland web page on the internet and we would like to know who set it up.

ANCHORAGE: Asked if we are doing anything to stop the book "Into the Abyss".

GENERAL BUSINESS

BOBBY (Long Island) and GEORGE (Ventura) had a meeting with 2 Banditos (George and Lee).

BILLY (Salem) discussed the phone cards they are starting to produce. He will send us detailed information.

If any charter has any members newly committed to jail would you get their name and address to O.B. Dave (Dage). [Author's note: He is publisher of the Hells Angels *Big House Crew* (B.H.C.) newsletter for gang members behind bars.]

*   *   *

April 12, 1997, Oakland

OAKLAND: Memo read from Tim Bobbit ATF, trying to get funding to set us up again. [Author's note: Tim Bobbit is a high-ranking supervisor in the California Bureau of Narcotics Enforcement. The Hells Angels' intelligence network obviously is well connected in the agency's higher levels, as a memorandum requesting funds is seen by a handful of people only and is not accessible by anyone outside the agency's top echelon.]

GENERAL BUSINESS

GEORGE (Ventura) talked with George (Banditos) about several issues. They are upset that we copyrited their name in New Zealand. Johnny A. will discuss this at the next EURO meeting.

MOTION MADE BY: Dago
DATE: 4-12-97
PRESENTED TO: United States
  1) Reason for Request: That we vote to make the "Renegades, Reno" a prospective Hells Angels charter.
  2) Motion or Request: That we vote to make the "Renegades, Reno" a prospective Hells Angels charter.

MOTION MADE BY: SFV
DATE: April 12, 1997
PRESENTED TO: United States
  1) Reason for Request: Request charters to vote to make Red Demons Las Vegas, Nevada, a Hells Angels prospective charter. Number of members— 7. How long hangaround—2 yrs.
  2) Motion or Request: Make Red Demons prospect Hells Angel charter.

*   *   *

May 17, 1997, Oakland

OAKLAND: One of the bars in Byron was blown up and SONNY and the club was blamed for it. SONNY's book is still being worked on.

SONOMA CO: Raymond's ex wife Donna Folkes is 86'ed because she is a rat.

VALLEJO: Investigators are reopening the case of Harry the Horse from 1977. [Author's note: Hells Angels chapter president Harry (The Horse) Flamburis was killed by fellow Hells Angels in 1977 for not wanting the gang to sell drugs. Flamburis was an old-time biker who believed in brotherhood and the biker lifestyle. He had little interest in crime and money. He was shot, welded into a 55-gallon drum, and dumped into the ocean. His body has never been found.]

GENERAL BUSINESS:
GEORGE (Ventura) talked with George (Banditos) about several issues (copy-rite, Sturgis and Iron Lords M/C). The Banditos will not take any more ex Hells Angels into their club.

MOTIONS for 5-17-97
By Nomads: Hells Angels Nomads New York would like permission from the H.A.U.S. to allow any Hells Angels members with their own charter consent to wear United States bottom rockers.

[Author's note: A list of major mandatory runs and host chapters until the year 2003 was handed out.]

1999 U.S.A
FUN RUN—SHASTA CO.
MEMORIAL DAY—SONOMA CO.
JULY 4th—VENTURA
LABOR DAY—RICHMOND
2000 U.S.A.
FUN RUN—FRISCO
MEMORIAL DAY—DAGO
JULY 4th—OAKLAND
LABOR DAY—DALY CITY
2001 U.S.A.
FUN RUN—MONTEREY
MEMORIAL RUN—VALLEJO
JULY 4th—SACTO
LABOR DAY—BERDOO
2002 U.S.A.
FUN RUN—SAN JOSE
MEMORIAL DAY—NOMADS
JULY 4th—S.F.V.
LABOR DAY—SHASTA CO.
2003 U.S.A.
FUN RUN—SONOMA CO.
MEMORIAL DAY—VENTURA
JULY 4th—RICHMOND
LABOR DAY—FRISCO

*   *   *

June 21, 1997, Oakland

OAKLAND: We will not sell anymore support items to the Red Legions M/C Hawaii because the people over there are assholes.

GENERAL BUSINESS

GEORGE (Ventura) talked with George (Banditos) he said that they want to resolve any problems we may have. They will meet in Sturgis.

*   *   *

July 19, 1997, Oakland

GENERAL BUSINESS

GEORGE (Ventura) will meet with George (Banditos) at Sturgis. A proposal by
    Europe regarding the Banditos is attached.

Fritz Clapp will get ahold of New Zealand's lawyer to stop the copywrite of the Banditos name.

*   *   *

August 23, 1997, Spokane, Washington

ANCHORAGE: Our clubhouse was broken into and MONTY's bike and our
    club books were stolen and nothing else.

GENERAL BUSINESS

GEORGE met with George in Sturgis but, nothing was resolved.

MOTION MADE BY: Berdoo

DATE: 8-23-97

PRESENTED TO: United States

  1) Reason for Request: Our Arizona prospects have prospects have been prospecting for more than 13 months and we feel they are now ready for full membership.

  2) Motion or Request: That we vote all 5 of our Arizona prospect charters in as full members.

*   *   *

September 13, 1997, Oakland

RICHMOND: We are filing suit against the NHRA because they will not allow members to wear patches when racing. [Author's note: The National Hot Rod Association, like many organizations, bars, and other establishments, bans all biker colors because of the threat posed to spectators and the event by clashes between gangs.]

    DALY CITY: Snowboard found with Hells Angels on it and it was turned over to the corporation.

    S.F.V. Whorehouse run is October 4th and 5th. [Author's note: The whorehouse run is a two- to three-day event during which the bikers travel from one whorehouse to another in Nevada on the California border and sample the wares. The establishments are legal in Nevada. Jack Kerouac's daughter once worked in one.]

SHASTA CO. Motion brought up to help PHIL fight a case against gang terrorism and it is attached.

MOTIONS

By Berdoo, To vote our Arizona prospects in as members   Yes 201   No 3

MOTION MADE BY: Shasta Co.

DATE: 9-13-97

PRESENTED TO: California

1) Reason for Request: Because of charges filed following arrest in August of this year of 186.22 (B) (1) P.C. Special Allegations - Street Terror and 11370.2 C HS Special Allegation - Narcotics Prior.

2) Motion or Request: If convicted on Street Terror charges "that were written for street gangs" may allow other counties to do the same against other members and or clubs, in California and other states.

3) Amendments: Donation of $50.00 per member in California to help pay legal costs in the above case.

*   *   *

October 18, 1997, Oakland

FRISCO: We will clarify what is meant by "not talking about charter business to other charter" to our younger members.

RICHMOND: We received a letter of apology from the owner of Sears Point raceway for not allowing members to wear their patches when racing.

SAN JOSE: STEVE is in jail for murder with enhancments. JIM is in jail for manufacturing with child endangerment enhancments. No patches in the courtroom. There were numerous raids at other members homes.

SACTO: Fun Drags are next weekend. Gang task force will be there. [Author's note: The Hells Angels know well ahead of time, from their informants within police departments, when and where police special teams will be. They probably get their information through administrative offices, as police departments require so much paperwork for budget and overtime approval before projects are authorized. Every cop works in secret and doesn't even tell his wife, then all the paperwork is handed over to a civilian clerk whose desk and computer are accessible to anyone in the office. DUH.]

*   *   *

November 22, 1997, Oakland

BERDOO: Toy Run December 14th.

OAKLAND: Oakland will put up our clubhouse for bail for San Jose.

SAN JOSE: We need any instance where club minutes were taken by the cops in raids and returned, call FRANK. If anyone has property they can put up for bail we would appreciate it. We need about $800K more. We will be raffling a new bike for defense money. We will have a fund raising dinner on February 21st.

S.F.V. Asked what is allowed to be used on the Internet regarding our club name and deathhead. A motion should be written to regulate our use of our name and deathhead.

VALLEJO: Anyone that has any dirt on Charlie or Mike contact Sonoma or us.

NOMADS: Trekkies are wearing red and white "Hells Aliens" patches. We have a video of bandito George with the rock machine in Canada.

BRITISH COLUMBIA: New Canadian bill C95 in effect that resembles RICO.

GENERAL BUSINESS

TEDDY (NYC) attended for the East Coast. He was stopped on his way home from Jo'burg and all his paperwork was confiscated and copied.

Discussed the continuing peace with the banditos GEORGE (Ventura) will call bandito George one more time.

* * *

December 20, 1997, Oakland

S.F.V. More Internet discussion. We will contact Tony from S&S enterprises about separating his SS website from our merchandise.

SHASTA CO: Gang enhancment was dropped on PHIL.

NOMADS, WA: George (Washington) is the new head of the Banditos.

GENERAL BUSINESS

GEORGE (Ventura) talked to George from the Banditos.

Would all charters compile copies of all the parole restrictions on all of its members and send them to Richmond to help fight non-association.

* * *

January 17, 1998, Oakland

BERDOO: Our 50-year anniversary party will be celebrated March 14th. If anyone has any trouble using the 8181 code to get rooms for the Fun Run call WAYNE.

SAN JOSE: JETHRO was charged with obstruction of justice and steroids and his wife were arrested for steroids. Be careful of what you write when writing to the jail. BOB B. was arrested for possession of a firearm after being convicted of domestic violence.

GENERAL BUSINESS

GEORGE (Ventura) talked to George from the Banditos.

MOTION MADE BY: Richmond
DATE: 2/14/98
PRESENTED TO: West Coast
1) Problem or reason: Our Death Head being used in advertising support items on the Internet.
2) Solution: Don't use it.
3) Motion: No one be allowed to use our DEATH HEAD for advertising on the Internet.
4) Penalty: Immediate removal from the Internet and $1000 fine for Charter responsible.

*   *   *

February 14, 1998, Oakland
OAKLAND: We want everyone to know that Margaret from SFV is 86ed from Oakland, and it is our wishes that she be 86'd from the club because she refuses to stop communicating with Branda, Steve Browns ex-wife, who ratted on him, after she was told to stop. Don't buy any more snowboards, and don't take them either. *People* magazine wants to do an interview with Sonny and Norm Green, WAYNE (Berdoo) will discuss it with Sonny.

SAN JOSE: We were all raided by several agencies for 187, 211 and 186.22 and all club property was confiscated from the clubhouse and members and associates homes. We are going to need financial help with this case against our club. (approximately $5 to $7K for the return of our property.)

S.F.V. Asked why the 50-year-anniversary picture is scheduled for 9:00 am.

NOMADS, WA: There might have been 4 Montana Banditos in town. We should rethink CHUCK ZITO's toy idea.

GENERAL BUSINESS
GEORGE (Ventura) talked to George from the Banditos again.

MOTION MADE BY: Richmond
DATE: 2/14/98
PRESENTED TO: West Coast
1) Problem or reason: The words HELLS ANGELS being used in advertising support items on the Internet.
2) Solution: Don't use our name in advertising without permission.
3) Motion: No one be allowed to use the name HELLS ANGELS for advertising on the Internet without first getting an O.K. from an O.M.
4) Penalty: Immediate removal from the Internet & Charter responsible put on carpet.

MOTION MADE BY: Richmond

DATE: 2/14/98

PRESENTED TO: West Coast

1) Problem or reason: Our Death Head being used in advertising support items on the Internet.
2) Solution: Don't use it.
3) Motion: No one be allowed to use our DEATH HEAD for advertising on the Internet.
4) Penalty: Immediate removal from the Internet and $1000 fine for Charter responsible.

*　　*　　*

March 7, 1998, Oakland

OAKLAND: Sonny wants to remind people that the cover of his book will have a Deathhead and Hells Angels on it and it will be advertised on the Internet. The Outlaws contacted us for help. CISCO will talk to them and keep the East Coast notified. Everybody keep it off the phone.

SAN JOSE: The cops are taking bikes from citizens with support stickers on them unless they take the stickers off. Easyriders wants to do an article on our civil rights violations. Discuss this with your membership and bring any objections to the next WCOM.

MONTEREY: February 19th 6 of us were arrested for robbery and receiving stolen property with a gang enhancement. We are expecting 6 more arrests and may need help with bail.

ORANGE CO: A production company is doing a documentary and would like to do some filming at the swap meet.

GENERAL BUSINESS

GEORGE (Ventura) talked to George from the Banditos and thins are working on a positive note. George (Banditos, Washington) moved to Texas.

*　　*　　*

EAST COAST OFFICERS MEETINGS

June 12, 1996, Omaha, Nebraska

NEW YORK CITY: There's an artist's picture/article in *Easy Rider* magazine (Aug. '96) that The City feels is very offensive. Same artist has a book out w/ picture included, will get w/ West Coast to resolve. The Movie proposal is not a dead issue. Any items for *The Big Red Machine Catalog* go thru N.Y.C.

GENERAL BUSINESS

Discussed Vietnam Vets USA, meeting @ West Coast. Each E.C. Charter related the specifics of the the Vets pertaining to their geographical area & compiled a list for the W.C. to have for future meeting.

*   *   *

August 31, 1996, Long Island, New York

NEW YORK CITY: Picture in Easy Rider was an oversight. They apologized, won't happen again. Movie motion shot down by Canada.

    CHARLESTON: Found club related material on Internet.

GENERAL BUSINESS

E.C. asked for advance notice of another meeting on W.C. w/ Vietnam Vets M.C.

*   *   *

November 23, 1996, Omaha, Nebraska

MINNEAPOLIS: Lost first court case against local police. Now liable for their costs. Two (2) more cases still pending.

    ROCKFORD: Passed around a patch from the cops "Operation Fallen Angel."

*   *   *

January 4, 1997, Cleveland

GENERAL BUSINESS

Motion PASS for Bobby and George to talk with Banditos   142 yes to 29 no

MOTION MADE BY: Hells Angels Nomads, New York, East Coast

DATE: January 4th, 1997

PRESENTED TO: Hells Angels Motorcycle Club East Coast And a copy to be givin to the Hells Angels Motorcycle Club West Coast Representative.

1. Problem or reason: No other motorcycle club wears a United States bottom rocker.
2. Solution: Hells Angels Motorcycle Club would be the first major motorcycle club to wear a United States bottom rocker.
3. Motion: Hells Angels Nomads, New York, would like the authority from the Hells Angels United States, to let the Hells Angels Nomads, East Coast, and the Hells Angels Nomads, West Coast "IF THEY CHOOSE" and any future Nomads that may start in any state, and any charter, in the United States who wishes, to wear a United States bottom rocker.

    "NOMADS" means just that, we go anywhere we want in the United States, and I that matter the world, like any and all Hells Angels!

    "BUT!" Nomads would be able to show it by wearing a United States bottom rocker with a Nomads chest tag!

    A good example for some Charters to change to a United States bottom rocker would be: new states will wear there state rocker for 2 yrs. Before using U.S. if they choose.

Recently Chuck Zito, HAMC, Nomads, New York was filming a movie in Memphis, Tenn. For three weeks, where there are two major motorcycle clubs in that city. Chuck wore his patch every day and went to local bike shops, other shops and went to a strip club where colors are not allowed and the two major motorcycle clubs are not welcome.

Chuck, refused to take off his patch, and after a short conversation with the owner of the bar, Chuck was allowed in and everything was on the house, he did the exact same thing in Daytona and Miami Florida.

There were a lot of bike people inside, who they were, who knows. But we're sure they went and told the local assholes tha they saw a Hells Angel with a New York bottom rocker. The locals might of said that's just Chuck Zito, making a movie, He'll be leaving soon?

Solution: If some Charters changed to a United States bottom rocker, and those Hells Angels are seen in other states where there are major motorcycle clubs, they won't know if we started a new charter; if we're thinking about starting a new charter; or if we're already there.

"LET THE ASSHOLES AND THE COPS KEEP GUESSING!"

HELLS ANGELS HAVE ALWAYS SET THE TREND . . . LETS NOT STOP THE TRADITION!

*   *   *

February 22, 1997, Charleston, South Carolina

LOWELL: George at home on bracelet. [Author's note: Some prisoners must wear an electronic bracelet when let out on parole so police can track them.]

ROCKFORD: The CLUBHOUSE, ROGER'S RICK'S house where all raided, ROGER and his Ol'lady where the only ones charged, they were charged with a controled substance. The Clubhouse was condemned on a code violation, they are working to fix.

NEW BUSINESS

There is a 25.00 fine for late or missed Tuesday night fax This will be back into affect immediately [Author's note: The Hells Angels set specific times for all chapters to communicate with each other so that all members are simultaneously informed of major events and can take action if needed.]

MOTION MADE BY: NOMADS N.Y.

DATE: 2/22/97

PRESENTED TO: UNITED STATES

1) Reason for request: To make it harder to single out and identify individuals, and or charter strength.

2) Motion or request: Hells Angels Nomads New York, would like permission

from the Hells Angels United States to allow any Hells Angels members, with their own charter consent, to wear United States bottom rockers.

3) Amendments: New charters will be required to wear their state bottom rockers for two years to identify themselves as a new charter before having the option to wear United States bottom rockers.

* * *

April 19, 1997, Cape Cod, Massachusetts

CLEVELAND: May 17th Blessing of the bikes, and Jail house Rock.

BRIDGEPORT: Wants to bring up Maine for membership, CAPE COD seconded. Motion to be written up. And brought to a U.S. vote. Call in vote to be called into BOBBY LONG ISLAND in two weeks from today's date, May 3rd.

MOTION MADE BY: LONG ISLAND

DATE: 4/19/97

PRESENTED TO: UNITED STATES

1) Reason for Request: When a member is kicked out of the Club in bad standings their is a need to know. There have cases in the past were this was not so, and other charters now knowing their statice, have had association with ex-members. To put an end to this a 24 hour notice must be send out to all charters on the East Coast, informing them of the ex-members statice.

2) Motion or Request: 24 hour notification of ex-members statice by their charter, to all East Coast charters.

* * *

May 24, 1997, South Bend, Indiana

CHICAGO: We have a new clubhouse, hope to be in it in a month.

ROCKFORD: Paul conv. On 2nd degree murder, sentancing july 2.

* * *

August 2, 1997, USA RUN

SALEM: The Clubhouse was raided, they said that they would be back, with warrants for members.

CAPE COD: A Lawyer looking into the property in Laconea for the Run site, paper work should be at next ECOM.

* * *

October 25, 1997, Durham, North Carolina

ROCKFORD: The city of Rockford will assess our Clubhouse, after this happens they will make us a money offer, if it is acceptable we'll start looking for a new location.

MAINE: Book proposal was discussed.

NEW BUSINESS

Vote taken on whether BOBBY, LONG ISLAND, needs to talk to certain MC's. The East Coast vote was a unanimous—no

There are two new information sheets. These forms will keep out country uniform. They are attached to these minutes, take these forms and make copies for your charter. One is a member info. sheet, the other to be used for ex-member info., This form will be sent out (with a photo, within 24 hours of that member/prospect leaving the club, regardless of his status.)

*   *   *

February 7, 1998, Charleston, South Carolina

LOWELL: Bucky got 6 months for civil rights violation case.

SALEM: BILLY is out of the Club in band standings. MONTY has been busted to prospect. DON is in jail on a rape case, bond is set at $50.000.00. JOHN and TONY still waiting on trial.

BRIDGEPORT: DANNY got charged with 1st degree murder, out on bond.

NOMADS: CHANCE also arrested for rape in Massachusetts. Motion discussed about HA toys.

*   *   *

HELLS ANGELS OAKLAND CHAPTER MEETINGS

July 30, 1989

Sonny called, said he's doing great. [Author's note: Barger was in jail for his part in a scheme to murder Outlaws in Chicago in 1987.]

September 17, 1989

Viet-Nam Vets met bogus Hells Angel, accepted his patch (Omaha has it) and accompanied him to the tattoo shop.

September 24, 1989

The bogus Hells Angel involved with the Viet-Nam Vets M/C did not get his tattoo's covered, but Omaha does have the bogus patch.

Viet-nam Vets do have one cop in thier club in Alska.

October 1, 1989

Fuki's indictment postponed until next Thursday. Government wanted Fuki to plead guilty to 2 machine guns and forfiet all cash confiscated.

Michael Malve needs old motor cycle magazines to copy club articles for proposed Hells Angels magazine.

October 8, 1989

Fuki may plead guilty to 1 machine gun and forfiet all cash confiscated.

Flash had meeting with corporation lawyers about revising corporation by-laws in relation to our law suit against producers of "Nam Angels" movie.

Everyone to get thier belt buckle redone that is not happy with it.

October 15, 1989

Fuki will plead guilty to possesion of a short barreled rifle and forfiet all cash confiscated.

Law suit will be filed Tuesday 10-17-89 against producers of "Nam Angels" movie.

Last Friday Mark's bike got knocked over in the clubhouse driveway and his gas cap with the club logo on it was stolen.

October 29, 1989

Donnie will organize our Thanksgiving dinner and Pop will get our usual 4 turkey's and 4 ham's and no ducks.

November 19, 1989

Retraction was printed in the Modesto Bee that only said that we weren't sponsoring the Toy Run in the article. Cisco tried calling the person the article was about [Kelcie Blades] again and will continue to do so.

Eddie and Deakon went to South Dakota and have a chance to buy some land for U.S.A. Run site near Sturgis.

November 26, 1989

We will be in trial on the law suit that was filed against producers of the "Nam Angels" movie by March 8, 1990. To start with we are asking for attorney's fee's, $10,000 up front, and to stop the movie immediately. Flash is on top of it.

Judge Johnstone (KY) wrote a good letter for Sonny but, denied a couple of his motions.

The book "Taking Care of Business" has been republished under the name "Three Can Keep a Secret if Two are Dead," Flash needs a copy.

December 17, 1989

The first of each month we will accept donations for our brother's in the joint. Be aware that the fed's always has put on a media blitz against us just before they come down on us with some phoney bust.

December 21, 1989
Flash talked about a possible deal with Roget Gorman on the movie lawsuit. Which would be to destroy all remaining copies and $50,000.00 of which $35,000.00 would go to attorneys.

Fuzzy picked up copy of the new reissued book "Taking Care of Business" for Flash and the corporation.

Dick would like a copy of the unedited version of the 60 Minutes interview.

Nick (White Rock) and a Bandito member got busted for 12 counts of trying to buy drugs from a federal agent.

December 29, 1989
Flash read a letter from out trademark attorney's to the publisher of the new book "Three Can Keep a Secret if Two Are Dead" by Yves Lavigne. (Reissue of "Taking Care of Business") We all agreed to send it.

Fuzzy is pissed off because someone is throwing away the smut magazines in the shitter and wants to know who it is.

January 14, 1990
Everyone from Monterey was raided last Tuesday.

January 28, 1990
Mark tried to buy a handgun and the gun dealer was denied permission to sell it by the A.T.F. and has no felony record. He is going to find out why.

May 13, 1990
Submit ideas for a plaque or headstone in the cemetary as a memorial to brothers such as Norton and Lovely Larry.

No one except Hells Angels or Oakland prospects are allowed to open the cash register for any reason.

May 20, 1990
Fuki is riding down to the Lompoc Camp on June 9th to turn himself in on June 11th. Anyone wanting to ride down with him will leave the clubhouse at 10:00 am.

A jacket that Mickey Rorke wore in the movie "Year of the Dragon" has an old army patch on it not a "Death Head". Chuck (Nomads, N.Y.) has the jacket now.

July 15, 1990
We are talked with Dennis Hopper about doing a movie that will be a true story about SONNY and everyone here voted unanimously for it.

July 22, 1990
Motion: Any member caught using a needle for any purpose other than a life threatening situation will lose his patch.

August 19, 1990
MIKE SHEELY (Richmond) got shot in the leg last Wednesday and is O.K.
   A bomb was found in SAM's (Akron) driveway at home.

October 7, 1990
Cisco talked with SONNY about the "movie" vote. He also talked with WILLIAM (Durham) at length about it. The main objection is actors wearing patches.
   Motion: That all our HELLS ANGELS patches be made in Austria from the same computer program or design that Austria is now using.

October 21, 1990
Letter read from Auckland and a letter from Bogus Hells Angels in Johanesburg Africa requesting information on how to become prospects.
   Bring up letter from Auckland about Johanesburg Africa. We should get ahold of both Auckland and France to see what their thoughts are.

November 4, 1990
We talked about Red on White Membership cards and will vote on it next week. We will then decide weather to: destroy last years membership cards; hang them collectively in the club house; or let members keep them.

February 2, 1992
We decided that the 25 year members would decide what the 25 year plaque would look like. The 25 year members decided to use the "Oakland Forever" centerpiece with laser pictures surrounding it and SONNY's picture in the top center.
   SEND LETTERS TO OUR BROTHERS IN JAIL.
   We will exclude anyone under the age of 18 years old from attending our club party's (excluding Thansgiving, Christmas, or other family orientated gatherings).

February 16, 1992
Gary has a price of $1200.00 for a new fence behind the garage.
   CISCO is checking on new letters for the front of the clubhouse.
   FLASH is mounting the cameras and monitors.

February 23, 1992
The people that are writing the screen play for SONNY's movie will be invited to our anniversary party.

February 28, 1992
We read a letter from Australia asking for donations to fight the immigration laws keeping out of the country.

The Orleans, France chapter is out on the streets.

The hearing down south regarding the helmet law was lost and will now go to the appeals court.

March 13, 1992
MIKE LESSARD was sentenced to 5 years under the old guidelines with 5 years probation and a $200.00 fine and has to turn himself in on April 1st to Big Spring, Texas.

We need blankets, pillows, pillow cases, sheets and towels for the clubhouse.

April 3, 1992
The feds are out and about trying to keep their phoney jobs.

January 3, 1993
Our 1993 membership cards will be red, white and blue.

GUINEA is on top of HELLS ANGELS vs. Marvel Comics [Author's note: The Hells Angels sued Marvel Comics for a new comic book heroine called Hell's Angel. The company changed the book's title to Dark Angel after five issues.]

Oregon is prosecuting "Bug eyed" Bob McClure and then BUCK (Nomads) for the Margoe Compton murder and feds will be running the show, so be ready for a big smear campaign against the club with or without conviction.

CISCO will check on a toy run for inmates in state prisons for next year.

Guinea will have Fritze contact Gorman about the Peter Fonda movie "Wild Angel."

Rick Talbot was arrested in front of his shop for possession of a concealed weapon and he was set up for possession of a controlled substance.

January 8, 1993
Steve is setting a date for a C.P.R. class here at the clubhouse in February.

January 15, 1993

Hells Angels vs. Marvel Comics status is; Marvel Comics will donate $35,000.00 to Ronald McDonald House in both our names and agrees to not use the name Hell's Angel or Hell's Angel with any of their characters or publications.

January 22, 1993

HELLS ANGELS vs. Marvel Comics status: We will issue a joint statement with Marvel Comics that Marvel Comics will donate $35,000.00 in both our names.

EDDIE and WILLIE checked out Julie's house in San Jose. She owes way too much in back payments and has no way of repaying a loan and does not seem to be making much headway towards a job.

ROBERT (Daly City) is having a blood drive on Saturday April 10, in Palo Alto for OATS (Charleston).

The prospect club from Aarhus Denmark became a charter December 31, 1992.

Hells Angels World has a new hangaround club called "Overkill M/C" from Helsinki Finland.

February 12, 1993

We will arrange to have everyone that goes to the U.S.A. run ride through Sturgis together in a pack. Suggestion: We do it after the U.S.A. run picture is taken.

We want to enforce the decision that was made at the last W.C.O.M. that states; "The West Coast wants any charter that has any members in Virginia to have their members return immediately and forget about Virginia for now." This means to forget about Virginia until the West Coast officers change their decision regardless of whatever the East Coast decides. If any member does not want to abide by the West Coast officers decision we want them brought up for their patches.

March 5, 1993

Mickey Roarke is going to film at the next "Sturgis Rally". He also wants to film Hells Angels in exchange for an uncertain dollar amount. We would like CISCO to negotiate the deal and bring it back to the club.

March 12, 1993

Manaus, Brazil is now a charter.

South Africa will be voted on this World Run for full membership, so all chapters should have their votes ready.

April 22, 1993

Motion: That our charter adopt a "Bullion Crest" gold wire "Hells Angels, deathhead, MC, and Oakland bottom Rocker" badge to wear on the front of our patch.

Motion: That we all wear this "Bullion Crest" directly under our enamel pin.

We want to bring up that we sponser the fuel for the helicopter that is going to go up on Mt. Everest to retreve the garbage that has been left on it by climbers, over the last 30 years.

April 30, 1993

THINGS $ ARE COMING MISSING FROM THE C.H. WE WILL SOLVE THIS AGAIN.

Mike Musick got a separate electric meter put in for the tenants next door.

SONNY had a great trip to the NCOM convention in Oklahoma. He received an award for Lifetime Achievement For Motorcycle Riding.

June 18, 1993

There is a baby shower at the C.H. on July 24th.

Where are the two missing couch cushions.

June 11, 1993

There is a new H.A.M.C. chapter in Darwin, Australia since April 2, 1993.

June 25, 1993

Ex fed Bertoloni is now a P.I.

August 6, 1993

Johnny B. is starting on the membership cards, the deathhead will be full color like our patch.

We are all in favor of the club paying for teeth for ALBERT and he will let us know the cost.

The parole board told HOWIE he would have to quit the club to get an early release date, he refused and they gave him the earliest possible date anyway in 1996. They changed their mind, HOWIE's parole date is now 1999.

August 13, 1993

2 Mass. members were jumped by someone (we believe it was the cops) in Janesville, Wisconsin and beat up pretty bad. The papers said it was the Outlaws, but we think that that's bullshit.

August 20, 1993

The Banditos in Washington are snivelling about our prospect charter there. We need to talk about the Banditos at the O.M. tommorow.

From GEORGE (Ventura): Taco from the Outlaws swears they do not have a new charter in Jainesville, Wisconsin and that he would go there with us to help us find out who did it.

September 3, 1993

The Banditos were told they better not have any problems with our prospect charter in Washington.

September 24, 1993

The Whorehouse Run will be on Oct. 2nd and 3rd.

October 1, 1993

MARK's house was raided yesterday by the O.P.D. they took his new bike and some guns and killed his dog. No one was charged.

October 8, 1993

Muscular Dystrophy ride in Santa Clara next Saturday.

October 22, 1993

Ex-member Rick Risner's time is up to get his club tattoo out dates. If you see him, escort him to the tattoo parlor.

A couple of members will start to keep a record ("the Keepers of the BIG BOOK") of what members are or are not doing for the club after the beginning of the year. [Author's note: Live Free, Ride Free, eh?]

December 3, 1993

The small bedroom in the back will only contain corporation and trademark materials only and therefore no one will have any need to go in there any more.

We are going to strive to keep our meetings more positive in the future.

We paused the meeting and pretended it was over, then we called the prospects and hangarounds in to put tables away. About ten minutes later Cisco mentioned that we had forgotten something. He then mentioned a barbeque at the Dragons tomorrow then read the minutes to refresh his memory, Then he told Little Robert and Fry "Oh yea, You Guys are New Oakland Hells Angels.!"

December 10, 1993

If someone does not want to to get bailed out of jail right away it is up to that person to notify the bondsman or he will get bailed automatically.

Oakland Business for the W.C.O.M.

December 11, 1993

Our trademark attorney is filing suit against 8 Tiawanese companies using our logo.

We need to get some more club flags made. Where?

Grateful Dead at the Coliseum this weekend. Leave clubhouse XSaturday at 8:00 pm.

*   *   *

The following pages contain an FBI "WANTED" poster for Outlaws national president Harry Joseph (Taco) Bowman, who was caught in March 1999, and a variety of Hells Angels documents. Read them carefully.

WANTED BY THE FBI

Racketeering Influenced Corrupt Organizations (RICO); RICO Conspiracy;
Conspiracy to Distribute Controlled Substances; Use of Violent Crimes in Aid of
Racketeering; Distribution and Possession with Intent to Distribute Controlled
Substances; Malicious Damage or Destruction by Explosive of Property Affecting
Interstate Commerce; Possession of a Firearm by a Convicted Felon

**ARMED AND
EXTREMELY
DANGEROUS**

Harry Joseph Bowman

Aliases: Harry Bouman; David Bowman; Harry Bowman; Harry J.
Bowman; Harry Joe Bowman; David Charles Dowman; Harry
Douman; Harry Tyree; "Taco"; and "T"

THE CRIME

Harry Joseph Bowman, international president of the Outlaws
Motorcycle Club, is wanted for his alleged involvement in violent
racketeering acts to include murders, bombings, drug trafficking,
extortion, firearms violations, and other acts of violence.

Bowman was allegedly involved in the murders of two Outlaws'
members and may have participated in the murder of a rival
motorcycle club member. The indictment alleges that he ordered the
bombings of rival motorcycle clubhouses.

DOB: July 17, 1949
Sex: Male
Height: 5'10"
Weight: 190 pounds
Race: White
Hair: Black
Eyes: Brown

REMARKS

Bowman heads the Outlaws' operations in more than 30 cities in the
United States and some 20 chapters in at least four other countries.
Bowman may be guarded by members of the Outlaws.

Bowman has multiple tattoos reflecting his association with the
Outlaws Motorcycle Club. He has tattoos on his back and upper right
arm of a skull and crossed pistons with the word "Outlaws" in black
above and the word "Detroit" in black below. He also has a swastika
tattoo on his right forearm, a "Merlin the Magician" figure on his left
forearm, and several other tattoos on both arms. Bowman has scars on
his chin, right arm, and abdomen and sometimes has a mustache,
goatee, or beard.

REWARD

The FBI is offering $50,000 for information leading to the
apprehension of Harry Joseph Bowman.

HELLS ANGELS MOTORCYCLE CLUB
FUNERAL INFORMATION & INSTRUCTIONS

Name:_____   Date:_____

AKA:_____   Military Service:_____

D.O.B.:_____   Birth Place:_____

SS#:_____   DL#:_____   State:_____

Date Joined Hells Angels:_____
Original Charter:_____
Charter at Time of Death:_____

Wife/Girlfriend's Name:_____

Mothers Name_____   Phone:_____
Mothers Address_____
Fathers Name_____   Phone:_____
Fathers address_____

List names of Brothers, Sisters, X-wife(s), Children, and addresses if
known:
_____
_____
_____
_____
_____

There is always a chance of your untimely death, so please fill out
the following:

Preferred Place of Burial:
1st Choice:_____
2nd Choice:_____
Type of Service:_____
Special song Request:_____

Pall Bearors:_____
_____
_____
_____

                                        Favorite Picture

SPECIAL INSTRUCTIONS: Use this space to briefly mention any special
request concerning the Funeral itself - especially important where a
Hells Angel's Funeral is requested.
_____
_____
_____
_____
_____
_____

Signature:_____Witness:_____

HELLS ANGELS MOTORCYCLE CORPORATION
4021 FOOTHILL BLVD.
OAKLAND, CA. 94601

I, _____ do hereby acknowledge and agree with the HELLS ANGELS MOTORCYCLE CLUB, hereinafter referred to as HAMC, and it's Licensed Charters hereinafter referred to as "LICENSEES", to the following:

1. The right to ownership of any and all articles bearing the name "HELLS ANGELS" and/or the winged skull insignia/logo known as a "DEATH HEAD" (both of which are registered with the United States Patent Office, the numbers being listed below in this document but, not limited to) are the sole and legal property of HAMC.

2. I may from time to time or on an ongoing basis, subject to termination at any time be permitted to have in my possession, to wear or display in accord with rules of the HAMC and its charter items bearing the above described terms and Logo. I agree that the permission to possess on a temporary basis, to wear and display these articles is subject to revocation at any time and for any or not reason at the sole option and discretion of the HAMC.

3. I agree that by granting me the permission to possess, display or wear these articles, the ownership of said articles and or logo shall in no way vest in me. These articles constitute, but are not limited to, the HELLS ANGELS vest/jacket commonly referred to as "colors", belt buckles, jewelry, T-shirts, hats and/or any other material item(s) bearing the afore-mentioned name and/or insignia/logos.

4. It is further agreed that possession by me, of any above mentioned article whether created or by me personally or at my direction, does not in any way, shape or form constitute legal ownership of the item(s) in question, but merely identifies me as a member in good standing of HAMC and it's licensees.

5. I specifically agree that in the event I am permitted to create, design or manufacture any article, item of clothing, patches or any other item whatsoever which shall display said logo icon or name, the ownership of said items will be solely vested in the HAMC, or its authorized Chapter.

6. I further grant a power of attorney to the HAMC or its designated Chapter the right and authority to claim said property at any time whether in my possession or that of another.

7. I agree that the HAMC or its designated chapter shall have the absolute right to institute any and all legal proceedings necessary to retake or to obtain possession of said articles, logo's or items and I agree to cooperate fully in any proceedings which may be instituted.

8.   I further agree to grant Power of Attorney to a duly appointed representative of HAMC, to sign, correspond or engage in any necessary action to retrieve any and all of the aforementioned items, seized by any law enforcement agency and/or their representatives.

9.   It is also understood and agreed, that in the event of my death, or at any point in time at which I am no longer a member in good standing of HAMC and it's licensees, all articles in my possession and control, which are designated by this agreement to be the legal property of HAMC, shall immediately be relinquished to a duly appointed representative of the HAMC, by either myself or my surviving heirs.

United States Registrations	Foreign Registrations	Foreign Registrations	Foreign Applications
1,130,494	85,916 Austria	A-1305 Hong Kong	58-063290 Japan
1,213,647	85,962 Austria	2337/1985 Hong Kong	
1,214,476	A384,045 Australia	233761 Taiwan	
1,243,951	A384,046 Australia	300301 Taiwan	
1,294,586	A384,047 Australia	2056292 Japan	
1,301,050	A384,048 Australia	2056293 Japan	
1,582,050	A384,049 Australia	354,187 Canada	
	A394,453 Australia	356,389 Canada	
	1,200,008 Great Britain	356,390 Canada	
	1,241,283 France	356,391 Canada	
	812870468 Brazil		

EXECUTED this _____ day of_____, 19_____,

at _____, County of_____,

in the State of_____,

_____
Signed (member)

Page 2 of 2

```
HELLS ANGELS MOTORCYCLE CLUB                              INFORMATION
OAKLAND, CA

Date:_____

Full Name:_____

Address:_____

City:_____ State:_____ Zip:_____

D.O.B.:_____ SS#:_____ DL#:_____

Place of Birth:_____

Single/Married/Divorced_____Spouse:_____

Names of Children, if any,_____
_____

Military Service ID#:_____Branch:_____Rank:_____

Dates of Service:_____to_____

Health Insurance:_____ Blood Type:_____

Have you ever been convicted of a felony?_____

Have you ever been incarcerated? If yes, where and when:_____
_____

Inmate/prison I.D.#:_____

Are you currently on parole or probation?_____

Have you ever been AN INFORMANT or WORKED for LAW ENFORCEMENT IN ANY
CAPACITY? (jailer, guard, MP etc.) If so, explain_____
_____

Have you ever belonged to any other MOTORCYCLE CLUBS in the past? If
yes, name the club, location & last year of membership:_____
_____

Identifiable Tattoo's or Scars, state location on body:_____
_____


    -------------------------------------
   |                                     |
   |                                     |
   |                                     |
   |      attach passport photo here     |
   |                                     |
   |                                     |
   |                                     |
    -------------------------------------


SIGNATURE_____DATE:_____

HAMCIF94- use separate sheet if necessary for answers or tattoo photos
```

H.A.M.C. VENTURA
SECURITY FILE

C.D.L.

Front & side
Passport Picture

Social Security
Card

DATE _____ / ___ / _____

NAME _____
     (first)   (last)   (m.

A.K.A. _____
_____

Current Address _____
_____
(city)   (state)   (zip)

STATUS: _____
_____
_____

Comments: _____
_____
_____

By _____
   (SECURITY MAN)
DATE _____ / ___ / _____

KICKED OUT
3/21/97 FROM
HELLS ANGELS OAKLAND

KICKED OUT 5-2-97 FOR
LYING, STEALING & ACTIONS
UNBECOMING OF A HELLS ANGEL.

BAD STANDING

NON ASSOCIATION

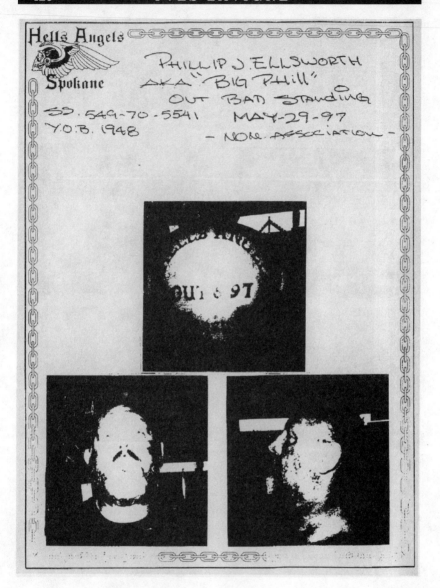

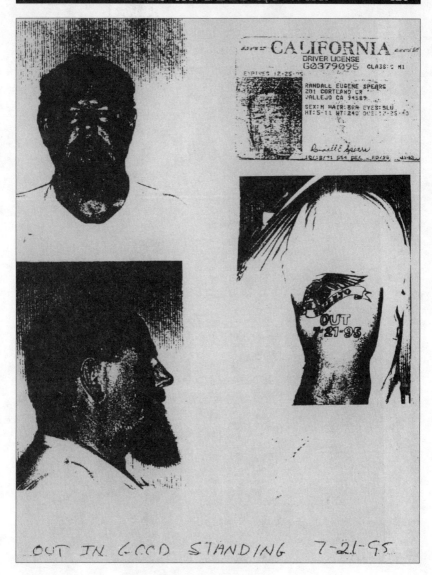

OUT IN GOOD STANDING 7-21-95

H.A.M.C. SHASTA CO.

SECURITY FILE

OUT PHOTO/INFORMATION

NAME____Joseph Donald Grant, "JOE"___

DOB_____April 22, 1950_____

SSN_____572-84-9084_____

OUT DATE_____FEBRUARY 1, 1998_____

CAL.DRIVERS LIC.____S0887462_____

REASON____LYING & STEALING_____

STATUS____BAD STANDING_____

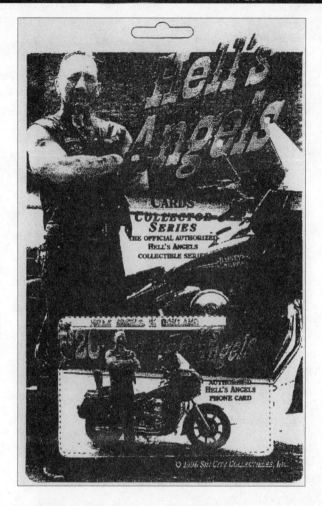

Hells Angel leader Sonny Barger markets himself as "an American legend" and sells countless items bearing his likeness, from bronze busts, to T-shirts, to collector phone cards.

Letter of TRANSFER EXAMPLE

LETTER OF TRANSFER

Date 00/00/00

    This letter is to varify that _____ has
been a member in good standing of HELLS ANGELS MONTEREY
since _____. _____ has the approval and
blessing of HELLS ANGELS MONTEREY to transfer to HELLS
ANGELS _____ within 10 days of this dated letter.

    Further information regarding club participation,
punctuality etc. may be obtained by writing to H.A.M.C.
P.O.Box 1279 Seaside, CA 93955

                         Love & Respect

                         _____
                         SECRETARY
                         H.A.M.C.M.

Has no outsanding debts w/ HAMCM or its membership

CC: H.A.M.C.M.

FORM FOR A MOTION TO PASS A RULE

(This side for Sect'y use only

MOTION MADE BY: United States   MOTION TYPE:

DATE: 12-8-96   DESCRIPTIVE NAME:

PRESENTED TO: United States   MOTION NUMBER:

1) **Problem or reason**: Irresponsible actions around campfires or campsites such as throwing explosive items in fires can cause injury or uncontrolled wildfires and unnecessary Red Alert situations.

2) **Solution**: Make a rule that keeps members from throwing any fireworks, paint cans, bullets or anything that may explode into any fire.

3) **Motion**: No potential explosives will be thrown into any fire at a Hells Angels function.

4) **Penalty**: $500.00 fine and put on carpet.

5) **Exceptions**:

6) **Amendments**:

OSLO

MC

NORWAY

Prospect Chapter Oslo Mc Norway

Po.box 87. Alnabru
0614 Oslo Norway
Phone:+47 22 65 86 66. Fax:+47 22 65 87 81

Visiting address :Strømsvn.222. 0668 Oslo.

WE WOULD LIKE TO INFORM.
YOU ABOUT A BOMB ATTACK
ON OUR CLUB HOUSE TO
NIGHT. IT'S ONLY MATERIAL
DAMAGE. EVERYBODY ARE
DOING FINE!

BE AWARE!

WITH RESPECT

SUPER PROSPECT

Oslo MC
Norway

Fuck em all

WOFJ.DRULES

If a prospect is voted member when he is in jail he receives
his colours only when he leaves jail on his first free time
ore ending his jail sentence.

If a member is in jail and is dishonourable discharged from
the club is it left to the club discretion if the member in
question is removed when he is in jail or when he comes out

Member cards are only given to members.

By producing from H.A. posters + H.A. support stickers
+support items is a registration print compulsory.

H.A. clubs are present on the world meeting.
When not present they pay $ 2000,— fine. When there exuse
is good enough for not appearing the fine is cancelled.
When the club is 3 times not present the club will be
dishournable discharged.

Vote on worldmeeting is 1 man — 1 vote

At the world meeting must H.A. clubs be present ore else
they have no vote.

H.A. clubs must have a steady postadres (Postbox ore
clubhouse) A new adres must be given thru immediate.

Problems among members will be sorted out 1 man to 1 man
It counts for member — member
               prospect — member
No use of ringa — no kicking when hels down.
When seen other wise $ 100 dollar fine.

There must be a 100 % favor vote from the world clubs when a
hangaround-club in an other world(!!!) part want to become
prospectclub.

The same is for becoming H.A. club from prospect club.

Prior U.S. Cl.: 200

United States Patent and Trademark Office

Reg. No. 1,301,050
Registered Oct. 16, 1984

COLLECTIVE MEMBERSHIP
Principal Register

Hells Angels Motorcycle Club (California corporation), a.k.a. Hells Angels
9308 Golf Links Rd.
Oakland, Calif. 94605

For: INDICATING MEMBERSHIP IN A MO-
TORCYCLE CLUB, (U.S. Cl. 200).
First use 1948; in commerce Nov. 1966.
Owner of U.S. Reg. Nos. 1,156,494 and 1,213,647.
The stippling in the drawing is for shading
purposes.

Ser. No. 433,063, filed Jul. 5, 1983.

CRAIG R. GILBERT, Examining Attorney

U.S. Cl.: 200

U.S. Patent and Trademark Office

Reg. No. 1,136,494

Registered May 27, 1980

COLLECTIVE MEMBERSHIP MARK
Principal Register

Hells Angels, Frisco, inc. (California corporation)
1606 12th Ave
San Francisco, Calif. 94122

For: INDICATING MEMBERSHIP IN AN ASSOCI-
ATION OF MOTORCYCLE DRIVERS (U.S. CL. 200)

First use Jul. 1966; in commerce Jul. 1967

Ser. No. 174,567 Filed Jun. 15, 1978

M. E. BODSON, Primary Examiner

Int. Cls.: 25 and 41

Prior U.S. Cls.: 39 and 107

United States Patent and Trademark Office

Reg. No. 1,294,586

Registered Sep. 11, 1984

TRADEMARK
SERVICE MARK
Principal Register

HELLS ANGELS

Hells Angels Motorcycle Club (California
corporation), a.k.a. Hells Angels
9508 Golf Links Rd.
Oakland, Calif. 94605

For: T-SHIRTS, in CLASS 25 (U.S. CL. 39).
First use Jun. 1983; in commerce Jun. 1983.
For: ENTERTAINMENT SERVICES—NAME-
LY, ARRANGING AND CONDUCTING CON-
CERTS FOR THE BENEFIT OF OTHERS, in

CLASS 41 (U.S. CL. 107).

First use Jun. 1983; in commerce Jun. 1983.

Owner of U.S. Reg. Nos. 1,136,494 and 1,213,647.

Ser. No. 435,328, filed Jul. 20, 1983.

DOMINICK J. SALEMI, Examiner

Nina Conti

...ng used by the proprietor

8262232. 23 August 1996. Class 25: ladies clothing. NINA CONTI LTD, a New Zealand company of Unit 12, Ngauranga Business Park, Tyers Road, Ngauranga Gorge, Wellington, New Zealand, importers, manufacturers and distributors. Address for service, c/- Unit 12, Ngauranga Business Park, Tyers Road, Ngauranga Gorge, Wellington, NZ.

DEMI

Application under Section 28(1)(a)

266296 28 August 1996. Class 25: articles of clothing, headwear, footwear and neckwear. PHILIP AUBYN BERTRAM THOREAU, a New Zealand citizen of 106 Mayoral Drive, Auckland, New Zealand, manufacturers and merchants. Address for service, c/- Baldwin Son and Carey, Level 14, NCR House, 342 Lambton Quay, Wellington 1, NZ. Associated with 266296.

MAZZONI

Proposed to be used by the proprietor

266276 26 August 1996. Class 25: clothing, footwear and headgear. THE FARMER'S TRADING COMPANY LIMITED, a New Zealand company of 270 Neilson Street, Te Papapa, Onehunga, Auckland, New Zealand, manufacturer and merchant. Address for service, c/- A J Park & Son, 8th Floor, Huddart Parker Building, Post Office Square, Wellington, NZ.

Being used by the proprietor

266542 2 September 1996. Class 25: articles of clothing including boots, shoes and slippers; football boots; studs for football boots; ties; T-shirts, shirts, jackets and pants; waterproof jackets and pants; tracksuits; football shorts; jumpers, jerseys and socks; caps and hats; gymnastic and other sporting articles included in this class; headbands; headgear; gloves; socks; scarves and all other goods included in this class. AUSTRALIAN RUGBY UNION LIMITED, an Australian company of Level 7, Rugby House, 12-14 Mount Street, North Sydney, New South Wales 2060, Australia, manufacturers and merchants. Address for service, c/- McCabe & Company, Fraser House, 180-182 Willis Street, Wellington, NZ.

Class 25 — continued

Proposed to be used by the proprietor

A translation of the word "BANDIDOS" is "bandits" or "outlaws"

Registration of this mark shall give no right to the exclusive use, separately, of the combination "1%" and the letters "MG"

266657 4 September 1996. Class 25: clothing and headgear. HELLS ANGELS MOTORCYCLE CORPORATION, a Californian corporation of 6521 Foothill Boulevard, Oakland, California 94601, United States of America, merchant. Address for service, c/- A J Park & Son, 8th Floor, Huddart Parker Building, Post Office Square, Wellington, NZ.

Advertised before acceptance, Section 37(1) (proviso)
Proposed to be used by the proprietor

266656 4 September 1996. Class 25: clothing and headgear. HELLS ANGELS MOTORCYCLE CORPORATION, a Californian corporation of 6521 Foothill Boulevard, Oakland, California 94601, United States of America, merchant. Address for service, c/- A J Park & Son, 8th Floor, Huddart Parker Building, Post Office Square, Wellington, NZ.

ZILCH

Being used by the proprietor

266640 4 September 1996. Class 25: articles of clothing including neckties. DESMOND ROBERTSHAW, a New Zealand citizen of Mark Road, RD 2, Hastings, New Zealand, manufacturer and merchant. Address for service, c/- Henry Hughes, Colenso House, 138 The Ter...

Christchurch 8001, New Zealand, manufacturer. Address for service, c/- 335 Gloucester Street, Christchurch 8001, NZ.

Novelli

Being used by the proprietor

267768 1 October 1996. Class 25: clothing. BARRY GILES PINKER, CATHERINE ANNE PINKER and DAVID PINKER, New Zealand citizens of 40 Rennie Drive, Airport Oaks, Mangere, Auckland, New Zealand, apparel merchants. Address for service, c/- 40 Rennie Drive, Airport Oaks, Mangere, Auckland, NZ.

WUZ-UP

Being used by the proprietor

268224 11 October 1996. Class 25: clothing; headgear. PENIAMINA MATAIO NONOA and ALISON LYNDA NONOA trading in partnership, New Zealand citizens, of 37 Campbell Road, Royal Oak, Auckland, New Zealand, merchants. Address for service, c/- 37 Campbell Road, Royal Oak, Auckland 6, NZ.

NEW ROCK

Being used by the proprietor

268278 14 October 1996. Class 25: clothing, footwear and headgear. SHOE-BIZ NEW ZEALAND LIMITED, a New Zealand company...

The Hells Angels copyrighted the Bandidos and Outlaws colors in New Zealand to prevent the gangs from wearing them in that country. They relinquished the copyrights after they signed truces with the gangs in 1997 and 1999.

**HAMCVA
P.O. BOX 8
A-6842   KOBLACH
VORARLBERG
AUSTRIA**

Howdy Bro´s!

Price List for Patch

Item	# in catalog	Price for one in Swiss currency		In US$ for one
Top Rocker + Deathhead	# 1	80,00 Sfr		64,00 US $
Bottom Rocker	# 2	47,00 Sfr		37,60 US $
Flag	# 4	480,00 Sfr		384,00 US $
All Front Flashes	# 5 till 28	8,00 Sfr		6,40 US $
1 Set Small Deathhead Left & right	# 29 till 31	22,00 Sfr		17,60 US $
Small Patch	# 32 + 33	11,00 Sfr		8,80 US $
Side Rocker	# 34	47,00 Sfr		37,60 US $
		100,00 US $ =		125,00 Sfr.
The exchangerate at the moment:		100,00 Sfr		80,00 US $

Hope this list will help you. For custom we send a special invoice with the order. So the import tax is not that high.

We ship the order UPS collect.

As the exchange rate of the US $ changes every day, please call your local Bank for the exchange rate of today.

If you need the price in another currency, call your local Bank also.

L & R

Werry Sect´y Vorarlberg
A.F.F.A.

PATCH-CATALOGUE

1 **Top Rocker +**
Deathhead

2 **Bottom Rocker + MC**
specify Country
minimum Order 10

4 **Flag** specify
Country

It is possible that it takes a while
till we can supply the flag, because we have to produce 4
flags at once, to keep the price
cheap. So we wait till we have 4
orders of Flags, than we start
production !

Front Flashes Big lettering

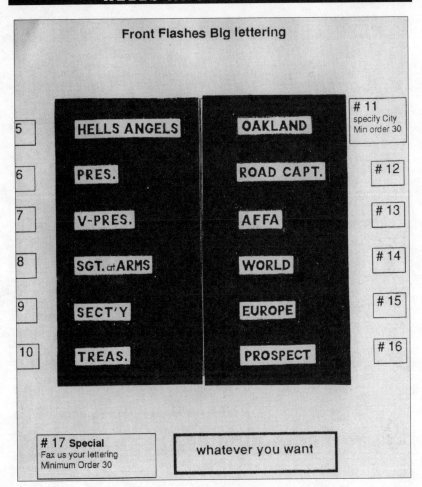

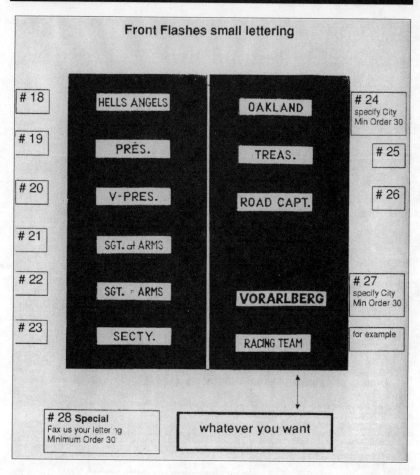

Front Flashes small lettering

18   HELLS ANGELS

19   PRÉS.

20   V-PRES.

21   SGT. at ARMS

22   SGT. = ARMS

23   SECTY.

OAKLAND   # 24 specify City Min Order 30

TREAS.   # 25

ROAD CAPT.   # 26

VORARLBERG   # 27 specify City Min Order 30

RACING TEAM   for example

↕

28 Special
Fax us your lettering
Minimum Order 30

whatever you want

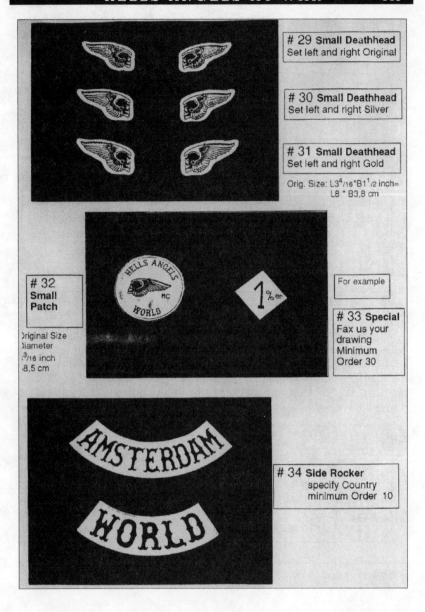

29 **Small Deathhead**
Set left and right Original

30 **Small Deathhead**
Set left and right Silver

31 **Small Deathhead**
Set left and right Gold

Orig. Size: L3^4/16*B1^1/2 inch=
L8 * B3,8 cm

32
**Small
Patch**

Original Size
Diameter
,^{3}/16 inch
8,5 cm

For example

33 **Special**
Fax us your
drawing
Minimum
Order 30

34 **Side Rocker**
specify Country
minimum Order 10

I included a list of Hells Angels chapters and their formation dates in *Hells Angels: Taking Care of Business*. In 1987, there were 1,200 Hells Angels in 67 chapters in 13 countries on 4 continents. There are now 1,700 Hells Angels in 137 chapters (138 if you count the Hamburg chapter which moved to Mallorca, Spain) in 21 countries on 5 continents. The gang is expanding so quickly that several prospective chapters will have been granted full status by the time this list is published.

HAMC Ålborg, Denmark ....October 14, 1996
HAMC Århus, Denmark ....December 31, 1992
HAMC Adelaide, Australia ....October 01, 1983
HAMC Amsterdam, Netherlands ....October 28, 1978
HAMC Anchorage, Alaska ....December 18, 1982
HAMC Antwerp, Belgium.......................................January 15, 1998
HAMC Ashfield, England ....May, 31, 1986
HAMC Auckland, New Zealand ....July 01, 1961
HAMC Barcelona, Spain..April 19, 1997
HAMC Berdoo, California ....March 17, 1948
HAMC Berkshire County, Massachusetts, U.S.A. ....April 24, 1982
HAMC Berlin, Germany ....February 03, 1990
HAMC Bridgeport, Connecticut, U.S.A. ....February 18, 1975
HAMC Brisbane, Australia ....March 21, 1997
HAMC Calgary, Alberta, Canada ....July 23, 1997
HAMC Canaan, Maine, U.S.A..June 13, 1997
HAMC Cape Cod, Massachusetts, U.S.A..........................May 01, 1996
HAMC Cave Creek, Arizona, U.S.A. ....October 18, 1997
HAMC Charleston, South Carolina, U.S.A..............February 07, 1976
HAMC Chicago, Illinois, U.S.A. ....December 02, 1994
HAMC Cleveland, Ohio, U.S.A. ....December 16, 1967
HAMC Copenhagen, Denmark............................December 31, 1980
HAMC Dago, California, U.S.A. ....May 30, 1966
HAMC Daly City, California, U.S.A. ....February 19, 1966
HAMC Darwin, Australia ....April 02, 1993
HAMC Durban, South Africa...............................September 06, 1997
HAMC Durham, North Carolina, U.S.A. ....July 24, 1973
HAMC East End (Vancouver),
   British Columbia, Canada ....December 22, 1983
HAMC East Side, Sweden (Stockholm chapter split) 1998
HAMC Edmonton, Alberta, Canada ....July 23, 1997
HAMC Essex, England ....August 15, 1976

HAMC Fairbanks, Alaska, U.S.A. ....December 18, 1982
HAMC Flagstaff, Arizona, U.S.A. ....October 18, 1997
HAMC Frisco, California, U.S.A. ....August 01, 1954
HAMC Fulton, Kentucky, U.S.A...................................June 29, 1985
HAMC Ghent, Belgium ....July 15, 1997
HAMC Göteborg, Sweden ....May 15, 1999
HAMC Haarlem, Holland ....January 19, 1980
HAMC Halifax, Nova Scotia, Canada ....December 05, 1984
HAMC Hamar, Norway..May 8, 1999
HAMC Hamburg, Germany ....March 16, 1973
HAMC Haney, British Columbia, Canada ....June 13, 1987
HAMC Helsingborg, Sweden ....February 27, 1996
HAMC Helsinki, Finland ....March 23, 1996
HAMC Johannesburg, South Africa ....August 14, 1993
HAMC Kajaani, Finland ....December 6, 1998
HAMC Kent, England...December 04, 1976
HAMC Kiel, Germany ....September 17, 1994
HAMC Lea Valley, England ....March 30, 1985
HAMC Liechtenstein ....December 06, 1996
HAMC London, England ....July 30, 1969
HAMC Long Island, New York, U.S.A. ....October 04, 1994
HAMC Lowell, Massachusetts, U.S.A............................April 17, 1967
HAMC Malmoe, Sweden ....February 27, 1993
HAMC Mallorca, Spain ....(moved from Hamburg)
HAMC Manaus, Brazil ....February 27, 1993
HAMC Manchester, England ....April 04, 1998
HAMC Melbourne, Australia.....................................August 23, 1975
HAMC Merced County, California, U.S.A................October 17, 1998
HAMC Mesa, Arizona, U.S.A. ....October 18, 1997
HAMC Middlesex, England ....January 04, 1994
HAMC Milan, Italy ....December 16, 1995
HAMC Minneapolis, Minnesota, U.S.A. ....September 18, 1982
HAMC Mission City, British Columbia, Canada ....July 10, 1999
HAMC Monterey, California, U.S.A. ....April 04, 1981
HAMC Montreal, Quebec, Canada ....December 05, 1977
HAMC Nanaimo, British Columbia, Canada ....July 23, 1983
HAMC New York City, New York, U.S.A...............December 05, 1969
HAMC Nomads, Argentina ....June 1999
HAMC Nomads, Arizona, U.S.A. ....October 18, 1997
HAMC Nomads, Australia ....August 14, 1980

HAMC Nomads, British Columbia, Canada ....July 23, 1998
HAMC Nomads, California, U.S.A. ....June 01, 1965
HAMC Nomads, Denmark ....August 28, 1996
HAMC Nomads, England..February 25, 1989
HAMC Nomads, Holland..September 17, 1986
HAMC Nomads, New York, U.S.A. ....November 15, 1984
HAMC Nomads, Quebec, Canada ....June 24, 1995
HAMC Nomads, South Africa.................................February 22, 1999
HAMC Nomads, Sweden ....November 01, 1996
HAMC Nomads, Washington, U.S.A.............................July 16, 1994
HAMC North Coast, Holland...................................October 28, 1992
HAMC North End, Germany ....April 13, 1990
HAMC Oakland, California, U.S.A. ....April 01, 1957
HAMC Odense, Denmark...August 27, 1996
HAMC Omaha, Nebraska, U.S.A.........................November 27, 1966
HAMC Orange County, California, U.S.A. ....October 18, 1997
HAMC Orleans, France ....April 18, 1987
HAMC Oslo, Norway...September 14, 1996
HAMC Paris, France...April 18, 1981
HAMC Phoenix, Arizona, U.S.A. ....October 18, 1997
HAMC Providence, Rhode Island,U.S.A. ....September 05, 1992
HAMC Quebec City, Quebec, Canada ....May 26, 1988
HAMC Reno, Nevada, U.S.A. ....November 14, 1998
HAMC Richmond, Virginia, U.S.A. ....February 14, 1962
HAMC Rio de Janeiro, Brazil ....June 16, 1984
HAMC Rochester, New York, U.S.A. ....December 05, 1969
HAMC Rockford, Illinois, U.S.A. ....December 02, 1994
HAMC Rome, Italy..February 1999
HAMC Roskilde, Denmark ....August 27, 1996
HAMC San Fernando Valley, California, U.S.A. ....January 01, 1978
HAMC Sacramento, California, U.S.A.........................August 09, 1973
HAMC Salem, Massachusetts, U.S.A. ....July 17, 1969
HAMC San Jose, California, U.S.A...................................July 14, 1969
HAMC Saskatoon, Saskatchewan, Canada ....September 18, 1998
HAMC Shasta County, California, U.S.A. ....July 09, 1994
HAMC Sherbrooke, Quebec, Canada ....December 05, 1984
HAMC Sonoma County, California, U.S.A. ....October 21, 1972
HAMC South-Quebec, Quebec, Canada ....March 01, 1997
HAMC South Bend, Indiana, U.S.A. ....December 02, 1994
HAMC South Coast, England ....February, 26, 1977

HAMC South End, Denmark ....October 30, 1997
HAMC Stockholm, Sweden ....February 27, 1997
HAMC Stavanger, Norway.....................................September 14, 1996
HAMC Stuttgart, Germany ....December 04, 1981
HAMC Sydney, Australia..August 23, 1975
HAMC Trois-Rivières, Quebec, Canada.........................June 14, 1991
HAMC Trondheim, Norway ....August 01, 1992
HAMC Tuscon, Arizona, U.S.A.................................October 18, 1997
HAMC Tyne and Wear, England.................................June 02, 1979
HAMC Valencia, Spain ....April 19, 1997
HAMC Vallejo, California, U.S.A. ....February 11, 1984
HAMC Vancouver, British Columbia, Canada ....July 23, 1983
HAMC Ventura, California, U.S.A..................................May 06, 1978
HAMC Vienna, Austria...November 23, 1985
HAMC Vorarlberg, Austria....................................November 19, 1975
HAMC Wanganui, New Zealand ....June 23, 1992
HAMC Wessex, England ....January 29, 1977
HAMC West Coast, England ....August 17, 1974
HAMC West End, Denmark ....August 27, 1996
HAMC West Rand, South Africa...............................January 31, 1994
HAMC West Side, Germany......................................February 15, 1999
HAMC White Rock, British Columbia, Canada ....July 23, 1983
HAMC Windsor, England......................................December 22, 1984
HAMC Winston/Salem, North Carolina, U.S.A ....June 06, 1979
HAMC Wolverhampton, England ....October 23, 1985
HAMC Zurich, Switzerland ....December 20, 1970

EPILOGUE

Epilogue:
In the Aftermath of War,
the True Battle Begins

The millennium marks a new and deadlier stage in the war against outlaw motorcycle gangs. Now that the gangs are no longer at war with each other, they will focus on their common enemy: society. The gangs have entered an era of rapid expansion and involvement in increasingly sophisticated crime. We have seen the end of large-scale battles between the most powerful outlaw motorcycle gangs. There may be skirmishes with smaller gangs and inevitable paybacks, but most acquisitions of territory will now be done with money rather than blood. The large gangs decided to divide the world among themselves when they signed their truces in 1999. Gang leaders understood that the violent ways of the past could cause panicked politicians to legislate them out of existence. They are too street-wise and flexible to let pride get in the way of survival.

But gangs have also opened new avenues for law enforcement and legislators to attack them. Money now means more to them than their colors. Special teams of income-tax investigators and prosecutors can do more damage to the new-era outlaw biker than police have. The era of the paper chase has begun. If investigators had tackled biker profits decades ago, they could have wiped them out. They didn't, so the battle must be fought now, before their accumulated wealth renders them untouchable. There will always be those in politics, law enforcement, and the justice system who can be bought. They must be severely dealt with. When organized crime gangs become so wealthy they contemplate buying a seat on a stock exchange—as the Hells Angels did in Vancouver—then the country's financial integrity and security are at stake.

The Scandinavian countries allow their national security agencies to participate in the war against outlaw bikers and other forms of organized crime. Their expertise in electronic surveillance and their access to the most current high-tech devices and communications systems, including satellites, enable them to collect essential intelligence from the most secretive criminals.

We spend countless billions funding civilian and military intelligence agencies whose employees would relish the opportunity to join the fight against organized crime. There is no logical reason these resources cannot be used under the scrutiny of a responsible agency to stave off the criminal threat to national security. If left unchecked, outlaw motorcycle gangs such as the Hells Angels will inevitably influence all walks of life. I have spent many years of my life writing about this gang, in the hope of awakening the public to the enemy in its midst. We have failed to prevent the spread of the cancer which is outlaw motorcycle gangs. We must take decisive and drastic measures against them now before they corrupt and destroy society as we know it. No one will fight the battle for us. It is a war we can't afford to lose.

The Hells Angels have proven they have mastered the subtleties of politics and manipulation to a degree most people would not expect from a gang whose main source of power for more than fifty years has been intimidation. Though fear will always be the lever the Hells Angels use to pry loose from the weak the money or favors they desire, the gang's greatest advances during the past year and in the years to come will be achieved through cunning.

It is no coincidence that the three major conflicts between outlaw motorcycle gangs in the world started about the same time in 1994: the Hells Angels challenged the upstart Bandidos in Scandinavia; the Hells Angels ordered the Rock Machine to surrender their territory in Montreal; the Hells Angels deliberately insulted the Outlaws by courting the Hells Henchmen on their home turf in Illinois and Indiana. Each of those wars saw unprecedented violence between the gangs and created a severe public backlash against outlaw motorcycle gangs to the point where Canada and four Scandinavian countries enacted laws that allowed the seizure of clubhouses, and Denmark verged on banning bikers outright.

Sonny Barger has always had a plan to assimilate all outlaw motorcycle gangs into one juggernaut. The Hells Angels have planned this for nearly fifteen years. Sonny Barger decided upon his release from jail in 1992 to proceed with his scheme. The Hells Angels instigated the violent biker wars of the 1990s. They pushed society's tolerance for outlaw biker gangs to the limit. And when legislators threatened to eliminate the problem, the Hells Angels used the fear of extermination to open the door to talks, negotiations, and finally truces with their enemies.

The Hells Angels knew they could never negotiate with their enemies as long as decades of bad blood flowed between them. The need for survival stanched the flow. The Hells Angels approached the Bandidos, the Outlaws, and the Pagans as friends. They pretended to be good guys, saviors. They offered them the chance to continue their existence as bikers. And all the gangs succumbed to the Hells Angels' ruse.

The Bandidos will gradually assimilate into the Hells Angels, starting in Europe. The Hells Angels will trade territory with the other gangs. The Outlaws may be willing to give up their Ontario chapters to the Hells Angels, in return for territory elsewhere. But in the decades to come, most of these gangs will blend into one large monolithic Big Red Machine. They may not adopt the name, but their allegiance will be unquestioned.

The Hells Angels ruthlessly sacrificed members in Scandinavia, Canada, and Illinois, as well as innocent bystanders, to achieve their goal of world domination. They started out wanting to control street corners in 1948, cities in the mid-1960s, states in the 1970s, countries in the 1980s, and now the world. Some forward-looking Hells Angels tattooed their backs with the bottom rocker "World" in the mid-1980s. The bottom rocker "United Nations" has been suggested in the 1990s.

The Hells Angels have seized power bit-by-bit, using each foothold to climb to greater heights. In this they have followed the path predicted by Athenian historian Thucydides: "A man will go to the limit of his power." Will we have the courage and the will to limit the growth and control of the Hells Angels? Or will we surrender to them the freedom for which so many have died? And who should lead the war against outlaw motorcycle gangs?

The new millennium does not belong to the short-sighted, the self-serving, or those who compromise. Law enforcement has failed society with its unwillingness to curb the growth and spread of outlaw motor-cycle gangs, especially the Hells Angels. We must look at and treat our police differently at the end of the century. They resist change, scrutiny, and accountability; they fight society with spies who try to dig up information to silence police critics; they hire lawyers to stymie legitimate investigations into their actions; they intimidate those who question them, with threats of newspaper ads exposing their lives to the world; and they manipulate the media to scare society into giving them money.

Some of them have succumbed to corruption and there seems to be a systemic acceptance of deception calculated to increase budgets and the commission of crimes in the course of investigating others.

Our law enforcement agencies have mutated into bureaucracies that have less to do with enforcing the rule of law and more to do with creating secure niches, jobs, and power-bases from which to exercise political clout and shape public policy. Bureaucracies kill. They smother initiative, drive, self-respect and, ultimately, the society that fostered them and allowed them to fester. The time has come to dismantle the police bureaucracy that burdens and stifles true law enforcement. The police should not be allowed to take control of public policy they were created to implement, enforce, and defend. Our police, who are supposed to be public servants, are now at war with society in a grab for power and control.

This is illustrated by the failure of law enforcement agencies to prevent the spread of the Hells Angels across the country. The same police officers under whom the Hells Angels flourished now want more money to manage a problem they admit has become so entrenched it will never be exterminated. These cops have never been part of the solution. Why should we allow them jurisdiction over the problem?

As the Hells Angels evolve and become more sophisticated, the police fail to keep up with the times. Just as bikers use wannabes to do their dirty work and take the blame, the police have taken to using fawning wannabe writers and journalists to push their public relations efforts. These unquestioning stenographers transcribe as gospel everything given to them. The police are not to be worshipped or adored. What they do is a job. If they do it well enough, they merit respect. The police think the media are theirs to manipulate to influence public opinion. The media are supposed to be an independent component in a system of checks and balances that keeps society stable. They should report what works and what doesn't, and give voice to ideas that will make the system work better. Too many media outlets and reporters curb criticism and commit stenography for fear of alienating so-called sources. They let themselves be used as mouthpieces and have weakened their own power. Journalism is not a matter of filling space or time: it is consciousness, conscience, compassion and combativeness.

Persistently false and inaccurate stories and predictions about the Hells Angels planted by the police during the past twenty years have desensitized the public to the issue and given the bikers the opportunity to seduce society with their own public relations efforts. The Hells

Angels now point to a growing number of false stories in their arsenal, and a jaded, suspicious public sides with them because they are tired of being lied to and manipulated by the police.

The police have increased the seriousness of the Hells Angels problem by laying ridiculous, needless, or groundless charges to satisfy their egos. The Hells Angels keep track through their expensive lawyers of each charge that is beaten in court and use it as support or precedent in other cases. Bad investigations and cases by police have served as an inoculation for the Hells Angels. Repeated small exposures to irritating charges that flopped in court helped build up their immunity to prosecution. The time will come when the scales of justice will weigh in their favor, and they will be untouchable.

The police have engaged in too little detective work and too much speculation and surmising. They have relied too much on guesswork, stilted, biased analysis, and unsubstantiated rumors of their own creation. When a cop says he knows someone is dirty but he can't prove it, he knows nothing. Even a biker is innocent until proven guilty. We cannot allow the rule of law to be watered down and weakened by lazy and ineffectual police.

Quebec police have asked for an anti-gang law that overrides the Charter of Rights and Freedoms. Giving police the power to arrest someone they can't prove committed a crime is an abdication of the rule of law. Anti-gang laws should require police to provide more facts, proof, and evidence, as they risk infringing on more than individual liberties, but also on the right to free association and speech. An anti-gang law should be a law for good cops, not lazy cops. Laws cannot be selective. A Charter of Rights and Freedoms must apply equally to all, for anyone to have rights and freedoms.

There is a despicable movement among some journalists that parallels attempts by police to reverse the burden of proof in law. Some journalists have banded together to lobby for a change in the libel law so that they can say or write anything about anybody and that person has to prove them wrong. As the law stands, anyone who publishes untruths about a person is liable for defaming them. A journalist taken to task in court must prove what he has written is indeed fact. And that is how the law should stand. There is no place in journalism or law enforcement for lazy conspiracy theorists who would rush to judgment with their contrived yarns without sweating their way toward the truth. These people prefer to create false realities that fit the narrow confines of their minds and satisfy their needs to control and exercise hurtful power over others. Doesn't anyone want to do an honest day's work anymore?

Many police actions seem driven by intellectual sloth and the lack of a sense of justice. Rather than uncover the truth, they contrive to cover up their ineptitude. The RCMP lied, back-stabbed other police agencies, and faked reports during the investigation of the Hells Angels / Rock Machine war in Quebec; the OPP and the RCMP lied when they predicted bloody biker wars in Ontario during the past two decades; the RCMP and Edmonton police in Alberta when they warned of a Hells Angels' invasion in 1996, then asked for money to protect Albertans; the RCMP and Vancouver police must account for their failure to combat the Hells Angels in British Columbia; the Canadian Association of Chiefs of Police plotted to frighten the public with horror stories about the Hells Angels to create political pressure that would fatten their coffers. This is a systemic problem. Our police agencies are sick.

The police have become a law unto themselves and have let organized crime, especially the Hells Angels, spread so they can create self-serving, career-generating bureaucracies to manage the problem. The police are not at war with the bikers. They are at war with society. The RCMP needs to be put under civilian control. The police who have incorrectly failed to predict the movements of the Hells Angels for twenty years and who have failed to halt or even slow their growth, and who now want money to manage the "biker problem," need to move on to other jobs and let more talented and professional police handle the task of fighting organized crime. We can no longer afford to let the inept, fearful, and weak pretend to protect our destinies. In the battle for our economic health, safety in our streets, and peace of mind in our homes, we cannot pin our survival on the hollow, malleable promises of the weakest. Failure in prediction, action, and results is not acceptable when the stakes are so high. Careerists and criminals see the fight against organized crime as a game in which society is a pawn to be used and abused.

We must not allow our police to stray into the gray zone that paramilitary groups use to judge, sentence, and execute their opponents in other parts of the world. The police must always be accountable and held accountable. The police must serve and protect, not be self-serving and self-promoting. The ability to recognize, admit, and correct failings is a sign of capability, maturity, and professionalism. Cops who shield their mistakes and incompetent or corrupt officers are the worms that feed off bad apples.

When a public institution such as a law enforcement agency sets out to manipulate public perception and fears through control of the media, no one is being served. This abuse of power and distortion of reality harms society, undermines attempts by more responsible media to expose the truth, and blinds the public to the facts they need to know to formulate informed opinions that can sway political thought and action. Police have taken law enforcement out of the arena of reality into the realm of politics. They have politicized themselves and forsaken their mandate to serve and protect when they try to manipulate the public with fear and intimidation. Even the Hells Angels have learned that scaring the public is counter-productive. Rather, the bikers woo the public. The Hells Angels have shown more intelligence and political astuteness than the police. They have learned from their mistakes, and benefit from those made by the police.

The police are causing irreparable damage to law enforcement and eroding public trust in the institution. Police officers are not elected. They have no right to play politics. They are public employees bound to obey orders. Police who seek to control issues, intimidate or manipulate the public into supporting them, and silence their critics, are driven by a pathological sense of impotence fed by their unwillingness to do their job. Their task is to enforce, not control. Police could best influence the public through actions, not rhetoric and deceit; by doing their jobs, rather than contriving and conspiring.

The manipulation of the public through fear rather than reason does not educate or create a thoughtful climate. This is not an effective way to build public consensus and will. The media and public continually need fresh fodder and will quickly get bored with the police scare tactics, especially when their predictions don't pan out. Then the police will be left with no support from either the media or the public.

The RCMP, the Criminal Intelligence Service of Canada, the Sûreté du Québec, the Edmonton police, and other law enforcement agencies across Canada have made the unpardonable error of playing the information game with intelligence. By using intelligence in public manipulation campaigns, the police have told the Hells Angels what they know and don't know about them; they have revealed to the Hell Angels how they work; they have allowed the Hells Angels to stay well ahead of them by revealing their edge and setting themselves back; they have exposed their underbelly to the Hells Angels. In the art of war, the fighter must always capitalize on his strengths and hide his weaknesses. Anyone who tries to capitalize on his weaknesses is doomed.

Police have a duty to accurately and legally collect proof of criminal activity, charge people, and assist in their prosecution to secure a conviction. The media games played by some police agencies and officers investigating the Hells Angels are a dangerous weakness in the intelligence business. Men who work in the shadows should not seek the public spotlight, because the light that illuminates can also burn.

Index

HA or Hells Angels MC = Hells Angels Motorcycle Corporation
OMG = Outlaw Motorcycle Gangs